Finance for Sustainability in a Turbulent Economy

Abdul Rafay
University of Management and Technology, Pakistan

A volume in the Advances in Finance, Accounting, and Economics (AFAE) Book Series

IGI Global
PUBLISHER of TIMELY KNOWLEDGE

Published in the United States of America by
IGI Global
Business Science Reference (an imprint of IGI Global)
701 E. Chocolate Avenue
Hershey PA, USA 17033
Tel: 717-533-8845
Fax: 717-533-8661
E-mail: cust@igi-global.com
Web site: http://www.igi-global.com

Library of Congress Cataloging-in-Publication Data

Names: Rafay, Abdul, 1973- editor.
Title: Finance for sustainability in a turbulent economy / Abdul Rafay, editor.
Description: Hershey, PA : Business Science Reference, [2022] | Includes bibliographical references and index. | Summary: "This book provides international financial strategies to achieve sustainable business practices within a turbulent economy, covering topics such as low-cost clean energy for transportation, energy alternatives, and policy-based cost solutions"-- Provided by publisher.
Identifiers: LCCN 2022003075 (print) | LCCN 2022003076 (ebook) | ISBN 9781668455807 (hardcover) | ISBN 9781668455814 (paperback) | ISBN 9781668455821 (ebook)
Subjects: LCSH: Finance--Environmental aspects. | Sustainable development--Finance. | Clean energy industries--Finance.
Classification: LCC HG101 .F546 2022 (print) | LCC HG101 (ebook) | DDC 333.7--dc23/eng/20220126
LC record available at https://lccn.loc.gov/2022003075
LC ebook record available at https://lccn.loc.gov/2022003076

This book is published in the IGI Global book series Advances in Finance, Accounting, and Economics (AFAE) (ISSN: 2327-5677; eISSN: 2327-5685)

British Cataloguing in Publication Data
A Cataloguing in Publication record for this book is available from the British Library.

For electronic access to this publication, please contact: eresources@igi-global.com.

Advances in Finance, Accounting, and Economics (AFAE) Book Series

Ahmed Driouchi
Al Akhawayn University, Morocco

ISSN:2327-5677
EISSN:2327-5685

MISSION

In our changing economic and business environment, it is important to consider the financial changes occurring internationally as well as within individual organizations and business environments. Understanding these changes as well as the factors that influence them is crucial in preparing for our financial future and ensuring economic sustainability and growth.

The **Advances in Finance, Accounting, and Economics (AFAE)** book series aims to publish comprehensive and informative titles in all areas of economics and economic theory, finance, and accounting to assist in advancing the available knowledge and providing for further research development in these dynamic fields.

COVERAGE

- Economics of Risks, Uncertainty, Ambiguity, and Insurance
- Health Economics
- Fiscal Policy
- Economic Theory
- Investments and Derivatives
- Economics of Natural and Environmental Resources
- International Economics
- E-finance
- Wages and Employment
- Corporate Finance

IGI Global is currently accepting manuscripts for publication within this series. To submit a proposal for a volume in this series, please contact our Acquisition Editors at Acquisitions@igi-global.com or visit: http://www.igi-global.com/publish/.

The Advances in Finance, Accounting, and Economics (AFAE) Book Series (ISSN 2327-5677) is published by IGI Global, 701 E. Chocolate Avenue, Hershey, PA 17033-1240, USA, www.igi-global.com. This series is composed of titles available for purchase individually; each title is edited to be contextually exclusive from any other title within the series. For pricing and ordering information please visit http://www.igi-global.com/book-series/advances-finance-accounting-economics/73685. Postmaster: Send all address changes to above address.

Titles in this Series

For a list of additional titles in this series, please visit: http://www.igi-global.com/book-series/

Handbook of Research on Changing World Economic Order in the Post-Pandemic Period
Sushanta Kumar Mahapatra (IBS Hyderabad, The ICFAI Foundation for Higher Education, India) and Vishal Sarin (Lovely Professional University, India)
Business Science Reference • © 2022 • 470pp • H/C (ISBN: 9781799868965) • US $325.00

Opportunities and Challenges for Multinational Enterprises and Foreign Direct Investment in the Belt and Road Initiative
Miraj Ahmed Bhuiyan (Guangdong University of Finance and Economics, China) and Isidora Beraha (Institute of Economic Sciences, Serbia)
Business Science Reference • © 2022 • 323pp • H/C (ISBN: 9781799880219) • US $250.00

Advanced Machine Learning Algorithms for Complex Financial Applications
Mohammad Irfan (CMR Institute of Technology, India) Mohamed Elhoseny (American University in the Emirates, UAE) Salina Kassim (International Islamic University of Malaysia, Malaysia) and Noura Metawa (University of Sharjah, UAE)
Engineering Science Reference • © 2022 • 335pp • H/C (ISBN: 9781668444832) • US $270.00

AI-Enabled Agile Internet of Things for Sustainable FinTech Ecosystems
Sandeep Kautish (Lord Buddha Education Foundation, Nepal) and Guneet Kaur (Independent Researcher, UK)
Engineering Science Reference • © 2022 • 271pp • H/C (ISBN: 9781668441763) • US $270.00

Applications, Challenges, and Opportunities of Blockchain Technology in Banking and Insurance
S. L. Gupta (Birla Institute of Technology, Noida, India) Pooja Kansra (Mittal School of Business, Lovely Professional University, India) and Gagan Kukreja (College of Business Administration, University of Bahrain, Bahrain)
Business Science Reference • © 2022 • 303pp • H/C (ISBN: 9781668441336) • US $250.00

IGI Global
PUBLISHER of TIMELY KNOWLEDGE

701 East Chocolate Avenue, Hershey, PA 17033, USA
Tel: 717-533-8845 x100 • Fax: 717-533-8661
E-Mail: cust@igi-global.com • www.igi-global.com

This book is dedicated to **Dr. Amjad Saqib**, a person of impeccable reputation and a visionary pioneer of sustainable social entrepreneurship model based on interest free micro financing. His scholarly and practical contribution in the respective fields made him a person of great depth and integrity.

He holds a master's degree in public administration from the American University, Washington D.C. Previously he completed his bachelor's degree in Medicine (M.B.B.S) from King Edward Medical College, Pakistan. In 2001, he established Akhuwat Foundation in Pakistan and became known for introducing the world's largest Islamic microfinance organization that provides interest-free loans to the most deserving segments of society. Akhuwat Foundation expanded its work into the field of education, health, and supporting the most marginalized segments of society.

He was awarded numerous awards such as Sitara-i-Imtiaz (2010) by Government of Pakistan, Lifetime Achievement Award by Abu Dhabi Islamic Bank and Thomson Reuters (2014), 35th Human Rights Award by Human Rights Society of Pakistan (2015), Pace Award by Pakistani American Community (2017), Social Entrepreneur of the year Award by the World Economic Forum (2018), Commonwealth's 31st Point of Light Award (2018), Pride of Pakistan Award (2020) and Ramon Magsaysay Award (2021). In 2022, he was nominated for the Nobel Peace Prize.

Currently he is the Executive Director of Akhuwat Foundation.

Editorial Advisory Board

Table of Contents

Detailed Table of Contents

This chapter examines the relationship between the water sector of the equity markets. It includes the world market and markets of different individual countries such as China, Hong Kong, Singapore, Germany, France, the UK, Brazil, Chile, and the US for the period 2001-2020. Investment returns and volatility of these markets are analyzed to understand investment decision-making in these water markets. The OLS and quantile regressions show that China, Hong Kong, Singapore, Germany, France, the UK, Brazil, Chile, and the US are positively related to the world market. The results confirm simultaneous interactions between the world market and the other nine markets. The ARMA (1,1)-GARCH (1,1) model shows a high degree of persistency in the conditional volatility of stock returns for these water markets which means "explosive" volatility. Moreover, the VAR analyses show that the nine markets positively and negatively affect the world market. The findings may assist the international institutions while deciding investment in water portfolios.

This study investigates the impact of financial development on green energy demand in Africa for the period 1990-2018. Using the dynamic generalized method of moments (GMM) technique, the findings of this study reveal that financial development reduces the share of renewable energy demand and increases environmental pollution in Africa. FDI inflows also hamper renewable energy demand and positively contribute to carbon dioxide emission. It is further evident from the results that although trade openness does not significantly enhance green energy demand, it matters for carbon dioxide emission. In line with these findings, appropriate policies are recommended.

Human activities to boost economic wellbeing have degraded the environment on many fronts to the extent that earth has reached its planetary boundaries by sabotaging its self-regulating equilibrium system. This study investigates the impact of air pollution (proxied by various indicators) on health expenditure over a panel consisting of 188 countries for the period 2000-2018. The impact of air pollution on health expenditures was analyzed using the GMM estimations. Findings suggest that health expenditures are increased due to air pollution caused by economic activities. The study urges that governments should reconsider their policies by creating a balance between economic growth and environmental sustainability. While spending on a sustainable environment, humans can have better health and working capacities that will ultimately contribute to the overall economy. A carbon taxing system on businesses that use obsolete technologies can also contribute towards a sustainable environment and reduced air pollution.

The global environment and climatic systems are heating up due to increased human activities. Making it happen due to technology and the availability of natural resources would be one of the greatest challenges that the cleantech revolution would be facing in the global market. In a short span of time, funding cleantech projects without sacrificing profitability and improving quality of life for a sustainable community has been understood to be a viable solution to the problem. In this context, it may be mentioned that a new stream of finance has emerged called environmental finance. The chapter throws light on the typology of funding agencies engaged in providing environmental finance and the role of governments in formulating relevant policies to promote lending for environmental projects. An array of financing instruments for environmental projects has been discussed to indicate the mobilizing potential for such projects with special reference to India.

Financial reporting without integration of environmental issues is not sustainable. The purpose of this chapter is to discuss the need for financial environmental reporting and also to provide empirical evidence for environmental financial

Preface

The editing of a book on sustainability is more exciting and challenging than ever before. The past few decades have been an eventful one for sustainability. This terminology has become a buzzword from G20[1] to World Economic Forum[2] to global and national economic agendas. Today tackling the problems of sustainability is being considered a key issue in developed and developing countries alike.

INTRODUCTION

Regardless of the size of business, industry, or country, sustainability is one of the biggest problems that countries and organizations are facing today at the macro and micro levels. The famous Brundtland Commission[3] in its report "Our Common future" defines:

"Sustainable development is the development that meets the needs of the present without compromising the ability of future generations to meet their own needs." (UN, n.d)

The Intergovernmental Panel on Climate Change (IPCC)[4] warns how climate change is a threat to a sustainable future:

"The cumulative scientific evidence is unequivocal: Climate change is a threat to human wellbeing and planetary health. Any further delay in concerted anticipatory global action on adaptation and mitigation will miss a brief and rapidly closing window of opportunity to secure a livable and sustainable future for all." (IPCC, 2022a)

The Council on Foreign Relations[5], warns:

"Exposure to a sustained wet-bulb temperature of 35°C (95°F), a point of intense heat with extreme humidity (90+), has been identified as the limit for human survival. When wet-bulb conditions develop, sweat can no longer evaporate off a person's skin and the body cannot cool down. Just a few hours of this kind of heat exposure can lead to death... Some regions, including southwestern North America, South Asia, and the Middle East have already endured conditions at or near this limit, and certain areas will experience the effects more intensely than others." (Hill, Babin & Baumgartner, 2021)

SUSTAINABLE ENVIRONMENT: AN OVERVIEW

The first Earth Summit in Sweden in 1972 adopted an action plan for environmental protection and led to the creation of the United Nations Environment Program. Since then, the world is on the forefront of exponential climate and environmental change which is here to stay. The climate changes are taking place faster than the projection by IPCC. Earth is hotter today than it's been in at least 1,000 years, and probably much longer (Rosen 2021). As reported by the National Oceanic and Atmospheric Administration (NOAA)[6], July 2021 was the hottest month in recorded history (Roy, 2021). Argentina, Uruguay and Paraguay are experiencing the hottest summer in 2022.

Today, fossil fuels contribute 64% of the world's CO_2 emissions (IPCC, 2022b). In 2021, carbon emissions into the atmosphere reached an alarming figure of 36.3 billion tons due to burning oil, gas and coal (IEA, 2022). Methane is contributing to one-third of human-generated warming. As recorded by Global Monitoring Laboratory, the methane concentration in the atmosphere exceeded 1900ppb for the first time in history (Stallard, 2022).

Figure 1. Global temperatures compared to a 1850-1900 baseline
Data Source: Copernicus Climate Change Service (2022)
Graph Source: John Keefe, CNN

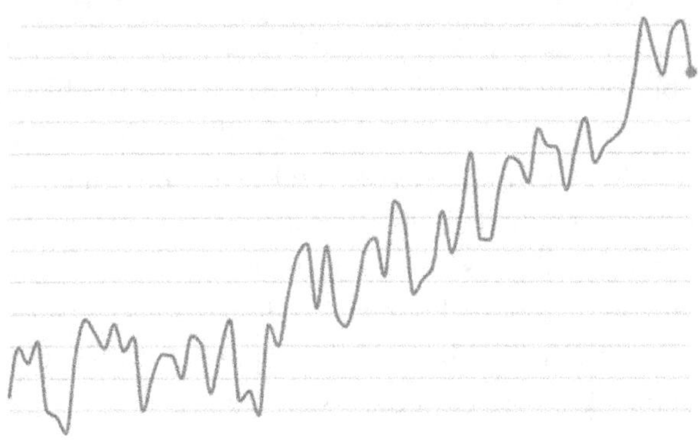

Global warming leads to a chain reaction that results in catastrophic effects like extreme/torrid heatwaves, floods due to fast melting of glaciers, wildfires, dying vegetation, insect infestations, decrease in the spring season, extraordinary powerful storms, rise in sea levels, acidification of oceans, deforestation, water degeneration drought and desertification, species extinction to name a few (Fountain, 2022). Rapid deforestation is being witnessed from Amazon in South America, tropical rainforests in Africa and green lands in Australia to mangroves in coastal areas of South Asia (Shahzar, 2022). In Brazil, Amazon deforestation is up to 69% last year (Stallard, 2022). Yellow cedars in Alaska died due to early snowmelt because of global warming (Hunziker, 2022). Widescale forest fires are another outcome of rising temperatures that result in loss of human lives, loss of livelihood for local residents, killing of animal species and destruction of precious trees on thousands of hectares (Bhatti, 2022). Russia lost 6.5 million hectares of forest to fires last year (Stallard, 2022). Moreover, global heat and surging temperatures are outpacing infrastructure capacities. La Niña[7], has also aggravated the weather conditions. Climate change will result in thousands of new viruses spread among animal species by 2070 (Carlson *et al.*, 2022).

Food insecurity creates a grave threat to humanity and is a cause of poverty, hunger, poor health and conflict (Khan, 2022). Due to abrupt changes in climate, many countries are becoming food insecure which put around 50 million people in 46 countries at the risk of famine, starvation and acute malnutrition (IRC, 2022). The crop yields may decrease substantially in case nitrogen dioxide crosses the limit of 5% (Lobell, Tommaso & Burney, 2022). All these climatic changes lead to seasonal migrations, long and high-gauge droughts, low water reservoirs, dried-up wells and low underground water tables. It is estimated that in Northern Hemisphere outside the tropics, summer warming will decline the plant productivity within the next half-century (Zhang *et al.,* 2022).

The dark side is that since the first assessment of IPCC in 1990, governments, industries and financial institutions consistently failed to take necessary steps. Financial institutions are continuously investing in climate-chocking industries. As reported by Oil Change International, fossil fuel financing from the world's 60 largest banks has reached USD3.8 trillion in 2021 alone (Falcon, 2021). Heavy state investments have been made in fossil fuel infrastructures and coal mining (Suzuki, 2022). USD844 billion are required annually to combat the biodiversity loss out of which the poor nations need at least USD60 billion (AFP, 2022). Currently, in 2022, only about 12% of green/environmental investment funds are aligned with global climate goals set by the famous Paris agreement (MacFarland *et al.*, 2022). Energy Treaty Charter (ETC)[8] is being considered an obstacle to phase-out fossil fuels because it enables fossil fuel companies to sue governments for lost profits. Recently young victims of the climate crisis approached the European Court of Human Rights against ETC (Rankin & Neslen, 2022).

Figure 2. Hunger hotspots due to conflicts and extreme whether
Data Source: FAO-WFP
Graph Source: Financial Times (2022)

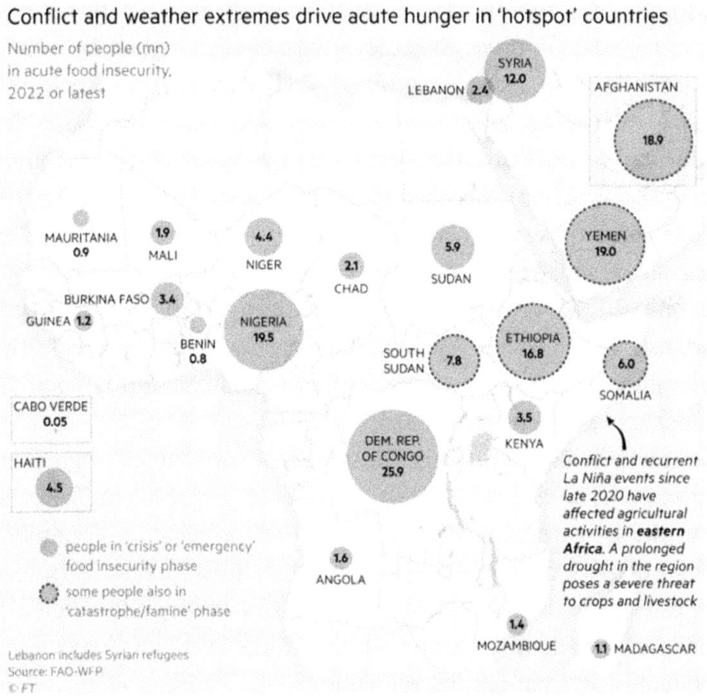

Figure 3. Climate Finance mobilized by developed countries
Data Source: OECD (2022)
Graph Source: BBC

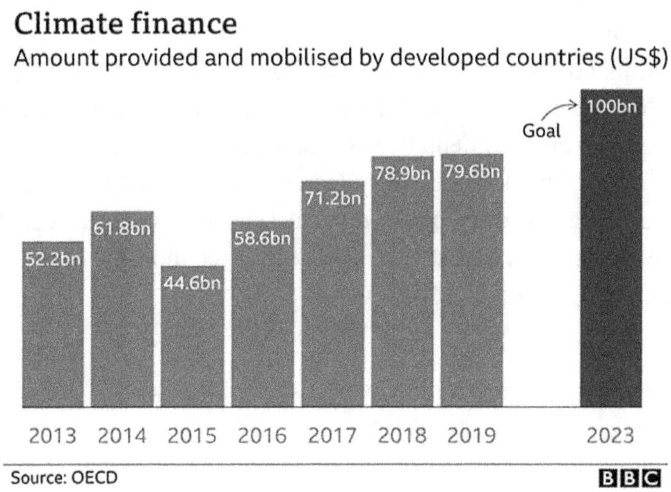

SUSTAINABLE ENVIRONMENT: CURRENT STRATEGIES

Many governments are receptive to the initiatives for long-term sustainability. Since 2005, wind and solar energy have been the fastest-growing forms of electricity generation every year. In order to achieve the net-zero carbon by 2050, wind and solar must hit 70% of global energy by 2050 (IEA, 2022). In April 2022, the US generated 20% of its electricity from wind and solar (Jacobs, 2022). In 2021, the first-ever blue carbon estimation study was completed in Pakistan through the World bank (Amin & Khan, 2022). Another example is Costa Rica, a country that markets itself as green and biodiverse. The lush high-elevation forest in Monteverde, Costa Rica is declared a jewel in the crown of cloud forests reserve by national geographics (Ocha & Smith, 2022). The Center for Agriculture and Biosciences International (CABI) and the UN's Food and Agricultural Organizations are working on Climate-Smart Agriculture (CSA) solutions for agriculture sustainability, food security and safe use of pesticides (Ahmed, 2022).

Transportation is also among the most significant sources of greenhouse gases (GHG)[9] emissions (Hannon *et al.,* 2022). In order to ensure the highest sustainability standards in the construction and transportation projects, environmental impact assessment specialists, ecologists, air and noise scientists and forestry specialists are playing key roles in devising strategies for terrestrial ecology, ecological restoration habitat conservation, animal protection, wildlife corridors, species movement routes, replantation of trees/shrubs, relocation of native/high-value trees and design/construction of culverts. The 1200 km long railway project in UAE is an ideal example of a sustainable transportation project (Kumar, 2022).

To become an agent of sustainable change, the private sector, conservation groups and carbon-neutral advocacy groups also started working with governments for clean energy development and nature-based solutions. In 2022, Wärtsilä Corporation in Finland established the Sustainable Technology Hub by spending Euro 250m to foster innovation, collaboration and development of green technologies (Wärtsilä, 2022). In this regard, Wärtsilä and Wasaline collaborated on one of the world's most energy-efficient and environmentally sustainable passenger ferries "Aurora Botnia". IHI Corporation of Japan successfully tested a subsea turbine that can generate the renewable energy in deep ocean current (Papadopoulos, 2022). In Pakistan, old brick kilns are being converted to new zigzag technology. Many countries are successfully floating green bonds.

Figure 4. Solar and Wind Power by country
Source: Visualcapitalist.com (2022)

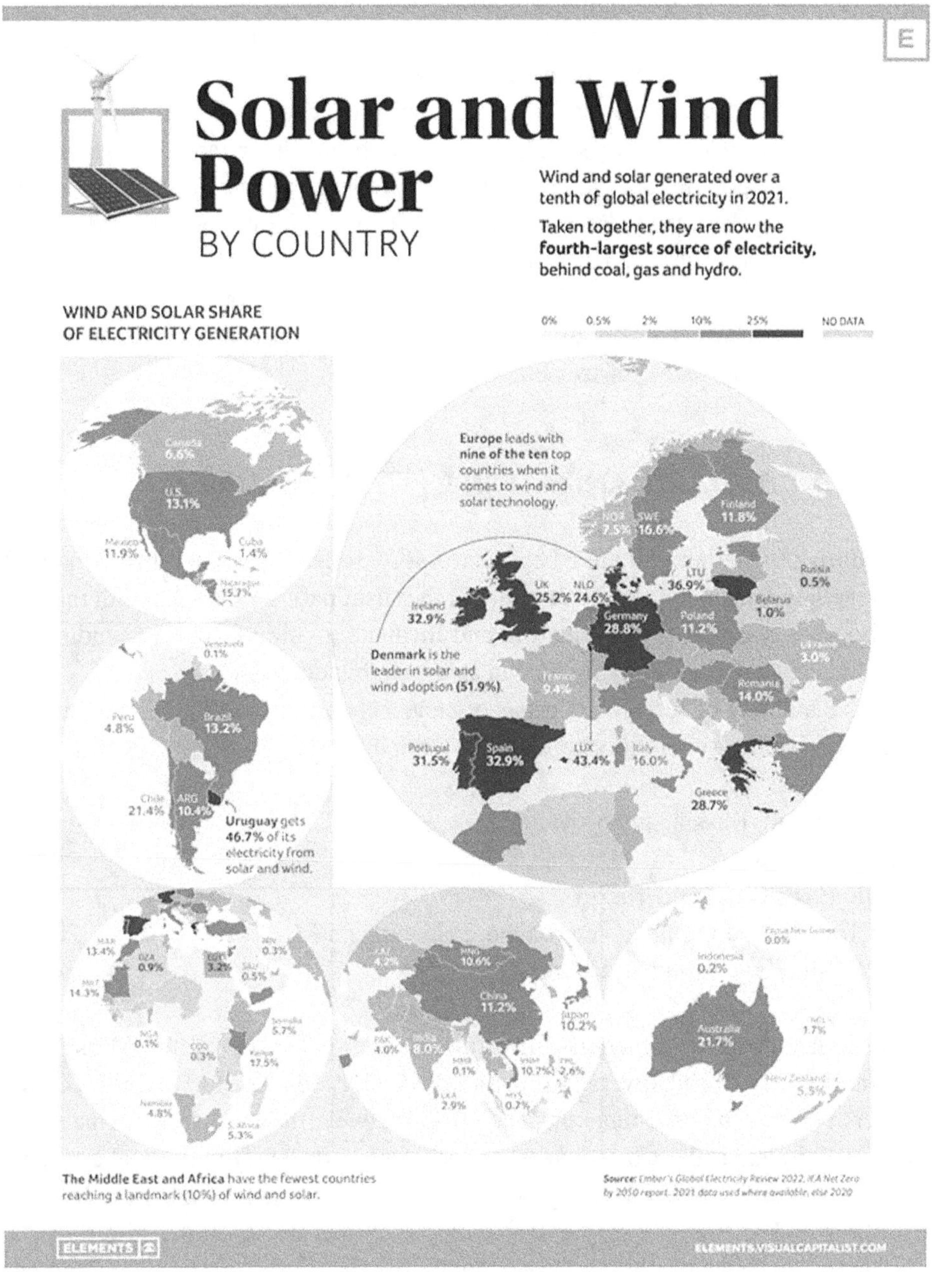

CONCLUDING REMARKS

The sustainability of the planet is at risk. Mobilizing the financial support for developing countries is required by developed nations in order to reduce the emission of greenhouse gases (Figueres, de Boer & Cutajar, 2022). Collective action is urgently needed to save the water, soil, air and forests for future generations. In this regard, the global vision for sustainability should be clear, crisp and understandably articulated. Climate change policies should be dynamic in order to create a synergy among the mitigation and adaptation plans. It is important to accelerate the decarbonization journey to demonstrate that a carbon-neutral future is achievable. Sustainable fuels are the cornerstone to achieving the targets for carbon neutrality. Climate-safe future is a more prosperous one economically. Societies will be more prosperous in a world where climate change is constrained.

CONTEXT AND ORGANIZATION OF THIS VOLUME

Regardless of whether you are a beginner or a seasoned researcher, this handbook of research will deepen the discourse about the sustainability. I am hopeful that this handbook of research is a fascinating and invaluable guide for understanding the theory, practice and cases of finance in a sustainable environment.

This handbook of research consists of eleven chapters by writers from fourteen countries. Twenty-six authors contributed from disparate parts of the world;

Europe: Spain, Russia, and Slovenia
ANZ: Australia
Middle East: Israel and Turkey
Asia: Taiwan, China, India, Azerbaijan, Pakistan and Malaysia
Africa: Nigeria, Ghana and Uganda

The first chapter "Financial Investments in the Global Water Market" by Rajibur Reza (Griffith University, Australia) and Gurudeo Anand Tularam (Griffith University, Australia), examines the relationship between the water sector of the equity markets. It includes the world market and markets of different individual countries such as China, Hong Kong, Singapore, Germany, France, the UK, Brazil, Chile, and the US. The findings may assist the international institutions while deciding investment in water portfolios. The second chapter "Green Energy Demand and Financial Development: Evidence from Africa" by Alhassan Bunyaminu (University of Professional Studies, Ghana) and Ibrahim Nandom Yakubu (Ankara Yildirim Beyazit University, Turkey) investigates the impact of financial development on green energy demand in Africa. It is evident from the results that although trade openness does not significantly enhance green energy demand, it matters for carbon dioxide emission. The third chapter "Global Oil Price Shocks and Sustainability: The Case of Post-Soviet Resources-Rich Countries" by Vugar Bayramov (Center for Economic and Social Development, Azerbaijan) and Nigar Islamli (Center for Economic and Social Development, Azerbaijan), discusses for countries, whose economies are largely based on oil revenues, the impacts of global oil price shocks play a significant role. The drop in oil prices caused the economic slowdown, however, Azerbaijan was able to prevent the negative impact with a social package. The fourth chapter "Oil Prices, Macroeconomic Performance and Sustainability: The Case of Turkey" by Nurcan Kilinc-Ata (Institute of Economics and Utility Regulation, Russia), examines the effect of oil prices on selected macroeconomic variables such as economic growth, inflation, interest rate, unemployment, and import in Turkey. It is recommended that Turkey (which is a developing oil-dependent country and where macroeconomic variables are vulnerable to oil shocks) should spread its oil providers, focus on domestic energy resources, develop advanced technology to raise the usage of renewable energy resources, and implement energy-saving policies. The fifth chapter chapter "Wealth at the Expense of Health: The Outcome of Environmental Degradation" by Awais Ur Rehman (University of Central Punjab, Pakistan), Arsalan Haneef Malik (Universiti Malaysia Sarawak, Malaysia), Aasia Kanwal (University of Health Sciences, Pakistan) and Naveed Aslam Lashari (PAF Hospital, Pakistan), discusses that human activities to boost economic wellbeing have degraded the environment on many fronts to the extent that earth has reached its planetary boundaries by sabotaging its self-regulating equilibrium system. A carbon taxing system on businesses that use obsolete technologies can also contribute towards a sustainable environment and reduced air pollution. The sixth chapter "Environmental Finance for a Sustainable Society: An Overview" by Kiranmai J., Ram Kumar Mishra (Institute of Public Enterprise, India), Maschendar M. Goud (Institute of Public Enterprise, India), Abdul Rafay (University of Management & Technology, Pakistan) and Marie G Nakitende (Uganda Martyrs University, Uganda) examines that the global environment and climatic systems are heating up due to increased human activities. Making it happen due to technology and the availability of natural resources would be one of the greatest challenges that the cleantech revolution would be facing in the global market. The seventh chapter "Environmental Financial Reporting Adoption Lag: The Case of Uganda" by Mary Maurice Nalwoga Mukokoma (Kyambogo University, Uganda), Kisenyi Vincent (Uganda Christian University, Uganda), Peter Masaba Nangayi (Uganda Revenue Authority, Uganda) and George Kasule (National Water and Sewerage Cooperation, Uganda) examines the need for financial environmental reporting and also to provide empirical evidence for Environmental Financial Reporting Disclosure (EFRD) of listed companies in Uganda. It is concluded that a low EFRD level demonstrates the lag in the adoption of environmental financial reporting. It is suggested that certain actions are required by the entities to publish environmental financial information and to reduce the lag. The eighth chapter "Social Responsibility for a Sustainable Environment" by Živko Bergant (College for Accounting and Finance, Slovenia), highlights the notion of social responsibility is abused for various political and business purposes and only left to various civil initiatives. It remains at the level of declarations, voluntary thinking, and philanthropy, albeit it has some impact on corporate practice. The ninth chapter "Sustainability Risks for ESG: An Investor's perspective" by Gil Cohen (Western Galille College, Israel) examines three sustainability risks: Environmental, Social, and Governance (ESG) which the investors take into consideration before any decision making. The Results insinuate that investors value the solar energy production method as the most cost-effective green energy production technique. The tenth chapter "Crowdfunding for Sustainable Utilities Tunnel Projects: The Case of China" by Feng Sun (South China Normal University, China), Tayo Oke (Afe Babalola University, Nigeria) and Marie G Nakitende (Uganda Martyrs University, Uganda), explains that organizations/Individuals (G part) and Profitable Social Organizations/Individuals (S part) are the counterparties to the G-S interactive finance framework. Choice of suitable funding mode (like debt funding, equity funding, Internet finance) is important to acquire enough construction capital for these types of projects. The eleventh chapter "Renewable Energy Framework for Sustainability: The Case of Spain" by Maria Jesus Garcia (University of Valencia, Spain) explains how clean energy is represented by the low level of emissions into the atmosphere. Energy efficiency must be accompanied by a policy of diversifying the sources used in energy production to open the door to the use and promotion of renewable energies.

I thank the contributors and also the external reviewers who have patiently critiqued these chapters to meet the minimum acceptable standard. While the publisher and the Editor (myself) have used their best efforts in preparing this book, they make no representations and warranties with respect to the accuracy or completeness of the contents of this book and specifically disclaim any implied warranties of merchantability or fitness for a particular purpose. The strategies or suggestions or whatsoever contained in this book may not be suitable for any specific situation for which anyone should consult with a professional, where appropriate. Neither the publisher nor the Editor shall be liable for any loss of profit or any other commercial damages, including but not limited to special, incidental, consequential, or other damages.

Abdul Rafay
University of Management and Technology, Pakistan
August 2022

REFERENCES

AFP. (2022, March 2). Poorer nations need $60b a year to protect biodiversity, nature: NGOs. *Global Times*. Retrieved from https://www.globaltimes.cn/page/202203/1253718.shtml

Ahmed, M. (2022, April 19). Climate-smart initiatives. *The News International*. Retrieved from https://www.thenews.com.pk/print/951381-climate-smart-initiatives

Amin, M., & Khan, A. (2022, April 27). Irreversible Climate. *The News International*. Retrieved from https://www.thenews.com.pk/print/953644-irreversible-climate

Bhatti, K. (2022, June 7). Protect the forest. *The News International*. Retrieved from https://www.thenews.com.pk/print/963966-protect-the-forest

Carlson, C. J., Albery, G. F., Merow, C., Trisos, C. H., Zipfel, C. M., Eskew, E. A., Olival, K. J., Ross, N., & Bansal, S. (2022). Climate change increases cross-species viral transmission risk. *Nature*, 1–1. doi:10.103841586-022-04788-w PMID:35483403

Falcon, J. K. (2021, March 24). World's 60 largest banks have poured $3.8 trillion into fossil fuels since Paris agreement. *Common Dreams*. Retrieved from https://www.commondreams.org/newswire/2021/03/24/worlds-60-largest-banks-have-poured-38-trillion-fossil-fuels-paris-agreement

Figueres, C., de Boer, Y., & Cutajar, M. Z. (2022, June 2). For 50 years, governments have failed to act on climate change. No more excuses. *The Guardian*. Retrieved from https://www.theguardian.com/commentisfree/2022/jun/02/for-50-years-governments-have-failed-to-act-on-climate-change-no-more-excuses

Fountain, H. (2022, June 3). Carbon Dioxide Levels Are Highest in Human History. *The New York Times*. Retrieved from https://www.nytimes.com/2022/06/03/climate/carbon-dioxide-record.html

Hannon, E., Krishnan, M., Patel, J., & Sahdev, S. (2022). *Mobility's net-zero transition: A look at opportunities and risks*. McKinsey & Company. Retrieved from https://www.mckinsey.com/industries/automotive-and-assembly/our-insights/mobilitys-net-zero-transition-a-look-at-opportunities-and-risks

Hill, A. C., Babin, M., & Baumgartner, S. (2021, October 18). A world overheating. *Council of Foreign Relations*. Retrieved from https://www.cfr.org/article/climate-change-world-overheating-how-countries-adapt-extreme-temperature

Hunziker, R. (2022, Apr. 18). Climate Change is killing trees. *Counterpunch*. Retrieved from https://www.counterpunch.org/2022/04/18/climate-change-is-killing-trees/

IEA. (2022, March 8). *Global CO2 emissions rebounded to their highest level in history in 2021*. International Energy Agency. Retrieved from https://www.iea.org/news/global-co2-emissions-rebounded-to-their-highest-level-in-history-in-2021

IPCC. (2022a). *Climate change 2022: Impacts, adaption and vulnerability*. The Intergovernmental Panel on Climate Change. Retrieved from https://report.ipcc.ch/ar6wg2/pdf/IPCC_AR6_WGII_SummaryForPolicymakers.pdf

IPCC. (2022b). *Climate change 2022: Mitigation of Climate Change*. The Intergovernmental Panel on Climate Change. Retrieved from https://report.ipcc.ch/ar6wg3/pdf/IPCC_AR6_WGIII_FinalDraft_FullReport.pdf

IRC. (2022). More than 50 million people are facing starvation. *Islamic Relief Canada*. Retrieved from https://www.islamicreliefcanada.org/emergencies/hunger-crisis-appeal/

Jacobs, F. (2022, June 2). World map reveals wind and solar power winners (and losers). *Big Think*. Retrieved from https://bigthink.com/strange-maps/wind-solar-world-map/

Khan, A. (2022, June 11). Migrating for water. *The News International*. Retrieved from https://www.thenews.com.pk/print/964505-migrating-for-water

Kumar, A. (2022, June 5). UAE: Sustainability at the heart of Etihad Rail network. *Khaleej Times*. Retrieved from https://www.khaleejtimes.com/environment/uae-sustainability-at-the-heart-of-etihad-rail-network

Lobell, D. B., Di Tommaso, S., & Burney, J. A. (2022). Globally ubiquitous negative effects of nitrogen dioxide on crop growth. *Science Advances*, *8*(22), eabm9909. doi:10.1126ciadv.abm9909 PMID:35648854

MacFarland, M., Stella, M. G., & Whieldon, E. (2022). Green funds have a Paris alignment problem. *S&P Global*. Retrieved from https://www.spglobal.com/esg/insights/green-funds-have-a-paris-alignment-problem

Ocha, A. E., & Smith, J. R. (2022, April 24). Costa Rica has reaped dividends by protecting biodiversity- and making it accessible. *Common Dreams*. Retrieved from https://www.commondreams.org/views/2022/04/24/costa-rica-has-reaped-dividends-protecting-biodiversity-and-making-it-accessible

Papadopoulos, L. (2022, June 4). Japan's trial of a deep ocean turbine could offer limitless renewable energy. *Interesting Engineering*. Retrieved from https://interestingengineering.com/japan-deep-ocean-turbine-limitless-renewable-energy

Rankin, J., & Neslen, A. (2022, June 21). Young people go to European court to stop treaty that aids fossil fuel investors. *The Guardian*. Retrieved from https://www.theguardian.com/environment/2022/jun/21/young-people-go-to-european-court-to-stop-treaty-that-aids-fossil-fuel-investors

Rosen, J. (2021, April 19). The Science of Climate Change Explained: Facts, Evidence and Proof. *The New York Times*. Retrieved from https://www.nytimes.com/article/climate-change-global-warming-faq.html?action=click

Roy, A. (2021, August 14). July 2021 was the hottest month in recorded history. *Backpacker*. Retrieved from https://www.backpacker.com/news-and-events/news/july-2021-was-the-hottest-month-ever/

Shahzar, E. (2022, April 26). Pakistan's climate crises. *The News International*. Retrieved from https://www.thenews.com.pk/print/953332-pakistan-s-climate-crisis

Stallard, E. (2022, June 5). COP26: Are nations on track to meet their climate goals? *BBC*. Retrieved from https://www.bbc.com/news/science-environment-61494531

Suzuki, D. (2022, April 15). Fossil Fuel Funding is a disastrous investment. *Common Dreams*. Retrieved from https://www.commondreams.org/views/2022/04/15/fossil-fuel-funding-disastrous-investment

UN. (n.d.). *Our Common Future: Report of the World Commission on Environment and Development*. Retrieved from http://www.un-documents.net/ocf-02.htm

Wärtsilä. (2022, June 1). *Wärtsilä opens world-leading Sustainable Technology Hub to* accelerate marine and energy decarbonization. Retrieved from https://www.wartsila.com/cyp/news/01-06-2022-wartsila-opens-world-leading-sustainable-technology-hub-to-accelerate-marine-and-energy-decarbonisation-3112015

Zhang, Y., Piao, S., Sun, Y., Rogers, B. M., Li, X., Lian, X., Liu, Z., Chen, A., & Peñuelas, J. (2022). Future reversal of warming-enhanced vegetation productivity in the Northern Hemisphere. *Nature Climate Change*, *12*(6), 581–586. doi:10.103841558-022-01374-w

ENDNOTES

1 **Group of Twenty (G20):** It is an inter intergovernmental forum comprising of the European Union and nineteen industrialized and developed countries. It is a primary venue for international economic and financial cooperation.

2 **World Economic Forum (WEF):** It is an international non-governmental forum based in Switzerland, to discuss the state of the world by engaging business, political, academic, and other leaders of society.

3 **Brundtland Commission (BC):** It was an independent organization established in 1983 to focus on the environment and sustainable development. It formally dissolved in 1987, after releasing the famous Brundtland Report.

4 **Intergovernmental Panel on Climate Change (IPCC):** It is an intergovernmental body of the United Nations, established in 1988. It is responsible for advancing knowledge on human-induced climate change.

5 **The Council on Foreign Relations (CFR):** It is an independent American think tank founded in 1921. It focuses on US foreign policy and international relations.

6 **National Oceanic and Atmospheric Administration (NOAA):** It is a US regulatory agency that forecasts and monitors weather, oceanic and atmospheric conditions, charts the seas, conducts deep-sea exploration, and manages fishing and protection of marine mammals and endangered species in the US.

7 **La Niña:** It is a climate pattern that changes ocean surface currents and brings cooler water up from the depths of the Pacific Ocean.

8 **Energy Treaty Charter (ETC):** It is a charter signed by 54 countries in 1994 to protect investors who were investing in fossil fuels.

9 **Greenhouse Gases (GHG):** The GHGs are gases that absorb and emit infrared radiation emitted by the earth. The main greenhouse gases whose rising concentrations are creating global warming are carbon dioxide (CO2), methane (CH4), nitrous oxide (N2O), and Tropospheric ozone (O3).

Chapter 1
Financial Investments in the Global Water Market

Rajibur Reza
Griffith University, Nathan, Australia

Gurudeo Anand Tularam
Griffith University, Nathan, Australia

ABSTRACT

This chapter examines the relationship between the water sector of the equity markets. It includes the world market and markets of different individual countries such as China, Hong Kong, Singapore, Germany, France, the UK, Brazil, Chile, and the US for the period 2001-2020. Investment returns and volatility of these markets are analyzed to understand investment decision-making in these water markets. The OLS and quantile regressions show that China, Hong Kong, Singapore, Germany, France, the UK, Brazil, Chile, and the US are positively related to the world market. The results confirm simultaneous interactions between the world market and the other nine markets. The ARMA (1,1)-GARCH (1,1) model shows a high degree of persistency in the conditional volatility of stock returns for these water markets which means "explosive" volatility. Moreover, the VAR analyses show that the nine markets positively and negatively affect the world market. The findings may assist the international institutions while deciding investment in water portfolios.

DOI: 10.4018/978-1-6684-5580-7.ch001

INTRODUCTION

It is well accepted that water is an issue of great concern worldwide given that there are water shortages in many countries (Reza *et al.*, 2021; Tularam & Marchisella, 2014). Acute potable water availability shortages and problems exist in regions such as South Asia, Middle East, Mexico, Southern Spain, and Northwest Africa just to name a few (Reza *et al.*, 2021; Jin *et al.*, 2015; Wild, *et al.*,2007). The data analyses by many continue to show that 3.9 billion people will be affected by severe water stress by 2030 (OECD, 2008; Tularam & Reza, 2016). The potable water usage has increased around; for example, almost seven times in terms of daily usage over the past 100 years (Tularam & Krishna, 2009; UN, 2015). This is not surprising given that there has been an unsustainable population growth that is further driving the higher water demand. Moreover, other factors such as climate volatility with changing weather patterns are not helping the serious shortages and excessive availability of the fresh water that cannot be safely captured or stored (Tularam & Reza, 2017; Tularam & Murali, 2015).

Evidently, water is a vital commodity where the world is facing a water supply-demand imbalance because of increasing water scarcity (Reza *et al.* 2017; Tularam & Properjohn, 2011). Tularam (2014) stated in the "Australian Planner" Journal: *"By 2030, under an average economic growth scenario and if no efficiency gains are assumed, global water requirements would grow from 4500 billion m^3 today to 6900 billion m^3 This is about 40% above the current accessible, reliable supply. This global figure is really the aggregation, and other such estimations show an even worse situation: one-third of the population, concentrated in developing countries, will live in basins where this deficit is larger than 50%* "(p. 372).

Currently, the world's population is approximately 7.3 billion people (UN, 2015). The population growth rates are increasing in fact in many countries and the numbers would be larger within the next few decades – for example, UN (2015) is expecting the global population may be 9.6 billion by the next 30 years (RobecoSAM., 2015) and therefore, the freshwater demand is predicted to increase by more than 50%. To meet the increasing demand, some solutions may be considered. One possible is the solution is to majorly finance in the water sector - both public and private water industry around the world (Reza & Tularam, 2021; Roca *et al.*, 2015). It is estimated that US$ 1 trillion is needed globally for the ailing water infrastructure[1] - about USD 6.7 trillion and 22.6 trillion are needed by 2030 and 2050, respectively for water infrastructure and security of investment (Winpenny, 2015).

To fund such a large amount, Governments, companies, individuals, domestic and foreign institutional investors have all noted the possibility of investment in water for not only to forward the ethically based investment but the stability and rise of water use may lead to substantial returns for investors. A critical examination of such investing has led to the private water sector investment groups to take up the challenge (Reza, 2017; Roca & Tularam, 2012).

Given the water sector needs funds, the consequent expanding of the water market including the added investment into water will grow further due to the ethical and so-called "green investing" has been becoming a focus for larger investors as well due the changing humanitarian aspect of the marketplace. Not surprisingly, the demand conditions should ultimately lead to a better set of financial returns from the global water industry as-a-whole (Roca *et al.*, 2015; Reza, 2017, Reza *et al.*, 2021).

The expanded demand of water and related assets has aided the increase in the number of the financial water assets developed (For example, water managed funds water exchange-traded-funds (ETFs), and water indices and their components), which have been introduced to provide opportunities for reasonable returns. Some examples of such are - S&P Global Water Index (S&P), S-Network Global Water Index (S-Net), MSCI World Water Index (MSCI), ISE Clean Edge Water Index (ISE), World Water Index (WOWAX), NASDAQ OMX Global Water Index, NASDAQ OMX US Water Index (Reza & Tularam, 2021). Water related managed funds also appeared after 2000. Some examples are - Pictet Global Water Fund, Swiss-based Sustainable Asset Management (SAM) water fund, KBC Eco water fund etc. (Roca and Tularam, 2012; Roca *et al.*, 2015; Reza *et al.*, 2018). Additionally, the water ETFs such as Invesco Water Resources ETF (PHO), Invesco Global Water ETF (PIO), First Trust Water ETF (FIW) and Invesco S&P Global Water Index ETF (CGW) were introduced to investors in 2007. According to Tularam and Reza (2016), "*Water EFTs are baskets of water-related shares aimed at replicating the performance of the water market...*" (p. 2).

This study investigates the water sector in various countries concerning the equity markets; in particular, relationships among the World, China, Hong Kong, Singapore, France, German, UK, Brazil, Chile, and US. The aim is to examine relationships between water indices - world market, and different individual countries' markets such as with China, Hong Kong, Singapore, Germany, France, UK, Brazil, Chile, and US. Volatility of the returns and indices are together analysed to understand how the global water sector incorporates China, Hong Kong, Singapore, Germany, France, UK, Brazil, Chile, and US markets in decision making. The contributions of this chapter are twofold. Firstly, this is one the first studies to investigate the relationships between world market returns, and different individual countries' market returns concerning water. Secondly, the results of the analyses concerning the investment returns and volatility of the global water sector would be beneficial to global water investors as well as managers. The findings will help individual investors, institutional investors, and foreign investors in making important investment decisions.

LITERATURE REVIEW

In the finance literature, several studies have examined in the issue of returns and volatility using the ARMA-GARCH model (Karanasos, 2000; Liu *et al.*, 2011; Mohammadi, 2017), and the dynamic relationships among equity, bonds, money, and commodity markets (Berbena & Jansen, 2009; Roca *et al.*, 2010). In terms of water investment literature, there are only a few studies on systematic literature review (Reza *et al.*, 2021), price integration (Roca & Tularam, 2012; Reza *et al.*, 2017), portfolio diversification benefits (Gilroy *et al.*, 2013; Jin *et al.*, 2015; Zeneli, 2016), fundamental analysis (Roca *et al.*,2015), regulatory risk and returns of water companies' stocks (Pescetto, 2008; Buckland and Williams, 2013; Buckland *et al.*, 2015, Jin *et al.*, 2019) returns and volatility (Geman & Kanyinda, 2007; Rompotis, 2016; Tularam & Reza, 2016), risk and return relation relationships of water companies' stocks (Buckland & Fraser, 2000; Jin *et al.*, 2016; Romano & Guerrini, 2019) and relationships between water assets and other precious commodities assets (Fiorelli & Mele, 2017; Vandone *et al.*, 2018, Piñeiro-Chousaa *et al.*, 2020). Unfortunately, despite of the above research and the importance to water investment, authors do not appear to initiate studies that systematically investigate the possible relationships among the global water sector of markets.

It is important to note that the private water sector include only three studies that have examined the relations in private water sector of markets' (Asia, Europe, Latin America, North America, and US) return and volatility. Even though Roca and Tularam (2012) study the relationship among the Asia, Europe and US water sector of markets using VAR analysis, their work does not reflect volatility aspect concerning the global water sector of markets. Also, they only investigate three water market indices whereas the present study involves ten water market indices. Peri *et al.* (2017) examine the dynamic relationships among the water, energy and food sectors and investigate the volatility from four water sector of markets (Asia, Europe, Latin America, and North America) using VARMA and DCC-GARCH (1, 1) models. Indeed, Reza *et al.* (2018) investigate four water indices (WOAX, S&P, S-Net and MSCI ACWI), four water sector of markets (Asia, Europe, Latin America, and US) and two water managed funds (Pictet and KBC Eco) returns and volatility during full, pre-GFC, GFC and post-GFC periods using ARMA (1, 1)-GARCH (1, 1) and EGARCH (1, 1) models. However, it appears that none of these studies have focused on relationships between global water sector in terms of their interactions across individual countries' water sector markets and returns together with the relevant volatility information. This study therefore attempts to fill some important gaps. Further, regarding the motivation, this is one of the first study to systematically analyse the relationships between world market and other nine countries' markets – focusing on the returns and volatility information.

DATA AND METHODOLOGY

Data

This study uses the DataStream (DS) Water Index data base for the water sector of the world stock markets information concerning - World, China, Hong Kong, Singapore, France, German, UK, Brazil, Chile, and US markets, which relate to capital markets and help investment in the private water sector in the form of water indices. It is important to note that one water market index encompasses private water companies, which represents 75%-80% of the market capitalization (Roca and Tularam, 2012). The quantitative data for these ten markets are collected from the Thomson Reuters DataStream database[2] for the period of 17 January 2001 to 30 June 2020. Figure 1 displays the trend in water equity markets prices. All equity markets prices are measured on daily basis in US dollars; and estimated by using the formula in the form of returns –

$$R_t = \ln(Price_t / Price_{t-1}) \times 100$$

Figure 1. Movement of water sector of ten markets - World, China, Hong Kong, Singapore, France, German, UK, Brazil, Chile, and US.
(Data Source: Thomson Reuters DataStream database) Time (2001-2020)

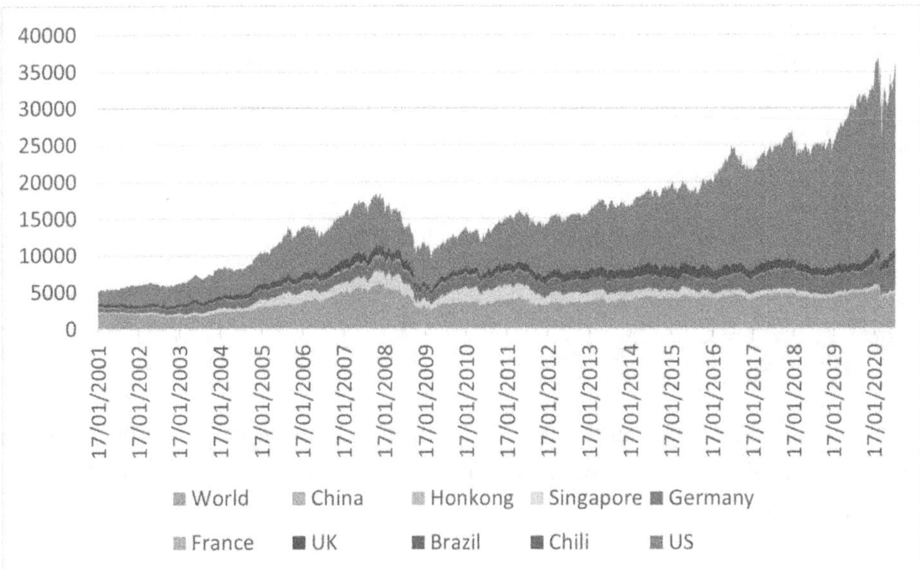

METHODOLOGY

Ordinary Least Square (OLS) Regression Model

This study examines the relationships between world market and other nine (China, Hong Kong, Singapore, France, German, UK, Brazil, Chile, and US) markets using Ordinary Least Square (OLS) regression model.

$$World_{rt} = \alpha_{rt} + \beta_1 China_{rt} + \beta_2 Hong\,Kong_{rt} + \beta_3 Singapore_{rt} + \beta_4 Germany_{rt} + \beta_5 France_{rt} + \beta_6 UK_{rt} + \beta_7 Brazil_{rt} + \beta_8 Chile_{rt} + \beta_9 US_{rt} + \varepsilon_t \tag{1}$$

where world is the dependent variable, and China, Hong Kong, Singapore, France, German, UK, Brazil, Chile, and US water markets are independent variables while εt is error term.

Quantile Regression Model

This study also uses the quantile regression methodology (Koenker and Bassett, 1978). The quantile regression model is also a way of studying the relationship between world market and other nine markets - China, Hong Kong, Singapore, France, German, UK, Brazil, Chile, and US. Let (x,y_i), i=1,…,n, be a sample from these markets, where x_i is a k x 1 vector of regressors. From Tularam and Reza (2017), the quintile regression model may be described as follows.

$$y_i = x_i'\beta_\theta + \varepsilon_{\theta i} \tag{2}$$

$$Quant_\theta\left(y_i \middle| x_i\right) \equiv \inf\left\{y : F(y|x)\,\theta\right\} = x_i'\beta_\theta \tag{3}$$

$$Quant_\theta\left(\varepsilon_{\theta i} \middle| x_i\right) = 0 \tag{4}$$

where $Quant_\theta(y_i|x_i)$ represents the θth conditional quantile of y_i on the regressor vector. β_θ is evaluated for different coefficient values of F and $\varepsilon_{\theta i}$ is the distribution of the error term.

Autoregressive Moving Average (ARMA) Model

This study also investigates the relationships between world market return, and China, Hong Kong, Singapore, Germany, France, UK, Brazil, Chile and US market returns using the ARMA (p, q) model (Reza et *al.*, 2018; Tularam & Saeed, 2016) with the provisional mean, used to all variance models. The ARMA model involving the autoregressive (AR) and the moving average (MA) frameworks in terms of p and q is used. Following Reza et *al.* (2018) and Tularam and Saeed (2016); the AR, MA and ARMA models are written as follows:

AR model: $y_t = \varphi_i y_{t-1} + \varphi_i y_{t-2} + \ldots + \varphi_i y_{t-p} + \varepsilon_t = \sum_{i=1}^{p} \varphi_i y_{t-i}$ (5)

MA model: $y_t = \gamma_j \varepsilon_{t-1} + \gamma_j \varepsilon_{t-2} + \ldots + \gamma_j \varepsilon_{t-p} + \varepsilon_t = \sum_{i=1}^{p} \gamma_j \varepsilon_{t-j}$ (6)

ARMA model: $y_t = \sum_{i=1}^{p} \varphi_i y_{t-i} + \sum_{i=1}^{p} \gamma_j \varepsilon_{t-j}$ (7)

This equation can also be written in compact form as follows:

$$\varphi(L)(y_t - \mu) = \varphi(L)\varepsilon_t \quad (8)$$

when all the roots of $\gamma(z)=1-\gamma_1 z-\gamma_2 z\ldots-\gamma_p z=0$, *ARMA* (*p*, *q*) process are stationary, and invertible; if the roots of the characteristic equations: $\varphi(z)$.

ARMA-GARCH Model

This study utilizes the autoregressive moving average–generalized autoregressive conditional heteroscedasticity (ARMA-GARCH) to model the water sector of ten water markets (Reza et al., *2018*). The ARMA-GARCH model is the mixed form of an ARMA model, which can be applied to model mean behaviour, and a GARCH model, which is used to estimate the volatility of the residual series from the ARMA. TA general form of an ARMA (p, q)-GARCH (p, q) model is given as:

$$\varphi(L)(y_t - \mu) = \varphi(L)\varepsilon_t \quad (9)$$

$$\sigma_t^2 = \omega + \sum_{i=1}^{p} \alpha_i \sigma_{t-1}^2 + \sum_{j=1}^{q} \beta_j \rho_{t-j}^2 + \varepsilon_t \qquad (10)$$

where $\varphi(L)$ is lag polynomials, and $\varepsilon_t = Z_t \rho_t$. Importantly, $\alpha_i, \ldots, \alpha_p, \beta_i, \ldots, \beta_p$ are constant coefficients. When modelling conditional variances, the values of ω, α_i and β_j are non-negative.

EMPIRICAL RESULTS

Descriptive Statistics

Table 1 exhibits the descriptive statistics of world and the nine countries markets. The data shows the mean returns are positive for the eight markets, but it is noted that two (China and Chile) markets' mean returns are negative. It is noted that Hong Kong market mean return (0.048) is the highest, whereas China market mean return is the lowest mean return (-0.010) among ten markets. World, China, France, UK, Brazil, and Chile markets skewness values are negative – suggesting an asymmetric tail. However, Hong Kong, Singapore, Germany, and US markets skewness values are positive. Hence, these countries skewness values are the symmetric. The kurtosis values of all market returns are fat-tailed because the kurtosis values are higher than three. Figure 1 summarizes results on a graph.

Correlation Analysis

In Table 2, the correlation coefficients among water indices are found to be relatively positive. The results show that China market is the less associated (0.010) to US market (lowest correlation); whereas the highest correlation (0.806) occurs between world market and France market. The results are indicating long-term association and contemporaneous interactions between world market and France market, and world market and UK market. It is important to note that China, Hong Kong, Singapore, Germany, France, UK, Brazil, Chile and US market returns are significantly linked with world water market at the 1% level. Thus, the results confirm that all markets coefficients are significant i.e., nine markets are significantly correlated with world water market. In sum, the correlation matrix results show that the markets are noticeable related over the last twenty years.

Table 1. Descriptive statistics

Variables	Observations	Mean	Std. Dev.	Minimum	Maximum	Skewness	Kurtosis
World	5091	0.016	1.053	-10.952	11.011	-0.391	9.202
China	5091	-0.010	2.134	-19.398	9.602	-0.616	5.775
Hong Kong	5091	0.048	2.172	-14.848	18.877	0.745	8.295
Singapore	5091	0.031	2.392	-28.207	23.140	0.505	12.539
Germany	5091	0.037	1.947	-12.597	15.661	0.312	6.066
France	5091	-0.009	2.034	-25.035	17.297	-0.530	11.526
UK	5091	0.021	1.371	-9.540	12.891	-0.025	7.119
Brazil	5091	0.007	2.667	-20.266	16.892	-0.358	4.628
Chile	5091	-0.006	1.481	-19.004	14.994	-0.876	21.968
US	5091	0.053	1.375	-13.088	17.462	0.608	16.769

Notes: Table 1 displays the descriptive statistics for the water sector of ten stocks market - World, China, Hong Kong, Singapore, France, German, UK, Brazil, Chile, and US.

Figure 2. Movements of mean

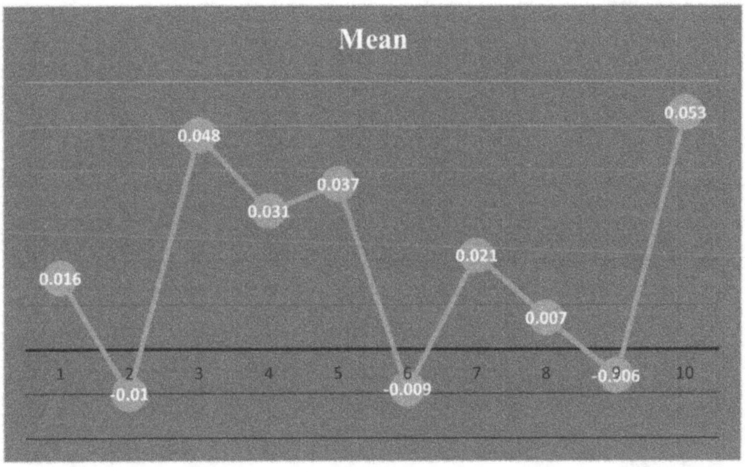

Regression Analysis

This study examines the relationships between world market returns, China, Hong Kong, Singapore, Germany, France, UK, Brazil, Chile and US market returns using OLS and quantile regression models. Table 6 presents the OLS estimated coefficients and it is noted that China, Hong Kong, Singapore, Germany, France, UK, Brazil, Chile, and US are positively significant at the 1% level. The specific quantile (25%,

50% and 75%) regression results further show the positive relationships between world market and other nine markets at the 1% level of significance. These results are line in (Tularam & Reza, 2017). The correlations and the set of regression results confirm that simultaneous interactions exist between world water market and the nine water markets. The global water sector has a long-term set of associations that is needs to be consulted when managers and investors make critical decisions.

Table 2. Correlation matrix

World	World	China	Hong Kong	Singapore	Germany	France	UK	Brazil	Chile	US
World	1									
China	0.119 (0.000)	1								
Hong Kong	0.270 (0.000)	0.180 (0.000)	1							
Singapore	0.228 (0.000)	0.102 (0.000)	0.169 (0.000)	1						
Germany	0.207 (0.000)	0.014 (0.000)	0.043 (0.091)	0.052 (0.008)	1					
France	0.806* (0.000)	0.060 (0.000)	0.107 (0.000)	0.157 (0.000)	0.135 (0.000)	1				
UK	0.746 (0.000)	0.051 (0.009)	0.135 (0.000)	0.139 (0.000)	0.138 (0.000)	0.463 (0.000)	1			
Brazil	0.488 (0.000)	0.070 (0.000)	0.121 (0.000)	0.146 (0.000)	0.062 (0.000)	0.240 (0.000)	0.266 (0.000)	1		
Chile	0.403 (0.000)	0.068 (0.000)	0.100 (0.000)	0.109 (0.000)	0.073 (0.000)	0.237 (0.000)	0.256 (0.000)	0.282 (0.000)	1	
US	0.450 (0.000)	0.010 (0.000)	0.080 (0.000)	0.061 (0.000)	0.024 (0.000)	0.216 (0.000)	0.284 (0.000)	0.240 (0.000)	0.174 (0.000)	1

Notes: Table 2 displays the correlation results among the water sector of ten markets. The results show that water sector of France market is highly and positively correlated with the world water market.

*Correlation above 0.800

ARMA Model

After investigating and testing the following ARMA(1,0), ARMA(0,1), ARMA(1,1), ARMA(1,2), ARMA(2,1) and ARMA(2,2) models in addition to the Autocorrelation Functions (ACF) and Partial Autocorrelation Functions (PCF), the ARMA (1,1) model of the conditional mean based on the minimum Akaike information criterion (AIC) was chosen; based on significant levels of the estimated ARMA(p,q) coefficients. The ARMA (1, 1) model p-values are significant at 1% level for the water sector of markets except China, which was significant at 10% level. Table 4 exhibits the ARMA model fitted results.

Table 3. Regression results

	OLS	25th Quant	50th Quant	75th Quant
China	0.013 (0.000)***	0.010 (0.000)***	0.007 (0.000)***	0.008 (0.000)***
Hong Kong	0.053 (0.000)***	0.054 (0.000)***	0.060 (0.000)***	0.061 (0.000)***
Singapore	0.011 (0.000)***	0.013 (0.000)***	0.013 (0.000)***	0.012 (0.000)***
Germany	0.032 (0.000)***	0.032 (0.000)***	0.033 (0.000)***	0.034 (0.000)***
France	0.265 (0.000)***	0.270 (0.000)***	0.263 (0.000)***	0.261 (0.000)***
UK	0.278 (0.000)***	0.270 (0.000)***	0.266 (0.000)***	0.273 (0.000)***
Brazil	0.071 (0.000)***	0.070 (0.000)***	0.071 (0.000)***	0.068 (0.000)***
Chile	0.063 (0.000)***	0.055 (0.000)***	0.062 (0.000)***	0.061 (0.000)***
US	0.127 (0.000)***	0.122 (0.000)***	0.122 (0.000)***	0.118 (0.000)***
C	0.001 (0.722)	-0.139 (0.000)***	0.002 (0.414)	0.147 (0.000)***
R-squared	0.933	-	-	-
Pseudo R2	-	0.738	0.733	0.729
Number of obs	5091	5091	5091	5091

Notes: Table 3 displays OLS and Quantile regressions results of Equations (1), (2), (3) and (4) to study the relationship between the world market, and China, Hong Kong, Singapore, France, German, UK, Brazil, Chile, and US markets. Here, world market is the independent variable. p-values are given in parentheses.

*, ** and *** represent significance at 10%, 5% and 1% levels, respectively; and p-values are given in brackets.

Ljung–Box Q Test

Table 5 presents the Ljung-Box Q test results based the residuals and squared residuals to confirm the ARMA-GARCH model fitting. The maximum p-values are above 0.05 for standardized residuals and 0.01for squared residuals. Thus, the standardized residuals and squared residuals results showed that p-values are statistically significant. Hence, ARMA-GARCH model is deemed to be a good fit model of the daily stock returns of ten markets.

Autocorrelation and Partial Autocorrelation Functions

The analyses show that the graphs of the Autocorrelation Functions (ACF) and Partial Autocorrelation Functions (PCF) become much smoother as ARMA can effectively deteriorate due to the autoregressive procedure and moving average mechanisms, after which stationary residuals are calculated as well. The ACF and PACF plots show that maximum values are within bounds (95% confidence interval for Gaussion white noise) - no discernible pattern is noted in the ACF and PACF in

Table 4. ARMA (1,1) model results

	World	China	Hong Kong	Singapore	Germany	France	UK	Brazil	Chile	US
Constant	0.001 (0.691)	-0.019 (0.533)	0.032 (0.139)	0.031 (0.764)	0.034 (0.010)	-0.012 (0.000)	0.002 (0.813)	-0.016 (0.529)	-0.015 (0.327)	0.033 (0.000)
AR (1)	0.639 (0.000)***	-0.475 (0.060)***	0.512 (0.000)***	1.000 (0.000)***	0.299 (0.000)***	0.995 (0.000)***	0.707 (0.000)***	0.749 (0.000)***	0.912 (0.000)***	0.477 (0.000)***
MA (1)	0.690 (0.000)**8	-.512 (0.038)***	0.608 (0.000)***	0.999 (0.000)***	0.628 (0.000)***	1.000 (0.000)***	0.748 (0.000)***	0.776 (0.000)***	0.926 (0.000)***	0.587 (0.000)***
R-squared	0.934	0.053	0.216	0.074	0.173	0.811	0.746	0.405	0.215	0.365

Notes: Table 4 exhibits the results of the forecast for ten water markets which is obtained from the ARMA (1,1) model.
*, ** and *** represent significance at 10%, 5% and 1% levels, respectively; and p-values are given in brackets.

the daily return data. The ACF shows that the row data are basically uncorrelated, but the variances are interesting - close to being non-stationary suggesting a GARCH-type model to be appropriate. Figure 3 and Figure 4 display the ACF and PACF of daily returns, respectively.

Table 5. Ljung–Box Q test results for ARMA (p, q) models

Ljung–Box Statistic	Residuals		Squared Residuals	
	Test Statistic	p-Value	Test Statistic	p-Value
Q(4)	14.402	0.006	387.84	0.000
Q(8)	26.341	0.001	592.09	0.000
Q(12)	31.143	0.002	644.19	0.000
Q(16)	35.880	0.003	742.46	0.000
Q(20)	42.929	0.002	841.53	0.000
Q(24)	46.551	0.004	874.44	0.000
Q(28)	48.646	0.009	923.26	0.000
Q(32)	49.743	0.024	940.77	0.000
Q(36)	52.875	0.034	969.98	0.000

Notes: Table 5 exhibits the Ljung-Box Q test results for the standardized residuals and squared residuals with 36 lagged values included.

ARMA (1, 1)-GARCH (1, 1) Model

Therefore, this chapter has used the ARMA (1,1)-GARCH (1,1) model for the water sector of ten markets using the conditional volatility technique. From Table 6, it is noted that parameters for the Singapore, UK, Brazil, and Chile markets AR (1) are not significant and the parameters for Singapore, Brazil, and Chile in the case of MA (1) are not significant - omitting orders of the AR (p) and MA (q) process results in a higher AIC-value. The results of the water sector of ten markets show that the parameters of GARCH (1, 1) model are statistically significant at 1% level. The ARMA (1,1)-GARCH (1,1) model results find a high degree of persistency in the conditional volatility from α and β of the ten market stock returns – that is, "volatile". The results are in line with the work of Reza et *al.* (2018). However, the results show that the p-values of the France, UK and Brazil markets are not significant.

Figure 3. Autocorrelation function (ACF) of water sector of ten equity market daily returns.

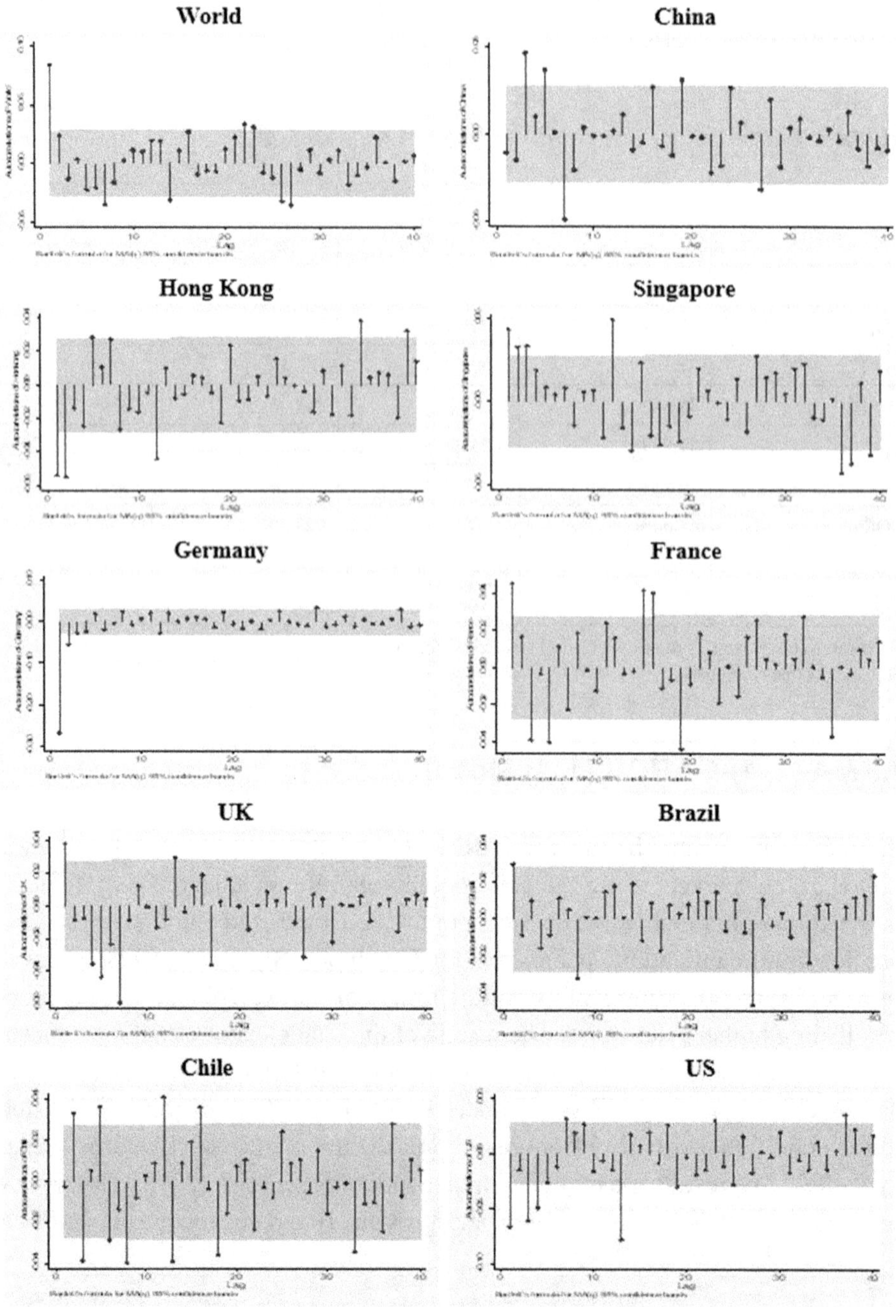

Figure 4. Partial autocorrelation (PACF) of water sector of ten equity market daily returns.

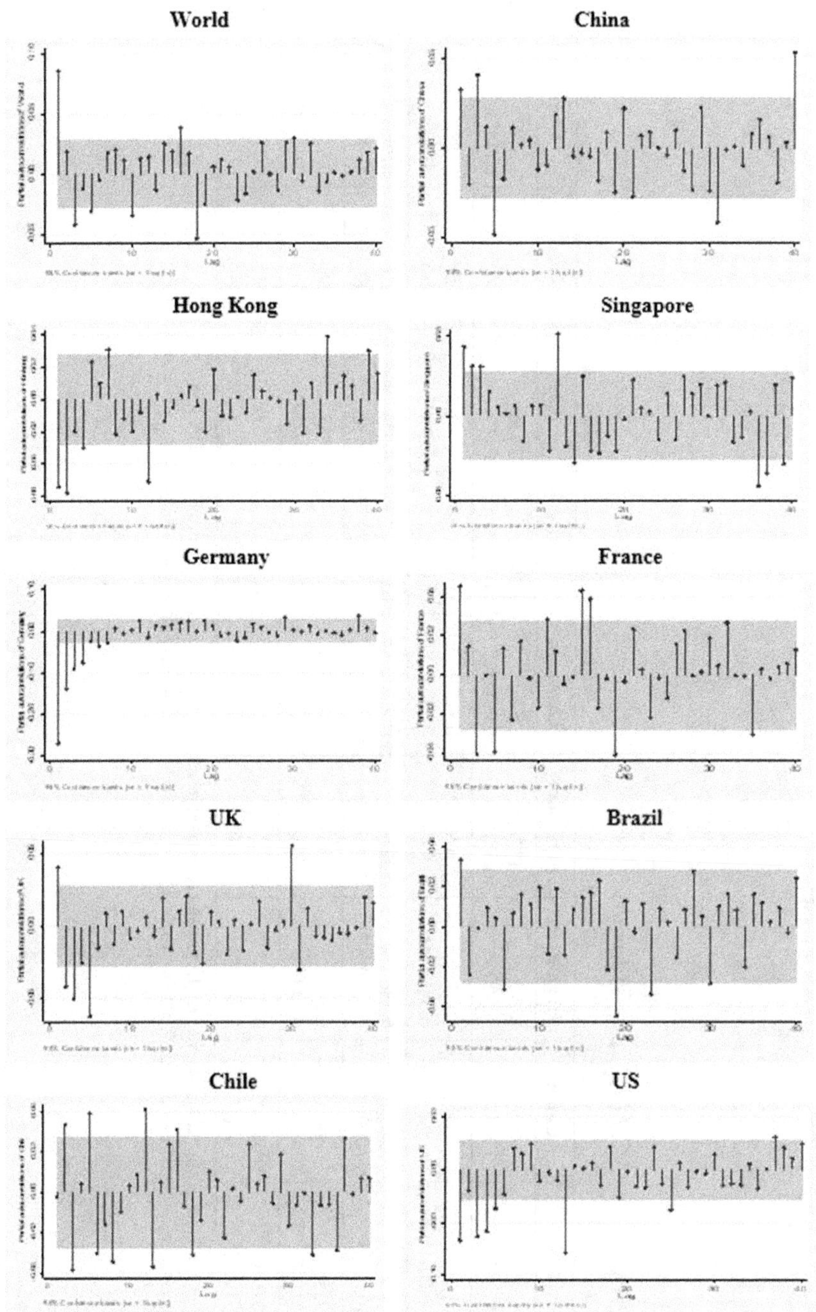

Table 6. ARMA-GRACH (1,1) model results

	World	China	Hong Kong	Singapore	Germany	France	UK	Brazil	Chile	US
AR	1.192 (0.002)**	4.056 (0.000)***	0.749 (0.000)***	2.112 (0.561)	0.208 (0.001)***	1.363 (0.000)***	0.736 (0.107)	0.627 (0.264)	1.879 (0.485)	0.563 (0.023)**
MA	-1.217 (0.001)***	-4.055 (0.000)***	-0.837 (0.000)***	-2.109 (0.563)	-0.528 (0.000)***	-1.396 (0.000)***	-0.764 (0.087)	-0.655 (0.236)	-1.882 (0.483)	-0.624 (0.009)***
α	0.227 (0.000)***	0.241 (0.000)***	0.386 (0.000)***	0.372 (0.000)***	0.180 (0.000)***	0.239 (0.000)***	0.364 (0.000)***	0.210 (0.000)***	0.296 (0.000)***	0.330 (0.000)***
β	0. 563 (0.000)***	0.599 (0.000)***	0.589 (0.000)***	0.531 (0.000)***	0.535 (0.000)***	0.796 (0.000)***	0.718 (0.000)***	0.866 (0.000)***	0.518 (0.000)***	0.514 (0.000)***
ω	0.016 (0.000)***	0.646 (0.000)***	0.306 (0.000)***	0.692 (0.000)***	0.922 (0.000)***	-0.011 (0.678)***	-0.012 (0.197)***	-0.215 (0.145)***	0.373 (0.000)***	0.221 (0.000)***

Notes: Table 6 displays the ARMA-GARCH (1,1) model estimated results for ten water market returns and volatility.
*, ** and *** denote significance at 10%, 5% and 1% levels, respectively; and p-values are given in brackets.

Vector Autoregression (VAR) Model

This study conducts the VAR analyses to determine variables whether there are interactions and significant links. The VAR optimum lag is found to be persistent based on the AIC test results. Table 7 shows the optimal lag test results - lag of 1 is statistically significant. Then VAR (1) is conducted to assess the interaction between world water markets and other nine water markets i.e., how one country's water index can link with world water index.

Table 7. Optimal lag determination

	Lags		
	1	2	3
AIC	36.326*	36.383	36.622
HQIC	36.387	36.532	36.937
SBIC	36.497	36.797	37.479

Note: *Denotes lowest AIC.

Table 8 shows the VAR results of the ten private sector water market indices. The VAR results show that the independent variables-China, Germany, and Chile water indices (lag 1) negatively affect the world water index at the 5%, 10% and 1% respectively. However, Brazil and US (lag 1) positively and statistically impact on world market at 10% and 1% levels. The VAR model results suggest that predictions can be made regarding the world, China, Hong Kong, Singapore, Germany, France, UK, Brazil, Chile, and US markets using set of Equations 11. There is one limitation noted in the VAR model – the seven water market indices show a negative relationship with world water market index — the forecast variables of seven water market indices are prejudiced by the predictor variables. The results for model fitting for the VAR model are in Table 9.

$$\begin{aligned} World_t &= 0.011 - 0.015China_{t-1} - 0.006Hong\,Kong_{t-1} \\ &+0.005Singapore_{t-1} - 0.014Germany_{t-1} + 0.002France_{rt} \\ &-0.016UK_{rt} + 0.012Brazil_{rt} - 0.028Chile_{rt} + 0.079US_{rt} + \varepsilon_t \end{aligned} \tag{11}$$

Table 8. VAR coefficients

World	Lag	Coef.	P-Value
World	L1.	0.062	0.245
China	L1.	-0.015	0.023**
Hong Kong	L1.	-0.006	0.357
Singapore	L1.	0.005	0.376
Germany	L1.	-0.014	0.066*
France	L1.	0.002	0.891
UK	L1.	-0.016	0.391
Brazil	L1.	0.012	0.070*
Chile	L1.	-0.028	0.010***
US	L1.	0.079	0.000***
C	-	0.011	0.432

Note: *, ** and *** each represent significance findings at the 10%, 5% and 1% levels.

Table 9. Model fitting for VAR coefficients

Equation	Parms	RMSE	R-sq	chi2	P>chi2
World	11	1.010	0.024	103.419	0.000***
China	11	2.048	0.007	29.547	0.001***
Hong Kong	11	2.106	0.035	149.276	0.000***
Singapore	11	2.396	0.029	121.638	0.000***
Germany	11	1.841	0.084	373.374	0.000***
France	11	1.974	0.016	68.709	0.000***
UK	11	1.346	0.020	83.155	0.000***
Brazil	11	2.643	0.007	28.722	0.001***
Chile	11	1.452	0.005	24.040	0.007***
US	11	1.353	0.013	54.256	0.000***

Note: *, ** and *** represent significance findings at the 10%, 5% and 1% levels.

Granger Causality

The 'Granger causality' tests are conducted between world market and other nine water markets (see Table 10). The results suggest that a significant Granger causality exists between the water sector of world market and the water sector of China market (significant at the 10% (low) level). These results are in line with those of Reza *et al.* (2017); while the world market Granger causing Brazil and Chile markets at the 5%

(medium) level. The Granger causality is stronger at the 1% level from world market to Germany and US markets - these two water markets appear to be significantly linked with world market. Moreover, a combined granger causality appears to exist in a combined manner with the world market at the 1% (highly significant) level i.e., the nine water markets are suggestively related with world water markets. There appears to be no substantial Granger causality between world market and Hong Kong, Singapore, and UK water markets.

Table 10. Granger causality test results

Equation	Excluded	chi2	df	Prob > chi2
World	China	3.369	1	0.066*
World	Hong Kong	2.619	1	0.106
World	Singapore	0.124	1	0.724
World	Germany	6.496	1	0.011***
World	France	0.029	1	0.865
World	UK	1.008	1	0.315
World	Brazil	4.491	1	0.034**
World	Chile	3.988	1	0.046**
World	US	21.925	1	0.000***
World	ALL	57.046	9	0.000***

Note: *, ** and *** represent significance findings at the 10%, 5% and 1% levels.

CONCLUSION

This study investigates the relationships between water sector of world market and water sector of nine countries' markets, studying their volatility and returns using well accepted statistical analysis methods and a comprehensive data set. The empirical tests show that a long-term association between world market and nine countries markets. The correlation analysis results show that nine countries markets are positively correlated with world market. However, France and UK are more highly correlated with the world market. As all countries' markets are positively correlated there is little possibility for international portfolio diversification between markets. The OLS and quantile regression (25%, 50% and 75%) results confirm causative relationships between world market and other nine markets. The findings indicate that the markets include a long-term association, a finding that may be helpful for managers and investors when making decisions.

In this chapter, although the ARMA (1, 1) model is applied to the ten markets daily returns. Petrică *et al.* (2016) claim that the normality assumption for residues is not fulfilled and that this happens often to residues of ARMA models. To contend with this limitation, this study is extended by applying ARMA-GARCH (1, 1) models including robustness tests. It is found that the LB-Q statistics are significant at 1% level – possible to estimate the expected and unexpected volatility. ARMA-GARCH (1, 1) model shows both the daily volatility and returns for the water sector of ten market. The motivation for this chapter has been justified in that the findings has addressed the questions that financial management often ask such as whether or not markets are desirable tools in water investment - the findings also help water investors improve their knowledge of whether higher returns' opportunities are available from investment when considering the different individual water indices around the world.

In studying interactions and developing robustness test of results, VAR analysis is applied and to determine the impact of water sectors of China, Hong Kong, Singapore, Germany, France, UK, Brazil, Chile, and US markets' investment upon the world markets' returns. The results show that only Brazil and US markets returns positively influence the world markets returns. The 'Granger causality' further shows that the nine markets are significantly related. However, no significant Granger causality is observed between world water market and Hong Kong, Singapore, and UK markets. The results and findings of this chapter could be more implacable for managers and investors in the global water sector. The findings assist the international institutions when decision making - the influence of investment in the water portfolios. The results and findings are for scholars, policy makers, and individual and institutional investors worldwide to examine in terms of their interests whether it is the use of model such as ARMA, GARCH, VAR etc. Moreover, given the large sample of countries studied the applications of findings are particularly useful for the relevant water indices. Future research could investigate the associations between water indices and commodity market indices to evaluate whether the water market could be a reasonably safe haven for trillions of dollars available from the ethically influenced investors.

DISCLAIMER

The contents and views of this chapter are expressed by the authors in their personal capacities. It is not necessary for the Editor and the Publisher to agree with these viewpoints, and they are not responsible for any duty of care in this regard.

ACKNOWLEDGMENT

The authors extend sincere gratitude to

- The Editor and the International Editorial Advisory Board (IEAB) of this book who initially desk reviewed, arranged a rigorous double/triple blind review process, and conducted a thorough, minute, and critical final review before accepting the chapter for publication.
- All anonymous reviewers who provided very constructive feedbacks for thorough revision, improvement, extension, and fine tuning of the chapter.
- All colleagues, assistants and well-wishers who assisted the authors to complete this task.

REFERENCES

Berbena, R., & Jansen, W. (2009). Bond market and stock market integration in Europe: A smooth transition approach. *Applied Economics, 41*(24), 3067–3080. doi:10.1080/00036840701367572

Buckland, R., Beecher, J., & Williams, J. (2015). Risk and regulation in water utilities: A cross-country comparison of evidence from the CAPM. *Journal of Regulatory Economics, 47*(2), 117–145. doi:10.100711149-014-9261-z

Buckland, R., & Fraser, P. (2000). *Abnormal returns in the UK water industry since privatisation* (Working Paper No. 00-10). Aberdeen Papers in Accountancy, Finance and Management. University of Aberdeen.

Buckland, R., & Williams, J. (2013). *Volatility and regulation in water supply and distribution: A post-privatization comparison of UK and US water utilities*. University of Aberdeen. Retrieved from https://aura.abdn.ac.uk/bitstream/2164/2968/1/WaterUtilityPaperforAURA.pdf

Fiorelli, C., & Mele, M. (2017). Water gain: As a common good becomes a financial opportunity. *International Journal of Economics and Financial Issues, 7*(2), 626–630.

Geman, H., & Kanyinda, A. (2007). Water as the next commodity. *Journal of Alternative Investments, 10*(2), 23–30. doi:10.3905/jai.2007.695264

Gilroy, B. M., Schreckenberg, H., & Seiler, V. (2013). *Water as an alternative asset* (Working Paper No. 2012-09). Center for International Economic. Retrieved from http://groups.unipaderborn.de/fiwi/RePEc/Working%20Paper%20neutral/WP55%20-%20 2012-09.pdf

Jin, Y., Li, B., Roca, E., & Wong, V. (2016). Water as an investment: Liquid yet illiquid. *Applied Economics*, *48*(9), 731–745. doi:10.1080/00036846.2015.1085646

Jin, Y., Reza, R., Li, B., Roca, E., & Wong, V. (2019). Water as an investment and the impact of regulatory risk. *Financial Planning Research. Journal*, *5*(1), 55–81.

Jin, Y., Roca, E., Li, B., Wong, V., & Cheung, A. (2015). Sprinkle your investment portfolio with water! *International Journal of Water*, *9*(1), 43–59. doi:10.1504/IJW.2015.067445

Karanasos, M. (2001). Prediction in ARMA models with GARCH in mean effects. *Journal of Time Series Analysis*, *22*(5), 555–576. doi:10.1111/1467-9892.00241

Koenker, R., & Bassett, G. (1978). Regression quantiles. *Econometrica*, *46*(1), 33–50. doi:10.2307/1913643

Liu, H., Erdem, E., & Shi, J. (2011). Comprehensive evaluation of ARMA–GARCH(-M) approaches for modeling the mean and volatility of wind speed. *Applied Energy*, *88*(3), 724–732. doi:10.1016/j.apenergy.2010.09.028

Ljung, G. M., & Box, G. E. P. (1978). On a measure of a lack of fit in time series models. *Biometrika*, *65*(2), 297–303. doi:10.1093/biomet/65.2.297

Mohammadi, M. (2017). Prediction of α -stable G.A.R.C.H. and ARMA-G.A.R.C.H.-M models. *Journal of Forecasting*, *36*(7), 859–866. doi:10.1002/for.2477

OECD. (2008). *OECD environmental outlook to 2030*. Organisation for Economic Co-operation and Development. Retrieved from https://www.OECD-ilibrary.org/environment/OECD-environmental-outlook-to-2030_9789264040519-en

Peri, M., Vandone, D., & Baldi, L. (2017). Volatility Spillover between Water, Energy and Food. *Sustainability*, *9*(6), 1071. doi:10.3390u9061071

Pescetto, G. M. (2008). Regulation and Systematic Risk: The Case of the Water Industry in England and Wales. *Applied Financial Economics*, *18*(1), 61–73. doi:10.1080/09603100601057847

Petrică, A. C., Stancu, S., & Tindeche, A. (2016). Limitation of ARIMA models in financial and monetary economics. *Theoretical and Applied Economics*, *23*(4), 19–42.

Piñeiro-Chousaa, J., López-Cabarcosb, M. A., & Ribeiro-Soriano, D. (2020). Does investor attention influence water companies' stock returns? *Technological Forecasting and Social Change*, *158*, 120115. doi:10.1016/j.techfore.2020.120115

Reza, R. (2017). *An investigation of water investment performance: Analysis of the global water industry [PhD Thesis]*. Griffith University. Retrieved from https://research-repository.griffith.edu.au/handle/10072/371256

Reza, R., & Tularam, G. A. (2021). The Determinants of capital structure: evidence from the global water industry. In K. Marleau (Ed.), Advances in Capital Structure Research (pp. 119–149). Nova Science.

Reza, R., Tularam, G. A., & Li, B. (2017). An investigation into the interdependence of global water indices: A VAR analysis. *Applied Economics*, *49*(8), 769–796. doi:10.1080/00036846.2016.1205725

Reza, R., Tularam, G. A., & Li, B. (2018). Returns and volatility of water investments. *Cogent Economics & Finance*, *6*(3), 1438724. doi:10.1080/23322039.2018.1438724

Reza, R., Tularam, G. A., & Li, B. (2021). A review of global research on private investment in the water sector. *Utilities Policy*, *72*, 101283. doi:10.1016/j.jup.2021.101283

Robeco, S. A. M. (2015). *Water: The market of the future*. Zurich: Carbon Neutral Publication. Retrieved from http://www.RobecoSAM.com/images/Water_ Study_en.pdf

Roca, E., Tularam, G. A., & Reza, R. (2015). Fundamental signals of investment profitability in the global water industry. *International Journal of Water*, *9*(4), 395–424. doi:10.1504/IJW.2015.072155

Roca, E. D., & Tularam, G. A. (2012). Which way does water flow? An econometric analysis of the global price integration of water stocks. *Applied Economics*, *44*(23), 2935–2944. doi:10.1080/00036846.2011.568403

Romano, G., & Guerrini, A. (2019). Paying Returns to Shareholders of Water Utilities: Evidence from Italy. *Sustainability*, *11*(7), 2033. doi:10.3390u11072033

Rompotis, G. G. (2016). Evaluating a new hot trend: The case of water exchange-traded funds. *The Journal of Index Investing*, *6*(4), 103–128. doi:10.3905/jii.2016.6.4.103

Tularam, G. A. (2014). Investing in water for a green economy. *Australian Plants*, *51*(4), 372–373. doi:10.1080/07293682.2014.948987

Tularam, G. A., & Krishna, M. (2009). Long term consequences of groundwater pumping in Australia: A review of impacts around the globe. *Journal of Applied Sciences in Environmental Sanitation*, *4*(2), 151–166.

Tularam, G. A., & Marchisella, P. (2014). Water scarcity in Asia and its long-term water and border security implications for Australia. In R. M. Clark & S. Hakim (Eds.), *Securing Water and Wastewater Systems* (pp. 189–211). Springer. doi:10.1007/978-3-319-01092-2_9

Tularam, G. A., & Murali, K. K. (2015). Water security problems in Asia and longer-term implications for Australia. In W. L. Filho & V. Sümer (Eds.), *Sustainable Water Use and Management Green Energy and Technology* (pp. 119–149). Springer. doi:10.1007/978-3-319-12394-3_7

Tularam, G. A., & Properjohn, M. (2011). An investigation into water distribution network security: Risk and implications. *Security Journal*, *24*(4), 283–301. doi:10.1057j.2010.4

Tularam, G. A., & Reza, R. (2016). Water exchange traded funds: A study on idiosyncratic risk using Markov switching analysis. *Cogent Economics & Finance*, *4*(1), 1139437. doi:10.1080/23322039.2016.1139437

Tularam, G. A., & Reza, R. (2017). The Critical Importance of Groundwater in Coastal Areas: Impact of Climate Change on Bangladesh Freshwater Resources. *Journal of Climate Change*, *3*(1), 59–70. doi:10.3233/JCC-170006

Tularam, G. A., & Reza, R. (2019). Subsurface Acid Sulphate Pollution and Salinity Intrusion in Coastal Groundwater Environments. In N. Narayanan, B. Mohanadhas & V. Mangottiri (Eds.), Flow and Transport in Subsurface Environment (pp. 189–214). Springer.

Tularam, G. A., & Saeed, T. (2016). Oil-price forecasting based on various univariate time-series models. *American Journal of Operations Research*, *6*(3), 226–235. doi:10.4236/ajor.2016.63023

UN. (2015). *World population projected to reach 9.7 billion by 2050.* Department of Economic and Social Affairs, United Nations.

Vandone, D., Peri, M., Vandone, D., Baldi, L., & Tanda, A. (2018). The impact of energy and agriculture prices on the stock performance of the water industry. *Water Resources and Economics*, *23*, 14–27. doi:10.1016/j.wre.2018.02.002

Wild, D., Francke, C. J., Menzli, P., & Schon, U. (2007). *Water: A Market of the Future*. Switzerland, Zurich: SAM Sustainable Asset Management. Retrieved from https:// venturecenter.co.in/water/pdf/Sam%20Group-Water%20Market%20 Report%202007.pdf

Winpenny, J. (2015). *Water: Fit to Finance? Catalyzing National Growth through Investment in Water Security*. Report of the High-Level Panel on Financing Infrastructure for a Water-Secure World. Water Council, OECD. Retrieved from https://www.worldwatercouncil.org/en/publications/water-fit-finance

Zeneli, F. (2016). Analysis of risks and investments' opportunities in water sector. *Academicus International Scientific Journal*, *7*(13), 128–137. doi:10.7336/academicus.2016.13.10

ADDITIONAL READING

Alvarez, M., & Rodríguez, A. (2015). Water-related mutual funds: Investment performance and social role. *Social Responsibility Journal*, *11*(3), 502–512. doi:10.1108/SRJ-08-2013-0104

Antoniou, A., Barr, D. G., & Priestley, R. (2000). Abnormal stock returns and public policy: The case of the UK privatised electricity and water utilities. *International Journal of Finance & Economics*, *55*(2), 93–106. doi:10.1002/(SICI)1099-1158(200004)5:2<93::AID-IJFE124>3.0.CO;2-T

Buckland, R., & Fraser, P. (2001). Political and regulatory risk in water utilities: Beta sensitivity in the United Kingdom. *Journal of Business Finance & Accounting*, *28*(7-8), 877–904. doi:10.1111/1468-5957.00397

Morana, C., & Sawkins, J. W. (2000). Regulatory uncertainty and share price volatility: The English and Welsh water industry's periodic price review. *Journal of Regulatory Economics*, *17*(1), 87–100. doi:10.1023/A:1008105405621

Reza, R., & Tularam, G. A. (2017). An analysis of the relationships between ownership structure and capital structure of the global water industry. In *22nd International Congress on Modelling and Simulation*, Australia.

ENDNOTES

1 http://www.justmeans.com/blogs/investing-in-water-0

2 Thomson Reuters DataStream is the world's highest inclusive financial historical time series database from the 1950s, which is designed for the financial researchers.

Chapter 2
Green Energy Demand and Financial Development:
Evidence From Africa

Alhassan Bunyaminu
University of Professional Studies, Ghana

Ibrahim Nandom Yakubu
https://orcid.org/0000-0003-4424-996X
Ankara Yildirim Beyazit University, Turkey

ABSTRACT

This study investigates the impact of financial development on green energy demand in Africa for the period 1990-2018. Using the dynamic generalized method of moments (GMM) technique, the findings of this study reveal that financial development reduces the share of renewable energy demand and increases environmental pollution in Africa. FDI inflows also hamper renewable energy demand and positively contribute to carbon dioxide emission. It is further evident from the results that although trade openness does not significantly enhance green energy demand, it matters for carbon dioxide emission. In line with these findings, appropriate policies are recommended.

DOI: 10.4018/978-1-6684-5580-7.ch002

INTRODUCTION

Demand for green energy sources (GES) and related technology has become a subject of scientific research in the 21st century. Although, experts have espoused several dependable, and leading-edge strategies in leveraging GES, the process of navigating from non-green energy sources to GES, particularly in emerging economies, has been quite sluggish. Though, some of the emerging economies have vast potential and significant GES, as evidenced in the availability of immense wind and solar energies. These wind and solar energies extend to wide ecological areas and may not require a centralized method of distribution. In spite of this prospect, utilization of green energy has not been maximized by these emerging economies. With rising population in these countries accompanied by a surge in energy and spiralling energy cost, an energy crunch has ensued resulting in the reliance on non-green energy sources. Even though traditional energy is the main source of worldwide energy mix, it is nonetheless the principal means of releasing greenhouse gases into the atmosphere.

The consequence of this is the atmospheric catastrophe happening lately like global warming. The advancement of GES is considered as one of the vital initiatives meant to reduce CO_2 emissions. This is to complement the search for alternatives in powering the mining sector where the use of gas, coal, radioactive ore and oil has remained dominant with its attendant contribution greenhouse emissions.

Small hydropower, geothermal and wind energies are used alternatively in other countries to stem the tide of CO_2 emissions. The years 2014-2024 have been declared by the UN General Assembly as the year of Sustainable Energy for All. The UN General Assembly has highlighted the impact of energy on long-term growth and the strengthening of the post-2015 expansion plan. Thus, green energy strategies, production, and financing of green energy sources have taken centre stage in emerging economies. Investment strategies have drifted from conservative governments and foreign sponsors to private, typically local commerce and financial institutions (Martinot *et al.*, 2002; REN21, 2014).

The adoption of green energy sources is rising between public organizations, industry, NGOs, and businesses. Presently, the outbreak of the COVID-19 pandemic is hampering the world of energy. As there has been a rapid increment in the level of conventional fuel prices, the machines and engines that use a large share of green energy sources are operating effectively and not been affected by the pandemic.

The need to achieve sustainable development has sparked the quest for embracing development initiatives that put climate change in the spotlight. Consequently, countries are adopting development blueprints will lead to sustainable development through the use of GES that can accelerate economic growth with minimum adverse impact on the climate. Using the GES enables us to classify the energy mix and enhance energy security, resulting in the reduction of reliance on conventional fuels and greenhouse gases (Rifkin, 2011). When it comes to curtailing reliance on traditional fuels, technology is the answer (Nasreen & Rafay, 2022). the International Energy Agency has proffered GES technology as the ultimate solution to finding a lasting solution. The GES is considerably being regarded as an asset that is able to offer economic potential by reducing reliance on imported fossil fuels, increasing air quality and health care, improving access to energy safety, enhancing economic growth, and decreasing unemployment. In several developing nations, the creation of helpful actions for the enactment of the GES is considered paramount. These nations accept support policies and conduct experiments. By 2013, developing nations and states in which a market economy was developing were at the forefront in enhancing policies to aid renewable energy sources (REN21, 2014). GES assistance policies usually entail the use of administrative and economic instruments such as direct investments towards enhancing infrastructure, which comprises greenhouse gas emission shares (GHGs) or green certificates, tax or financial inducements, and market initiatives. It has been discovered that economic in addition to financial instruments have a solid impact on other energy creation in developing countries (Pfeiffer & Mulder, 2013). The renewable energy space is wide and offer opportunities for investment to curb climate change. However, it is mostly bedevilled by inadequate financial investments with most developing economies suffering from gaps in alternative energy financing (Lindlein & Mostert, 2005).

Financing green energy projects is fundamental to the start and adoption of green energy technologies (GETs) for sustained economic growth and combating climate change. The provision of finance for investment in Green Energy Projects (GEPs) has an intense influence on the level of adoption of green energy (GE). Africa as a continent is greatly affected by low energy access and weak energy security. It is affirmed that the issue of access to clean energy sources is associated with the rural nature of African communities (Liming, 2009; Karekezi, 2002; Rashed *et al.*, 2022). This does not suggest that urban communities in Africa are not affected by energy access. As the population of countries increases, traditional energy sources are constrained (Painuly, 2001). This brings the issue of increasing energy availability together with its security in Africa.

Toke and Lauber (2007) indicate that financing GETs and GEPs offers vital access to a country to adequately respond to the problems of global warming and climate change. As countries enhance their financial investments in the development of GE and support for GEPs, they intensify the chances of reducing their carbon emissions. Presently, a lot of African countries satisfy their energy needs from sources like fossil fuels, which when burned emits greenhouse gases (GHGs) that are detrimental to the environment. Environmental pollutants in the form of GHGs such as methane, carbon dioxide, and chlorodifluoromethane (CH4, C02, and

HCFC-22, respectively) are identified to be drivers of climate change (Oji, 2015). The call for countries by the United Nations Framework Convention on Climate Change (UNFCCC) to reduce and screen the atmospheric releases of greenhouse gases in recent times has become apparent.

Financing is a key factor for the widespread distribution of GETs in Africa. It gives an opportunity for borrowers to secure affordable credit over a reasonable time span, at the same time creating an avenue to invest in systems that enhance the quality of life of the people. As a result, access to finance plays a crucial role in stimulating the penetration of GETs to aid resolve the energy problem that is prevalent in several nations in African. Researchers have associated sustainable economic development with finance, signifying that positive changes in the condition of an economy come with innovative financial interventions (Schumpeter, 1911; McKinnon, 1973; Shaw, 1973; Oji, 2015).

GE development may be funded from a number of sources. Researchers have classified these sources into two distinct categories; namely traditional source, alternatively called conventional financing and innovative financing (Ma *et al.*, 2010; Konstantinos *et al.*, 2011; Shrestha, 2007). These methods of funding may be used in projects as the only means of providing finance. However, disparities in these methods may occur depending on the aims of funding the project. Traditionally, in the private sector, it is recognized that GE investment projects may be funded through equity or debt (Oji, 2015).

There are viewpoints that traditional funding approaches are not suitable for funding GEPs, especially given the challenges investors are confronted with in accepting GEPs (Derrick, 1998). There exist numerous uncertainties concerning profit-making on invested capital, owing to inherent risks associated with GEPs; the uncertainty of the trade-off between the risk of investing and returns on investment; uncertainty with the rate of altering technologies; and the result of policy on market dynamics (Wiser *et al.*, 1997; Shrestha, 2007; UNEPFI, 2012; Justice, 2009). Traditional funding for GEPs is mostly favoured by investment banks, development banks, commercial banks, multilateral institutions, and non-governmental institutions. In traditional financing, the main avenues which comprise of models by which funds are directed into GEPs are project financing, corporate financing, and lease financing. These days Islamic financing is also available for green projects (Rafay *et al.*, 2017)

This research is motivated by two vital factors. Spending on green energy generation strategies offer prospects of decreasing energy deficiency in Africa, stimulate economic growth, and safeguard paucity in energy. Green energy generation permits nations to graduate from reliance on fossil fuels to fresh energy sources, thus decreasing greenhouse gas dissipation (Panwar *et al.*, 2011). Additionally, the function of financial development on green energy generation in Africa is visibly missing. Prior empirical studies connecting financial development and the energy sector are fixated on energy consumption. The studies on finance and green energy production are constrained notwithstanding the essential function carried out by financial growth in the aspect of green energy generation (Scholtens & Veldhuisa, 2015). The limited research that exists are focused on developed economies in Europe and America. Extant literature on green energy financing in Africa is not only narrow, but the relevance of financial development on green energy demand is conspicuously missing (Da Silva *et al.*, 2018; Lokonon & Salami, 2017; Brunnschweiler, 2010). The significance of this study on financial development and green energy demand within the African perspective and its associated barriers to investment cannot be overemphasized.

LITERATURE REVIEW

Factors Influencing Financial Development

There is plethora of theories in the finance growth research. The prominent theories include the finance-led growth (Schumpeter, 1911; Patrick, 1966; McKinnon, 1973; Shaw, 1973) and growth-led finance theory (Robinson, 1952, Lewis, 1956). Apart from these two theories, other researchers detect that the relevance of financial growth in economic activities is exaggerated (Lucas, 1988, De Gregorio & Guidotti, 1995; Arcand *et al.*, 2015) whereas other researchers consider finance as unhelpful to steps of economic growth (Minsky, 1974; Tobin, 1984; Cihak *et al.*, 2012). The theory of finance-led growth posits that, if financial institution embarks on plausible financial initiatives, it will deliver adequate returns on investment, and consequently boosts economic development. Functions of financial systems encompass organizing and mobilizing savings, distribution of funds, enhancing risk-taking, implementation of organizational control together with the acceleration of buying of goods and services (Levine, 1997). Although extensive discussion has gone into this school of thought, there are dissenting views about the function of financial development in investment, economic growth, and human well-being. The position of the growth-led finance theory is that financial development is synonymous to economic growth (Robinson, 1952). When economic activities increase it bolsters demand for financial instruments culminating in overall improvement of the financial industry. The disruptive hypothesis in financial studies stipulate that, financial development is considered to be a disruptive instrument of economic expansion as financial development could engender macroeconomic uncertainty, affecting society's savings, resulting in weaknesses in bank lending (Cihak *et al.*, 2012; Minsky, 1974). Apart from creating weaknesses in bank lending, excessive complicated financial instruments may lead to financial uncertainty which can bring about an economic downturn (Gennaioli *et al.*, 2012). The fact that economic growth nosedived following the banking sector crisis bears testimony to the importance of the financial services sector (Reinhart & Reinhart, 2015; Arcand *et al.*, 2015). The financial industry diverts resources from the actual industries resulting in weaknesses and hampering progress to economic growth (Tobin, 1984). Prior to the 2008 global economic downturn, resources in developed nations were channelled to the financial sector at the expense of more productive areas of the economy (Dabla-Norris & Narapong, 2013). However, other researchers consider finance as an unbiased medium towards economic growth, but Lucas (1988) argued that the role of finance in economic growth has been overstated. The standpoint of (Arcand *et al.*, 2015; Cecchetti & Kharroubi, 2015) is that financial development does not result in economic progress. De Gregorio and Guidotti (1995) opine that developed nations may reach a level of growth at which financial abundance is no more a panacea to the efficiency of investment and eventually to economic development. According to the finance-led growth hypothesis, when finance reaches a particular level its positive impact on economic prosperity may diminish considerably (Arcand *et al.*, 2015). Churchill and Saunders (1989) suggested that more ground-breaking financing research should be conducted to enhance performance and investment in the energy sector particularly, those from the private sector. Similarly, Kim and Park (2015) express similar opinions by stating that the financial industry should mobilize savings, improve risk, and institute corporate control and transmission of resources that will lead to improvement in the renewable energy industry.

Financial Development and Green Energy

A pioneering study by Sadorsky (2010) connecting financial development to the energy industry was supported by a number of research examining the nexus between financial growth and demand for energy in varying geographical areas based on different techniques (Çoban & Topcu, 2013; Ali *et al.*, 2015; Roubaud & Shahbaz, 2018). The results of these studies have mixed findings as some researchers have found a positive association between financial development and demand for energy whereas other researchers have revealed a negative association. Other related literature concentrates on financial development and emissions of carbon (Abbasi & Riaz, 2016). These related studies suggest that financial development results in economic growth and an increase in household wealth which subsequently leads to an upward rise in energy consumption and carbon emissions. However, the prior empirical studies on determinants of investment in renewable energy based on this hypothesis appeared indecisive. Investigations by Kim and Park (2015) established that financial development results in a significant positive impact on the investment of green energy. Brunnschweiler (2010) conducted a study on the impact of financial development on green energy production. The study employed data from the period 1980-2006 using 119 non-OECD countries. The study the general methods of moments (GMM) approach. The outcome of the research revealed that there exists a significant positive effect between financial development and the amount of green energy output. The impact was high on non-hydropower sources like wind, biomass, geothermal and solar. In a related study, Fangmin and Jun (2010) studied the association that exists between financial systems and green energy using panel data within the period 1980-2008 for 55 countries. The outcome of the research indicates that there exists a positive association between the development segment of financial intermediation and the total power production of green energy projects in those countries. Also, a study conducted by Kim and Park (2015), examined the function of financial growth in total energy generated using a range of data from 2000-2013 for 30 countries from the Americas, Asia and Oceania, and Europe. The results indicate that financial development has a positive and significant impact on renewable energy output. Countries with robust financial structures experience uneven growth in green energy production as against countries with ailing financial structures. A study undertaken by Scholtens and Veldhuisa (2015) also examined the impact of financial growth and energy sector expansion using data from 198 countries from 1980 - 2008. The research employed random and fixed effects together with the GMM estimation methods. The outcome of the study revealed that financial development proxy as the size of the commercial banking sector, commercial bank credit to the private sector, and the size of the financial sector depict a positive impact of green energy size. A greater chunk of the existing literature connecting finance and the energy industry mostly focuses on financial development and green energy intake. Additionally, most of the studies relating to financial development and green energy have a narrow concentration on Africa. Some of the researchers examining the determinants of green energy in Africa mostly omit financial development in terms of their investigation. Meanwhile, with the goal to make the world carbon-free by swapping from fossil fuels to green energy, it is imperative the function of financial development in green energy is scrutinized. This research thus tries to add to the pool of studies on financial development and green energy development by concentrating on Africa.

In recent times, due to barriers associated with obtaining financing through traditional means, some GEP designers are coming out with inventive models of financing. Some researchers have proclaimed that fresh inventive financing techniques enable GEP inventors lots of flexibility as far as credit resettlements are concerned arguing that these models are crafted to properly take into account the risks associated with GEPs (Saunders *et al.*, 2012). Innovative financing models are decent means for widespread dissemination of GETs as they are intended to solve the issue of access to energy and comprehensive sustainable development, especially in rural areas (Sarkar & Singh, 2010).

According to Konstantinos *et al.*, (2010), in Africa, there are a number of innovative green energy financing models used by GETs such as renting schemes, revolving funds, credit co-operatives, hire purchase, and utility leasing. Other relevant inventive financing techniques comprise the consumer credit model, energy service company model, Clean Development Mechanism (CDM), dealer credit model, the Global Environmental Facility (GEF), supplier credit model and (Derrick, 1998; Enzensberger *et al.*, 2003; Oji, 2015; Martinot 2003; Shrestha, 2007).

This study contends that green energy development requires a comprehensive financial structure that can galvanize both local and external financial capital for investment. In consonance with the finance-industry growth connection research (Beck *et al.*, 2004; 2007; Rajan & Zingales, 1998) which was propounded by Bagehot (1873) and Schumpeter (1911), financial growth expedites quick entry of new firms and spurs the development of existing companies. Companies and corporations which rely heavily on outside financing develop quicker in countries with well-structured financial structures than those nations with feeble systems and financial architecture (Rajan & Zingales, 1998).

A study carried out by Fisman and Love (2013) reveal that highly grown financial organizations quicken the flow of wealth. Green energy area in Africa is one of the sectors with vibrant growth and investment potential. It is estimated that green energy will bring forth almost half of Africa's power generation growth by the year 2040 (IEA, 2014). A study by Gielen *et al.* (2019) affirmed that green energy is made up of more than half of all worlds' energy volume additions.

Investment in the green energy sector is stagnated by lack of independent creditworthiness, under-developed financial systems which do not provide sufficient wealth and suitable financial instruments, expensive start-up costs, high economic risk of infrastructure projects, and information asymmetry (Brunnschweiler, 2010; Ba *et al.*, 2010). Nonetheless, well-structured financial systems can conquer these challenges by savings mobilization, improvement of risk, and information dissemination (Levine, 1997). When these purposes are sufficiently achieved, well-structured financial systems will overawe moral hazards and adverse selection issues, therefore inspiring investment and development of the green energy area (Kim & Park, 2015).

Financial Development vs. Carbon Emission

Borio (2011) examined the effect of financial development on the growth and stability of an economy. The outcome of the study indicates that financial development accelerates economic growth . By implication, a rise in economic growth stirs demand for energy to drive the growth and with non-green sources of energy currently holding sway in most economies, carbon emissions will worsen (Borio, 2011; Nasir *et al.*, 2015; Zhang, 2011; Rafay, 2022) clarifies that financial development increases FDI and stimulates economic growth which also increases the use of energy. The growth of the financial industry greatly helps in securing credit and increases the acquisition of energy products and services. Consequently, the growth of the capital market surges the investment in the energy sector for energy creation and usage. As the financial sector grows, it is imperative to take into account the environment to prevent degradation (Shahbaz *et al.*, 2013, 2016a, 2016b, 2018). The debate on the nexus between financial growth and carbon emissions appears in diverse places; some researchers affirm that financial development is not adversely affecting carbon emissions, instead assists in the decrease of carbon emissions (Dogan & Seker, 2016; Abbasi & Riaz, 2016; Tamazian *et al.*, 2009; Tamazian & Rao, 2010; Jalil & Feridun, 2011). Another aspect of the debate indicates that financial development impacts positively on carbon emissions (Salahuddin *et al.*, 2018; Javid & Sherif, 2016; Zhang, 2011). In another point of view, some researchers indicate that the connection that exists between financial development and carbon emissions are insignificant and that there is no strong connection between the two (Bekhet *et al.*, 2017; Charfeddine and Khediri, 2016; Omri *et al.*, 2015; Coban & Topcu, 2013; Ozturk & Acaravci, 2013). To elaborate on the varied arguments as far as the financial development and carbon emission in prior research are concerned, academics on the positive relationship harangued that financial development moderately enhances economic growth which brings about ecological and environmental repercussions through energy intake and reduction of environmental quality (Tamazian *et al.*, 2009; Boutabba, 2014). Furthermore, the financial development of a country turns as a base for foreign direct investment which runs into productive areas to upturn growth (Shahbaz *et al.*, 2013). In effect, financial industry development changes the living standard of the citizenry in a country due to availability of finances and economic bustling in the energy intake which increase carbon emission (Charfeddine & Ben Khediri, 2016; Shahbaz *et al.*, 2013). Conversely, other researchers are of the point that financial development is relevant to the environment, hence negatively impacting carbon emission (Charfeddine & Ben Khediri, 2016). A study conducted by Tamazian *et al.* (2009) examined the effect of financial development on carbon emission in China; they established that they exist an inverse relationship between the two for the period of 1992 to 2004. Implies, financial development has contributed negatively to carbon emission in China. To buttress their discoveries, Jalil and Feridun (2011) studied the nexus that exists between environmental quality and financial development and their findings revealed that an upsurge in financial development in developing economies reduces carbon emission. Also, Shahbaz *et al.* (2013)

validated in their study that reveals that financial development inversely impacts carbon emissions in countries such as Indonesia and South Africa.

Relationship Between Foreign Direct Investment and Carbon Emission

To examine the presence of the Factor Endowment and Pollution Haven Theories, some researchers discovered that FDI inflow causes carbon emissions to rise. Evidence authenticates the presence of Factor Endowment and Pollution Haven Hypotheses in countries like China, Malaysia, Indonesia, the United States of America, and several other countries (Chandran & Tang, 2013). In contrast, some researchers endorse the presence of the Halo Effect hypothesis in some countries which in their studies suggest that FDI has a negative impact on carbon emissions by way of investment in greener technologies in those countries (Zhang & Zhou, 2016; Zhu *et al.*, 2016; Jiang *et al.*, 2017; Baskurt, *et al.*, 2022). This research considers these areas worthwhile in view of the implausible and mixed findings discovered in existing literature to examine the impact of financial development and foreign direct investment on carbon emissions in the Southern Africa and West Africa areas in a comparative study. This study used the dynamic panel data and panel quantile regression techniques to deduce several findings using financial development as an explanatory variable and carbon emissions per capita as a predicted variable as well as trade openness, foreign direct investment, and financial openness as control variables to measure the effect on carbon emissions.

METHODOLOGY

Data and Variables

This study employs a panel method, pooling data from a cross-section of units across periods. The authors employed data from 46 African countries which spanned from 1990-2018. The data for each variable is collected from the World Development Indicators of the World Bank. The main dependent variable is green energy demand, measured by renewable energy consumption (REN) as a share or percentage of the total energy consumption. Carbon dioxide emission (CO_2 emission) is also considered as an additional dependent variable to test how finance decreases emissions if there is any significant impact of finance on renewable energy demand. CO_2 emission is measured by emissions in kilotons. The main independent variable in this study is finance indicated by financial development (FINDEV). Financial development is measured by domestic credit to the private sector (% of GDP). The study also controlled for the effect of foreign direct investment (FDI), trade openness (TRADE), and economic growth (GDP) on renewable energy demand. FDI is the amount of FDI inflows (% of GDP). Trade is measured as import and export of goods and services (% of GDP) and GDP growth indicates economic growth.

Model and Analytical Approach

The following is a general specification of the panel data model:

$$Y_{it} = \alpha + \beta' X_{it} + \varepsilon_{it} \quad (1)$$

where *i* is the cross-sectional dimension and *t* is the period dimension, respectively. Model variables Y and X are respectively represented by the dependent and independent variables. Constant is noted by α. The regression coefficients of the explanatory factors are indicated by β and ε defines the error term.

In order to take care of the possibility of endogeneity, the study employs the dynamic generalized method of moments (GMM) approach developed by Arellano and Bond (1991). As a result, dynamic model is expressed in the following form:

$$Y_{it} = \alpha Y_{it-1} + \beta' X_{it} + \varepsilon_{it} \quad (2)$$

To observe the effect of financial development (FINDEV) on green energy demand and carbon dioxide emission, while controlling for FDI, trade, and economic growth, equation (2) can be extended as follows:

$$lnREN_{it} = \alpha lnREN_{it-1} + \beta_1 lnFINDEV_{it} + \beta_2 ln\ lnFDI_{it} + \beta_3 TRADE_{it} + \beta_4 lnGDP_{it} + \varepsilon_{it} \quad (3)$$

$$lnCO_{2it} = \alpha lnCO_{2it-1} + \beta_1 lnFINDEV_{it} + \beta_2 ln\ lnFDI_{it} + \beta_3 TRADE_{it} + \beta_4 lnGDP_{it} + \varepsilon_{it} \quad (4)$$

Where all acronyms are defined. The variables used are converted into their logarithms for data normalization.

EMPIRICAL FINDINGS

Descriptive Statistics

The descriptive statistics of all the variables are displayed in Table 1. This shows the mean, maximum, minimum, and standard deviation values of each variable. The variables are presented in their raw form and not their logarithms. The mean value of renewable energy consumption is 72.929 from the share of the final energy consumption. Carbon dioxide has a mean of 17743.590 kilotons. Financial development's average is 16.986 with a maximum value of 160.125 in terms of private sector to the domestic credit. The mean value of FDI inflows is 3.071. Trade and economic growth are averaged at 66.994 and 3.819, respectively. For the independent variables, trade has the largest standard deviation value indicating high volatility.

Table 1. Descriptive statistics

	REN	*CO_2*	*FINDEV*	*FDI*	*TRADE*	*GDP*
Mean	72.929	17743.590	16.986	3.071	66.994	3.819
Maximum	98.343	503112.400	160.125	103.337	311.354	35.224
Minimum	5.352	132.012	0.000	-8.703	11.087	-50.248
Std. Dev.	21.495	71510.370	23.285	7.390	34.485	5.387

4.2 Correlation Analysis

Table 2 indicates the correlation level of the independent factors in the study. It is important to examine the correlation level among the variable to ensure that there is no multicollinearity problem in the study. The presence of multicollinearity leads to unreliable model estimates. Kennedy (2003) argued that for variables to show free multicollinearity, the correlation coefficients should be below 0.80. It can be observed from the results that there exists a weak or low correlation among the factors and based on the standard of Kennedy (2003), the authors suggest that there is no multicollinearity problem in the study.

Regression Results

Table 3 presents the results of the GMM estimation. Before discussing the main findings, the study tests for serial correlation in the data validity of the research instruments. The results show that the study instruments are valid as indicated by the Sargan test. Also, second-order autocorrelation is absent as portrayed by the Arellano-Bond test for AR(2). Overall, models are highly significant as indicated by the Wald test statistics and their p-values.

Table 2. Correlation analysis

	lnREN	*lnFINDEV*	*lnGFDI*	*lnTRADE*	*lnGDP*
lnREN	1.000				
lnFINDEV	-0.497	1.000			
lnFDI	-0.111	-0.039	1.000		
lnTRADE	-0.362	0.255	0.381	1.000	
lnGDP	-0.330	0.412	0.158	-0.064	1.000

Table 3. Regression results

Variables	Renewable Energy Consumption	CO_2 Emission
Lag_{t-1}	0.759***	0.661***
	(0.018)	(0.023)
lnFINDEV	-0.011***	0.111***
	(0.004)	(0.020)
lnFDI	-0.005***	0.012***
	(0.001)	(0.002)
lnTRADE	0.001	0.056***
	(0.004)	(0.016)
lnGDP	0.004***	0.013***
	(0.001)	(0.003)
Constant	0.443***	0.892***
	(0.032)	(0.088)
Diagnostics		
Wald χ^2 (pro.> χ^2)	31556.11 [0.000]	4105.92 [0.000]
Sargan test (pro.> χ^2)	30.861 [1.000]	39.0116 [1.000]
AR(2)	-1.252 [0.211]	-0.204 [0.838]

Standard errors in parentheses and p-values are in [ ] *** p<0.01

The first model shows the impact of the independent variables on renewable energy consumption. The results show that financial development has a negative significant impact on the demand for renewable energy. This suggests that finance does not promote the renewable energy drive in Africa. This result is similar to the findings of He *et al.* (2019). The implication is that financial development through credit advancement is insufficient for renewable energy investment efficiency in Africa. This can be ascribed to the underdeveloped nature of the financial system in the continent. FDI is also observed to reduce the demand for renewable energy. This suggests that technology transfer and the use of heavy equipment which are mostly imported by African countries increases the utilization of other energy sources such as fossil fuels and lowers renewable energy consumption. The finding agrees with the result of Kang *et al.* (2021) in the case of South Asian Countries. The impact of trade on renewable energy consumption is positive but insignificant. Economic growth positively and significantly influences renewable energy usage. This suggests that as economic activities surge the demand for clean energy rises.

The impact of the independent factors on carbon dioxide emission is examined in the second model. The findings revealed that financial development has a positive significant effect on carbon dioxide emission. This suggests that a boom in credit to the private sector encourages spending on emission-related machinery including heavy factory equipment and automobiles that rely heavily on non-renewable energy sources. The influence of FDI is positive and significant, suggesting that FDI in the form of technological and other transfers increase carbon dioxide emission. Trade openness significantly and positively affects carbon dioxide emission, indicating that as trade policies are relaxed, which enable the flexibility in the movement of goods and services (including environmental unfriendly technologies), pollution increases. Finally, an increase in economic activity promotes emission levels in Africa. A plausible implication is that as the economy grows, production and industrialization also boom which increases energy consumption from non-renewable energy sources, and thus pollution levels.

CONCLUSION AND RECOMMENDATIONS

This chapter explored whether finance measured by financial development influences green energy proxied by renewable energy demand in Africa. The study used a panel dataset of 46 countries in Africa covering from 1990 to 2018. The study also analyzed how finance influences the emission of carbon dioxide. In addition, the paper controlled for the effect of trade openness, foreign direct investment, and economic growth on green energy demand. The study applied the generalized method of moments (GMM) technique which controls for endogeneity problems. The results showed that finance significantly reduces the demand for green energy in Africa. It is established that foreign direct investment also affects green energy negatively. Trade openness and economic growth positively enhance green energy though the effect of trade is insignificant. The outcome of the analysis further reported that financial development and the other independent factors positively and significantly increase environmental pollution measured by carbon dioxide emission.

This study presents some policy recommendations. Given the negative effect of financial development on green energy and the positive impact on carbon dioxide emission, the researchers recommend that the direction of private sector credit should be reconsidered towards investment in renewable energy sources. Specifically, credit to the private sector for the purchase and financing of machinery and equipment that exacerbate pollution should be limited. The financial sector should rather encourage investment in renewable energy sources by granting more credit for the purchase of environmentally-friendly equipment required for production by the private sector. The fact that FDI also reduces demand for renewable energy and promotes pollution, the respective governments in Africa can place restrictions on the transfer of pollution generation equipment into Africa. Similarly, to decrease the adverse impact of trade openness on the environment, trade restrictions should be placed on the import of certain types of technologies and machinery, specifically those that consume more non-renewables such as fossil fuels.

DISCLAIMER

The contents and views of this chapter are expressed by the authors in their personal capacities. It is not necessary for the Editor and the Publisher to agree with these viewpoints and they are not responsible for any duty of care in this regard.

ACKNOWLEDGMENT

The authors extend sincere gratitude to

- The Editor and the International Editorial Advisory Board (IEAB) of this book who initially desk reviewed, arranged a rigorous double/triple blind review process and conducted a thorough, minute and critical final review before accepting the chapter for publication.
- All anonymous reviewers who provided very constructive feedbacks for thorough revision, improvement, extension and fine tuning of the chapter.
- All colleagues, assistants and well-wishers who assisted the authors to complete this task.

REFERENCES

Abbasi, F., & Riaz, K. (2016). CO_2 emissions and financial development in an emerging economy: An augmented VAR approach. *Energy Policy, 90*, 102–114. doi:10.1016/j.enpol.2015.12.017

Ali, H. S., Yusop, Z. B., & Hook, L. S. (2015). Financial development and energy consumption nexus in Nigeria: An application of autoregressive distributed lag bound testing approach. *International Journal of Energy Economics and Policy, 5*(3), 816–821.

Arcand, J. L., Berkes, E., & Panizza, U. (2015). Too much finance? *Journal of Economic Growth, 20*(2), 105–148. doi:10.100710887-015-9115-2

Arellano, M., & Bond, S. (1991). Some tests of specification for panel data: Monte Carlo evidence and an application to employment equations. *The Review of Economic Studies, 58*(2), 277–297. doi:10.2307/2297968

Ba, L., Gasmi, F., & Noumba, P. (2010). *Is the level of financial sector development a key determinant of private investment in the power sector?* (Working Paper No. 5373). World Bank.

Bagehot, W. (1873). *Lombard Street: A description of the money market*. Wiley & Sons.

Baskurt, B. B., Celik, S., Oke, T., & Rafay, A. (2022). FDI and Environmental Degradation: Evidence from a developed country. In A. Rafay (Ed.), *Handbook of Research on Energy and Environmental Finance 4.0* (pp. 446–471). IGI Global. doi:10.4018/978-1-7998-8210-7.ch018

Beck, T., Demirguc-Kunt, A., Laeven, L., & Levine, R. (2004). *Finance, firm size, and growth* (Working Paper No. 10983). NBER.

Beck, T., Demirguc-Kunt, A. S. L. I., Laeven, L., & Levine, R. (2008). Finance, firm size, and growth. *Journal of Money, Credit and Banking, 40*(7), 1379–1405. doi:10.1111/j.1538-4616.2008.00164.x

Bekhet, H. A., Matar, A., & Yasmin, T. (2017). CO_2 emissions, energy consumption, economic growth, and financial development in GCC countries: Dynamic simultaneous equation models. *Renewable & Sustainable Energy Reviews, 70*, 117–132. doi:10.1016/j.rser.2016.11.089

Borio, C. (2011). Rediscovering the macroeconomic roots of financial stability policy: Journey, challenges, and a way forward. *Annual Review of Financial Economics, 3*(1), 87–117. doi:10.1146/annurev-financial-102710-144819

Boutabba, M. A. (2014). The impact of financial development, income, energy and trade on carbon emissions: Evidence from the Indian economy. *Economic Modelling*, *40*, 33–41. doi:10.1016/j.econmod.2014.03.005

Brunnschweiler, C. N. (2010). Finance for renewable energy: An empirical analysis of developing and transition economies. *Environment and Development Economics*, *15*(3), 241–274. doi:10.1017/S1355770X1000001X

CecchettiS. G.KharroubiE. (2015). *Why does financial sector growth crowd out real economic growth?* (Discussion Paper No. DP10642). CEPR. Retrieved from https://ssrn.com/abstract=2615882

Chandran, V. G. R., & Tang, C. F. (2013). The impacts of transport energy consumption, foreign direct investment and income on CO_2 emissions in ASEAN-5 economies. *Renewable & Sustainable Energy Reviews*, *24*, 445–453. doi:10.1016/j.rser.2013.03.054

Charfeddine, L., & Khediri, K. B. (2016). Financial development and environmental quality in UAE: Cointegration with structural breaks. *Renewable & Sustainable Energy Reviews*, *55*, 1322–1335. doi:10.1016/j.rser.2015.07.059

Chitioui, S. (2012). Does economic growth and financial development spur energy consumption in Tunisia? *Journal of Economics and International Finance*, *4*(7), 150–158. doi:10.5897/JEIF12.014

Churchill, A. A., & Saunders, R. J. (1989). *Financing the energy sector in developing countries* (Working Paper Energy Series No. 14). World Bank.

Cihak, M., Demirgüç-Kunt, A., Feyen, E., & Levine, R. (2012). *Benchmarking financial systems around the world* (Policy Research Working Paper No. WPS6175). World Bank.

Çoban, S., & Topcu, M. (2013). The nexus between financial development and energy consumption in the EU: A dynamic panel data analysis. *Energy Economics*, *39*, 81–88. doi:10.1016/j.eneco.2013.04.001

Da Silva, P. P., Cerqueira, P. A., & Ogbe, W. (2018). Determinants of renewable energy growth in Sub-Saharan Africa: Evidence from panel ARDL. *Energy*, *156*, 45–54. doi:10.1016/j.energy.2018.05.068

Dabla-Norris, M. E., & Srivisal, M. N. (2013). *Revisiting the link between finance and macroeconomic volatility* (Working Paper No. 13/29). International Monetary Fund.

De Gregorio, J., & Guidotti, P. E. (1995). Financial development and economic growth. *World Development*, *23*(3), 433–448. doi:10.1016/0305-750X(94)00132-I

Derrick, A. (1998). Financing mechanisms for renewable energy. *Renewable Energy*, *15*(1-4), 211–214. doi:10.1016/S0960-1481(98)00159-1

Dogan, E., & Seker, F. (2016). The influence of real output, renewable and non-renewable energy, trade and financial development on carbon emissions in the top renewable energy countries. *Renewable & Sustainable Energy Reviews*, *60*, 1074–1085. doi:10.1016/j.rser.2016.02.006

Enzensberger, N., Fichtner, W., & Rentz, O. (2003). Financing renewable energy projects via closed-end funds—A German case study. *Renewable Energy*, *28*(13), 2023–2036. doi:10.1016/S0960-1481(03)00080-6

Fangmin, L., & Jun, W. (2011). Financial system and renewable energy development: Analysis based on different types of renewable energy situation. *Energy Procedia*, *5*, 829–833. doi:10.1016/j.egypro.2011.03.146

Fisman, R., & Love, I. (2004). Financial development and intersectoral allocation: A new approach. *The Journal of Finance*, *59*(6), 2785–2807. doi:10.1111/j.1540-6261.2004.00716.x

Gennaioli, N., Shleifer, A., & Vishny, R. (2012). Neglected risks, financial innovation, and financial fragility. *Journal of Financial Economics*, *104*(3), 452–468. doi:10.1016/j.jfineco.2011.05.005

Gielen, D., Boshell, F., Saygin, D., Bazilian, M. D., Wagner, N., & Gorini, R. (2019). The role of renewable energy in the global energy transformation. *Energy Strategy Reviews*, *24*, 38–50. doi:10.1016/j.esr.2019.01.006

He, L., Liu, R., Zhong, Z., Wang, D., & Xia, Y. (2019). Can green financial development promote renewable energy investment efficiency? A consideration of bank credit. *Renewable Energy*, *143*, 974–984. doi:10.1016/j.renene.2019.05.059

IEA. (2014). *Africa Energy Outlook. A Focus on Energy Prospects in Sub-Saharan Africa.* World Energy Outlook Special Report. Retrieved from https://www.usaid.gov/sites/default/files/documents/1860/IE47A-Africa-Energy-Outlook-2014.pdf

Jalil, A., & Feridun, M. (2011). The impact of growth, energy and financial development on the environment in China: A cointegration analysis. *Energy Economics*, *33*(2), 284–291. doi:10.1016/j.eneco.2010.10.003

Javid, M., & Sharif, F. (2016). Environmental Kuznets curve and financial development in Pakistan. *Renewable & Sustainable Energy Reviews*, *54*, 406–414. doi:10.1016/j.rser.2015.10.019

Jiang, L., Zhou, H.-F., Bai, L., & Zhou, P. (2017). Does foreign direct investment drive environmental degradation in China? An empirical study based on air quality index from a spatial perspective. *Journal of Cleaner Production*, *176*, 864–872. doi:10.1016/j.jclepro.2017.12.048

Justice, S. (2009). *Private financing of renewable energy – A guide for policymakers*. Retrieved from https://www.chathamhouse.org/sites/default/files/public/Research/Energy,%20Environment%20and%20Development/1209_financeguide.pdf

Kang, X., Khan, F. U., Ullah, R., Arif, M., Rehman, S. U., & Ullah, F. (2021). Does Foreign Direct Investment Influence Renewable Energy Consumption? Empirical Evidence from South Asian Countries. *Energies*, *14*(12), 3470. doi:10.3390/en14123470

Karekezi, S. (2002). Renewables in Africa—Meeting the energy needs of the poor. *Energy Policy*, *30*(11-12), 1059–1069. doi:10.1016/S0301-4215(02)00058-7

Kennedy, P. (2003). *A guide to econometrics* (5th ed.). MIT Press.

Kim, J., & Park, K. (2015). *Financial development and deployment of renewable energy technologies* (Working Paper No. 2015-023). KAIST College of Business.

Konstantinos, D., Patlitzianas, A., & Christos, K. (2011). Sustainable energy investments in Hellenic urban areas: Examining modern financial mechanisms. *Renewable & Sustainable Energy Reviews*, *15*(9), 5186–5188. doi:10.1016/j.rser.2011.03.006

Levine, R. (1997). Financial development and economic growth: Views and agenda. *Journal of Economic Literature*, *35*(2), 688–726.

Liming, H. (2009). Financing rural renewable energy: A comparison between China and India. *Renewable & Sustainable Energy Reviews*, *13*(5), 1096–1103. doi:10.1016/j.rser.2008.03.002

Lindlein, P., & Mostert, W. (2005). *Financing Renewable Energy. Instruments, Strategies, Practice Approaches* (Discussion Paper No. 38). Frankfurt: KfW.

Lokonon, B. O. K., & Salami, A. O. (2017). *Climate Change and Renewable Energy Generation in Africa* (Working Paper No. 269). Abidjan: African Development Bank.

Lucas, R. E. Jr. (1988). On the mechanics of economic development. *Journal of Monetary Economics*, *22*(1), 3–42. doi:10.1016/0304-3932(88)90168-7

Ma, H., Oxley, L., Gibson, J., & Li, W. (2010). A survey of China's renewable energy economy. *Renewable & Sustainable Energy Reviews, 14*(1), 438–445. doi:10.1016/j.rser.2009.07.029

Martinot, E. (2004). Global Renewable Energy Markets & Policies. *New Academy Review, 3*, 56–67.

McKinnon, R. I. (1973). *Money and capital in economic development*. The Brookings Institution Press.

Minsky, H. P. (1974). The modeling of financial instability: An introduction. *Modelling and Simulation (Anaheim), 5*(1), 267–272.

Nasir, M., Ahmad, F. K., Ahmed, M., & Wu, J. (2015). Financial and economic stability as 'two sides of a coin': Non-crisis regime evidence from the UK based on VECM. *Journal of Financial Economic Policy, 7*(4), 327–353. doi:10.1108/JFEP-01-2015-0006

Nasreen, S., & Rafay, A. (2022). Technological Innovation and Financialization for Environment: The Case of Pakistan. In A. Rafay (Ed.), *Handbook of Research on Energy and Environmental Finance 4.0* (pp. 333–353). IGI Global. doi:10.4018/978-1-7998-8210-7.ch013

Oji, K. C. (2015). *Models of Financing Renewable Energy for Sustainable Development: An African Perspective* [Ph.D. thesis]. Faculty of Commerce, Law and Management, University of the Witwatersrand, Johannesburg, South Africa.

Omri, A., Daly, S., Rault, C., & Chaibi, A. (2015). Financial development, environmental quality, trade and economic growth: What causes what in MENA countries? *Energy Economic, 48*, 242–252. doi:10.1016/j.eneco.2015.01.008

Ozturk, I., & Acaravci, A. (2013). The long-run and causal analysis of energy, growth, openness and financial development on carbon emissions in Turkey. *Energy Economics, 36*, 262–267. doi:10.1016/j.eneco.2012.08.025

Painuly, J. P. (2001). Barriers to renewable energy penetration; a framework for analysis. *Renewable Energy, 24*(1), 73–89. doi:10.1016/S0960-1481(00)00186-5

Panwar, N. L., Kaushik, S. C., & Kothari, S. (2011). Role of renewable energy sources in environmental protection: A review. *Renewable & Sustainable Energy Reviews, 15*(3), 1513–1524. doi:10.1016/j.rser.2010.11.037

Patrick, H. T. (1966). Financial development and economic growth in underdeveloped countries. *Economic Development and Cultural Change, 14*(2), 174–189. doi:10.1086/450153

Pfeiffer, B., & Mulder, P. (2013). Explaining the diffusion of renewable energy technology in developing countries. *Energy Economics*, *40*, 285–296. doi:10.1016/j.eneco.2013.07.005

Rafay, A. (Ed.). (2022). *Handbook of Research on Energy and Environmental Finance 4.0*. IGI Global. doi:10.4018/978-1-7998-8210-7

Rafay, A., Sadiq, R., & Ajmal, M. M. (2017). Uniform Framework for Sukuk-Al-Ijara – A proposed model for all Madhahib. *Journal of Islamic Accounting and Business Research*, *8*(4), 420–454. doi:10.1108/JIABR-09-2015-0042

Rajan, R. G., & Zingales, L. (1998). Financial dependence and growth. *The American Economic Review*, *88*(3), 559–586.

Rashed, A., Chen, Y. C., & Soon, S. (2022). FDI and the Gap of Clean Power Finance: The Case of Africa. In A. Rafay (Ed.), *Handbook of Resaerch on Energy & Environmental Finance 4.0*. IGI Global. doi:10.4018/978-1-7998-8210-7.ch009

REN21. (2014). *Renewables 2014: Global Status Report 2014*. Paris: Renewable Energy Policy Network for the 21st Century (REN21).

Reinhart, C. M., & Reinhart, V. R. (2015). Financial crises, development, and growth: A long-term perspective. *The World Bank Economic Review*, *29*(suppl_1), S53–S76. doi:10.1093/wber/lhv011

Rifkin, J. (2011). *The third industrial revolution: how lateral power is transforming energy, the economy, and the world*. Macmillan.

Robinson, J. (1952). *The Generalisation of the General Theory in the Rate of Interest and Other Essays*. Macmillan.

Roubaud, D., & Shahbaz, M. (2017). Financial development, economic growth, and electricity demand: A sector analysis of an emerging economy. *Journal of the Energy Division*, *43*(1/2), 47–98.

Sadorsky, P. (2010). The impact of financial development on energy consumption in emerging economies. *Energy Policy*, *38*(5), 2528–2535. doi:10.1016/j.enpol.2009.12.048

Salahuddin, M., Alam, K., Ozturk, I., & Sohag, K. (2018). The effects of electricity consumption, economic growth, financial development and foreign direct investment on CO_2 emissions in Kuwait. *Renewable & Sustainable Energy Reviews*, *81*, 2002–2010. doi:10.1016/j.rser.2017.06.009

Sarkar, A., & Singh, J. (2010). Financing energy efficiency in developing countries—Lessons learned and remaining challenges. *Energy Policy*, *38*(10), 5560–5571. doi:10.1016/j.enpol.2010.05.001

Saunders, R. W., Gross, R. J. K., & Wade, J. (2012). Can premium tariffs for micro-generation and small scale renewable heat help the fuel poor, and if so, how? Case studies of innovative finance for community energy schemes in the UK. *Energy Policy*, *42*, 78–88. doi:10.1016/j.enpol.2011.11.045

Scholtens, B., & Veldhuis, R. (2015). *How Does the Development of the Financial Industry Advance Renewable Energy? A Panel Regression Study of 198 Countries Over Three Decades*. Retrieved from http://www.hdl.handle.net/10419/113114

Schumpeter, J. A. (1911). *The Theory of Economic Development*. Harvard University Press.

Shahbaz, M., Jam, F. A., Bibi, S., & Loganathan, N. (2016a). Multivariate Granger causality between CO_2 emissions, energy intensity and economic growth in Portugal: Evidence from cointegration and causality analysis. *Technological and Economic Development of Economy*, *22*(1), 47–74. doi:10.3846/20294913.2014.989932

Shahbaz, M., Nasir, M. A., & Roubaud, D. (2018). Environmental degradation in France: The effects of FDI, financial development, and energy innovations. *Energy Economics*, *74*, 843–857. doi:10.1016/j.eneco.2018.07.020

Shahbaz, M., Shahzad, S. J. H., Ahmad, N., & Alam, S. (2016b). Financial development and environmental quality: The way forward. *Energy Policy*, *98*, 353–364. doi:10.1016/j.enpol.2016.09.002

Shahbaz, M., Solarin, S. A., Mahmood, H., & Arouri, M. (2013). Does financial development reduce CO_2 emissions in Malaysian economy? A time series analysis. *Economic Modelling*, *35*, 145–152. doi:10.1016/j.econmod.2013.06.037

Shaw, E. (1973). *Financial Deepening in Economic Development*. Oxford University Press.

Shrestha, R. M. (2007). *Financing mechanisms for renewable energy, extract of course on bio-energy for achieving MGDs*. Asian Institute of Technology.

Tamazian, A., Chousa, J. P., & Vadlamannati, K. C. (2009). Does higher economic and financial development lead to environmental degradation: Evidence from BRIC countries. *Energy Policy*, *37*(1), 246–253. doi:10.1016/j.enpol.2008.08.025

Tamazian, A., & Rao, B. B. (2010). Do economic, financial and institutional developments matter for environmental degradation? Evidence from transitional economies. *Energy Economics, 32*(1), 137–145. doi:10.1016/j.eneco.2009.04.004

Tobin, J. (1984). On the Efficiency of the Financial System. *Lloyds Bank Review*, 1-15.

Toke, D., & Lauber, V. (2007). Anglo-Saxon and German approaches to neoliberalism and environmental policy: The case of financing renewable energy. *Geoforum, 38*(4), 677–687. doi:10.1016/j.geoforum.2006.11.016

UNEPFI. (2012). *Financing renewable energy in developing countries – Drivers and barriers for private finance in sub-Saharan Africa*. United Nations Environmental Program Finance Initiative.

Wiser, R. H. (1997). Renewable energy finance and project ownership: The impact of alternative development structures on the cost of wind power. *Energy Policy, 25*(1), 15–27. doi:10.1016/S0301-4215(96)00115-2

Zhang, Y. J. (2011). The impact of financial development on carbon emissions: An empirical analysis in China. *Energy Policy, 39*(4), 2197–2203. doi:10.1016/j.enpol.2011.02.026

Zhu, H., Duan, L., Guo, Y., & Yu, K. (2016). The effects of FDI, economic growth and energy consumption on carbon emissions in ASEAN-5: Evidence from panel quantile regression. *Economic Modelling, 58*, 237–248. doi:10.1016/j.econmod.2016.05.003

ADDITIONAL READING

Babbar, S., & Schuster, J. (1998). *Power project finance: experience in developing countries*. (RMC Discussion Paper No. 119). World Bank.

Beck, T. (2006). *Creating an efficient financial system: challenges in a global economy*. (Working Paper No. 3856). World Bank.

Head, C. R. (2000). *Financing of private hydropower projects* (Discussion Paper No. 420). World Bank.

REN21. (2009). *Renewables 2009: Global Status Report 2009*. Paris: Renewable Energy Policy Network for the 21st Century (REN21).

Chapter 3
Global Oil Price Shocks and Sustainability:
The Case of Post-Soviet Resources-Rich Countries

Vugar Bayramov
Center for Economic and Social Development, Azerbaijan

Nigar Islamli
https://orcid.org/0000-0002-2095-7681
Center for Economic and Social Development, Azerbaijan

ABSTRACT

For countries whose economies are largely based on oil revenues, the impacts of global oil price shocks play a significant role. This research aims at investigating the impacts of the post-2014 oil price shock on the post-soviet resources-rich countries of the Caspian Basin, namely Azerbaijan, Russia, and Kazakhstan. The drop in oil prices caused the economic slowdown in all three countries. In comparison with the other two countries, Azerbaijan was able to prevent the negative impact with a social package. The post-shock social package was implemented by the Azerbaijani government in 2019, which covered more than 3 million people. This package can be considered as an "Azerbaijani model" for the stability of macroeconomic indicators during the devaluation period.

DOI: 10.4018/978-1-6684-5580-7.ch003

INTRODUCTION

The most affected countries due to the shock of global oil prices are oil-rich countries (Sheng & Gupta, 2022). For three oil resource rich countries, namely the Republic of Azerbaijan, the Republic of Kazakhstan, and the Russian Federation, the sharp drop in oil prices has led to interrelated slowdowns in the economy. This is the most important event for countries whose economies are governed by public spending and final consumption. It also affects the currency along with other challenges, resulting in devaluations.

The first country to be affected by this shock was Kazakhstan, which also has close ties to the Russian economy. As a result of the devaluation of the Russian ruble, the national currency of Kazakhstan was also affected. The Russian ruble lost up to 50% of its value against the dollar by November 2014. For this reason, the Central Bank of Russia resolved to move to a freely floating exchange rate. On December 31, 2014, the official exchange rate dollar against the ruble was set by the Central Bank at the level of 56.26 RUB with 72.26% losing value.[1] Kazakhstan's national currency - the tenge - fell twice in 2014, depreciating by more than 40% of its original value. And in 2014, 1 USD = 182.51 KZT.[2] However, the Central Bank of Azerbaijan switched to a floating exchange regime on December 21, 2015, as lower oil prices increased costs. On the same day, the official exchange rate became 1 USD=1.55 AZN, a 49.4% devaluation of the national currency within a year. Additionally, GDP growth rates also changed across countries. The countries that differed the most from these changes were Russia, then Kazakhstan, and then Azerbaijan. Even in Russia, the result was negative. Inflation remained stable in Kazakhstan and doubled in Azerbaijan and Russia. There is a small difference in unemployment rates. While there is very little growth in Russia and Azerbaijan, in Kazakhstan, on the contrary, there is a very small decrease. While GDP tax revenues increase in Azerbaijan, there is a slight decrease in Russia and Kazakhstan. The number of exports of goods and services decreased significantly in Russia and Kazakhstan, but Azerbaijan should also be noted. If we look at the extent of diversification, the economic diversification index or concentration ratio is the same extent for 2014 and 2015, however, Russia gets lower in it. On the other hand, the Herfindahl Hirschman Index for exports of three countries shows a high concentration.

The aim of this chapter paper is to evaluate the impacts of the global oil shock on diversification, unemployment, inflation rate, GDP growth rate, export of goods and services, and the currency exchange rate of those countries. The chapter structure consists of literature review which contains the latest literature on the effects of a sharp drop in oil prices, and the currency crisis in Azerbaijan, Kazakhstan, and Russia. The next section is the Calculation of Diversification which gauging the economic and export diversification in three countries using Concentration Ratio

(CR_n) and Herfindahl-Hirschman Index (HHI); Next is the discussion about the damage caused by the global oil shock to these three countries through inflation, GDP growth, unemployment, exports, and currency fluctuations.

LITERATURE REVIEW

This part reviews an overview of recent literature on the impacts of the global oil shock on Azerbaijan, Kazakhstan, and Russia. The impact of falling oil prices on resource-rich countries will be examined. Since the export of these countries is based on one type of product, their economic sustainability also depends on export revenues and domestic spending. In some countries, economic diversification is a force for economic stability. However, in the long run, economic diversification has a better effect. (Gelb, 2010; Kilinc-Ata, 2022)

Guliyev (2016) noted that after the drop of June 2014, Azerbaijan was forced to collapse by a long-term oil boom, and terms such as "economic crisis" and "post-oil period" began to be used more often in terminology. Citizens borrowed from banks during the boom to meet their various needs. Some of these loans were in dollars, and the rise in foreign exchange and the depreciation of the manat made it difficult for people to repay these loans. The rise in inflation rates continued to rise rapidly, from 4% to 12% in 2015. All these indicators began to indicate that the situation in the social sphere is becoming increasingly sensitive. Ahmadov (2016) adds social implications which said that the new socio-economic environment created by the situation has affected virtually all members of society. The state budget was used to finance investment projects, and the State Oil Company's capital-intensive investments were reduced and frozen. After the devaluation of the national currency, the annual GDP per capita in Azerbaijan dropped by 56%. CESD (2019) investigated that the situation has also affected countries' public spending. The recommendations to solve the impacts are heaving the local demand, the diversification of export, expanding social protection.

Rahimli and Nazirov (2020) searched the effects of the oil prices and real exchange rate fluctuations on the activity of the economy. They state that there is a positive relationship between oil price and exchange rate. The rise in oil prices raise real effective exchange rate. This finding might also be seen as one of the indications of the Azerbaijani economy's "Dutch Disease." In addition, Mammadov (2016) noted the financial impact of falling oil prices. The fall in oil prices has led to the depreciation of the national currency. This in itself created the potential for foreign investment in Azerbaijan. And this process can be a ground for reimbursing local investments and getting down the interest rates.

Humbatova *et al.* (2019) stated that the world price of oil and oil products and the volume of the production in Azerbaijan influence the exchange rate of the national currency of Azerbaijan. Identically, authors- Mukhtarov *et al.* (2021) also talked about evaluating the impacts of oil price shock on macroeconomic indicators such as GDP per capita, exchange rate, and total trade turnover for Azerbaijan. It was noted that oil prices bring an advantage for total trade turnover and GDP per capita, but anti positive impact on exchange rates for Azerbaijan.

On the other side, Aslanli (2016) investigated the impact on the budget and stated that the price shock led to declines in Azerbaijan's financial and budget revenues and led to a growing deficit in the Azerbaijani government's budget. Due to the situation on world markets, the country's foreign exchange reserves have declined and fiscal factors have fluctuated. At the same time, the government does not have the financial capacity to keep public debt low.

Bayramov and Orujova (2017) searched that the unexpected drop in oil prices for all three countries showed that Azerbaijan and Kazakhstan, as well as other oil-dependent countries are not ready for this. According to statistics, economic and export diversification is weak in resource-rich countries. The calculated HHI showed that economic diversification is moderate for Kazakhstan, as other countries, with the exception of Kazakhstan, are more economically dependent on oil and gas. Identically, Bayramov and Abbas (2017) stated the diversification policy and subsidized economy of affected by falling oil prices countries. Azerbaijan, Kazakhstan, and Russia are supply-based countries, in this regard, their economy relies on government capital and expenditures. There is a need for a transition from the supply-based economy to the demand-based economy in order to form a sustainable economy through diversification reforms. On the other side, Dikkaya and Doyar (2017) noted that after the collapse of the Soviet Union, Kazakhstan and Azerbaijan achieved their development thanks to the oil and gas industry. This means that Azerbaijan and Kazakhstan have made more progress in GDP growth than other countries. The decline towards the end of 2014 showed how sensitive both countries are to oil revenues. There was a devaluation, Kazakhstan switched to a free currency regime, and Azerbaijan had a floating exchange rate. Bayramov, Breban, and Mukhtarov (2019) concluded that Russia firmly depends on energy revenues.

Kazakhstan was examined by Asian Development Bank (2017), the economy of Kazakhstan faced hardships due to the devaluation of the Russian ruble and increasing imports at the beginning. However, due to borders with Russia and integration into the Eurasian Economic Union, imports from Russia have not been reduced. This has had a negative impact on the trade balance. Back in 2009, Kazakhstan was expected to be hit by the oil shock again. Gronwald, Mayr, and Orazbayev (2009) said that Kazakhstan will suffer shock in the future, due to the vulnerability to the oil price shocks.

CALCULATION OF DIVERSIFICATION

Diversification of Export

This part consists of the export diversification and economic diversification extents for Azerbaijan, Kazakhstan, and Russia. Diversification of export constitutes one of the oldest concepts in the economic development theory. Traditional well-known models such as Smith (1776), Ricardo (1817), and Heckscher-Ohlin-Samuelson (HOS) stated that countries diversify and export due to their comparative advantage. Prebisch (1950) and Singer (1950) think otherwise. According to them, as less developed countries specialize in exports, their purchases of consumer goods from developed countries are increasing. In addition, they note that goods produced in terms of income elasticity outperform primary goods. This hinders the growth of less developed countries. Therefore, they must diversify their exports to ensure stability and growth in foreign exchange earnings. Export diversification minimizes trade downturns and price fluctuations. (Noureen and Mahmood, 2016)

Herfindahl Hirschman Index (HHI) is a common measuring index of the concentration of the market and shows the competitiveness of the market. A market with an HHI of less than 1,500 is considered a competitive market, a market with an HHI of 1,500 to 2,500 is considered a moderately concentrated market, and a market with an HHI of 2,500 or more is considered an extremely concentrated market.

$$HHI=S_1^2+S_2^2+S_3^2+\dots S_n^2 \quad (1)$$

where:

s_n=the market share percentage of firm n expressed as a whole number, not a decimal

The Standard International Trade Classification (SITC) is a widely used classification mostly applied for scientific and analytical purposes such as business data that deal with import, export etc. The Standard International Trade Classification (SITC) categories are used to compute the diversification index for each country. The product categories are agricultural raw materials, machinery and transport equipment, textiles, manufactures, food, chemical, ores and metals, and fuel. (Luttenberger and Zedlitz, 2018)

As shown in Figure 1, Figure 2, and Figure3, all three resource-rich countries are highly reliant on their hydrocarbon exports, as evidenced by higher HHI diversification index values. Until the 2014 oil crash, the value of this index in both Russia and Kazakhstan stayed around 0.4, suggesting low export diversification, and no significant shift is registered in this regard. Azerbaijan has the highest share in the exports, with HHI exceeding 0.8 between the Global Financial Crisis and the latest oil shock, exposing the country's troubling degree of resource dependence and very low diversification.

Furthermore, the Concentration Ratio (CR) of the top four export classes is determined for each of the three countries to have robustness tests. This ratio is a reasonably simple indicator of diversification that is determined by adding the shares of the top commodity groups as follows:

$$CR_n = S_1 + S_2 + \ldots + S_n \tag{2}$$

As seen (Figure 1, Figure 2, and Figure 3), the graphs of HHI and CR shift together, indicating that the findings are reliable. Nonetheless, based on CR estimates, the countries had slightly poorer results, with a concentration ratio of about 0.9.

Figure 1. Export Diversification in Kazakhstan.
Source: Author's calculations based on the data from the World Integrated Trade Solution (WITS, https://wits.worldbank.org/); Ministry of National Economy of the Republic of Kazakhstan

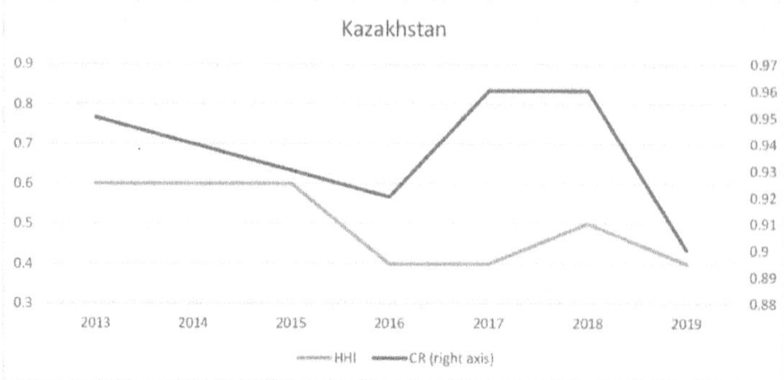

Figure 2. Export Diversification in Russia.
Source: Author's calculations based on the data from the World Integrated Trade Solution (WITS, https://wits.worldbank.org/); Federal Customs Service of Russia

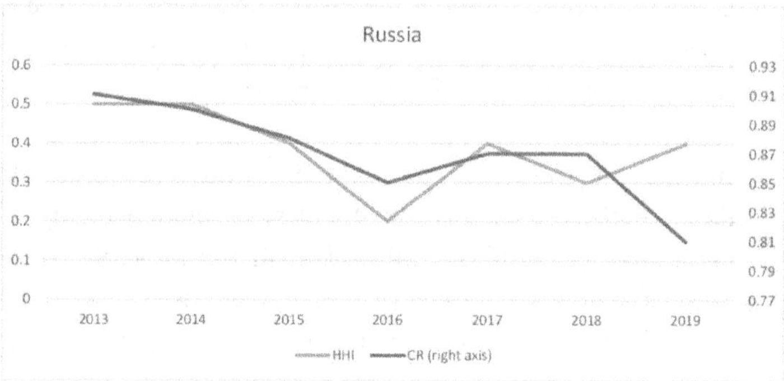

Figure 3. Export Diversification in Azerbaijan.
Source: Author's calculations based on the data from the World Integrated Trade Solution (WITS, https://wits.worldbank.org/); The State Customs Committee of the Republic of Azerbaijan

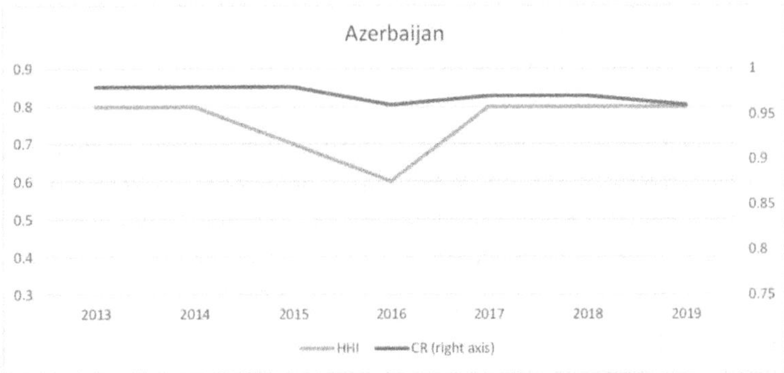

All three countries were not on the base of the diversification and they are vulnerable next possible shocks. They depend highly on mineral export which is demonstrated through the HHI index.

Economic Diversification

Economic diversification also needs to be measured to make the diversification more accurate and understandable and to expand research. To do this, similarly, the HHI formula is used. To measure the overall level of the economic diversification, the value-added of each economic sector in relation to total GDP must be calculated using United Nations Statistics Division data on the International Standard Industrial Classification (ISIC). According to the ISIC data set, ***A*** and ***B*** represent agriculture, hunting, forestry, and fisheries, ***C*** and ***E*** represent mining, manufacturing, and utilities, ***D*** represents manufacturing, ***F*** represents construction, and ***G*** and ***H*** represent wholesale trade, retail trade, restaurants, and hotels, and ***I*** represents transport, storage, and communication.[3] The formula is organized as follows:

$$HI = \left(\frac{A+B}{100}\right)^2 + \left(\frac{C+E}{100}\right)^2 + \left(\frac{D}{100}\right) + \left(\frac{F}{100}\right)^2 + \left(\frac{G+H}{100}\right)^2 + \left(\frac{I}{100}\right)^2 \quad (3)$$

It should be noted that Russia does well in terms of economic diversification than in terms of export diversification. The nation depends heavily on its natural resources, as its export structure dictates, but this dependency is not reflected in the GDP output structure. That is, the value-added of major economic sectors in the country show a reasonably balanced structure, with manufacturing value-added accounting for a greater share than mining over the time, except in 2015.

As can be seen in Figure 4, Figure 5, and Figure 6, Russia has shown a balanced value added of key economic sectors compared to other countries during the observed period. However, the high dependence on mineral resources does not allow to say the same for GDP.

According to the latest statistics, Kazakhstan has achieved positive results in economic diversification, mining and manufacturing compared to the last 5 years.

In Azerbaijan, on the other hand, there may be declines in the value added of the construction and domestic trade sectors from areas not related to economic trade. In addition, there was little decline in agriculture and forestry in 2015-2018.

It should be noted that there are no statistics for all years. For this reason, the calculations are until 2018.

Figure 4. Economic Diversification in Azerbaijan.
Source: Author's calculations based on the data from the United Nations Statistics Division 2019.

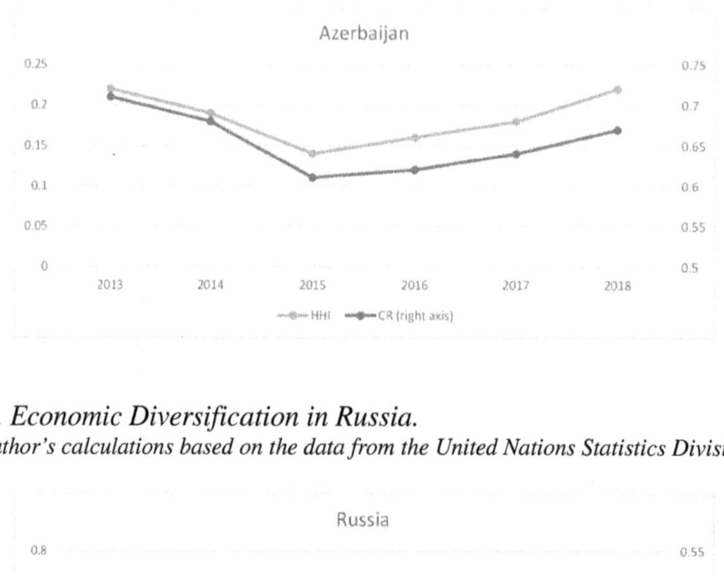

Figure 5. Economic Diversification in Russia.
Source: Author's calculations based on the data from the United Nations Statistics Division 2019.

Figure 6. Economic Diversification in Kazakhstan.
Source: Author's calculations based on the data from the United Nations Statistics Division 2019.

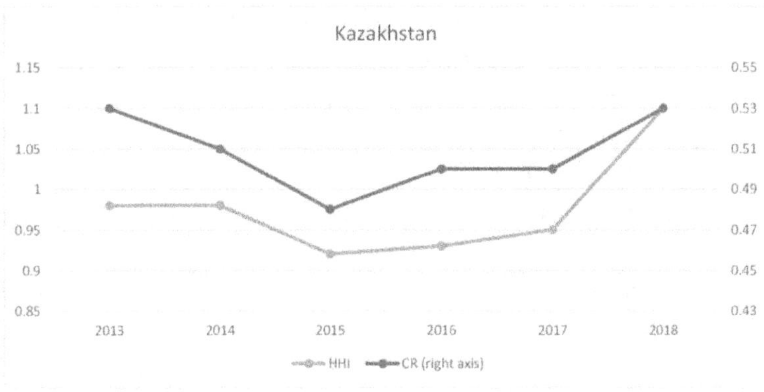

IMPACT OF GLOBAL OIL PRICE SHOCK

Russian Federation

Russia experienced an economic slowdown at the beginning of 2014, owing to a drop in oil prices and international tensions. As the world's top oil exporter, the oil crash and Western sanctions placed on Russia in the aftermath of the Ukraine crisis greatly diminished export receipts and government revenues in the Federation. Furthermore, speculative assaults on the ruble after the annexation of Crimea and the Ukraine war triggered a currency crisis in Russia, resulting in the national currency's exchange rate reaching a historical low. The Central Bank fixed the official exchange rate of the dollar against the ruble at 32.66 RUB on January 1, 2014, and it reached 56.26 RUB on December 31, losing 72.26 percent of its value. The ruble reached its low point on December 18, 2014, when it fell by 107.56 percent from its level on January 1, 2014. The next year, it fell even more against the US dollar.

To show the severity of the Russian recession and its effects on the region, the growth rate in emerging markets of Europe and Central Asia (ECA region as described by the World Bank) fell by 0.1 percent, while the regional growth rate was 2.5 percent without Russia, despite the fact that Russian national income is for more than 35 percent of the total.

The demand structure in Russia shows that differences between gross capital accumulation and final consumption were typically lower between 2009 and 2015. Though domestic spending fell by 1.1 percent in 2014, both public and private current expenditure increased by the same percentage points. Despite this, the share of capital accumulation and final demand in total production increased marginally in

2015, despite lower net exports. Throughout the time frame, these two components of GDP accounted for more than 90% of the total GDP.

Depreciation, contrarily, has benefited some of the country's export sectors, especially agriculture. This, in particular, has led to a slowdown in the economy's recession. The value-added in GDP by the agriculture sector rose from 3.6 percent in 2013 to 4.4 percent in 2015. Nevertheless, approximate changes in this and other industries have no discernible effect on economic development. According to the IMF staff study, a successful recovery seems extremely doubtful in the light of low oil prices. There is an immediate need for economic changes in order to benefit from greater competition relative to OECD countries as a result of exchange rate depreciation.

A supply-based economy is shown by the favorable association between overall government spending and non-oil and gas revenues. In other words, a parallel trend of these two factors shows that the non-oil and gas market seems to be dependent on government investment, and thus falling GDP is induced by the government.

A supply-based economy is shown by the favorable association between overall government spending and non-oil and gas revenues. Differently, a parallel trend of these two factors shows that the non-oil and gas market seems to be dependent on government expenditure, and thus falling GDP is induced by the government. The World Bank's forecast of 2016 depicts 1.2 percent contraction for the Russian economy is, contrarily, largely motivated by the decline in private sector demand. That is, the private sector is projected to reduce its expenditure and consumption spending, contributing to the expected negative economic outlook.

The Russian Federation's combined budget divides taxes into two categories: oil and gas revenues and non-oil and gas revenues. The "National Economy" division under the expenses column reflects the budget distributed to different economic operations, including both the oil and non-oil industries. As a result, this can be regarded as a proximate indicator for monitoring government investment in non-oil sector growth. During the time of high oil prices from 2011 to 2014, consolidated government deficits in this segment ranged from $95 billion to $120 billion.

As seen in Figure 7, the non-resource revenues sector comprised of gradual increase, in addition, crude oil price fluctuations are shown through a 3-year period.

With the implementation of new financial regulation in 2018, Russia is now authorized to compensate for oil price variations as long as the over mid-term average price stays over USD 50 and export volumes do not decrease. Russia's real GDP growth in 2018 surpassed projections and expectations, hitting 2.3 percent, compared to the 1.2 percent gain expected for 2019. Lower exports weighed on the Russia's current account surplus in the second quarter of 2019. As a result, the current account surplus dropped dramatically to USD 12.1 billion in the second quarter of 2019, down from USD 17.9 billion at the same time the previous year.

A fiscal policy limiting contribution to aggregate demand was made in early 2019. According to the Central Bank of Russia's statistics, the inflation rate in 2020 will be 3.4 percent.

Figure 7. Government expenditure, non-resource revenues and crude oil price in the Russian Federation.
Source: Federal State Statistics Service of the Russian Federation (https://eng.gks.ru/); World Bank; CBR

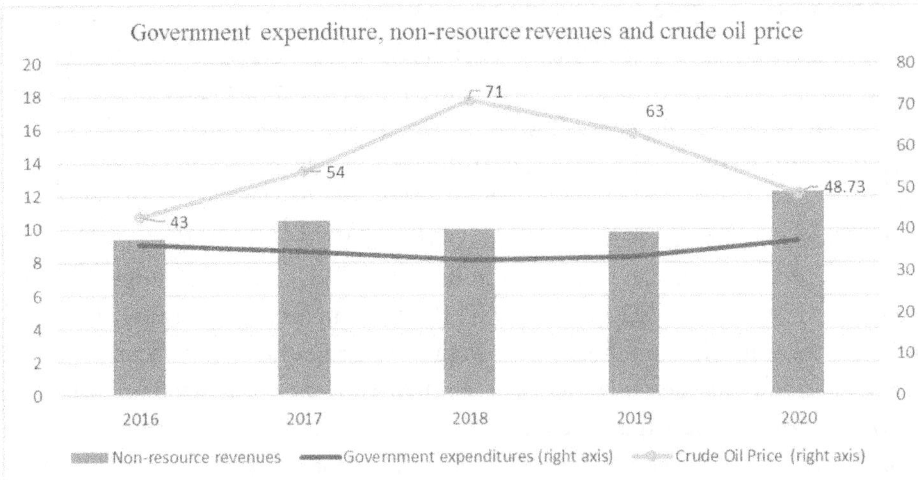

Oil price volatility is another major issue for oil exporting countries (Rafay & Farid, 2015). Russia was firmly urged to continue the audacious fiscal reform operation, with the primary goal of decoupling oil price volatility from the federal budget, which would lead to real exchange rate stability. In the course of the transition, critical areas such as health and education are largely bypassed. One of the primary causes of the economic recession is a decline in investment. For starting, the threat of economic sanctions has drastically limited the volume of foreign direct investment. Second, the financial crisis (which is also attributed to tariffs, when banks' international borrowing gets more expensive) has resulted in a rise in interest rates, significantly reducing private investment. To compensate, the Russian government must 1) right tax policy reforms toward consumption while resisting incentives spend and invest natural material incomes in sectors with long-term growth potential. It was also noticed that, predictably, the most intense periods of change coincided with periods of economic recession. As a result, the ongoing extended oil price crisis should be seen as an impetus to further changes in order to prevent potential crises. As a way of reducing budget deficits, the Russian government is also contemplating a progressive privatization program. Subsidies to the economy and intergovernmental transfers were major causes of reductions in spending, which were followed by an anticrisis package intended to alleviate the impact of restructuring on key economic sectors and disadvantaged households.

On the other hand, gas prices will have risen dramatically by the beginning of 2021 to be the same as they were in early 2019. The change in natural gas prices from the end of 2020 to the start of 2021 is expected to be 24.06 percent, or $7.27 per cubic meter. Furthermore, as a consequence of the globally signed deal through the IMF, income for Russian natural gas and oil are projected to return immediately owing to the order of lowering the amount produced as a result of the epidemic. As a result, hopes that the pandemic would have a long-term influence on oil and gas prices have been clearly reduced. That is, it is critical to remember that as long as the amount of the production is low, as well as prices, the economy will be severely harmed.

It is worth noting that the introduction of the COVID-19 spread resulted in lower fiscal receipts and a weaker ruble (World Bank, 2020). The federal budget deficit in the first five months of 2020 was USD 5 billion, compared to a surplus of USD 17 billion at the same time previous year. On the backdrop of COVID-19 on economic activity, a significant drop in trade and commodity prices was noticed in 2020. Over the first quarter of 2020, the trade balance surplus was USD 35.6 billion. Net private capital flows fell to USD 23.9 billion, while international reserves increased by just USD 2.6 billion. Meanwhile, it should be highlighted that the present crisis has mostly impacted small and medium-sized companies (SMEs), which are sensitive to supply-and-demand shocks and rely on service consumption. The Central Bank of the Russian Federation (CBR) has authorized a package of USD 6 billion to assist SMEs as a crisis-response measure. Because the Russian economy has been affected by an oil price downturn, a sliding ruble, and the COVID-19 epidemic, the government and the Central Bank have implemented a wide variety of policy measures to offset the socioeconomic consequences and maintain financial-sector stability. Diversification is critical for Russia as a transitional stage that allows for the development of new industrial capacities. As it is, the Russian economy is not diverse since many sectors continue to endure from poor productivity and transitions to higher-value-added industries have been constrained. Furthermore, there is no question that the initiatives have failed to adequately address basic barriers to private-sector-led company entrance, innovation, and development. When compared to other sophisticated economies, Russia spends substantially less on health and education. Rebalancing in favor of the aforementioned areas may increase the overall efficiency of government spending.

Kazakhstan

Kazakhstan's economy slowed significantly in 2015, with production growth slowing to a five-year low due to slower domestic and external demand, as well as oil price shocks. Although GDP grew at an annual rate of 6.5 percent from 2010 to 2013, it fell to 1.2 percent in 2015, down from 4.1 percent in 2014. During the oil shocks, the current account worsened, with a deficit of 2.2 billion USD in the last half of 2014, down from a surplus of 6.9 billion USD in the beginning, and a deficit of 5.8 per cent of GDP in 2015 (National Bank of Kazakhstan, 2019). Additionally, industrial output fell by more than 2 percentage points in 2014, owing primarily to a decline in oil production.

The national currency was devalued in February 2014, resulting in a 20% depreciation of the tenge, which remarkably reduced local demand and private investment (National Bank of Kazakhstan, 2019). In late September, the second devaluation caused the tenge to lose 40% of its value, and in August, the National Bank of Kazakhstan decided to switch to a floating exchange rate regime, thereby engaging in inflation targeting. Following the oil crisis, the main focus of economic policy was to connect shrinking monetary measures with some fiscal incentive. The breakdown of GDP by major sectors shows that trade, transportation, and real estate services were the primary drivers of output growth in 2014. Since Russia and China are Kazakhstan's main trading partners, spillovers from the Russian recession and the Chinese slowdown in the economy placed significant strain on the country's fiscal balance. To be noted, economic slowdowns in these countries reduced demand for Kazakh exports, resulting in a worsening of the country's current account. In 2015, the turnover of the foreign trade with Russia decreased by 27.8%, with imports falling to 10.2 billion USD (13.8 billion USD in the baseline period) and exports falling to about 4.3 billion USD (6.4 billion USD) (National Bank of Kazakhstan, 2019).

In Kazakhstan, the government's investment spending is a smaller proportion of overall expenses than prevailing spending, which includes government consumption and employee benefits. Capital expenditures accounted for 11.2 percent of overall central government expenditure in 2016, down from 17.6 percent in 2013. The revised budget reduced spending mostly at the cost of capital expenses, despite the fact that the 2015 budget aimed to commit 14.7 percent of overall expenditures to infrastructure spending. The budget cut was achieved to a greater degree by proroguing non-priority investment programs. Against all odds, a smaller share of capital expenses in the case of the budget can be seen as a risk to the non-oil sector's long-term growth.

Budget cuts, in another case, were offset by fiscal encouragement measures. To combat the negative impact of lower demand on the economy, the Kazakh government initiated two economic support programs. Due to the oil shock, additional economic support initiatives were implemented, including the "Nurly Zhol" program (USD 14 billion) for 2015–2017. It should be noted that payments from the Oil Fund rose to over 13 per cent of total revenues for the central government in 2015, up from 8 per cent in 2014.

It is important to note that the oil shock is only the nearest cause of Kazakhstan's economic downturn; more fundamental crisis drivers must be found in order to resolve the country's flow slowdown. The connection between crude oil costs and government expenditure shows in the Figure 8 that when oil prices are high, government spending rises in tandem, but when oil prices fall, the Kazakh government cuts back. The budget was reduced by around 15% in 2015, compared to less than 5% the previous year. As a result, a drop in crude oil costs in 2014 signaled the end of government spending that had been fueled primarily by resource benefits.

In Kazakhstan, non-resource sector production began to downfall in response to falling oil prices on global markets, as evidenced by a 5% drop in non-resource GDP in 2014. Non-oil output fell by 10% the following year. It can be assumed that non-resource GDP growth is influenced by crude oil costs on global markets. Since, as this paper argues, the non-resource sector in these countries is largely reliant on resource rentals, falling oil prices offer bleak prospects in this regard.

During the period 2009–2015, government spending and non-resource GDP in Kazakhstan followed similar paths (Figure 8). This explains the connection between government spending and non-resource sector development, implying that the non-oil sector was funded by government spending and had the ability to expand during boom times due to higher fiscal incomes. Both government spending and non-resource GDP dropped in 2014, with further drops of 15% and 10% in the following year.

The functional budget structure of Kazakhstan shows that during high commodity prices, the share of expenditures directed to the industry was relatively low, accounting for 0.23 percent in 2012 and 0.27 percent in 2013. Following a 0.37 percent rise in 2014 to 135 million USD, it experienced a substantial contraction in 2015, falling to 62 million USD. As a result, the oil shock made it difficult to sustain previously allocated investment levels, even though they were inadequate to underpin export-oriented non-resource sectors. Equivalently, agricultural expenses fell 4.24 percent in 2012, 3.1 percent in 2013, 2.43 percent in 2014, and 2.41 percent in 2015 as oil prices fell. Agriculture expenses have also decreased in real terms, falling to 741 million USD in 2013 from 1.5 billion USD in 2012.

Transportation and communications, contrarily, raised their share of overall budget spending in 2014 (from 6.07 percent to 7.6 percent) and suffered relatively minor shrinkages in the next year (at 7.26 percent), according to Kazakhstan's Statistical Office. It can be inferred that the oil shock primarily harmed the potential non-resource sector, with a minor effect on the non-tradable industry, as evidenced by insufficient government spending on the tradable non-oil industries. Furthermore, these expenditures resulted in a similar downward trend in manufacturing value-added and an upward trend in transportation and communication value-added from 2012 to 2015.

Figure 8. Government expenditure, non-resource revenues and crude oil price in Kazakhstan.
Source: World Bank; Statistical Office of Kazakhstan; IMF

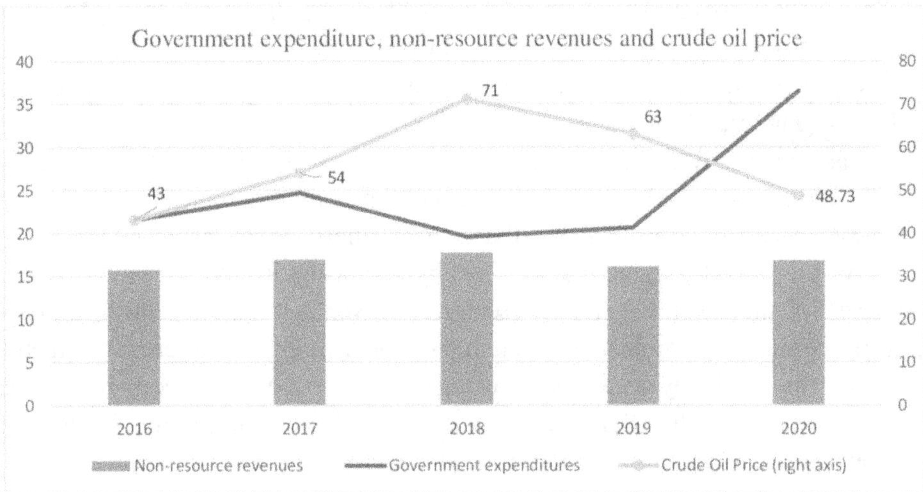

The economy was subsidized by the government of Kazakhstan through account of the government and investment spending dependent on high resource revenues, but the oil shock posed a challenge in this regard. As a result, the non-resource industry was robbed of its primary source of funding and struggled to serve as a source of diversification. It's worth noting that the Kazakh government's spending rose steadily and by more than 80% between 2009 and 2013. However, the subsequent oil shock reversed the tendency, as higher energy prices became the primary driver of increased government spending. As a result of the lower fiscal receipts in 2015, government spending decreased by 15%.

When it comes to the effects of the virus, the COVID-19 blow to Kazakhstan's economy is thought to be the worst in over two decades. The decline in global oil prices has had a significant impact on the government's budget. The trade channel and the decline in commodity prices have the greatest impact on the economy. The government has set aside USD 297 million for coordinated pandemic response operations, and "anti-crisis" measures equal to 5.7 percent of GDP. The stimulus plan includes tax breaks for small businesses, as well as increased investment on health care, cash transfers to households, and subsidized loans to businesses. Consumer expenditure and on the bae of mining investment have continued to support GDP but falling activity in the first quarter of 2020 is due to a significant decline in the service sector. Meanwhile, the NBK has sold USD 1.5 trillion from its reserves on the domestic market, as well as USD 0.9 billion by the National Oil Fund, to support the budget. Following a trade surplus in Q1 2020 and a rise in oil prices, the tenge has steadied and recovered some of its losses (World Bank, 2020). Annual inflation has risen to 7% in September 2020, up from 5.4 percent in December 2019, much over the NBK's goal range of 4–6%. It is worth noting, however, that inflation is anticipated to fall back to its target range in 2021. Meanwhile, the value of crude oil and gas condensate exports fell by 31% and 57%, respectively, in the second and third quarters.

Kazakhstan's government concentrated their emphasis on the growth of the agriculture sector in order to reduce reliance on natural resources and increase economic diversification. Kazakhstan might benefit from the Belt and Road Initiative proposed by Chinese authorities by increasing its exports and attracting Chinese investment in the agriculture sector. However, as is apparent, the oil and gas industry continue to dominate the country's economy. Extended-term sustainable development could only be achieved via the diversification of the economy and the rise of technology sector (Rafay, 2019). Kazakhstan has a lot of promise in terms of economic diversification, and the country's leaders need to pay greater attention to it.

Azerbaijan

Azerbaijan's economy also dependent on oil sales, with minerals responding for more than 90% of exports between 2009 and 2014. (Statistical Committee of the Republic of Azerbaijan, 2017). The last oil accident caused a significant drop in production, with GDP growth falling from 5.8% in 2013 to 2.8 percent in 2014, and then to 1.1 percent in 2015 (Statistical Committee of the Republic of Azerbaijan, 2017). Furthermore, budget incomes fell from 23.6 billion USD in 2014 to 16.9 billion USD in 2015. It should be noted that remittances from the Republic of Azerbaijan's State Oil Fund accounted for 60% of total budget incomes in 2015, or $10.2 billion USD.

The Central Bank's attempts to preserve the national currency's stability indicated expensive, as intercession operations depleted the Bank's foreign currency reserves. That is, intervention spending rose in December 2014, reaching 1.2 billion USD, and 1.08 billion and 1.68 billion USD were pumped into the economy in the following two months (Central Bank of the Republic of Azerbaijan, 2017). As a result, the Bank's currency reserves dropped to 11 billion dollars, a decrease of 26.6 percent in just three months.

As oil prices fell, the Central Bank of Azerbaijan moved to a floating exchange rate system on December 21, 2015, increasing intervention costs. The official exchange rate became 1 USD=1.55 AZN on the same day, a 49.4 percent depreciation of the national currency in a year. It is important to note that, despite the adoption of a floating exchange rate system, the Central Bank has not stopped enacting administrative steps. Officials from the Central Bank characterized it as the transition to a 'floating currency,' or 'regulated' floating currency.

Up until 2014, when oil prices were high, Azerbaijan's budget revenues grew in lockstep, reaching $25 billion USD in 2013. The oil crash, on the other hand, signaled the end of an upward trend in government incomes, with budget incomes falling by more than 33% in 2015, from 25 billion USD in 2013 to 16.9 billion USD. Budget receipts fell short of expectations, putting pressure on the government to slash spending. As a result, budget spending fell to 17.4 billion dollars in 2015, down from 24 billion dollars the year before. Since resource incomes are regarded as the primary source of funding for government spending, the government could not count on oil incomes to maintain the same level of spending in the face of declining oil prices. In order to achieve macroeconomic stability, the government announced structural reformations.

Figure 9 depicts the dynamics of the GDP growth, considering the dynamics of both oil and non-oil GDP growth. It is difficult not to note that, in compared to past years, the structure of oil and non-oil GDP in 2019 was reasonably balanced, demonstrating the successful execution of a diversification program.

Figure 9 depicts the trend of a consistent growth in non-recourse GDP over a three-year period, but in 2019 a significant fall in both non-resource GDP and government spending was seen.

Meanwhile, Azerbaijan is working on the development of a more efficient, diverse, and market-oriented economic structure. From 1994 to 2018, around 470 million tons of oil were produced. There is a need to execute a number of measures targeted at diversifying the Azerbaijani economy in order to ensure its long-term viability.

Infrastructure plans, social plans, and institutional plans are the three types of investment programs of the government mentioned in the Republic of Azerbaijan's budget. The Azerbaijani government has taken a big step to address this shock in the country in 2019 through a social anti-crisis program. This program covered a bulky social package of 3 million people and compensation for those who borrowed credit from the banks before the devaluation. Following the devaluation of the manat, it was a major step towards compensating for the difference between the dollar and loans in pre-2015 loans.

Figure 9. Government expenditure, non-resource revenues and crude oil price in Azerbaijan.
Source: State Statistical Committee of the Republic of Azerbaijan, IMF, Central Bank of the Republic of Azerbaijan

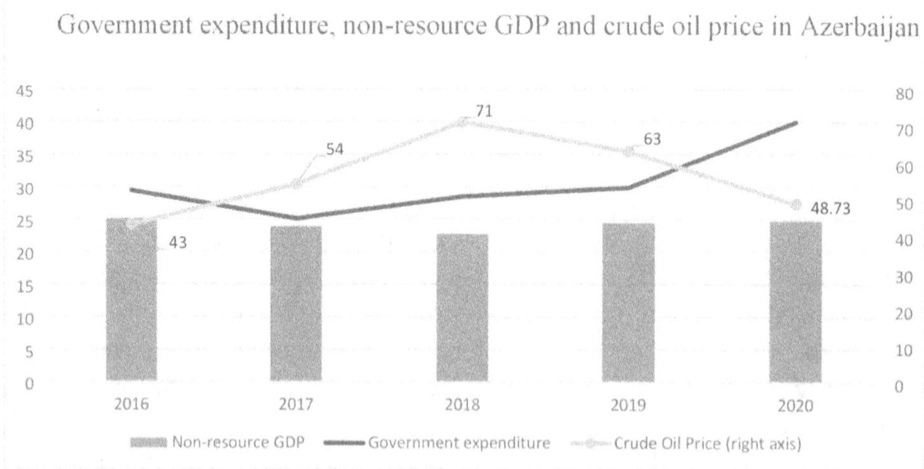

In 2015, infrastructure projects accounted for more than 60% of investment spending, with transportation accounting for the largest share (44 percent or 2.2 billion manat out of 5.1 billion manat). It is important to note that one of the factors limiting agriculture's export potential is the low share (12%) of investments directed to the sector in 2015.

In terms of the handy structure of budget expenses, funds directed to agriculture, forestry, and fishing increased by 8.5 percent in 2015, while spending on economic activities (as sorted by the Republic of Azerbaijan's Budget) increased by 10.2 percent. Transport and communications expenses, otherwise, increased by 35.4 percent, representing the non-tradable market with minimal export potential. General government spending increased by 24.4 percent, mostly due to current expenses.

In 2012, capital expenditures accounted for 34% of all budget outgoings, but this figure dropped to 32% in the 2015 budgetary program. During the implementation of the 2015 budget, however, this percentage dropped to just 24%. Agriculture's share of GDP remained relatively steady from 2012 to 2015, hovering about 2.7 percent, but it was insufficient to boost export ability. Other economic activities expenditures increased from 1.09 percent of budget costs in 2012 to 1.7 percent in 2015.

The rate of non-oil GDP growth also slowed in 2014, falling to 1.1 percent in 2015 from 10% in 2013. Oil GDP, on the other hand, declined by 2.9 percent in 2014, before rebounding to 1.2 percent growth the following year. It should be noted that the country's monetary and economic policies were previously tied to the oil price of 90 dollars (later reduced to 80 dollars), so an average price of 53.4 dollars resulted in an economic imbalance.

The non-oil sector expressed 69.3 percent of overall value added in 2015, up 8.4 percent from 2014. (60.9 percent, 2014). The share of non-oil production fell after the Baku-Tbilisi-Ceyhan pipeline was put into operation, but the end of the large inflow of oil in 2011 coincided with an increase in the non-oil market. In this way, after the shock, the country's GDP growth has been dependent on the non-oil sector's growth as seen from the Figure 10, but the non-resource sector's growth was funded by budget outgoings. As a result, non-oil production growth slowed to 1.1 percent in 2015, down from 7% the year before. It can be assumed that the government's inability to maintain previously high-level expenditures was the primary reason for the non-resource sector's failure to deliver the same development.

Present spending accounted for 58.2 percent of overall government spending in 2015, while capital spending accounted for 37.8%. Before the oil shock, capital expenditure accounted for 45.5 percent of overall budget expenses in 2013, while current spending accounted for 50.7 percent. The sum of government capital spending in 2015 was $4.9 billion, down 39% from the $8 billion reported in 2014 and 44% from the $8.8 billion recorded in 2013. To put it another way, the government's share of overall budget expenses allocated to capital projects fell to 28.1 percent in 2015, down from 33.5 percent the previous year. The oil shock appears to be to blame for a drop in government capital spending, which is considered important for the development of a long-term non-oil market. As a result of the failure to establish a sustainable and export-driven non-resource sector through the high flow of the oil era, oil shock was unavoidable.

Figure 10. GDP growth, oil and non-oil GDP growth in Azerbaijan.
Source: State Statistical Committee of the Republic of Azerbaijan, World Bank

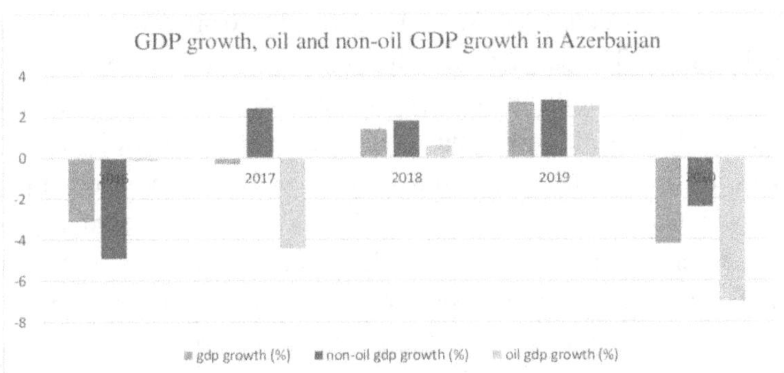

CONCLUSION

The drop in oil prices has caused the economic slowdown in the oil-exporting countries, Azerbaijan, Kazakhstan, and Russian Federation. Their account balances have weakened as a result of lower export revenues, and overall economic activity has decreased. All three countries were forced to transition to a floating exchange rate system to avoid exhaustion of foreign exchange reserves, resulting in significantly depreciated national currencies.

It can be argued that these countries struggled to attain economic diversification, which is regarded as a key component of effective resource management strategy. After all, the countries of the post-soviet have depended on resource windfalls while ignoring the more sustainable development of non-resource tradable spheres. In view of this, the HI diversification index shows that even these countries' export structures do not show a diversified basket. The findings show that all three countries' revenues are mainly generated on minerals. Besides, the prospects for Russia and Kazakhstan in terms of economic diversification, which is dependent on the economic value added by various sectors, are not so hopeless. Additionally, calculations and indexes have shown that post-Soviet countries, which are highly dependent on energy resources, have a significant impact on the country's economy during fluctuations in oil prices.

The recent oil shock, according to the data, signaled the end of higher budget spending in these countries, whose economies were dependent on resource windfalls. Said otherwise, government spending financed the economies of these resource-rich countries. Furthermore, the non-resource sector was reliant on this spending; as a result, lower non-oil and gas production followed lower budget expenses. The lack of attempts to diversify the economy and the reliance on windfall-financed government expenditure for non-resource sector development has been identified as the main underlying occasions of the post-soviet economic shrinkage.

Unlike the other two countries, Azerbaijan was able to prevent the negative impact with a social package. The package, which covers 3 million people in 2019, provides for compensation of the dollar-manat difference in loans before 2015. This package can be indicated like an ''Azerbaijani model'' for the stability of macroeconomic indicators during the devaluation period. Besides social attempts, other post-Soviet countries must introduce many economic reforms that will encourage a diversified economy in order to reduce their dependence on the resource sector and solve the economic crisis. Economic diversification is critical for these resource-rich countries to achieve long-term economic growth and development; as a result, the government should guarantee that diversification efforts are adequate to lead to the progress of non-resource sectors. To put it another way, the diversification reforms would make it easier to move from a supply-driven to a demand-driven economy, in which the non-resource market is defined by its ability to generate a stable degree of economic value-added.

In a nutshell, by encouraging an export-oriented non-oil market, economic liberalization would promote a more diversified economy. Non-resource exports are expected to increase as the business climate improves and funding for SMEs grows, as well as barriers to market entry are removed. Without active execution of the above policies, the post-soviet resource-rich countries are likely to face significant difficulties in overcoming current and future oil shocks.

DISCLAIMER

The contents and views of this chapter are expressed by the authors in their personal capacities. It is not necessary for the Editor and the Publisher to agree with these viewpoints and they are not responsible for any duty of care in this regard.

ACKNOWLEDGMENT

The authors extend sincere gratitude to:

- The Editor and the International Editorial Advisory Board (IEAB) of this book who initially desk reviewed, arranged a rigorous double/triple blind review process and conducted a thorough, minute and critical final review before accepting the chapter for publication.
- All anonymous reviewers who provided very constructive feedbacks for thorough revision, improvement, extension and fine tuning of the chapter.
- All colleagues, assistants and well-wishers who assisted the authors to complete this task.

REFERENCES

Ahmadov, I. (2016). Azerbaijan's New Macroeconomic Reality: How to Adapt to Low Oil Prices. *Caucasus Analytical Digest*, *83*, 2–6.

Asian Development Bank. (2017). *Responding to External Shocks Hitting the Economy of Kazakhstan*. Retrieved from https://www.adb.org/sites/default/files/project-documents/49045/49045-001-dpta-en_8.pdf

Aslanli, K. (2016). *Lower Oil Revenues, Higher Public Debt: The Fiscal Policy Implications of Low Oil Prices in Azerbaijan*. National Reports. Retrieved from https://www.socialwatch.org/node/17465

Bayramov, V., & Abbas, G. (2017). Oil shock in the Caspian Basin: Diversification policy and subsidized economies. *Resources Policy*, *54*, 149–156. doi:10.1016/j.resourpol.2017.10.006

Bayramov, V., Breban, D., & Mukhtarov, E. (2019). Economic effects estimation for the Eurasian Economic Union: Application of regional linear regression. *Communist and Post-Communist Studies*, *52*(3), 209–225. doi:10.1016/j.postcomstud.2019.07.001

Bayramov, V., & Orujova, L. (2017). Volatility, Diversification and Oil Shock in Resource-Rich Turkic Countries: Avenues for Recovery. *Bilig*, *83*, 303–329.

Central Bank of the Republic of Azerbaijan. (2017). *Annual Report*. Retrieved from https://www.cbar.az/home?language=en

CESD. (2019). *Social consequences of the oil price shock in the resource rich post-soviet countries*. Center for Economic and Social Development. Retrieved from https://www.cesd.az/

Dikkaya, M., & Doyar, B. V. (2017). Causality among Oil Prices, GDP and Exchange Rate: Evidence from Azerbaijan and Kazakhstan. *Bilig*, *83*, 79–98.

Gelb, A. (2010). Economic Diversification in Resource Rich Countries. Center for Global Development.

Gronwald, M., Mayr, J., & Orazbayev, S. (2009). *Estimating the effects of oil price shocks on the Kazakh economy* (Working Paper No. 81). ifo Institut – Leibniz-Institut für Wirtschaftsforschung an der Universität München.

Guliyev, F. (2016). Azerbaijan: Low Oil Prices and their Social Impact. *Caucasus Analytical Digest*, *83*, 16–25.

Humbatova, S., Tanriverdiyev, S., Garayev, A., & Hajiyev, N. (2019). Analysis of the oil, price and currency factor of economic growth in Azerbaijan. *Entrepreneurship and Sustainability Issues*, *6*(3), 1335–1353. doi:10.9770/jesi.2019.6.3(20)

Kilinc-Ata, N. (2022). Oil Prices, Macroeconomic Performance and Sustainability: The Case of Turkey. In A. Rafay (Ed.), *Finance for Sustainability in a Turbulent Economy*. IGI Global. doi:10.4018/978-1-6684-5580-7.ch004

Luttenberger, N., & Zedlitz, J. (2018). Standard International Trade Classification. *Business & Information Systems Engineering*, *60*(4), 305–316. doi:10.100712599-017-0495-z

Mammadov, J. (2016). Oil Price Shocks and Monetary Policy in Azerbaijan: Challenges and Opportunities. *Caucasus Analytical Digest*, *83*, 6–11.

Mukhtarov, S., Humbatova, S., Mammadli, M., & Hajiyev, N. (2021). The Impact of Oil Price Shocks on National Income: Evidence from Azerbaijan. *Feature Papers in Energy, Environment and Well-Being*, *14*(6), 1695.

National Bank of Kazakhstan. (2019). *Kazakhstan: Balance of Payments and External Debt*. Retrieved from https://nationalbank.kz/kz?switch=english

Noureen, S., & Mahmood, Z. (2016). Explaining Trends and Factors Affecting Export Diversification in ASEAN and SAARC Regions: An Empirical Analysis. *Nust Journal of Social Sciences and Humanities*, *2*(1), 1–28.

OECD. (2020). *Coronavirus (COVID-19): SME Policy Responses*. Retrieved from https://www.oecd.org/coronavirus/policy-responses/coronavirus-covid-19-sme-policy-responses-04440101/

Rafay, A. (Ed.). (2019). *FinTech as a Disruptive Technology for Financial Institutions*. IGI Global., doi:10.4018/978-1-5225-7805-5

Rafay, A., & Farid, S. (2015). An Analysis of Oil Price Volatility using VAR: Evidence from Pakistan. *Lahore Journal of Business*, *4*(1), 23–36. doi:10.35536/ljb.2015.v4.i1.a2

Rahimli, N., & Nazirov, M. (2020). Impact of Oil Price On Azerbaijan Economy: Relationship Between Oil Prices, Real Effective Exchange Rates and Real GDP. *Journal of Social and Economic Studies*, *3*(1), 37–45.

Sheng, X., & Gupta, R. (2022). Oil Price Shocks and Income Inequality: Evidence From the US. In A. Rafay (Ed.), *Handbook of Research on Energy and Environmental Finance 4.0* (pp. 144–158). IGI Global. doi:10.4018/978-1-7998-8210-7.ch005

Statistical Committee of the Republic of Azerbaijan. (2017). *Reports*. Retrieved from https://www.stat.gov.az/?lang=en

World Bank. (2020). *A Slow Recovery through the COVID-19 Crisis*. Retrieved from https://www.worldbank.org/en/country/kazakhstan

World Bank. (2020). *Navigating the crisis* (Working Paper 2020). Retrieved from https://www.worldbank.org/en/country/kazakhstan

World Bank. (2020). *The Global Economic Outlook during the COVID-19 pandemic: A Changed World*. Retrieved from https://www.worldbank.org/en/country/kazakhstan

ADDITIONAL READING

Bank of Russia. (2021). Inflation Expectations and Consumer Sentiment. *Information and Analytical Commentary, 3*(51). Retrieved from https://www.cbr.ru/eng/

Bank of Russia. (2021). *Russia's Economic Outlook and Monetary Policy*. Retrieved from https://www.cbr.ru/eng/

Bayramov, V., Hasanov, R., & Gasimova, N. (2021). Perspectives on the Analysis and Development of Social Policies in Azerbaijan. In *Social Policy in the Islamic World* (pp. 225–240). Palgrave Macmillan. doi:10.1007/978-3-030-57753-7_10

Bayramov, V., Rustamli, N., & Abbas, G. (2020). Collateral damage: The Western sanctions on Russia and the evaluation of implications for Russia's post-communist neighbourhood. *Inter Economics, 162*, 92–109. doi:10.1016/j.inteco.2020.01.002

Central Bank of the Republic of Azerbaijan. (2014-2020). *Annual Reports*. Retrieved from https://www.cbar.az/home?language=en

CESD. (2009). *Ending Dependency: How is oil revenues effectively used in Azerbaijan*. Center for Economic and Social Development. Retrieved from https://www.cesd.az/book.pdf

International Monetary Fund. (2019). *Kazakhstan: Staff Concluding Statement of the 2019*. Article IV Mission.

Ismayilov, A., & Yusifov, S. (2014). The Role of Energy Investments in Economic Development of Azerbaijan: Econometric Approach. *International Conference for Academic Disciplines*. 10.2139srn.2383223

World Bank. (2017). *Kazakhstan. The Economy is Rising: It is Still All About Oil*. Country Economic Update.

ENDNOTES

1 Bayramov, V., & Abbas, G. (2017). Oil shock in the Caspian Basin: Diversification policy and subsidized economies. https://www.sciencedirect.com/science/article/abs/pii/S0301420717300326

2 https://www.exchange-rates.org/Rate/USD/KZT/12-31-2014

3 https://unstats.un.org/unsd/snaama/Basic

Chapter 4
Oil Prices, Macroeconomic Performance, and Sustainability:
The Case of Turkey

Nurcan Kilinc-Ata
https://orcid.org/0000-0001-8780-1983
Institute of Economics and Utility Regulation, National Research University Higher School of Economics, Moscow, Russia

ABSTRACT

This chapter examines the effect of oil prices on selected macroeconomic variables such as economic growth, inflation, interest rate, unemployment, and import in Turkey. Johansen cointegration and vector error correction model (VECM) were used for yearly data from 1990 to 2020. According to the findings, the rise in oil prices in the short term has a positive impact on unemployment and economic growth, which are among the selected variables. However, it is observed that a rise in oil prices in the long term has an unstable volatile effect on selected macroeconomic variables. It is recommended that Turkey (which is a developing oil-dependent country and where macroeconomic variables are vulnerable to oil shocks) should spread its oil providers, focus on domestic energy resources, develop advanced technology to raise the usage of renewable energy resources, and implement energy-saving policies.

DOI: 10.4018/978-1-6684-5580-7.ch004

INTRODUCTION

Energy is fundamental for economic and social enlargement and improving the quality of life in all countries (Keser, 2003). However, most of the world's energy sources are produced and consumed yet unsustainably of technology remains stable and total amounts of energy demand increase significantly. Energy production and consumption vary according to the development levels of countries. Energy consumption in developed countries is much higher than it is in developing countries (Amri, 2016). At the same time, energy supply and demand, which decides the unit price of important energy sources such as oil, coal, and natural gas, varies depending on the global economic and political conjuncture. When energy resources are evaluated as an alternative investment tool, energy prices are shaped by non-market factors, speculative trends, and expectations as well as domestic market dynamics. In this context, price increases will inevitably affect the energy demand of most energy-consuming countries. However, the continuous increase in energy prices at the national or international level does not mean that the energy demand or consumption in these economies will decrease in the same way. Although energy prices in a country constantly increase, energy use in this country is not as low as the price elasticity of energy demand; in other words, energy demand is less sensitive to price changes (Esen and Bayrak, 2015).

Among the energy resources, oil has an important place in the economies of the countries because the relationship between the economic performance of the countries and oil prices is quite high. It is seen that the changes in oil prices according to the types of national economies affect the country's economies positively or negatively (Mukhtarov *et al.* 2020). When the literature is examined, some studies reveal a negative relationship between oil prices and economic growth (Mahmood and Murshed, 2021; Van Eyden, 2019; Aimer and Moftah, 2016; Nazir and Qayyum, 2014; Ghalayini, 2011; Bhusal, 2010; Hanabusa, 2009; Jiménez-Rodríguez and Sánchez, 2005). Nevertheless, some studies found oil prices to increase economic growth (Alkahteeb & Sultan, 2019; Benramdane, 2017; Akinlo and Apanisile, 2015; Okoro, 2014; Berument *et al.* 2010). According to the findings of the studies in the literature, oil prices affect the economy positively in oil-importing countries, and oil prices negatively affect economic growth in developing countries (Kiani, 2011). As can be seen, the change in oil price produces different results in oil-importing and exporting countries. The increase in oil prices increases the foreign exchange income in oil-exporting countries, raises the real income level, and creates a current account surplus (Gundogan and Tok, 2019). In other words, the rise in oil prices increases the input costs, decreases the foreign exchange reserves, increases the current account deficit, and decreases real incomes in importing countries with high oil dependency (Iwayemi and Fowowe, 2011). In countries such as Turkey, which is an oil-importing country, oil price increases can cause macroeconomic instability. It is seen that the fluctuation in oil prices has a great effect on Turkey's macroeconomic variables. In this context, the effect of oil price on economic growth, inflation, interest, unemployment, and import in Turkey is investigated in this study.

To shed light on the relationship between oil prices and macroeconomic factors, this section aims to present both theoretically and empirically the impact of the increase in oil prices on macroeconomic factors in Turkey. In other words, the presented chapter aims to provide empirically important information on the relationship between oil prices and macroeconomic performance in Turkey. For this purpose, the research question of the study is *"What is the effect of oil price on selected macroeconomic variables in the case of Turkey?"*. Particularly, the present chapter purposes to show the influence of oil prices on economic growth, inflation, interest rate, unemployment, and import. To reveal the effect of oil prices on macroeconomic variables, the period 1990-2020 was analyzed using the econometric approach. Hence, this chapter contributes to the existing literature in many ways. Firstly, it is one of initial studies that determines oil prices fluctuations while considering macroeconomic factors such as economic growth, inflation, interest rate, unemployment, and import to overcome the omitted variable bias in selected Turkey case to offer a broader outlook. Secondly, the core contribution of the present chapter is to scrutinize the influence of oil price volatilities on diverse macroeconomic variables, which employs the best available latest data set for the case of Turkey. Thirdly, this chapter utilized the effective technique that Johansen Cointegration and Vector Error Correction Model (VECM) test has been employed to find a relationship between oil prices fluctuations and selected macroeconomics variables.

LITERATURE REVIEW

There is a direct relationship between energy prices and macroeconomic variables. It is of great importance to reveal the sensitivity of macroeconomic variables to unexpected alterations in the supply and demand of the energy sector, to unexpected cuts in energy supply, energy supply prices, energy-saving, and the discovery of new energy resources. Today, the relationships between energy prices and macroeconomic variables such as gross domestic product and employment are examined in many studies in the literature. In other words, the energy prices literature generally treats the impact of macroeconomic variables on energy prices in an empirically framework context (Mukhtarov *et al.*, 2020; Asaleye *et al.*, 2019; Sağlam and Güresci, 2018; Narayan *et al.*, 2014; Kahn and Mansur, 2013; Kilian and Vega, 2011; Tang, 2010; Edelstein and Kilian, 2007; Brown *et al.*, 2003).

In this chapter, especially the impact of oil prices on macroeconomic variables was examined. Therefore, similar studies in the literature have been reviewed for different countries. Various studies are scrutinizing the effect of oil prices on macroeconomic variables. Thus, it is classified based on the relationship between oil prices and economic growth, inflation, interest rate, unemployment, and import. Furthermore, there are several empirical papers in the literature on the relationship between oil prices and economic growth. These papers found different results due to the method, time zone, and country they used. Some of the study has found a positive relationship between oil price and economic growth (Mukhtarov *et al.* 2020; Awolaja and Musa, 2017; Akinlo and Apanisile, 2015; Omojolaibi and Egwaikhide, 2013). For instance, Narayan *et al.* (2014) determined that oil prices positively affect economic growth in 16 developing countries and 21 developed countries. Differently, some studies have found that there is a negative relationship between oil prices and economic growth (Van Eyden *et al.* 2019; Aimer and Moftah, 2016; Nazir and Qayyum, 2014; Ghalayini, 2011). In another study investigating the effects of increases in oil prices on the economy, Sadorsky (1999) concluded that the said effects are quite deep, but that economic activities have little effect on oil prices. On the other hand, Brown and Yucel (2002) and Lardic and Mignon (2008), who examined the effect of the change in oil prices on economic activities, concluded that the effect of the increase in oil prices on economic activities is deeper than the effect caused by the decrease in prices.

In the literature, there are also studies examined the relationship between oil prices and inflation. For instance, Tang *et al.* (2010) found that oil prices have a positive effect on inflation in the case of China. Similarly, Qianqian (2011) and Chen *et al.* (2014) stated in their study that when oil prices increase, inflation increases. Unlike these studies, Katırcıoğlu *et al.* (2015) discovered that oil price had a negative impact on inflation. In another study in a similar direction, Zhao *et al.* (2016) indicated that fluctuations in oil prices cause inflation in the Chinese economy in the long run. Additionally, Sağlam and Güresci (2018) emphasized that price inflation is not caused by changes in oil prices in the short term; inflation has a negative impact on oil prices in the long term.

From the studies examined the relationship between oil prices and the interest rate, Tang *et al.* (2010) revealed that oil prices positively affect the interest rate in the case of China. Similarly, Wang and Chueh (2013) showed that interest rates have a positive impact on future crude oil prices, in the context of the US example. In the long term, there is a relationship in which interest rates affect the US dollar, which in turn affects international crude oil prices. As a result, international crude oil prices have a feedback effect on interest rates. With a different perspective, Wei and Guo (2016) discovered that the interest rate responds significantly to oil price shocks. In fact, interest rates decrease substantially in the second and third quarters after oil shocks. Later the interest rates steadily rise again and lastly converge to the trend level. Therefore, the fall in interest rates caused by oil price shocks is temporary. Arora and Tanner (2013) supported this opinion. Arora and Tanner (2013) argued that the oil price is constantly sensitive to international real interest rates in the short run and it becomes more sensitive to real interest rates in the long term.

Oil prices are effective on unemployment and employment. Developing countries are seriously dependent on oil as an input to the manufacturing sector. Therefore, the increase in oil prices raises the unemployment rate. For instance, Asaleye *et al.*, (2019) found in their study that the relationship between oil prices and employment is negative. Similarly, Kahn and Mansur (2013) examined the relationship between energy prices and employment for exact industries. The findings show that the increase in electricity prices increases unemployment. Differently, Dogrul and Soytas (2010) found in their study that oil prices reduce unemployment rates in the long term. In other words, oil shocks transmit oil price increases in Turkey to the labor market. Ahmad (2013) argued in his study that oil prices have a substantial effect on unemployment. It can be accomplished from the outcomes that oil prices can be used to expand the unemployment forecast in the long term.

Finally, the studies between oil prices and imports in the literature are examined. Gorus *et al.* (2019) found that oil imports are sensitive to alterations in oil prices in the long term. The rise in crude oil prices also leads to a growth in energy import prices. Therefore, the Turkish economy suffers from oil price shocks. In addition, the Turkish economy is vulnerable to oil price shocks in the market. Kilci (2019) showed that there is a causal relationship between Brent crude oil prices to energy imports in Turkey. Because energy imports constitute the largest share of the current account deficit and the increase in oil prices increases imports upwards. Differently, Marathe and Guntur (2020) looked at the effect of oil prices on imports for BRICS countries. In the example of Brazil and India, it was determined that crude oil prices and imports share a unidirectional relationship. For Russia, there is a bidirectional relationship between oil prices and imports.

While many studies conducted to date have examined the relationship between selected macroeconomic variables in developed countries, very few studies have addressed developing countries, including Turkey. For instance, Alagoz *et al.* (2017) investigated the effects of oil prices on macroeconomic variables in Turkey, China, South Africa, Mexico, Colombia, Costa Rica, Indonesia, and Kazakhstan. According to the results of the study, a one-dollar increase in the price of crude oil causes an increase of 0.04% on inflation across the countries studied. The increase in crude oil price has a negative effect on the current account balance and affects the current account deficit. In addition, there are studies in the literature on how the stocks related to crude oil prices traded in the Istanbul Stock Exchange are affected by macroeconomic variables. From these studies, Kocabiyik and Fattah (2020) selected several indices on *Borsa Istanbul* (BIST) that are expected to be related to oil prices, and how these indices are affected by oil and other macroeconomic variables. As a result, it has been determined that the effect of oil prices is quite low, while interest rates and exchange rates have a strong effect on most indices. Akyol and Baltaci (2018) examined the effects of Credit Default Swaps (CDS) premiums, oil prices, and selected macroeconomic variables on the *Borsa Istanbul* 100 index (BIST100). In the long run, CDS premiums, oil prices, inflation rate, real interest rates, monetary expansion, and economic growth have significant effects on the BIST100 index.

In conclusion, it is clear that studies examining the relationship between fluctuations in oil prices and selected macroeconomic variables such as economic growth, inflation, interest rate, unemployment, and import are limited in the Turkish case. In addition, since the studies primarily focus on the relationship between oil prices and economic growth, due importance is not given to the relationship between the fluctuations in oil prices of other selected macroeconomic variables. This study will fill these gaps especially investigating macroeconomic variables affected by oil prices.

DATA AND METHODS

Data

The present chapter analyzes oil prices (OP) effect of selected macroeconomics variables such as economic growth (GDP), inflation (INF), interest rates (IR), unemployment (UN), and imports (IMP) throughout 1990–2020 in case of Turkey. Data were collected from the World Bank database, Turkish Statistical Institute (TUIK), and Central Bank of the Republic of Turkey (CBRT). All variables were taken in logarithmic transformed form. The gathered data were analyzed using the Eviews software program. Information about the variables employed in the analysis is given in Table 1.

Method

In this chapter, it is targeted to reveal the impact of oil prices on economic growth, inflation, interest rate, unemployment, and import by using the VECM approach, impulse response analysis, and variance decomposition tests. In this context, the Augmented Dickey-Fuller (ADF) unit root test (Dickey and Fuller, 1981) was first used to test whether the data used in the study are stationary. In the ADF test, the fixed and trend-containing model is considered. The hypotheses are;

H_0 = Variables are not stationary (Variables contain unit root)
H_1 = Variables are stationary (Variables not contain unit root)

Table 1. Variable Description

Symbol*	Variables	Definition
OIL	Oil Price	Brent Oil Price in US dollars per barrel
GDP	Economic Growth (Gross Domestic Product)	GDP per capita (Current US$)
INF	Inflation	% (Percentage)
IR	Interest Rate (Turkish Lira Deposit Interest Rate)	% (Percentage)
UEM	Unemployment	% (Percentage)
IM	Import	Million $

* Variables with natural log transformations are lOIL, lGDP, lINF, lIR, lUEM, and lIM

Then, Johansen's cointegration analysis will be used to determine whether there is a relationship/correlation between the variables (Johansen, 1988). The main regression equation to be used in practice can be expressed as follows.

$$OIL_t = \beta_0 + \beta_1 MACROVARIABLES_t + \beta_2 TREND_t + U_t \tag{1}$$

The MACROVARIABLES series consists of GDP, inflation, interest rate, unemployment, and import. Considering the possibility that the series may contain a trend, the trend variable (TREND) has been added to the model.

Finally, after determining that there is cointegration between the variables, impulse-response analysis, and variance decomposition test were applied under the assumption of Vector Error Correction Model (VECM) to scrutinize the relationship between the variables. The error correction model reveals whether a deviation in the long-run cointegrated series is corrected. This approach investigates how the series moving away from equilibrium approach the mean. In the Error Correction Model (ECM), the lagged value (ECM_{t-1}) of the error terms obtained after the Ordinary Least Squares (OLS) estimation and the differences of the series are revealed. Accordingly, the relevant model can be expressed as follows.

$$\Delta OIL_t = \alpha_0 + \alpha_1 \Delta MACROVARIABLES_t + \alpha_2 TREND_t + \alpha_3 ECM_{t-1} + \varepsilon_t \tag{2}$$

EMPIRICAL RESULTS AND DISCUSSION

In this section, the findings obtained as a result of analyzes are presented in the form of tables and figures. In this beginning, firstly, the outcomes of the ADF unit root test for whether the variables used are stationary or not are presented in Table 2.

Table 2. Findings of ADF Unit Root Analysis

Variables	I(0)		Variables	I(1)	
	t-statistics	Probability		t-statistics	Probability
OIL	-1.2356	0.8844	Δ OIL	-4.4358	0.0077***
GDP	-1.0639	0.9187	Δ GDP	-5.7163	0.0003***
INF	-1.0240	0.9253	Δ INF	-5.0910	0.0016***
IR	-1.9207	0.6190	Δ IR	-4.2777	0.0111**
UEM	-2.5143	0.3194	Δ UEM	-4.6781	0.0042***
IM	-1.9257	0.6164	Δ IM	-6.3053	0.0001***

Notes: (*) Significant at the 10%; (**) Significant at the 5%; (***) Significant at the 1%.

According to Table 2, all variables are not stationary at the I(0) level. When the first differences of the variables are taken, all of them became stationary at the I(1) level. Thus, it can be tested whether there is cointegration between the variables. In the Johansen correlation analysis, the optimal lag number must first be determined. For determining the optimal lag interval in the study, a randomly selected lag interval including oil price, GDP, inflation, interest rate, unemployment, and import variables, and a Vector Auto-Regressive (VAR) model to examine the lag interval were determined. In this context, the lag interval test results obtained are displayed in Table 3.

According to Table 3, the appropriate lag length to be used to test the cointegration was chosen as VAR=0. That is, a VAR model was set up and the appropriate lag length was decided as 0 because four different criteria point in this direction. In addition, the Lagrangian Multiplier (LM) test was also applied to know whether there is an autocorrelation problem in the error terms of the VAR model. The results of the LM test are presented in Table 4.

The H_0 hypothesis of the LM test shows that there is no autocorrelation problem between the variables. According to Table 4, H_0 hypothesis is accepted since the p-value of the fifth lag is greater than 0.05. In other words, there is no autocorrelation problem between the variables. AR roots must be less than 1 to provide the stability and accuracy of the VAR model. In this context, the graph of the inverse roots AR characteristic polynomial is plotted and the result is shown in Figure 1.

Table 3. VAR Lag Order Selection Criteria

Lag	LogL	LR	FPE	AIC	SC	HQ
0	49.74750	NA*	1.58e-09*	-3.240555	-2.952592*	-3.154929*
1	77.05535	40.45607	3.23e-09	-2.596692	-0.580946	-1.997305
2	104.6947	28.66303	9.39e-09	-1.977385	1.766144	-0.864238
3	171.1038	39.35356	4.56e-09	-4.229913*	1.241398	-2.603006

* Specifies lag order selected by the criterion
LR: sequential modified LR test statistic (each test at 5% level)
FPE: Final prediction error
AIC: Akaike information criterion
SC: Schwarz information criterion
HQ: Hannan-Quinn information criterion

Table 4. VAR Residual Serial Correlation LM Tests Results

Lag	LM Statistics	Probability
1	32.94297	0.6148
2	44.81666	0.1488
3	47.29172	0.0986
4	49.17625	0.0705
5	42.32404	0.2167
6	39.76817	0.3059
7	28.88789	0.7941
8	48.29265	0.0827
9	49.50990	0.0663
10	27.00562	0.8607
11	36.32206	0.4536
12	45.38180	0.1359

As seen in Figure 1, it is determined that all inverse roots are within the unit circle. Depending on this condition, it is seen that the VAR model ensures the stability condition. In addition to these, the White Test was employed to specify whether there is a problem of varying variance (heteroscedasticity problem) in the model. In the White test, the H_0 hypothesis clarifies homoscedasticity. Results of the White test are presented in Table 5.

Figure 1. Inverse Roots of AR Characteristic Polynomial

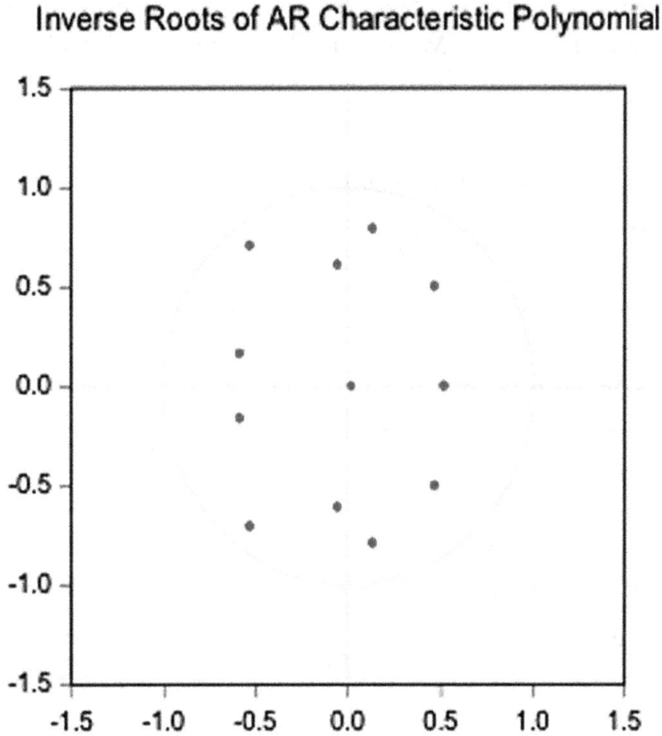

Table 5. Results of White Test

Chi-square	df	Probability (p-Value)
510.6083	504	0.4097

As seen in Table 5, the H_0 hypothesis is accepted since the p-value is greater than 0.05. That is to say, it is determined that there is no problem of varying variance (heteroscedasticity problem) in this model. Johansen's cointegration test was applied to test the cointegration relationship between the variables and the outcomes are shown in Table 6.

According to Table 6, the statistical value of the Trace test for r = 0 at the 5% significance level is greater than the table critical value. It specifies that there is a cointegration (long-term equilibrium) vector between the variables. It also shows that there are 3 cointegration equations at the 0.05 level in the trace test. In other words, there are three cointegrated vectors at the 5% significance level. Therefore, H0 (there is no cointegration between the variables) hypothesis is rejected and it is accepted that there is a long-term relationship between oil prices and the selected variables at the 5% significance level. Since there is a cointegration relationship between the variables, the VECM model has been applied and results for the VECM residuals diagnostics test are displayed in Table 7.

Table 6. Results of Johansen Cointegration Test

H_0	Eigenvalue	λt_{race}	%5 (0,05)	p-Value
None*	0.754265	124.9879	103.8473	0.0010
At most 1*	0.652156	85.68987	76.97277	0.0093
At most 2*	0.536513	56.12183	54.07904	0.0325
At most 3	0.463040	34.59050	35.19275	0.0580
At most 4	0.345239	17.17922	20.26184	0.1259
At most 5	0.173090	5.321654	9.164546	0.2500

Table 7. VECM Residuals Diagnostics Tests Results

	Chi-square	Probability (p-Value)
X^2_{HTR}	10.6083	0.44
$Q_{AR}(2)$	14.87130	0.24
LM_{SC}	34.97475	0.51

Notes: X^2_{HTR} : Chi-squared statistic for heteroscedasticity test; $Q_{AR}(2)$: Q statistic from testing *AR*(2) process; LM_{SC}: Lagrange multiplier statistic of serial correlation test

According to Table 7, VECM residuals do not have problems with instability, serial correlation, and heteroscedasticity issues. Therefore, the robustness of the prediction results has been demonstrated by the VECM residuals diagnostics test. To understand the impacts of shocks in oil prices on selected variables, impulse-response analysis was employed. Thus, with the impulse-response analysis, it can be seen which variables are impacted by the shocks in oil prices and how these variables react. The outcomes of the impulse-response test are given in Figure 2.

According to Figure 2, the response of the GDP to the single standard deviation shock to the oil price is positive until it reaches a stable level after the third quarter, and after the fourth quarter it is negative, and its negative effect continues in the following quarters. In other words, although the rise in oil prices caused an increase in the GDP in the first place, it had a negative effect after the fourth quarter. Although inflation reacts negatively to oil prices in the first place, it gives a positive reaction as of the second quarter. Inflation is not stable in the face of oil prices. The rise in oil prices generally causes a reduction in exports. It shows that interest rates decreased in the first place against oil prices, but increased steadily after the third quarter. While the unemployment figures were at the highest level in the third quarter, they decreased after the oil shocks, while the unemployment figures increased again after the fifth quarter. In general, shocks occurring in oil prices do not have a stable impact on the selected variables. In other words, selected variables against oil prices react as increases or decreases according to periods. Ultimately, a variance decomposition test was also performed to see the effect of oil price on selected macroeconomic variables, and the outcomes are given in Table 8.

Figure 2. The Results of the Impulse-Response Test

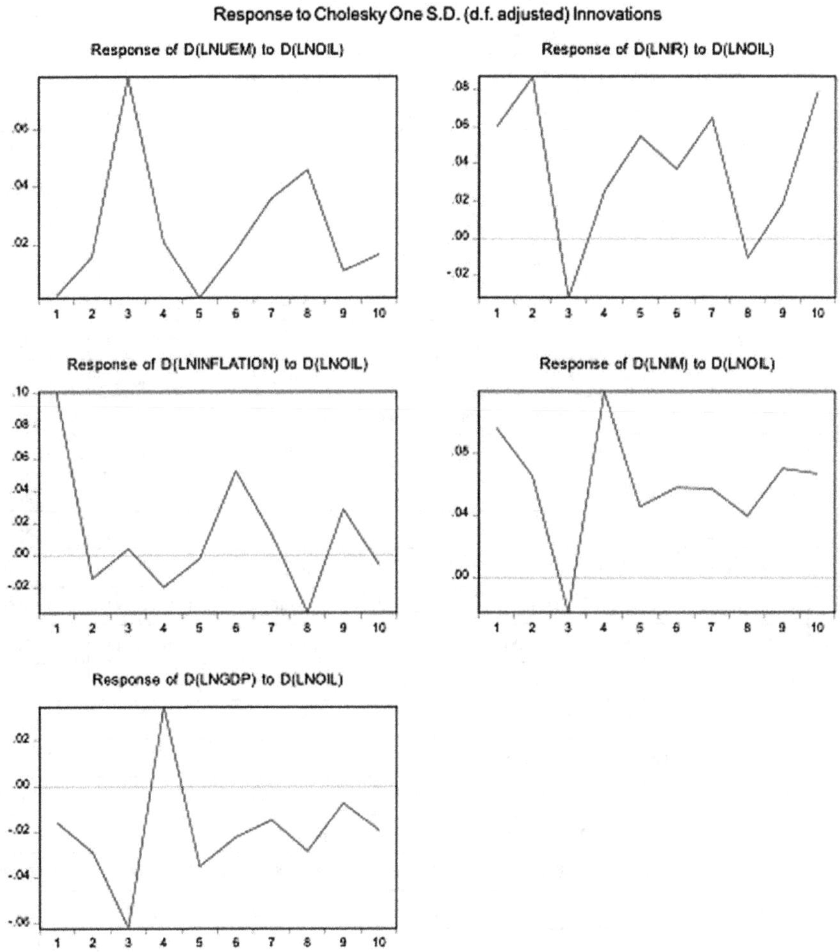

Table 8. Variance Decomposition Test Results

Period	S.E.	D(LNOIL)	D(LNUEM)	D(LNIR)	D(LNINFLATION)	D(LNIM)	D(LNGDP)
Variance Decomposition of GDP							
1	0.203982	0.586049	12.51721	4.236302	8.397877	66.57076	7.691803
2	0.267765	2.136698	18.22049	7.476823	7.724297	57.75309	6.688600
3	0.327402	6.304329	27.94724	7.004088	10.20887	43.46993	5.065546
4	0.351628	7.218810	26.33309	7.170664	9.473480	44.86229	4.941666
5	0.395371	7.035301	35.51644	6.443988	8.239804	38.45915	4.305316
6	0.421580	6.742157	33.92985	5.929724	9.640897	39.02379	4.733581
7	0.429619	6.586956	33.18210	5.632069	9.395889	40.58384	4.619151
8	0.458504	6.461621	36.81462	5.130581	9.398296	37.90340	4.291484
9	0.475777	6.125161	35.72023	5.251683	9.997900	38.32014	4.584889
10	0.487867	6.013827	35.67804	4.974488	9.447599	39.33945	4.546596
Variance Decomposition of Inflation							
1	0.279174	5.861809	1.946667	31.73855	60.45298	0.000000	0.000000
2	0.394092	4.932553	1.632968	31.02806	59.57000	0.223285	2.613140
3	0.502930	4.133480	2.144143	33.68164	57.19671	0.538853	2.305179
4	0.521785	3.694419	1.931786	29.03988	62.05122	0.959128	2.323570
5	0.588783	3.204683	1.683147	36.13837	55.57860	1.370673	2.024523
6	0.636609	3.242008	3.775283	32.51858	56.65985	2.078974	1.725299
7	0.647486	2.795399	5.268698	29.76611	56.59478	3.171363	2.403654
8	0.675207	2.987301	5.165780	30.47512	55.81988	3.189141	2.362770
9	0.697127	2.666602	6.047184	28.86783	57.44023	2.841779	2.136369
10	0.719250	2.475328	6.467574	29.52847	56.48134	2.806712	2.240583
Variance Decomposition of Interest Rate							
1	0.150554	4.604347	0.365223	95.03043	0.000000	0.000000	0.000000
2	0.208039	7.119791	0.925704	54.15975	27.26285	3.734187	6.797717
3	0.254571	4.770780	25.21235	35.34054	17.88231	10.90774	5.886287
4	0.259916	4.669257	26.53755	35.61860	16.93214	10.64936	5.593101
5	0.286893	4.527872	20.90605	37.88260	22.14613	8.871684	5.665664
6	0.308642	4.211605	24.13506	36.25190	19.31405	10.51943	5.567960
7	0.324873	5.067431	23.34459	36.11604	19.27030	10.58165	5.619982
8	0.347739	4.683279	23.28299	36.69259	19.58511	10.01680	5.739234
9	0.357684	4.466150	22.40445	38.72806	18.55890	10.21113	5.631305
10	0.372444	5.393089	21.05090	39.03422	18.86155	9.989945	5.670301
Variance Decomposition of Unemployment							
1	0.276553	0.018463	99.98154	0.000000	0.000000	0.000000	0.000000
2	0.360092	0.577249	82.71797	11.15657	0.694538	3.326756	1.526913

continues on following page

Table 8. Continued

Period	S.E.	D(LNOIL)	D(LNUEM)	D(LNIR)	D(LNINFLATION)	D(LNIM)	D(LNGDP)
3	0.413555	9.805148	77.21319	7.511354	2.217995	2.223468	1.028845
4	0.422741	10.05150	76.89206	7.327589	2.173930	2.556950	0.997974
5	0.450285	8.252212	78.91933	6.196137	1.785789	3.783705	1.062830
6	0.479758	7.463445	79.53935	6.858892	1.922056	3.297374	0.918883
7	0.490660	7.966745	79.40466	6.556526	2.135770	2.992678	0.943625
8	0.503493	8.698701	79.82194	5.795304	2.112899	2.688933	0.882226
9	0.519058	8.312183	80.16777	5.890541	2.129204	2.654248	0.846053
10	0.535788	7.863134	80.95757	5.843434	2.013548	2.510135	0.812178
Variance Decomposition of Import							
1	0.416766	22.33942	44.55119	0.192008	6.707664	26.20972	0.000000
2	0.458979	18.95165	44.00370	7.347229	4.979050	23.90661	0.811761
3	0.501751	13.15617	55.73447	6.949891	7.296966	16.21976	0.642747
4	0.540562	23.03899	48.70450	6.700258	6.688386	14.09982	0.768050
5	0.580542	19.56160	56.89422	5.690935	5.290389	11.49263	1.070223
6	0.645503	19.09105	57.74094	5.023136	7.008782	10.19285	0.943246
7	0.699530	20.16357	56.57540	4.882543	7.264082	10.08199	1.032413
8	0.707315	18.44876	60.28493	4.481673	6.420584	9.074896	1.289158
9	0.768805	19.31210	59.38222	4.265519	7.337371	8.486219	1.216576
10	0.798822	20.25149	59.14476	4.056929	7.212450	8.095152	1.239210

As presented in Table 8, the variance decomposition indicates that approximately 2% of fluctuations in Turkey's economic growth are explicated by a 58% deviation in oil price shock. Furthermore, 2% of the fluctuations in inflation is explained by 86% deviation in oil price shock. The variance decomposition of unemployment shows that the oil price shock explains around 1.8% of the unemployment change. The variance decomposition of interest rate shows that the oil price shock explains about 60% of the interest rate variation. The oil price shock explains about 33% of the import variation.

DISCUSSION

Turkey is a crude oil importing country. Therefore, it is a general opinion accepted by both the public and the government of the country that one of the important reasons for the change in other macroeconomic activities besides economic growth is the increase in oil prices. It is aimed to contribute to the literature by investigating how the changes in oil prices in oil-importing countries affect macroeconomic activities. As a result of the analysis, the rise in oil prices in the short term has a positive effect on economic growth. When the studies in the literature are examined, Atil *et al.* (2020), one of the studies that find results in the same direction as the findings obtained in the presented study, revealed that oil prices have a positive effect on economic development. Kurihara (2015) examined the relationship between oil prices and economic growth. According to the results, increases in oil prices cause positive economic growth in the United States, European Union, and Japan. Similarly, Mukhtarov *et al.* (2020) found that increases in oil prices positively affect economic growth for oil-exporting Azerbaijan. Contrary, Sodeyfi and Katircioglu (2016) emphasized that oil price has a negative effect on commercial activities in some countries. Bouzid (2012) stated that the increase in oil prices reduces economic growth for oil-importing Tunisia. Some studies have not found any relationship between economic growth and oil prices. For instance, Idrisov *et al.* (2015) found that a steady increase in oil prices cannot affect the long-term economic growth rate. Similarly, Rostin *et al.* (2019) explored that crude oil prices do not affect economic growth in both the short and long term for Indonesia.

When the results of the studies in the literature are evaluated, increases in oil prices affect the economy positively in oil-exporting countries, while increases in oil prices in oil-importing countries have a positive effect on the economy in the short term, but negatively affect the economy in the long term. In other words, the positive effects in developing and oil-producing countries in the short term are temporary.

Another finding is that increases in oil prices have a positive effect on unemployment in the short term. Similarly, Ahmad (2013) showed the significant impact of oil prices on unemployment. In other words, oil prices have a positive effect on unemployment in the long run for Pakistan. Dogrul and Soytas (2010) found that oil prices improve unemployment forecasts for Turkey in the long run, confirming Nusair's (2020) results for the USA and Canada. Senzangakhona and Choga (2015) showed that crude oil prices are positively related to unemployment in the long run for South Africa. It is displayed in the study that unemployment returns to equilibrium in the long run when the price of crude oil changes. Contrary, Kocaarslan *et al.* (2020) indicated that the increase in oil prices causes an increase in unemployment. Cuestas and Gil-Alana (2018) pointed out that there is not much correlation between oil prices and unemployment in the short run. In other words, they revealed that the effect of oil price shocks on the natural unemployment rate proceeds in the same direction so that increases or decreases in oil prices increase or decrease unemployment rates. Trang (2017) found that the effects of the increase in oil prices on unemployment in Vietnam are uncertain.

Lastly, increases in oil prices have an unstable and a volatile effect on inflation, interest rate, and import variables in the long run. While some studies in the literature found a positive relationship between oil prices and inflation, interest rate, and import variables, some studies found a negative relationship. Various studies reveal that there is no relationship between oil prices and these variables. For instance, Ayisi (2020) found that inflation responds asymmetrically to oil prices in the long run, but not in the short run. Choi *et al.* (2018) examined the impact of fluctuations in global oil prices on domestic inflation for 72 developed and developing countries. According to the results, a 10% increase in global oil inflation increases local inflation by about 0.4 percentage points on average. Similarly, LeBlanc and Chinn (2004) showed that increases in oil prices can have only a modest effect on inflation in the US, Japan, and Europe. In other words, increases of up to 10 percent in oil prices will lead to direct inflationary increases of about 0.1-0.8 percentage points in the USA and EU.

For the interest rate, Arora and Tanner (2013) showed the existence of an inverse relationship between the real interest rate and the real oil price in the long run. Mensi *et al.* (2013) found out important relationships between crude oil prices and interest rates. Also, co-movements between oil price and interest rate variables are particularly vulnerable during periods of anomalous political events and financial 'collapses'. When the relationship between oil prices and imports is examined, Gorus *et al.* (2019) found that oil imports are more sensitive to changes in income than to changes in oil prices in the long run. Marathe and Guntur (2020) revealed that there is a short-run relationship between imports and crude oil for BRICS countries.

As a result, it can be stated that imported crude oil prices have an impact on Turkey's macroeconomic performance. Therefore, both policymakers and businesses in Turkey should not ignore the risks arising from the above-mentioned oil price shocks.

CONCLUSION

Due to the effect of oil price fluctuations on macroeconomic variables, it is a significant issue for countries that import oil and petroleum products. In this context, this chapter examines the effects of oil price fluctuations on economic growth, inflation, interest rate, unemployment, and imports in Turkey. For this goal, the VECM method was employed for the period 1990-2020 years. First of all, the variables were stationarity with the ADF unit root test. Afterward, the Johansen cointegration test was employed to evaluate the long-term relationships between the variables. The findings revealed that there is a long-term relationship between the variables. Due to the cointegration between the variables, impulse-response and variance decomposition tests were performed under the assumption of VECM. According to the findings, the rise in oil prices in the short term has a positive impact on unemployment and economic growth, which are among the selected variables.

However, it is seen that rises in oil prices in the long term have an unstable volatile effect on selected macroeconomic variables.

In conclusion, since Turkey is an oil-importing country, the volatility in oil prices unstable affects macroeconomic variables and the Turkish economy is vulnerable to shocks/volatility in oil prices. Therefore, to ensure energy supply security, Turkey should spread its oil providers, focus on domestic energy resources, and develop advanced technology to raise the usage of renewable energy resources and should also implement energy-saving policies.

DISCLAIMER

The contents and views of this chapter are expressed by the author in her personal capacity. It is not necessary for the Editor and the Publisher to agree with these viewpoints and they are not responsible for any duty of care in this regard.

ACKNOWLEDGMENT

The author extends sincere gratitude to

- The Editor and the International Editorial Advisory Board (IEAB) of this book who initially desk reviewed, arranged a rigorous double/triple blind review process and conducted a thorough, minute and critical final review before accepting the chapter for publication.
- All anonymous reviewers who provided very constructive feedbacks for thorough revision, improvement, extension and fine tuning of the chapter.
- All colleagues, assistants and well-wishers who assisted the authors to complete this task.

REFERENCES

Ahmad, F. (2013). The effect of oil prices on unemployment: Evidence from Pakistan. *Business and Economics Research Journal*, *4*(1), 43–57.

Aimer, N. M. M., & Moftah, M. (2016). The effects of fluctuations of oil price on economic growth of Libya. *Energy Economics Letters*, *3*(2), 17–29. doi:10.18488/journal.82/2016.3.2/82.2.17.29

Akinlo, T., & Apanisile, O. T. (2015). The impact of volatility of oil price on the economic growth in sub-Saharan Africa. *Journal of Economics. Management and Trade*, *5*(3), 338–349.

Akyol, H., & Baltaci, N. (2018). Ülke Kredi Risk Düzeyi, Petrol Fiyatlari Ve Temel Makroekonomik Göstergelerin Hisse Senedi Getirilerine Etkisi: BIST 100 Örneği. *Kafkas Universitesi. Sosyal Bilimler Enstitu*, *22*, 459–476.

Alagoz, M., Alacahan, N. D., & Akarsu, Y. (2017). Petrol fiyatlarının makro ekonomi üzerindeki etkisi-ülke karşılaştırmaları ile panel veri analizi. *Karamanoğlu Mehmetbey Üniversitesi Sosyal Ve Ekonomik Araştırmalar Dergisi*, *19*(33), 144–150.

Alkahteeb, T. T. Y., & Sultan, Z. A. (2019). Oil price and economic growth: The case of Indian economy. *International Journal of Energy Economics and Policy*, *9*(3), 274–279. doi:10.32479/ijeep.7602

Amri, F. (2016). The relationship amongst energy consumption, foreign direct investment and output in developed and developing countries. *Renewable & Sustainable Energy Reviews*, *64*, 694–702. doi:10.1016/j.rser.2016.06.065

Arora, V., & Tanner, M. (2013). Do oil prices respond to real interest rates? *Energy Economics*, *36*, 546–555. doi:10.1016/j.eneco.2012.11.001

Asaleye, A. J., Aremu, C. O., Lawal, A. I., Inegbedion, H., Popoola, O., Adewara, S. O., & Obasaju, B. O. (2019). Oil price shock and macroeconomic performance in Nigeria: Implication on employment. *International Journal of Energy Economics and Policy*, *9*(5), 451–457. doi:10.32479/ijeep.7768

Atil, A., Nawaz, K., Lahiani, A., & Roubaud, D. (2020). Are natural resources a blessing or a curse for financial development in Pakistan? The importance of oil prices, economic growth and economic globalization. *Resources Policy*, *67*, 101683. doi:10.1016/j.resourpol.2020.101683

Awolaja, G. O., & Musa, D. C. (2017). Asymmetric Oil Price Shocks and Stock Prices in Nigeria. *MPRA Paper*, 1–27.

Ayisi, R. K. (2020). The asymmetry effect of oil price changes on inflation, and the welfare implication for Ghana. *African Journal of Economic and Management Studies*, *12*(1), 55–70. doi:10.1108/AJEMS-01-2020-0009

Benramdane, A. (2017). Oil price volatility and economic growth in Algeria. *Energy Sources. Part B, Economics, Planning, and Policy*, *12*(4), 338–343. doi:10.1080/15567249.2015.1128015

Berument, M. H., Ceylan, N. B., & Dogan, N. (2010). The impact of oil price shocks on the economic growth of selected MENA1 countries. *Energy Journal, 31*(1), 149–176. doi:10.5547/ISSN0195-6574-EJ-Vol31-No1-7

Bhusal, T. P. (2010). Econometric analysis of oil consumption and economic growth in Nepal. *Economic Journal of Development Issues, 11/12*, 135–143.

Bouzid, A. (2012). The relationship of oil prices and economic growth in Tunisia: A vector error correction model analysis. *The Romanian Economic Journal, XV*(43), 3–22.

Brown, S. P., & Yücel, M. K. (2002). Energy prices and aggregate economic activity: An interpretative survey. *The Quarterly Review of Economics and Finance, 42*(2), 193–208. doi:10.1016/S1062-9769(02)00138-2

Brown, S. P. A., Yucel, M. K., & Thompson, J. (2003). *Business cycles: the role of energy prices* (Working Paper 0304). Federal Reserve Bank of Dallas.

Chen, S., Chen, D., & Härdle, W. K. (2014). *The influence of oil price shocks on china's macroeconomy: a perspective of international trade*. Retrieved from https://papers.ssrn.com/sol3/papers.cfm?abstract_id=2634637

Choi, S., Furceri, D., Loungani, P., Mishra, S., & Poplawski-Ribeiro, M. (2018). Oil prices and inflation dynamics: Evidence from advanced and developing economies. *Journal of International Money and Finance, 82*, 71–96. doi:10.1016/j.jimonfin.2017.12.004

Cuestas, J. C., & Gil-Alana, L. A. (2018). Oil price shocks and unemployment in Central and Eastern Europe. *Economic Systems, 42*(1), 164–173. doi:10.1016/j.ecosys.2017.05.005

Dickey, D. A., & Fuller, W. A. (1981). Likelihood ratio statistics for autoregressive time series with a unit root. *Econometrica, 49*(4), 1057–1072. doi:10.2307/1912517

Dogrul, H. G., & Soytas, U. (2010). Relationship between oil prices, interest rate, and unemployment: Evidence from an emerging market. *Energy Economics, 32*(6), 1523–1528. doi:10.1016/j.eneco.2010.09.005

Edelstein, P., & Kilian, L. (2007). *Retail energy prices and consumer expenditures*. Retrieved from https://papers.ssrn.com/sol3/papers.cfm?abstract_id=1135493

Esen, O., & Bayrak, M. (2015). Enerji Açığının Belirleyicilerinin Teorik Perspektiften İncelenmesi. *Anemon Muş Alparslan Üniversitesi Sosyal Bilimler Dergisi, 3*(1), 45–61. doi:10.18506/anemon.26550

Ghalayini, L. (2011). The interaction between oil price and economic growth. *Middle Eastern Finance and Economics*, *13*(21), 127–141.

Gorus, M. S., Ozgur, O., & Develi, A. (2019). The relationship between oil prices, oil imports and income level in Turkey: Evidence from Fourier approximation. *OPEC Energy Review*, *43*(3), 327–341. doi:10.1111/opec.12159

Gundogan, H., & Tok, D. (2019). Petrole bağımlı ülkelerde petrol fiyatlarının sanayi üretimine etkisi: Panel nedensellik çalışması. *Ege Academic Review*, *19*(1), 131–140.

Hanabusa, K. (2009). Causality relationship between the price of oil and economic growth in Japan. *Energy Policy*, *37*(5), 1953–1957. doi:10.1016/j.enpol.2009.02.007

Idrisov, G., Kazakova, M., & Polbin, A. (2015). A theoretical interpretation of the oil prices impact on economic growth in contemporary Russia. *Russian Journal of Economics*, *1*(3), 257–272. doi:10.1016/j.ruje.2015.12.004

Iwayemi, A., & Fowowe, B. (2011). Impact of oil price shocks on selected macroeconomic variables in Nigeria. *Energy Policy*, *39*(2), 603–612. doi:10.1016/j.enpol.2010.10.033

Jiménez-Rodríguez, R., & Sánchez, M. (2005). Oil price shocks and real GDP growth: Empirical evidence for some OECD countries. *Applied Economics*, *37*(2), 201–228.

Johansen, S. (1988). Statistical analysis of cointegration vectors. *Journal of Economic Dynamics & Control*, *12*(2-3), 231–254.

Kahn, M. E., & Mansur, E. T. (2010). How do energy prices, and labor and environmental regulations affect local manufacturing employment dynamics? A regression discontinuity approach (No. w16538). National Bureau of Economic Research.

Katırcıoğlu, S. T., Sertoglu, K., Candemir, M., & Mercan, M. (2015). Oil price movements and macroeconomic performance: Evidence from twenty-six OECD countries. *Renewable & Sustainable Energy Reviews*, *44*, 257–270.

Keser, Ö. (2003). Energy, environment, and education relationship, in developing countries' policies: A case study for Turkey. *Energy Sources*, *25*(2), 123–133.

Kiani, A. (2011). Impact of high oil prices on Pakistan's economic growth. *International Journal of Business and Social Science*, *2*(17), 209–217.

Kilci, E. N. (2019). Analysis of the causality relationship between Brent crude oil prices and energy import in Turkey under structural breaks. *Business and Economics Research Journal*, *10*(4), 777–788.

Kilian, L., & Vega, C. (2011). Do energy prices respond to US macroeconomic news? A test of the hypothesis of predetermined energy prices. *The Review of Economics and Statistics*, *93*(2), 660–671.

Kocaarslan, B., Soytas, M. A., & Soytas, U. (2020). The asymmetric impact of oil prices, interest rates and oil price uncertainty on unemployment in the US. *Energy Economics*, *86*, 104625.

Kocabiyik, T., & Fattah, A. S. (2020). Makroekonomik Değişkenlerin Borsa Endeksleri Üzerine Etkisi: Türkiye Ve Abd Karşılaştırması. *Finansal Araştırmalar Ve Çalışmalar Dergisi*, *12*(22), 116–151.

Kurihara, Y. (2015). Oil prices and economic growth in developed countries. *International Journal of Business and Social Science*, *6*(11), 40–46.

Lardic, S., & Mignon, V. (2008). Oil prices and economic activity: An asymmetric cointegration approach. *Energy Economics*, *30*(3), 847–855.

LeBlanc, M., & Chinn, M. D. (2004). *Do high oil prices presage inflation? The evidence from G-5 countries* (Working Paper No. 561). Santa Cruz: University of California.

Mahmood, H., & Murshed, M. (2021). Oil price and economic growth nexus in Saudi Arabia: Asymmetry analysis. *International Journal of Energy Economics and Policy*, *11*(1), 29.

Marathe, S. R., & Guntur, A. R. (2020). Does Crude Oil Prices have Effect on Exports, Imports and GDP on BRICS Countries?-An Empirical Evidence. *International Journal of Energy Economics and Policy*, *10*(6), 524.

Mensi, W., Rehman, M. U., & Al-Yahyaee, K. H. (2020). Time-frequency co-movements between oil prices and interest rates: Evidence from a wavelet-based approach. *The North American Journal of Economics and Finance*, *51*, 100836.

Mukhtarov, S., Aliyev, S., & Zeynalov, J. (2020). The Effect of Oil Prices on Macroeconomic Variables: Evidence from Azerbaijan. *International Journal of Energy Economics and Policy*, *10*(1), 72–80.

Narayan, P. K., Sharma, S., Poon, W. C., & Westerlund, J. (2014). Do oil prices predict economic growth? New global evidence. *Energy Economics*, *41*, 137–146.

Nazir, S., & Qayyum, A. (2014). Impact of oil price and shocks on economic growth of Pakistan: Multivariate analysis. *MPRA Paper,* 1–24.

Nusair, S. A. (2020). The asymmetric effects of oil price changes on unemployment: Evidence from Canada and the US. *Journal of Economic Asymmetries*, *21*, e00153.

Okoro, E. G. (2014). Oil price volatility and economic growth in Nigeria: A Vector Auto-Regression (VAR) approach. *Acta Universitatis Danubius. Œconomica, 10*(1), 70–82.

Omojolaibi, J. A., & Egwaikhide, F. (2013). A panel analysis of oil price dynamics, fiscal stance and macroeconomic effects: The case of some selected African countries. *Economic and Financial Review*, *51*(1), 4.

Qianqian, Z. (2011). The impact of international oil price fluctuation on China's economy. *Energy Procedia*, *5*, 1360–1364.

Rostin, R., Adam, P., Nur, M., Saenong, Z., & Baso, J. N. (2019). The effect of crude oil prices on inflation, interest rates and economic growth in Indonesia. *International Journal of Energy Economics and Policy*, *9*(5), 14.

Sadorsky, P. (1999). Oil price shocks and stock market activity. *Energy Economics*, *21*(5), 449–469.

Sağlam, Y., & Güreşçi, G. (2018). Petrol Şoklarının Makroekonomik Göstergeler Üzerine Etkileri: OPEC İçin Yapısal VAR Analizi. *Finans Politik ve Ekonomik Yorumlar*, *55*(640), 27–47.

Senzangakhona, P., & Choga, I. (2015). Crude oil prices and unemployment in South Africa: 1990–2010. *Mediterranean Journal of Social Sciences*, *6*(2), 407.

Sodeyfi, S., & Katircioglu, S. (2016). Interactions between business conditions, economic growth and crude oil prices. *Economic Research-Ekonomska Istraživanja*, *29*(1), 980–990.

Tang, W., Wu, L., & Zhang, Z. (2010). Oil price shocks and their short-and long-term effects on the Chinese economy. *Energy Economics*, *32*, S3–S14.

Trang, N. T. N. (2017). The impact of oil price on the growth, inflation, unemployment and budget deficit of Vietnam. *International Journal of Energy Economics and Policy*, *7*(3), 42–49.

Van Eyden, R., Difeto, M., Gupta, R., & Wohar, M. E. (2019). Oil price volatility and economic growth: Evidence from advanced economies using more than a century's data. *Applied Energy*, *233*, 612–621.

Wang, Y. S., & Chueh, Y. L. (2013). Dynamic transmission effects between the interest rate, the US dollar, and gold and crude oil prices. *Economic Modelling, 30*, 792–798.

Wei, Y., & Guo, X. (2016). An empirical analysis of the relationship between oil prices and the Chinese macro-economy. *Energy Economics, 56*, 88–100.

Zhao, L., Zhang, X., Wang, S., & Xu, S. (2016). The effects of oil price shocks on output and inflation in China. *Energy Economics, 53*, 101–110.

KEY TERMS AND DEFINITIONS

Brent Oil Price: Brent oil is the fuel that the markets follow closely and directs the world oil market.

Economic Growth (GDP): Economic growth is a rise in the production of goods and services in an economy.

Import: Import, on the other hand, is the process of purchasing a product produced abroad by buyers in the country.

Inflation: The general rise in the prices of goods and services is expressed as inflation.

Interest Rate: Interest is the price of money loaned. In another definition, when a debt is borrowed over any amount, it is the remuneration process performed while paying the debt.

Macroeconomic Variables: It is expressed as indicators that a country considers to understand its economic reality compared to other countries. Basic macroeconomic data are GDP, inflation, unemployment/employment, interest rate, exchange rate, and imports.

Unemployment: Unemployment is defined as the situation in which some people want to work but cannot find a job in any economy. A person who cannot find a job is called unemployed.

Chapter 5
Wealth at the Expense of Health:
The Outcome of Environmental Degradation

Awais Ur Rehman
Faculty of Management Sciences, University of Central Punjab, Pakistan

Arsalan Haneef Malik
https://orcid.org/0000-0001-8940-4850
Faculty of Economics and Business, Universiti Malaysia Sarawak, Malaysia

Aasia Kanwal
University of Health Sciences, Lahore, Pakistan & Shalamar Medical and Dental College, Lahore, Pakistan

Naveed Aslam Lashari
Pakistan Air Force Hospital, Islamabad, Pakistan

ABSTRACT

Human activities to boost economic wellbeing have degraded the environment on many fronts to the extent that earth has reached its planetary boundaries by sabotaging its self-regulating equilibrium system. This study investigates the impact of air pollution (proxied by various indicators) on health expenditure over a panel consisting of 188 countries for the period 2000-2018. The impact of air pollution on health expenditures was analyzed using the GMM estimations. Findings suggest that health expenditures are increased due to air pollution caused by economic activities. The study urges that governments should reconsider their policies by

DOI: 10.4018/978-1-6684-5580-7.ch005

creating a balance between economic growth and environmental sustainability. While spending on a sustainable environment, humans can have better health and working capacities that will ultimately contribute to the overall economy. A carbon taxing system on businesses that use obsolete technologies can also contribute towards a sustainable environment and reduced air pollution.

INTRODUCTION

Concerning pollution and human health, a complex and long history has been cited in the literature. Urban populations of ancient Rome and Athens were the first to raise their voices for it (Colbeck, 2007). In comparison, the worsened situations regarding these issues were first felt during the Industrial Revolution era. Due to the extensive use of coal during this era, some historians have even used the term "Smoke Age" for this period (Mosley, 2014). But these concerns were not shaped to manage this issue with strong and efficient regulatory supervision at a global level (Stutz, 2010). It explains the reason that why humans have to face a series of environment-related health issues. This issue was restricted to limited geographic areas. Still, after World War II, the after-effects of armaments and wide-spread use of energy, fossil fuels, and industrialization resulted in frequent acid rains, chemical smog, ozone issues, and abrupt climate changes (Sieferle, 2001). Logically, these frequent environmental issues can impact human health conditions (Boogaard, *et al.*, 2019). Until recently, the human population cannot breathe clean air, and this issue is of greater concern in industrial and metropolitan urban areas.

On the other hand, to improve living standards, the world has witnessed intense competition to achieve economic growth. Though, because of the economic growth, mother nature has faced severe problems of environmental degradation and, most prominently, air pollution (Baloch, *et al.*, 2020). According to the World Health Organization (WHO), 3.8 million people per year suffer from premature death due to illness caused by air pollution (WHO, 2021a).

The adverse impact of air pollution can be quantified by considering health expenditure. Health expenditure has a significant role in formulating national health and environmental policy. The real challenge for policymakers is to manage health costs and accomplish economic growth at the same time. For instance, stringent regulations for environmental protection may reduce profits by firms, and on the other hand, relaxed regulations may affect the health of a population (Chen & Chen, 2021). Nieto (2017) explains that a sudden change in policies to switch towards a low-carbon economy will create uncertainty in a region. Giving an example of European banks, Nieto (2017) explains that as of December 2014, €1.35 trillion of lending amount belongs to a sector that has a sizable portion in causing environmental damage that is gas and oil exploitation companies. A sudden shift will not only harm these firms alone, but it would also affect the banks by losing their assets, impair GDP, and harm the overall economy (Nieto, 2017).

There is no doubt that acquiring the optimal solution, i.e., a balance between environmental and economic sustainability, is not an easy task due to a lack of accurate health cost estimations. Contrary to this, several studies have established that the impact of air pollution is different on every individual based on their economic conditions. For example, Jans, Johansson, and Nilsson (2018) found that children from high-income households are less affected by air pollution than children WHO belong to low-income households. Thus, it can be said that economic growth is necessary for a country that makes it capable of providing good health services to its citizen. On the other hand, rapid economic activities also create health problems for citizens by increasing air pollution and environmental degradation. Therefore, policymakers must assess that to what extent air pollution caused by economic activities increases health expenditures.

Few studies have assessed the impact of air pollution on economic output and health expenditure in a small number of regions (Selin, *et al.*, 2009; Xie *et al.*, 2016). However, based on Gaia theory and life history theory, this study is among the few that conducted cross-country analysis to assess the impact of greenhouse gas emissions and $PM_{2.5}$ air pollution exposure to a population exceeding the levels set by the World Health Organization (WHO) guidelines on health expenditure per capita.

This study would also help policymakers assess environmental degradation caused by economic activities on health-related issues. The cost of economic activities without considering the impact on the environment increases the health expenditures of the governments. In this context, policymakers need to create a balance between economic growth and environmental sustainability. If environmental sustainability is not considered while introducing policies for achieving economic growth. In that case, it will affect the economy itself eventually by increasing health expenditure, loss of GDP, and human capital as well.

LITERATURE REVIEW

Theoretical Underpinnings

Gaia theory, also known as Gaia Paradigm, establishes that life on Earth and inorganic substances in the environment are associated with each other so that they both can impact and can be impacted by each other (Lovelock & Margulis, 1974). The dynamics of human life, including their economic and ecological imprints, derive the operationalization of this causal linkage. At the same time, allocating resources from the environmental conditions to the extent that an allocation of resources, governed by the principles of ecological justice, can be favorable for both humans and their environment (Lynch, *et al.*, 2019).

Under the life history theory, life on the Earth is a phenomenon that presides over centuries with varying human needs and resources over time (Griskevicius *et al.,* 2011). The Earth under Gaia theory is presented as an entity that interacts with these varying human needs and resources and generates its response. This response is aligned to the human dynamic of ecological imprints; if the environment is damaged, the response is often a "natural response of revenge" (Lovelock, 2006; Lynch, *et al.*, 2019). Critically, over the past couple of centuries, the rise of capitalism has seen a devastating response to the environment. We argue that the adverse reaction of Earth can be felt in the form of new diseases like Covid-19, and the governments have to allocate resources in the form of health budgeting to cope with these issues. In other words, the economies at a higher ebb of polluting the environment are expected to shoulder a higher burden of health budgeting.

Based on Gaia theory, our argument becomes more significant to analyze in the current scenario since it has been observed that during the past two centuries, nearly half the capacity of the Earth to sustain its resources has been consumed. Gaia theory has been used to study the temperature and water salinity concerning the Earth's habitability for organisms (Beirne, 1999). While their interaction with human life has been discussed at scant levels (Lynch, *et al.*, 2019). In this wake, our study is also contributing to the literary ambit of Gaia theory since it is applying the theory on the economic dynamic of humans' life instead of other organisms. No gainsaying that humans are the critical organism to pollute the environment and have to face the after-effects.

Economic Activities and Health Expenditure

Rapid economic growth has upgraded people's technology and living standards, but it has also compromised the air quality. World Health Organization has declared air pollution a silent public health emergency (Manisalidis *et al.*, 2020). The air pollution can be indoor as well as outdoor and henceforth can impact human health at large and even the people staying indoors or working outside. In developing countries, 95% of the population burns wood to keep themselves warm and cook their food (Currie *et al.*, 2009, Khoshnevis Yazdi and Khanalizadeh, 2017) leading to indoor pollution. This indoor pollution makes women vulnerable to health issues, especially COPD (Hashim and Boffetta, 2014, Guo *et al.*, 2017).

Overcrowding of the cities and industrialization cause outdoor air pollution. People facing air pollution suffer from respiratory problems, including allergic asthma and obstructive pulmonary diseases, cardiovascular problems, and diabetes (Karl *et al.*, 2009, Kelishadi and Poursafa, 2010, Eze *et al.*, 2014). Cardiac issues are more prevalent in developed countries due to air pollution (Pena and Rollins, 2017). Studies from India and Nepal have also reported that air pollution is a serious concern due to overcrowded urbanization and an increase in industrial wastes (Kankaria *et al.*, 2014, Parajuli *et al.*, 2016). Multiple international studies from Australia, Japan and, Mexico have reported bad air quality in these countries and increasing health problems (Kassomenos *et al.*, 2012).

Including human capital loss, environmental degradation also damages the economy (Xie, *et al.*, 2019). Numerous studies have shown the $PM_{2.5}$ has caused massive adverse health impacts and economic losses in China (Bai, Lam, & Li, 2018). Furthermore, $PM_{2.5}$, the primary air pollutant, also adversely impacts human mental health and affects its performance (Zhang, Chen, & Zhang, 2018). In the long run, air pollution exposure has compromised individuals' mental health, which is a matter of prime concern (Manisalidis *et al.*, 2020, Genc *et al.*, 2012).

Additionally, ozone pollution caused by environmental degradation is also causing a rise in health expenditures of individuals and governments worldwide. For instance, ozone pollution increases hospital admissions due to respiratory, cardiovascular, and asthma diseases, restricted activity days, absenteeism in school, and premature deaths (Anenberg, *et al.*, 2017).

Numerous studies have assessed the impact of environmental degradation on economic output on a regional basis. For instance, Xie *et al.* (2016) observed that if steps are not taken to mitigate air pollution, the GDP will be impaired by 2.0% in China. Selin *et al.* (2009), in their study over sixteen countries of the world, anticipated the impact of ozone air pollution on economic and human health between 2000 to 2050. They estimated that health costs would be around $580 billion, and mortalities will go beyond two million.

The Organization for Economic Co-operation and Development (OECD) report also projected high health and economic cost caused by air pollution (OECD, 2016). Moreover, Xie, *et al.* (2019) established that air pollution significantly affects economic welfare. Furthermore, $PM_{2.5}$ pollution has a severely damaging impact on health and economic growth. Additionally, in China, the steps to improve air quality would help in reducing health expenditure by 157 billion CNY and 50 billion CNY by reducing $PM_{2.5}$ pollution (Xie, *et al.*, 2019).

Based on the literature review, we conclude that economic activities are causing severe adverse effects on human health, which further lay the burden on governments by increasing expenditures on health. This study also highlights that when governments attempt to boost economic activities without considering environmental aspects, these activities, contrary to the expectations, deteriorate the GDP.

DATA AND METHODOLOGY

Data Description

The study was conducted on a panel of 188 countries from 2000 to 2018. The selection of countries and time was based on the availability of the data. The list of countries included in the panel study is provided in the Appendix.

The economic condition may predict health expenditure; however, air pollution is usually associated with economic development. This study would use current health expenditure per capita (HCE) provided by the WHO as a health cost. While for air pollution, the study considered CO_2 emission (metric tons per capita), Methane emissions (metric tons of CO_2 equivalent per capita), Nitrous oxide emissions (metric tons of CO_2 equivalent per capita), $PM_{2.5}$ air pollution, population exposure to levels exceeding WHO guideline value (% of total) provided by the World Bank. GDP per capita growth (annual %) was employed as a control variable. Data for all variables of this was study gathered from the world development indicators (WDI) provided by the World Bank. The description of the variables considered in this study is presented in Table 1.

Table 1. Variables of the study from year 2000-2018

Variables	Min	Max	Mean	Std. Deviation	Abb
Current health expenditure per capita (current US$)	4.34	10623	866.95	1525.58	HEC
CO_2 emissions (Metric tons per capita)	0.02	67	5	6.42	CO_2
Methane emissions (Kt of CO_2 equivalent)	1.31	1752290	39572	128887.54	MTE
Nitrous oxide emissions (Thousand metric tons of CO_2 equivalent)	0.02	587166	16045	49224.29	NOE
$PM_{2.5}$ air pollution, population exposed to levels exceeding WHO guideline value (% of total)	0.00	100	93	23.06	$PM_{2.5}$
GDP per capita growth (annual %)	-62.38	122	2.35	5.10	GDP

Notes: Source of the data is the world development indicators database provided by the World Bank. Abb: Abbreviation used for variables in the study.

Source: Author's Calculations.

METHODOLOGIES

There can be fair chances of getting biased results in panel data due to endogeneity issues (Ahamed & Mallick, 2019; Vo, Nguyen, & Van, 2021) autocorrelation, heteroskedasticity, measurement error, and unobserved biases in the sample data (Dutta & Saha, 2020). To tackle these issues, there is a need to find suitable instrumental variables. However, finding an appropriate instrumental variable is challenging (Dutta & Saha, 2020). Besides, generalized method of moments (GMM) eradicates the need to find external and strictly exogenous instrumental variables by constructing an internal instrumental variable (Malik, Isa, Jais, Rehman, & Khan, 2021). In this wake, this study uses the GMM technique (Asongu & Nnanna, 2019; Asongu & Odhiambo, 2020a; Asongu & Odhiambo, 2020b). The results of diagnSostic tests reported in Table 2 validate heteroskedasticity and autocorrelation in the model. Hence, the use of a two-step GMM estimator with an instrumental technique (OECD, 2009), which is an extension of Arellano and Bover (1995), is considered suitable (Tran & Vo, 2020; Vo, Nguyen, & Van, 2021). The estimation model is illustrated in Equation 1.

$$\begin{aligned} HEC_{i,t} &= \sigma_0 + \sigma_1 HEC_{i,t-1} + \sigma_2 CO2_{i,t} + \sigma_3 MTE_{i,t} \\ &+\sigma_4 NOE_{i,t} + \sigma_5 PM2.5_{i,t} + \sigma_6 GDP_{i,t} + n_i + \xi_1 + \varepsilon_{i,t} \end{aligned} \quad (1)$$

Where,

HEC = Current health expenditure per capita (current US$) for country *i* at year *t*

$\sigma 0$ = a constant

CO_2 = CO_2 emissions (metric tons per capita)

MTE = Methane emissions (kt of CO_2 equivalent)

NOE = Nitrous oxide emissions (thousand metric tons of CO_2 equivalent)

$PM_{2.5}$ = $PM_{2.5}$ air pollution, population exposed to levels exceeding WHO guideline value (% of total)

GDP = GDP per capita growth (annual %)

n_i = country-specific effect

ξt = time-specific constant

$\varepsilon i_{,t}$ = an error term.

EMPIRICAL FINDINGS

The use of GMM was based on preliminary and post-estimation tests, as illustrated in Table 2. The results for Breusch and Pagan Lagrangian multiplier (BPL) signifies that ordinary least square (OLS) is not appropriate for the model (Equation 1). Moreover, modified Wald tests also identify heteroscedasticity problems in the model (Uyanto, 2019; Vo, Nguyen, & Van, 2021). Furthermore, the Wooldridge test indicates the presence of autocorrelation in the model (Tran, Van, & Vo, 2020; Vo, Nguyen, & Van, 2021). Hence to counter these problems, recent studies suggest using GMM (Sardo & Serrasqueiro, 2017; Anifowose *et al.*, 2018; Vo, 2018; Haris *et al.,* 2019; Van, Nguyen, & Vo, 2020; Malik, Isa, Jais, Rehman, & Khan, 2021). Moreover, the results of the Sargan test and Arellano-Bond tests also approve the validity of the instrumental variables in the GMM (Tran & Vo, 2020; Tran, Van, & Vo, 2020; Vo, Nguyen, & Van, 2021). Hence, we use GMM on the justifications of the above-mentioned shreds of evidence and diagnostic tests (see Table 2.

Table 2. Diagnostic Tests

Breusch and Pagan Lagrangian multiplier (Prob > chibar2) Existence of Heteroskedasticity	753.78 (0.000) YES
Modified Wald test (Prob > chibar2) Existence of Heteroskedasticity	7.0e+07 (0.000) YES
Wooldridge test (Prob > chibar2) Existence of Heteroskedasticity	49.311 (0.000) YES
Arellano Bond test Order 1 (Prob > z)	-4.4175 (0.000)
Arellano Bond test Order 2 (Prob > z)	-0.1504 (0.1256)
Sargan Test $\chi2$ Prob > $\chi2$	185.9133 (0.1770)

Source: Author's Calculations.

Table 3 represents the results for regressing health expenditures on different indicators of air pollution. The lag dependent variable was highly significant; it manifested that the data for air pollution was dynamic. Environmental sustainability is a long-term phenomenon; henceforth, the current values of air contaminations depend on their past values. It is also established that the environmental sustainability issues have their long-term impacts by year on years basis, and by now or later, the consequences of pollution have to be paid. The dynamic nature of environmental sustainability and post-estimation tests stressed that GMM was an appropriate choice for analyzing air pollution data.

It can be noted that CO_2 was positive and highly significant to infer that an increase in the amount of CO_2 in the air causes governments around the world to increase their health budgets. Similarly, a positive and highly significant relationship was observed for $PM_{2.5}$. It can be noted that the high magnitude was yielded for $PM_{2.5}$. This contamination is hazardous for human health, and it causes many health complications. Hence, it causes high levels of public spending on public health. The WHO has warned against $PM_{2.5}$ as a significant concern to human health. These contaminated particles can penetrate the airways and impair the breathing system and even the cardiovascular organs (WHO, 2021b). Studies have reported that $PM_{2.5}$ is the most dangerous of all pollutants after the Ozone depletion issue (Environmental Protection Agency, 2015). Therefore, it seems plausible that the quantity of these particles in the air is associated with higher health expenditures. While the smaller but significant beta was found with nitrous and methane had an insignificant impact on health budgeting. Moreover, these variables were robust after the inclusion of control variables.

Moreover, we also highlight the issue that air pollution does not affect governments only but also disturb the life of individuals. Zhang and Mu (2018) found that increase in polluted air quality results in a rise in the demand for anti-haze masks. Thus, apart from health expenditure by governments, it also increases the expenses of the population. Moreover, Yang and Zhang (2018); Chen and Chen (2021) also investigated the impact of air pollution on an individual's health expenditure. They argue that air pollution does not necessarily accumulate individual's expenses but also causes cardiovascular, respiratory diseases and an increase in medical insurance compensation. They further emphasize that the cost in terms of traffic accidents and mental health due to air pollution cannot be disregarded.

This study has demonstrated that negligence to tackle environmental issues can cause governments to increase their spending in the form of health budgeting, catastrophes, and deteriorating mental health of human capital. This increase in health costs can, off-course, cause a burden for governments to spend on alternative economic projects. Governments will have to face the negative consequences from the opportunity costs of those spending that may lead to lowering the GDP. Xie *et al.* (2016) has also documented the similar notion that an increase in environmental unsustainability and air pollution can cause a negative impact on GDP.

Table 3. Results of System Dynamic Panel-data Generalized Method of Moments Estimations

Variable	Estimate
Current health expenditure per capita (current US$) (D.V)	0.737*** [0.079]
Constant	0.0081*** [0.0005]
CO_2 emissions (metric tons per capita) (IV)	0.055*** [0.002]
Methane emissions (kt of CO_2 equivalent) (IV)	0.199 [0.130]
Nitrous oxide emissions (thousand metric tons of CO_2 equivalent) (IV)	0.073*** [0.0013]
$PM_{2.5}$ air pollution, population exposed to levels exceeding WHO guideline value (% of total) (IV)	0.474*** [0.025]
GDP per capita growth (annual %) (CV)	0.00206* [0.00125]
Number of observations	3350
Prob > chi2	(0.000)

Notes: Standard errors are in [ ]. *, **, *** denote statistical significance at 10%, 5%, 1% levels, respectively. Prob > Chi2: For Overall Model. DV: Dependent Variable. IV: Independent Variable. CV: Control Variable.

Source: Author's Calculations.

CONCLUSION

Human activities to boost economic wellbeing have degraded the environment at many fronts to the extent that Earth has reached her planetary boundaries by sabotaging her self-regulating equilibrium system under the Gaia theory (Carpejani, Assad, Godoi, Waters, & de Andrade, 2020). Despite the several indications as a warning, current industrial practices have shown lesser heeds to environmental concerns. This information or warning is often ignored by the policymakers (Lenton & Latour, 2018), and at the length of these damaging practices, nature takes its revenge in the form of human health issues. Governments must willy-nilly spend for the health issues on stakeholders' pressure. These expenditures have their opportunity cost and may cause negative pressure on economic growth. Therefore, this study stresses to the policymakers and other stakeholders that humans are facing a double edge loss both in health and economic development by damaging the environment. Policy insights recommended by this study include the extensive usage of green technology even if governments have to bear expenditures on them. This study underlines that these expenditures are better than spending on public health due to environmental degradation.

Moreover, administrations may compensate the individuals residing in low-air quality regions with health insurance. Additionally, governments can improve air quality through improved public Transportations by promoting green travel. The governments must formulate new legislation and implement regulations relating to health and reducing air pollution. Legislations can be further extended to encourage the population to opt for electric cars that considerably reduce air pollution. The governments are also recommended to boost their microeconomic institutes to follow environmental sustainability practices. In this scenario, this study applauds the carbon taxing system as a Penalty on the businesses not paying substantial heed to ecological issues. Hence, in a nutshell, governments, individuals, and firms must jointly contribute to environmental sustainability.

Under the direction for future research, this study recommends that data on the usage of green technology should be collected, and its importance should be analyzed in the nexus of environmental issues, public health issues, government expenditures, and GDP. This study deemed that the mortality rate due to air pollution is essential for its research model under its conceptual framework. However, due to data availability issues on a macro level, it can be recommended that regional studies can be brought forward where mortality rates have been quantitatively defined. The importance of corporate social sustainability practices by microeconomic entities should also be examined in this context. Moreover, further study can be conducted on the relationship between air pollution and related specific diseases.

DISCLAIMER

The contents and views of this chapter are expressed by the authors in their personal capacities. It is not necessary for the Editor and the Publisher to agree with these viewpoints and they are not responsible for any duty of care in this regard.

ACKNOWLEDGMENT

The authors extend sincere gratitude to:

- The Editor and the International Editorial Advisory Board (IEAB) of this book WHO initially desk reviewed, arranged a rigorous double/triple blind review process and conducted a thorough, minute and critical final review before accepting the chapter for publication.
- All anonymous reviewers WHO provided very constructive feedbacks for thorough revision, improvement, extension and fine tuning of the chapter.

- All colleagues, assistants and well-wishers WHO assisted the authors to complete this task.

REFERENCES

Ahamed, M. M., & Mallick, S. K. (2019). Is financial inclusion good for bank stability? International evidence. *Journal of Economic Behavior & Organization*, *157*, 403–427. doi:10.1016/j.jebo.2017.07.027

Anenberg, S. C., Miller, J., Minjares, R., Du, L., Henze, D. K., Lacey, F., & Heyes, C. (2017). Impacts and mitigation of excess diesel-related NO x emissions in 11 major vehicle markets. *Nature*, *545*(7655), 467–471. doi:10.1038/nature22086 PMID:28505629

Anifowose, M. A., Rashid, H. M., Annuar, H. A., & Ibrahim, H. (2018). Intellectual capital efficiency and corporate book value: Evidence from Nigerian economy. *Journal of Intellectual Capital*, *19*(3), 644–668. doi:10.1108/JIC-09-2016-0091

Arellano, M., & Bover, O. (1995). Another look at the instrumental variable estimation of error-components models. *Journal of Econometrics*, *68*(1), 29–51. doi:10.1016/0304-4076(94)01642-D

Asongu, S. A., & Nnanna, J. (2019). Foreign Aid, Instability, and Governance in Africa. *Politics & Policy*, *47*(4), 807–848. doi:10.1111/polp.12320

Asongu, S. A., & Odhiambo, N. M. (2020a). Governance, CO_2 emissions and inclusive human development in sub-Saharan Africa. *Energy Exploration & Exploitation*, *38*(1), 18–36. doi:10.1177/0144598719835594

Asongu, S. A., & Odhiambo, N. M. (2020b). Inequality thresholds, governance and gender economic inclusion in sub-Sahran Africa. *International Review of Applied Economics*, *34*(1), 91–114. doi:10.1080/02692171.2019.1645817

Bai, R., Lam, J. C., & Li, V. O. (2018). A review on health cost accounting of air pollution in China. *Environment International*, *120*, 279–294. doi:10.1016/j.envint.2018.08.001 PMID:30103126

Baloch, R. M., Maesano, C. N., Christoffersen, J., Banerjee, S., Gabriel, M., Csobod, E., & Dewolf, M. C. (2020). Indoor air pollution, physical and comfort parameters related to schoolchildren's health: Data from the European SINPHONIE study. *The Science of the Total Environment*, *739*, 139870. doi:10.1016/j.scitotenv.2020.139870 PMID:32544681

Beirne, P. (1999). For a nonspeciesist criminology: Animal abuse as an object of study. *Criminology*, *37*(1), 117–148. doi:10.1111/j.1745-9125.1999.tb00481.x

Boogaard, H., Walker, K., & Cohen, A. J. (2019). Air pollution: The emergence of a major global health risk factor. *International Health*, *11*(6), 417–421. doi:10.1093/inthealth/ihz078 PMID:31613318

Carpejani, G., Assad, A. S., Godoi, L. R., Waters, J., & de Andrade, J. B. (2020). The Anthropocene: Conceptual Analysis with Global Climate Change, Planetary Boundaries and Gaia 2.0. In Water, Energy and Food Nexus in the Context of Strategies for Climate Change Mitigation (pp. 301-314). Springer Nature.

Chen, F., & Chen, Z. (2021). Cost of economic growth: Air pollution and health expenditure. *The Science of the Total Environment*, *755*, 142543. doi:10.1016/j.scitotenv.2020.142543 PMID:33035980

Colbeck, I. (2007). Air pollution: history of actions and effectiveness of change. In *The Handbook of Environment and Society* (pp. 374–384). Sage. doi:10.4135/9781848607873.n26

Currie, J., Neidell, M., & Schmieder, J. F. (2009). Air pollution and infant health: Lessons from New Jersey. *Journal of Health Economics*, *28*(3), 688–703. doi:10.1016/j.jhealeco.2009.02.001 PMID:19328569

Dutta, K. D., & Saha, M. (2020). Nexus of governance, macroprudential policy and financial risk: Cross-country evidence. *Economic Change and Restructuring*, *54*(4), 1253–1298. doi:10.100710644-020-09301-9

Environmental Protection Agency. (2015). *Air Quality Index Report*. United States Environmental Protection Agency.

Eze, I. C., Schaffner, E., Fischer, E., Schikowski, T., Adam, M., Imboden, M., Tsai, M., Carballo, D., Von Eckardstein, A., Künzli, N., Schindler, C., & Probst-Hensch, N. (2014). Long-term air pollution exposure and diabetes in a population-based Swiss cohort. *Environment International*, *70*, 95–105. doi:10.1016/j.envint.2014.05.014 PMID:24912113

Griskevicius, V., Tybur, J. M., Delton, A. W., & Robertson, T. E. (2011). The influence of mortality and socioeconomic status on risk and delayed rewards: A life history theory approach. *Journal of Personality and Social Psychology*, *100*(6), 1015–1026. doi:10.1037/a0022403 PMID:21299312

Guo, Y., Zeng, H., Zheng, R., Li, S., Pereira, G., Liu, Q., Chen, W., & Huxley, R. (2017). The burden of lung cancer mortality attributable to fine particles in China. *The Science of the Total Environment*, *579*, 1460–1466. doi:10.1016/j.scitotenv.2016.11.147 PMID:27913022

Haris, M., Yao, H., Tariq, G., Malik, A., & Javaid, H. M. (2019). Intellectual capital performance and profitability of banks: Evidence from Pakistan. *Journal of Risk and Financial Management*, *12*(2), 56. doi:10.3390/jrfm12020056

Hashim, D., & Boffetta, P. (2014). Occupational and environmental exposures and cancers in developing countries. *Annals of Global Health*, *80*(5), 393–411. doi:10.1016/j.aogh.2014.10.002 PMID:25512155

Jans, J., Johansson, P., & Nilsson, J. P. (2018). Economic status, air quality, and child health: Evidence from inversion episodes. *Journal of Health Economics*, *61*, 220–232. doi:10.1016/j.jhealeco.2018.08.002 PMID:30193188

Kankaria, A., Nongkynrih, B., & Gupta, S. K. (2014). Indoor air pollution in India: Implications on health and its control. *Indian Journal of Community Medicine*, *39*(4), 203. doi:10.4103/0970-0218.143019 PMID:25364142

Karl, T. R., Melillo, J. M., Peterson, T. C., & Hassol, S. J. (2009). *Global climate change impacts in the United States*. Cambridge University Press.

Kassomenos, P., Kelessis, A., Petrakakis, M., Zoumakis, N., Christidis, T., & Paschalidou, A. (2012). Air quality assessment in a heavily polluted urban Mediterranean environment through air quality indices. *Ecological Indicators*, *18*, 259–268. doi:10.1016/j.ecolind.2011.11.021

Kelishadi, R., & Poursafa, P. (2010). Air pollution and non-respiratory health hazards for children. *Archives of Medical Science*, *6*(4), 483–495. doi:10.5114/aoms.2010.14458 PMID:22371790

Khoshnevis Yazdi, S., & Khanalizadeh, B. (2017). Air pollution, economic growth and health care expenditure. *Economic research-. Ekonomska Istrazivanja*, *30*(1), 1181–1190. doi:10.1080/1331677X.2017.1314823

Lenton, T. M., & Latour, B. (2018). Gaia 2.0. *Science*, *361*(6407), 1066–1068. doi:10.1126cience.aau0427 PMID:30213897

Lovelock, J. (2006). *The Revenge of Gaia: Earth's Climate Crisis & the Fate of Humanity*. Basic Books.

Lovelock, J., & Margulis, L. (1974). Atmospheric homeostasis by and for the biosphere: The Gaia hypothesis. *Tellus*, *26*(2), 2–10.

Lynch, M. J., Long, M. A., & Stretesky, P. B. (2019). Gaia and a Green Theory of Justice. In *Green Criminology and Green Theories of Justice* (pp. 127–149). Palgrave Macmillan. doi:10.1007/978-3-030-28573-9_6

Malik, A. H., Md Isa, A. H., Jais, M., Ur Rehman, A., & Ali Khan, M. (2021). Financial stability of Asian Nations: Governance quality and financial inclusion. *Borsa Istanbul Review*, *22*(2), 377–387. doi:10.1016/j.bir.2021.05.005

Mosley, S. (2014). Environmental history of air pollution and protection. In *The Basic Environmental History* (pp. 143–169). Springer. doi:10.1007/978-3-319-09180-8_5

Nieto, M. (2017). *Banks and Environmental Sustainability: Some reflections from the perspective of financial stability*. CEPS.

OECD. (2016). *Economic Consequences of Outdoor Air Pollution*. Organisation for Economic Co-operation and Development.

Parajuli, I., Lee, H., & Shrestha, K. R. (2016). Indoor air quality and ventilation assessment of rural mountainous households of Nepal. *International Journal of Sustainable Built Environment*, *5*(2), 301–311. doi:10.1016/j.ijsbe.2016.08.003

Pena, M. S. B., & Rollins, A. (2017). Environmental exposures and cardiovascular disease: A challenge for health and development in low-and middle-income countries. *Cardiology Clinics*, *35*(1), 71–86. doi:10.1016/j.ccl.2016.09.001 PMID:27886791

Roodman, D.OECD. (2009). How to do xtabond2: An introduction to difference and system GMM in Stata. *The Stata Journal*, *9*(1), 86–136. doi:10.1177/1536867X0900900106

Sardo, F., & Serrasqueiro, Z. (2017). A European empirical study of the relationship between firms' intellectual capital, financial performance and market value. *Journal of Intellectual Capital*, *18*(4), 771–778. doi:10.1108/JIC-10-2016-0105

Selin, N. E., Wu, S., Nam, K. M., Reilly, J. M., Paltsev, S., Prinn, R. G., & Webster, M. D. (2009). Global health and economic impacts of future ozone pollution. *Environmental Research Letters*, *4*(4), 044014. doi:10.1088/1748-9326/4/4/044014

Sieferle, R. (2001). *The subterranean forest: energy systems and the industrial revolution*. White Horse Press.

Stutz, J. (2010). The three-front war: pursuing sustainability in a world shaped by explosive growth. *Sustainability: Science. Practice and Policy*, *6*(2), 49–59.

Tran, N. P., Van, L. T.-H., & Vo, D. H. (2020). The nexus between corporate governance and intellectual capital in Vietnam. *Journal of Asia Business Studies*, *14*(5), 637–650. doi:10.1108/JABS-01-2020-0007

Tran, N. P., & Vo, D. H. (2020). Human capital efficiency and firm performance across sectors in an emerging market. *Cogent Business & Management*, *7*(1), 1738832. doi:10.1080/23311975.2020.1738832

Uyanto, S. S. (2019). Monte Carlo power comparison of seven most commonly used heteroscedasticity tests. *Communications in Statistics. Simulation and Computation*, 1–18.

Vo, D. H. (2018). Should bankers be concerned with Intellectual capital? A study of the Thai banking sector. *Journal of Intellectual Capital*, *19*(5), 897–914. doi:10.1108/JIC-12-2017-0185

Vo, D. H., Nguyen, N. T., & Van, L. T. H. (2021). Financial inclusion and stability in the Asian region using bank-level data. *Borsa Istanbul Review*, *21*(1), 36–43. doi:10.1016/j.bir.2020.06.003

WHO. (2021a). *Household air pollution and health*. Retrieved from https://www.who .int/news-room/fact-sheets/detail/household-air-pollution-and-health

WHO. (2021b). *Household air pollution: Disease impacts*. World Health Organisation.

Xie, Y., Dai, H., Dong, H., Hanaoka, T., & Masui, T. (2016). Economic impacts from PM2. 5 pollution-related health effects in China: A provincial-level analysis. *Environmental Science & Technology*, *50*(9), 4836–4843. doi:10.1021/acs.est.5b05576 PMID:27063584

Xie, Y., Dai, H., Zhang, Y., Wu, Y., Hanaoka, T., & Masui, T. (2019). Comparison of health and economic impacts of PM2. 5 and ozone pollution in China. *Environment International*, *130*, 104881. doi:10.1016/j.envint.2019.05.075 PMID:31200152

Yang, J., & Zhang, B. (2018). Air pollution and healthcare expenditure: Implication for the benefit of air pollution control in China. *Environment International*, *120*, 443–455. doi:10.1016/j.envint.2018.08.011 PMID:30142582

Zhang, J., & Mu, Q. (2018). Air pollution and defensive expenditures: Evidence from particulate-filtering facemasks. *Journal of Environmental Economics and Management*, *92*, 517–536. doi:10.1016/j.jeem.2017.07.006

Zhang, X., Chen, X., & Zhang, X. (2018). The impact of exposure to air pollution on cognitive performance. *Proceedings of the National Academy of Sciences of the United States of America*, *115*(37), 9193–9197. doi:10.1073/pnas.1809474115 PMID:30150383

APPENDIX

Table 4. Countries selected for Panel Data Analysis

1	Afghanistan	48	Djibouti	95	Lebanon	142	Samoa
2	Albania	49	Dominica	96	Lesotho	143	San Marino
3	Algeria	50	Dominican Republic	97	Liberia	144	São Tomé and Príncipe
4	Andorra	51	Ecuador	98	Libya	145	Saudi Arabia
5	Angola	52	Egypt, Arab Rep.	99	Lithuania	146	Senegal
6	Antigua and Barbuda	53	El Salvador	100	Luxembourg	147	Serbia
7	Argentina	54	Equatorial Guinea	101	Madagascar	148	Seychelles
8	Armenia	55	Eritrea	102	Malawi	149	Sierra Leone
9	Australia	56	Estonia	103	Malaysia	150	Singapore
10	Austria	57	Eswatini	104	Maldives	151	Slovak Republic
11	Azerbaijan	58	Ethiopia	105	Mali	152	Slovenia
12	Bahamas	59	Fiji	106	Malta	153	Solomon Islands
13	Bahrain	60	Finland	107	Marshall Islands	154	South Africa
14	Bangladesh	61	France	108	Mauritania	155	Spain
15	Barbados	62	Gabon	109	Mauritius	156	Sri Lanka
16	Belarus	63	Gambia, The	110	Mexico	157	St. Kitts and Nevis
17	Belgium	64	Georgia	111	Micronesia, Fed. Sts.	158	St. Lucia
18	Belize	65	Germany	112	Moldova	159	St. Vincent and the Grenadines
19	Benin	66	Ghana	113	Monaco	160	Sudan
20	Bhutan	67	Greece	114	Mongolia	161	Suriname
21	Bolivia	68	Grenada	115	Morocco	162	Sweden
22	Bosnia and Herzegovina	69	Guatemala	116	Mozambique	163	Switzerland
23	Botswana	70	Guinea	117	Myanmar	164	Syrian Arab Republic
24	Brazil	71	Guinea-Bissau	118	Namibia	165	Tajikistan
25	Brunei Darussalam	72	Guyana	119	Nauru	166	Tanzania
26	Bulgaria	73	Haiti	120	Nepal	167	Thailand
27	Burkina Faso	74	Honduras	121	Netherlands	168	Timor-Leste
28	Burundi	75	Hungary	122	New Zealand	169	Togo

continues on following page

Table 4. Continued

29	Cabo Verde	76	Iceland	123	Nicaragua	170	Tonga
30	Cambodia	77	India	124	Niger	171	Trinidad and Tobago
31	Cameroon	78	Indonesia	125	Nigeria	172	Tunisia
32	Canada	79	Iran, Islamic Rep.	126	North Macedonia	173	Turkey
33	Central African Republic	80	Iraq	127	Norway	174	Turkmenistan
34	Chad	81	Ireland	128	Oman	175	Tuvalu
35	Chile	82	Israel	129	Pakistan	176	Uganda
36	China	83	Italy	130	Palau	177	Ukraine
37	Colombia	84	Jamaica	131	Panama	178	United Arab Emirates
38	Comoros	85	Japan	132	Papua New Guinea	179	United Kingdom
39	Congo, Dem. Rep.	86	Jordan	133	Paraguay	180	United States
40	Congo, Rep.	87	Kazakhstan	134	Peru	181	Uruguay
41	Costa Rica	88	Kenya	135	Philippines	182	Uzbekistan
42	Cote d'Ivoire	89	Kiribati	136	Poland	183	Vanuatu
43	Croatia	90	Korea, Rep.	137	Portugal	184	Venezuela, RB
44	Cuba	91	Kuwait	138	Qatar	185	Vietnam
45	Cyprus	92	Kyrgyz Republic	139	Romania	186	Yemen, Rep.
46	Czech Republic	93	Lao PDR	140	Russian Federation	187	Zambia
47	Denmark	94	Latvia	141	Rwanda	188	Zimbabwe

Chapter 6
Environmental Finance for a Sustainable Society:
An Overview

J. Kiranmai
Institute of Public Enterprise, India

Ram Kumar Mishra
https://orcid.org/0000-0003-4370-8001
Institute of Public Enterprise, India

M. Maschendar Goud
https://orcid.org/0000-0002-6710-5021
Institute of Public Enterprise, India

Abdul Rafay
https://orcid.org/0000-0002-0285-5980
University of Management and Technology, Pakistan

Marie G. Nakitende
Uganda Martyrs University, Uganda

ABSTRACT

The global environment and climatic systems are heating up due to increased human activities. Making it happen due to technology and the availability of natural resources would be one of the greatest challenges that the cleantech revolution would be facing in the global market. In a short span of time, funding cleantech projects without sacrificing profitability and improving quality of life for a sustainable community has been understood to be a viable solution to the problem. In this context, it may be

DOI: 10.4018/978-1-6684-5580-7.ch006

mentioned that a new stream of finance has emerged called environmental finance. The chapter throws light on the typology of funding agencies engaged in providing environmental finance and the role of governments in formulating relevant policies to promote lending for environmental projects. An array of financing instruments for environmental projects has been discussed to indicate the mobilizing potential for such projects with special reference to India.

WHAT IS ENVIRONMENTAL FINANCE?

Environmental Finance (EF) is a new offshoot of 'finance' extending its contours typically to non- commercial, non-industrial and traditional ventures. Its emergence has added a new dimension to the field of finance. In common parlance, EF is used interchangeably with the terms "Green Finance" and "Sustainable Finance". As it is different in nature and deployment, its sources, applications, institutional mechanism too are different and so are the regulatory and public policies, and the processes and systems governing EF. The models belonging to environmental finance include traditional finance, low-carbon finance, climate finance, green finance, socio-environmental finance, and sustainable finance. EF is a paradigm shift in the field of finance and sustainable development impacting the humankind.

Environmental finance is a relatively new field of finance. Economists and international organizations have failed to establish a precise definition or agree upon one unanimously. However, workable definitions have been developed by various scholars, organizations, and governments (Labatt, 2003). An interesting variation in this is that specific organizations have coined the following phrase: a sustainable financial system (Hira, 2012). Nevertheless, their tools and mechanisms are the same. A sustainable financial system incorporates the development of values and aids in dealing with financial assets, so that actual wealth may be used to meet the demands of an ecologically sustainable and inclusive economy over time (Force, 2015).

Environmental finance concerns itself with the impact of environmental issues on financial decision making, which is essentially a three-step process. The first step is to identify sources of risk and opportunities to create value.

"Knowledge, on the whole, is an environmentally neural asset that can contribute to the future" (Solow, 1991).

In the context of the banking sector, PwC (2013) mentioned the following attributes of EF:

1. product and service innovation which promote responsible investments, and
2. support low–carbon technologies projects.

To quote *Finanças Brasileiras Sustentáveis*:

"EF refers to the integration of sustainability aspects in the decision-making processes of financial market actors, financial market policy and related institutional and market arrangements that contribute to the achievement of strong, sustainable, balanced and inclusive growth" (Sommer, 2020).

As defined by Nobel Laureate Robert Solow:

"Environmental finance concerns itself with the impact of environmental issues on financial decision making, which is essentially a three-step process. The first step is to identify sources of risk and/or opportunities to create value. This requires a better understanding of the interconnections between ecology and economics, which is a good thing" (Solow, 1991)

There is no one common definition of EF. However, keeping in view the above definitions, EF could be said to constitute the following:

- the financing of public and private green investments in water management or protection of biodiversity and landscapes;
- extending public policy related finance for choosing and implementing environmental activities;
- deal with that part of the financial system devoted to environmental projects.

ORIGIN OF ENVIRONMENTAL FINANCE

EF is an emerging field so far not much known to the financial experts, public policymakers, business and industry personnel, barring those engaged in emission trading. Sandor (2016) pointed out that EF concerns itself with economic and market analysis related to finance, used for funding conservation initiatives, create a symbiotic relationship between businesses and the environment and enhancing the quality of life for society without lowering profitability. EF combines insights across the social sciences, natural sciences and humanities disciplines to help combat critical environmental issues and connected societal risks. In this context it may be mentioned that climate change resulting from volatile weather conditions expose corporate assets to severe risks. In addition, regulatory resource constraints are affected by climate change (Linnenluecke *et al.*, 2016).

EF has recent origins in India. The Reserve Bank of India through its guidelines to Indian Banks and financial institutions (RBI, 2021) permitted them to consider lending for environmental projects. EF has found favor across various segments comprising businesses, commerce, public systems, organizations not for profit and family-owned entities. This happens through embedding green practices in business operations. The fusion between environmental management systems and finance provides these segments access to EF. The cost-benefit analysis is resorted to make this fusion happen. Emission trading currently holds the roost. Thus, it is clear that EF is a new breed of finance with new premises and characteristics (Schoenmaker, 2019). EF in its present form shuns shareholder value (Schoenmaker & Schramade, 2019) as asserted by Friedman (1970) who concluded that 'the business of business is business'. Criticized for its narrow approach, the traditional view of finance is losing its ground substantially. The fusion between finance and sustainability has gone beyond shareholder value and triple bottom line to stand on the premise of common good value.

INSTITUTIONS PROMOTING EF

EF in this form focuses on new innovative technologies to reduce the ills of climate, pollution and public health-related concerns. Green bonds are one example of positive EF. It is interesting to note that there has been a growing demand in blue bonds, which are resorted to finance the ocean and marine economy, and biodiversity. On the other hand, green transition bond is an example of negative EF resorted to by companies engaged in de-carburizing activities. Debt instruments mostly dominate capital markets involved in EF transactions. Development banks, global financial institutions, regional trading blocs, national and international associations provide medium- and long-term finance. EF instruments to access these institutions include corporate bonds, project bonds, asset-backed securities, municipal bonds, supranational/sub-sovereign/agency bonds, and equity flotation connected to ESG investments. Figure 1 displays the growth of sustainable bonds worldwide during 2013-2019. The amount raised through such bonds was a mere USD14.8 billion in 2013, and it registered a sharp increase to USD465 billion during 2019. As per the research studies, the returns earned by the ESG stocks, if not more, were as much as the returns secured by the non-ESG stocks (Barclays, 2020; Kennedy, 2020).

Projections estimate that global issuance of green bond is likely to reach USD450 billion this year (CBI, 2021) and that there is high possibility of issuance surpassing USD1 trillion in 2023 (Figure 2).

Figure 1. Forays in Sustainable Bonds
Source: Sustainable Debt Market: Summary H1 2021 (CBI, 2021)

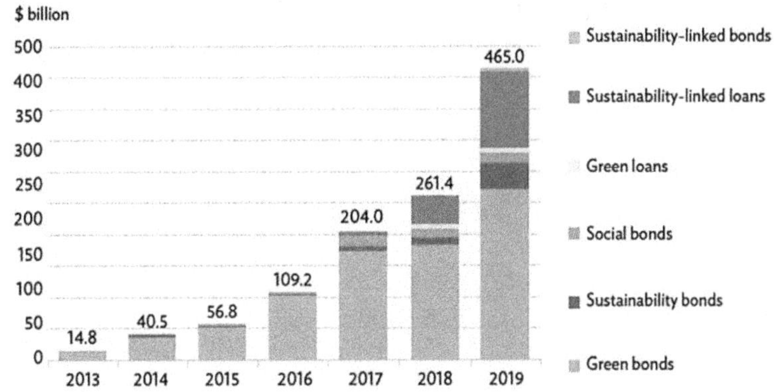

Figure 2. Annual Trillion in Green Bonds Within Reach by 2023
Source: CBI. (2021)

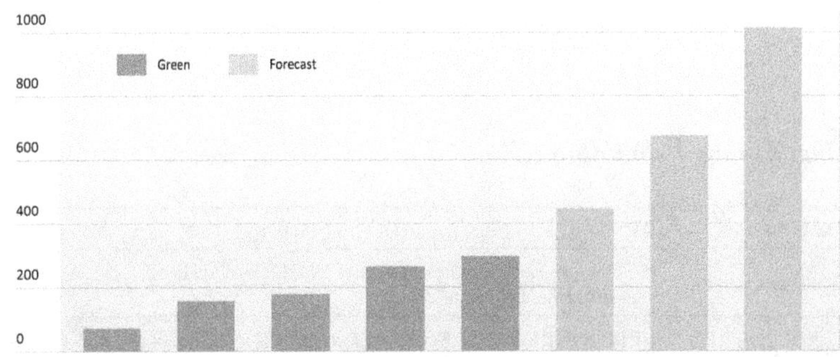

Overall, developed economies contributed major part of green bond issuance globally. Among the emerging economies, India occupies the 2nd spot (after China) in cumulative emerging market (IFC, 2021).

The following organizations have joined the pipeline for providing EF (Table 1). In addition, several products have been innovated in the realm of EF by multiple financial institutions, which are banking and insurance companies. Institutions offering such products could be classified in four categories: retail banking, corporate and investment banking services, asset management, and insurance products.

The value of global assets highlighting environmental, social and governance data to drive investment decisions is almost doubled over four years, and more than tripled over eight years, to USD40.5t in 2020. Green finance is a policy that refers to a set of policy and institutional arrangements aimed at attracting private money into green sectors, such as environmental preservation and energy conservation via financial services (Force, 2015). The notion of green financing is also different from the traditional banking approaches. It reflects the advantages of protecting the environment by taking environmental risk management strategies and the sustainability of plans into account (Jeucken, 2010).

Figure 3. Cumulative Emerging Market Green Bond Issuance 2012-2020 (USD million)
Source: Emerging Market Green Bonds Report, 2020 (IFC, 2021)

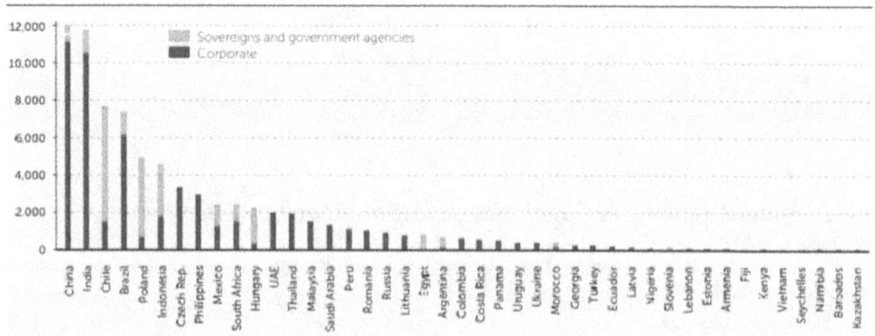

Table 1. Institutions Promoting EF

Name of the Agency	Activity
Bloomberg Philanthropies 2020	1700 organizations, representing over USD17.3 trillion in market capitalization, have endorsed these philanthropies.
Green Climate Fund (GCF) 2020	Paris Agreement is the world's largest climate fund. EF activities in developing countries enable them to raise their financial contribution for reducing carbon emissions and sustainable development programmes.
Adaptation Fund 2020	The Fund's Readiness Programme for Climate Finance (the Readiness Programme), was established by the Board through Decision to increase the capacity of parties of developing country to directly access climate adaptation finance and to develop and initiate implementation of concrete projects and programmes that increase the resilience of vulnerable communities to the impacts of climate change.
Global Environment Facility (GEF)	A learning initiative to constantly provide advice and inputs to the facility members to access EF through various means and diverse channels.
Climate Policy Initiative (CPI)	The mission is to prop up sustainable growth through EF.
European Bank for Reconstruction and Development (EBRD)	The bank finances private sector projects in the range of USD5 million to USD250 million by way of debt or risk capital
United Nations Environment Program Finance Initiative (UNEP FI)	UNEP FI is to educate financial services sector organizations about meshing sustainable development concept in their operations
United Nations Development Program (UNDP) 2019	UNDP provides financial support through voluntary contributions from its members, international organizations, financing institutions and philanthropic organizations.

Source: Authors' Compilation

Table 2 provides information about some leading financial institutions and their EF products. It can be seen from the table that the products offered are like short-term and long-term financing, secured and unsecured, and working capital and project finance. A novelty is about introducing securitization, which has the potential of opening flood gates for mobilizing EF. This would depend on the availability of expertise in valuation and public finance stipulations such as the stamp duty and location of the issuer's registered office. The prominent sectors developing products include retail, corporate banking, asset management and the insurance sector.

Table 2. EF: Products, Issuers and Potential

Sector	Product or Service Model	Banks Studied	Key Product(s) and Results or Potential
Retail Banking	Home, Energy Efficient and power oriented Mortgages	Dutch banks, CFS, Abbey, HBOS, Halifax, Bendigo Bank, Van City and Citigroup	It is a State directed green mortgage initiative for low and middle-income consumers offering free home energy rating and having high potential for environmental benefits incentivizing homeowners to use renewable power
	Commercial Building Loan, Home Equity, Auto, and Fleet Loans	NRB, Wells Fargo, TAF / Tridel® Wainwright Bank & Trust, CFS, Van City Mecu	These constitute green loans for condominium construction, Solar Financing, loans for low emitting vehicle types, go green auto loans, and small business administration express loans
	Sales	Barclays, HSBC	This relates to offsetting CO_2 emissions emanating to air travel
Corporate & Investment Banking	Project Finance	Standard Chartered Bank, Citigroup, West LB and Dexia	These relate to financing renewable energy projects and form a part of portfolio financing techniques
	Partial Credit Guarantees	IFC	It supports municipal endeavors to engage in environmental projects.
	Securitization	IFC and DFID	These include Eco-Securitization and Green Mortgage-Backed Securitization.
	Bond	BNP Paribas, Goldman Sachs, Lehman Brothers	These include Forest Bond and Cat Bonds issuance.
	Private Equity	Bank of America	This includes equity deals about forest conservation, preserving biodiversity and sequestering CO_2.
	Eco-Indices	ABN AMRO	This includes innovative eco-products concerning multiple asset classes
	Carbon Commodity Products	Barclays Capital, HSBC, Fortis, ABN AMRO, BNP Paribas, JPMorgan, Goldman Sachs, Citigroup, among others	They pertained to equity, loans and upfront or upon delivery payments to acquire carbon credits
Asset Management	Green and Cat Bond Funds	Dutch Banks, UBS, Credit Suisse	Investments in green and cat bonds, and equity fund – eco performance entitle for an income tax rebate and offering lower interest rates to investors and thereby giving loans at reduced interest rates to investors in such bonds

continues on following page

Table 2. Continued

Sector	Product or Service Model	Banks Studied	Key Product(s) and Results or Potential
Insurance	Auto, Home, and Commodity Insurance	Aviva, GMAC, Cooperative Insurance Services, California's Firemen Fund, ETA, Swiss Re, AIG and Marsh	These relate to carbon emissions, credit guarantees, climate neutral, home insurance policy, green building replacement and upgrade and discount for hybrid and fuel-efficient vehicles.

Source: Authors' Compilation

According to the Green Finance Study Group of the G20 (Berensmann, 2017), green financing promotes technologies that lower pollution. Further, green financing strives to promote a green economy. Regarding adaptation to climate change concerns, the European Banking Federation stated that green finance is not restricted to simply environmental or climate change-related factors, hence opening up opportunities for green insurance plans and green bonds (Mularova, 2021). In addition, the green economy has three-fold benefits. Firstly, the development of green finance strengthens the role of corporate governance factors and companies. Secondly, the green economy promotes environmental awareness and ensures. Thirdly, green financial development can effectively optimize the supply structure of production factors, reduce overcapacity in traditional industries, and promote economic transformation and upgrading (Bergset, 2015).

The most essential among natural resources is Water. Water investments have increased globally. One of the largest water resource company mutual funds provide additional ways to invest. The Calvert Global Water Fund and the Allianz GI Water Fund tap into water-based opportunities across the globe. Tesla is meeting the Green transportation requirements. General Electric, Next Era Energy Partner, Siemens Gamesa Renewable Energy are into wind power financing.

It is interesting to note that innovations in EF are still making headway. EF is providing ways and means for investments in the core assets. The ESG investments have a vast scope to grow. The unicorn and millennium investing are yet another golden source of EF. Islamic finance and finances under the aegis of other religious bodies with linkages to EF could make its pool very vast. Development banks and similar institutions could strategically add to this pool of resources with grants and guarantees to grow this innovative environment-friendly market (IFC, 2017). The investments by such institutions could be outcome-based. Similarly, small investors could influence banks, pension and insurance organizations' policies regarding investing in various instruments about EF.

CENTERS AND COURSES ON ENVIRONMENTAL FINANCE

EF has made its incursions in the programmes and courses in higher education institutions of repute. These institutions offer doctoral programmes, masters' programmes and various degree and diploma courses. Table 3 details the institutions across the globe that is offering special courses on environmental finance. The courses are high in demand. The courses range from foundation to advanced learning programmes such as Climate change, climate risk and management of finance. TERI, India is also offering programme in the area of energy, sustainable finance and green finance.

Table 3. Institutions Offering Environmental Finance Courses

University / Institute Name	Very High Demand	High Demand	Highlights of Programme
MACQUARIE University, Sydney, AUS	-	Environmental Finance	New standards of sustainable finance and investment
The Smith School of Enterprise and the Environment, University of Oxford	Sustainable Finance Foundation Course	Climate related Financial Risk Course	Emerging theories and practice of sustainable finance and investment
			Sustainable finance
UCD Michael Smurfit Graduate Business School, Cary fort Avenue, Blackrock, Co. Dublin	MSc - Renewable Energy & Environmental Finance	-	Advance understanding of financial markets, with a specific focus on SDGs and emerging legislation on environmental matte₹
University College Dublin, Michael Smurfit Graduate Business School		-	Sustainability factors to financial markets
Imperial College Business School, UK		MSc Climate Change, Management & Finance	Climate change and sustainability (Graduate level)
London School of Economics and Political Science	Environmental Economics & Sustainable Development	-	Fundamentals of rigorous economic analysis
Harvard University	Introduction to Sustainable Finance and Investments	-	Diverse aspects of sustainable investments include effective financial valuation and risk assessment
UN Climate Change Learning Partnership, United Nations Institute for Training and Research (UNITAR)	Introduction to Sustainable Finance	-	Trends in the area of sustainable finance

continues on following page

Table 3. Continued

University / Institute Name	Very High Demand	High Demand	Highlights of Programme
Tata Energy Resource Center (TERI)	Environmental Finance, Climate Risk and Management Energy Management	-	Energy, sustainable finance, green finance
Indian Institutes of Management (IIMs)	Sustainable Finance, Climate Change, Bond finance	-	Courses impart the connect between climate change and the role of financial institutions, green financing and capital markets
Central Universities in India	-	Sustainability, economic development, climate change and green finance	Renewable energy, sources of funding, renewable energy

Source: Authors' Compilation

Environmental Finance: The Case of India

It is clear from Figure 4 that environmental finance is an outgrowth of the financial industry devoted to environmental improvement propping economic growth. Such linkages indicate a bright future for environmental finance and the constant growth of the financial industry contributing to environmental improvement. The green bonds issued in several tranches supports this contention. India ranked as the second-largest market for Green Bonds with USD10.3 billion transactions in the first half of 2019. The Indian framework for EF in terms of backward and forward linkages of environmental finance is conceptualized in Figure 4.

India's initiative on green finance forming a part of EF commenced in 2007. In mentioning the role that green finance could play, the Reserve Bank of India (RBI) asserted that EF could be considered as a part of sustainable development embedding corporate social responsibility and non-financial reporting. The National Action Plan on Climate Change (NAPCC) was prepared and tasked with developing a broad policy framework to combat the effects of climate change. The Ministry of Finance, Government of India set up the Climate Change Finance Unit in 2011 for coordinating the work with various financial institutions engaged in providing EF. The top 100 listed companies were mandated to publish business responsibility reports annually since 2012. Securities Exchange Board of India (SEBI), 2017 issued guidelines for green bond issuance specifying the disclosure requirements.

Figure 4. Backward and Forward Linkages of Environmental Finance in India
Source: Authors' Compilation

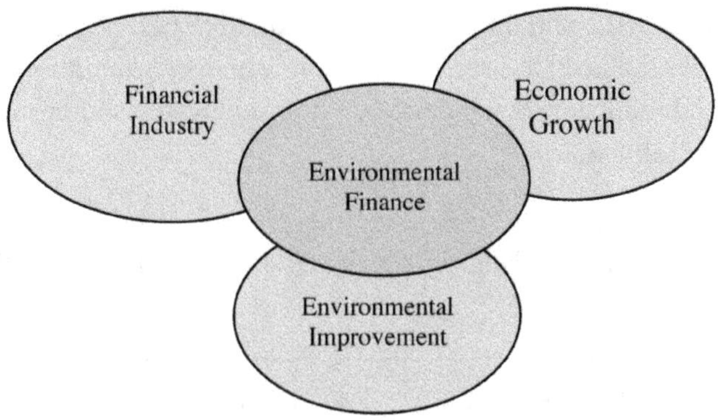

An emerging source of environmental finance is the commercial bank credit to the non-conventional energy projects. The outstanding bank credit in public sector banks is ₹21655 crore, while the percentage of the power sector is 6.2%. In the private sector, the bank credit accounted to ₹12,302 with 27.1% of power sector credit, while the foreign banks had ₹2,586 crore with 27.1% of power credit. However, EF is yet to make headway in the Indian capital markets by registering its presence through appropriately designed instruments. The one exception that merits mention is that of Green bond issues (Figure 5). The graph portrays 63 percent of the total issuances of green bonds in India by various companies in 2017. Greenko Investment Company was the largest issuer with USD1billion followed by Indian Renewable Energy Development Agency Limited (IREDA) and India Railways Finance Corporation (IRFC).

Figure 5. Green Bond Issues in India (figures in USD billions)
Source: Sustainable Debt Market: Summary H1 2021 (CBI, 2021)

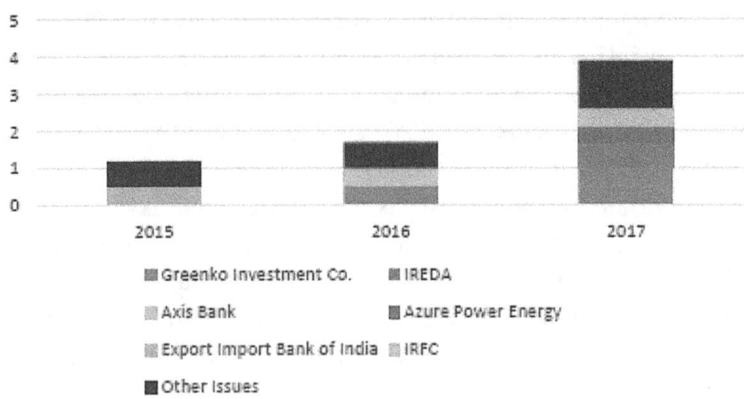

It is the renewable energy sector that has immensely benefited from EF. As per the plans of the Government of India, renewable energy generation was to go up to 21,761 MW in 2012 and 71,461 MW by 2022 (IREDA, 2021). The policy of India underscores the need to promote renewable energy generation for sustainable development and reduce its dependence on non-renewable sources in the long run, as evident from Table 4.

Table 4. Power Generation Capacity by Type in India in the New Policies Scenario (GW)

Sources	2000	2014	2020	2030	2040	Shares (%)		CAGR*
						2014	2040	2014-2040
Fossil fuels	84	204	280	419	576	71	53	4.1
Nuclear	3	6	10	24	39	2	4	7.6
Renewables	27	79	147	304	462	27	43	7
Total	113	289	436	746	1 076	100	100	5.2

Source: IEA (2015)
*Compound Average Annual Growth Rate

There are multiple stakeholders in the field of renewable energy investments in India. These constitute commercial banks, equity investors, institutional investors and development banks. It is interesting to note that private sector and foreign banks are also actively participating in these initiatives. Both private equity and venture capital are active in the field. Institutional investors and development banks have joined. However, the number of institutions in each category can vastly increase with greater participation. The banks and long-term financial institutions committed USD2,570 million towards the financing of renewable energy projects. The Infrastructure Development Finance Corporation (IDFC) financed a major chunk of this commitment, around 20%. There are various committees constituted by different financial institutions/banks for sourcing renewable energy. These include IDFC (20.2%), L & T Finance Holdings (13.7%), SBI (12.6%), IREDA (10.9%), Yes Bank (10.2%), Indus Bank, (9.2%) PTC India Financial Services (5.4%), Union Bank of India (5.3%) and Bank of Baroda (4.2%) (CFA, 2018)

The Reserve Bank of India (RBI) as the Central Bank is actively engaged in overseeing the practices that are being followed by the Indian Financial System. The Reserve Bank had advised commercial banks in 2007 to put in place an appropriate action plan towards making a meaningful contribution to sustainable development. The RBI has been incentivizing bank lending towards greener industries and projects.

It has been very strongly emphasizing the funding for renewable energy projects by including their financing under Priority Sector Lending. In 2020, Reserve Bank of India included loans sanctioned by banks directly to individuals for setting up off-grid solar and other off-grid renewable energy solutions for households.

Policy measures support EF for accelerating renewable energy generation in several ways. National Clean Energy and Environment Fund (NCEEF) was set up in 2011 to support renewable energy financing by supporting associated activities like clean energy technologies and promoting entrepreneurial ventures. The RBI provided access to priority sector lending to the renewable energy sector to provide a boost renewable energy generation programmes and activities. IREDA provides low interest-bearing loans to the renewable energy sector. Encouraged by the IREDA experience, the State Bank of India (SBI), joined by several other commercial banks in India, has also provided green finance loans. Green bonds in the aftermath of the guidelines issued by the SEBI have become a potential source of financing renewable energy and so far, yielded USD6.5 billion. Infrastructure Debt Fund (IDF) is yet to gain popularity as an innovative financing instrument for renewable energy financing in India. However, the finances from this fund are allocated only to the PPP projects. Larsen & Toubro Infrastructure Development Fund, Indiainfra debt, and IDFC infrastructure Development Fund belong to this category.

Crowd funding has emerged as a new source of green financing in India. The Information and Communication Technology (ICT) is playing a vital role. For example, crowd funding has been employed in India in financing the rural electrification programme. An instance of this could be found in the German crowd funding platform investing in 'MeraGao Power' and 'Bond Engineering' engaged in energizing rural India through renewable (Sarangi, 2018). However, these new financing instruments, EF faces formidable challenges from several quarters, which emanate from weak institutional, policy/regulatory frameworks, recognizing the renewable energy sector as a part of the power sector, costly debt financing, and lack of coordination among development banks. The Department of Economic Affairs (DEA), Ministry of Finance, Government of India has set up a group on climate finance. The Group deals with bi-lateral and multi-lateral funding for the projects selected by the Government of India and monitor such funding for the projects. Most of the projects relate to renewable energy. At home, the big corporates have made funding for renewable a strategic initiative. The Reliance Industries Limited has an investment plan of USD100 billion with the purpose to invest USD75 billion in green energy projects.

CHALLENGES

Despite the growing realization of its vitality and importance in the context of sustainable development, EF faces strong challenges impeding its fast progress. First, there are issues relating to the demand and supply sides. The supply-side constraint is a lack of investable deals and developing a group of investees who could continuously supply funds. This challenge could be met to a large extent by attracting venture capital, private equity, grants from public and private sectors, crowd funding and angel finance. The demand-side constraint also inhibits the growth of EF. The transaction costs of availing EF are high. Non-availability of performance data does act as a limitation to the entities providing EF. It may be mentioned that some large financial institutions have instituted their database for taking decisions about various facets of EF. This brings in the question of standards and data for EF as agreed standards for disclosure are conspicuous by their absence. However, the GRI, PRI, SASB, and UNDP have developed standards that ought to bring down the cost of the transactions.

Monetization of environmental assets could lead to a breathtaking upsurge in the pool of resources constituting EF. The national income accounting incorporating accounting for natural resources may help monetize environmental assets to a large extent. However, in most countries, the national income accounting does not provide for accounting for natural resources. Therefore, a cadre of environmental economists would come in very handy as they are well versed in applying the social rate of return by evaluating environmental projects.

Green washing is another formidable challenge to EF. There have been innumerable cases of companies going for IPOs, fundraising for Environment, Social and Governance (ESG) projects and public communication emphasizing green projects. However, once succeeded, the green aspects of the projects are either not attended to or only partially attended. This is not fully disclosed in the financial statements. Green washing, therefore, acts as a major limiting factor in the popularity and wide usage of EF. The green finance markets provide an opportunity for private sector investment to finance the new innovative projects. Public Private Participation (PPP) in environmental projects may also ensure participation of the private sector. However, investments by the private sector in environmental projects is challenging as potential investors perceive high financial risks and low returns. Private investors may shun participation in environmental projects simply by their risk-return profiles and non-scalability.

POLICY MEASURES AND IMPLICATIONS

Several programmes have been set up to increase awareness about EF and finance EF initiatives. These programmes incentivize financial and non-financial institutions to accord special treatment for financing EF activities. Some important programmes to financing EF activities include Responsible Investment; Equator Principles for financial institutions, United Nation's Environment Programme (UNEP). A variety of policy measures and actionable steps are required to promote EF. It is important to embed environmental requirements in laws concerning investment, lending, credit rating and accounting. The actionable step in this regard rests on financial institutions that should disclose environmental concerns and credit rating agencies to ensure that such concerns are instituted as an element of credit rating exercise. Corporate disclosures for environmental information are essential. While going in for Initial Public Offerings (IPOs), environmental information could be made as a requirement for listing and disclosure. Comprehensive environmental information has to be disclosed voluntarily as per the Global Reporting Initiative (GRI). Business associations and industries need to guide investment and lending to enterprises using such certified green technologies. On the part of financial institutions, they should rate environmental performance for lending. Green indices should be promoted to help decision making for investments in green enterprises. Lending institutions should develop a green risk index to promote investment in green bonds. As a policy measure system for providing green information, provision should be put in place. A network of institutions should be put in place for environmental information provisioning. Instituting green enterprise rating agencies and preparing a cadre of green financial professionals could yet be another policy measure. Innovest in the US is an example of a green enterprise rating agency. Higher Educational Institutions (HIEs) should create a space for producing green financial professionals. Conferences and Seminars should be organized for sensitizing the general public (Noh, 2018).

The policy implications of EF are varied, long term and vital for society, nations and geo-political scenario. Firstly, the quantum of EF has to be identified nationally and internationally. The United Nations is working on the sustainable development goals. The 17 sustainable development goals would require for India alone more than USD3 trillion. Much of it may come from external sources existing in the form of global organizations, regional organizations, international capital markets, and multi-lateral and bi-lateral agreements. However, COVID-19 would certainly obstruct this flow. Nationally, domestic capital markets, development banks, federal and sub national governments, and commercial/ development banks would have to be tapped to mobilize the requisite EF. New financing instruments would come in currency. They might even be floated as a part of the Environment, Social and Governance (ESG). The International and the domestic laws would require a fresh look to accommodate the concerns connected to EF. There have been initiatives in some countries to set up exclusive stock exchanges dealing with the ESG known as Social Stock Exchanges.

CONCLUSION

The UN Sustainable Development Goals (SDGs) have been unanimously endorsed as an approach for future development by countries across the globe. Enormous efforts have to be made to achieve sustainable development goals. In its traditional form, 'Finance' cannot match the financial requirements for sustainable development in this context. EF alone can fulfil the financial requirements of instruments with the requisite characteristics, processes, operations, and outcomes. EF has been defined variously. In its present form, it has come to be recognized as a stream of initiatives that engages itself in fathoming the impact of environmental issues on financial decision making. Its origins relate to outcomes borne of climate change and the need for green management. The Paris Agreement has acted as a watershed in the emergence and growth of EF.

The developed countries are way ahead than their counterparts in providing a congenial ecosystem for the growth of EF. Financial Institutions and Markets have designed suitable instruments to mobilize EF. The portfolio of such instruments is growing gradually bringing in finance for short term and long-term durations. Educational institutions of repute have introduced courses and programmes on EF to meet the requirements of human capital for EF. Recognizing the importance and significance of EF, the financial institutions and capital markets in India have been paying special attention for its growth and development. EF pipeline is being tapped vigorously by the renewable energy market to finance its needs. The future of EF is full of promise. The developed and developing countries could vastly step-up the availability of financial resources by designing suitable policies, institutions, instruments, and relevant courses. EF would go a long way in achieving the SDGs for a better, happy and prosperous humankind.

DISCLAIMER

The contents and views of this chapter are expressed by the authors in their personal capacities. It is not necessary for the Editor and the Publisher to agree with these viewpoints and they are not responsible for any duty of care in this regard.

ACKNOWLEDGMENT

The authors extend sincere gratitude to

- The Editor and the International Editorial Advisory Board (IEAB) of this book who initially desk reviewed, arranged a rigorous double/triple blind review process and conducted a thorough, minute and critical final review before accepting the chapter for publication.
- All anonymous reviewers who provided very constructive feedbacks for thorough revision, improvement, extension and fine tuning of the chapter.
- All colleagues, assistants and well-wishers who assisted the authors to complete this task.

REFERENCES

Barclays. (2020, August 13). *ESG funds: Looking beyond the label.* Retrieved from https://www.investmentbank.barclays.com/our-insights/3-point-perspective/esg-funds-looking-beyond-the-label.html

Berensmann, K., Volz, U., Alloisio, I., Bak, C., Bhattacharya, A., Leipold, G., Schindler, H., & MacDonald, L., Huifang, T., & Yang, Q. (2017). *Fostering Sustainable Global Growth through Green Finance—What Role for the G20.* The World Bank. Retrieved from https://collaboration.worldbank.org/content/usergenerated/asi/cloud/attachments/sites/collaboration-for-development/en/groups/green-finance-community-of-practice/documents/jcr:content/content/primary/blog/green_finance_educat-LVNC/Climate_Green-Finance_V2.pdf

Bergset, L. (2015). The rationality and irrationality of financing green start-ups. *Administrative Sciences*, *5*(4), 260–285. doi:10.3390/admsci5040260

CBI. (2021). Sustainable Debt Market: Summary H1 2021. *Climate Bonds Initiative.* Retrieved from https://www.climatebonds.net/files/reports/cbi_susdebtsum_h12021_02b.pdf

CFA. (2018). *Coal vs Renewables: Financial Analysis.* New Delhi: Centre for Financial Accountability. Retrieved from https://carboncopy.info/wp-content/uploads/COAL-VS-RENEWABLES-REPORT_NOV-19-2.pdf

Costanza, R., & Daly, H. E. (1992). Natural capital and sustainable development. *Conservation Biology*, *6*(1), 37–46. doi:10.1046/j.1523-1739.1992.610037.x

Force, G. F. T. (2015). *Establishing China's green financial system. Report of the Green Finance Task Force*. People's Bank of China & United Nations Environment Programme. Retrieved from https://2degrees-investing.org/wp-content/uploads/2015/04/Establishing-Chinas-green-financial-system-April-2015.pdf

Friedman, M. (1970, September 13). The Social Responsibility of Business is to Increase its Profits. *The New York Times*. Retrieved from https://link.springer.com/chapter/10.1007/978-3-540-70818-6_14

Hira, T. K. (2012). Promoting sustainable financial behaviour: Implications for education and research. *International Journal of Consumer Studies, 36*(5), 502–507. doi:10.1111/j.1470-6431.2012.01115.x

IEA. (2015). *World Energy Outlook Special Report: India Energy Outlook*. International Energy Agency. Retrieved from https://www.iea.org/reports/india-energy-outlook-2015

IFC. (2017). *Blended Concessional Finance for Private Sector Projects – Summary Report*. International Finance Corporation. Retrieved from https://www.ifc.org/wps/wcm/connect/ a8398ed6-55d0-4cc4-95aa-bcbabe39f79f/DFI+Blended+Concessional+Finance+for+Private+Sector+Operations_Summary+R.... pdf?MOD=AJPERES&CVID=lYCLe0B

IFC. (2021). *Emerging Market Green Bonds Report 2020*. The World Bank Group. Retrieved from https://www.ifc.org/wps/wcm/connect/publications_ext_ content/ifc_external_publication_site/publications_listing_page/emerging-market-green-bonds-report-2020

IREDA. (2021). *IREDA Annual Report*. New Delhi: Indian Renewable Energy Development Agency Limited. Retrieved from https://www.ireda.in/home

Jeucken, M. (2010). *Sustainable finance and banking: The financial sector and the future of the planet*. Routledge. doi:10.4324/9781849776264

Kennedy, B. (2020, May 6). The returns and fundamentals of ESG integrated investing. *DGFM*. Retrieved from https://www.davygfm.com/insights/esg-investing-series/the-returns-and-fundamentals-of-esg-integrated-investing.html

Labatt, S., & White, R. R. (2003). *Environmental Finance: A Guide to Environmental Risk Assessment and Financial Products*. Wiley.

Linnenluecke, M. K., Smith, T., & McKnight, B. (2016). Environmental finance: A research agenda for interdisciplinary finance research. *Economic Modelling, 59*, 124–130. doi:10.1016/j.econmod.2016.07.010

Mularova, D. (2017). *Towards a green finance framework: Opportunities and challenges for banks in the existing regulatory context*. Brussels: European Banking Federation. Retrieved from https://www.ebf.eu/ebf-media-centre/towards-a-green-finance-framework/

Noh, H. J. (2018). *Financial strategy to accelerate green growth* (Working Paper No. 866). Manila: Asian Development Bank.

PwC. (2013). *Exploring green finance incentives in China*. Shenzhen: PricewaterhouseCoopers Consultants. Retrieved from https://www.pwchk.com/en/migration/pdf/green-finance-incentives-oct2013-eng.pdf

RBI. (2021). Green Finance in India: Progress and Challenges. *RBI Bulletin*. Retrieved from https://rbidocs.rbi.org.in/rdocs/Bulletin/PDFs/ 04AR_2101202185D9B6905ADD465CB7DD280B88266F77.PDF

Sandor, R. L. (2016). *How I Saw It: Analysis and Commentary on Environmental Finance (1999–2005)*. World Scientific Publishing Company.

Sarangi, G. K. (2018). *Green Energy Finance in India: Challenges and Solutions* (Working Paper No. 863). Manila: Asian Development Bank.

Schoenmaker, D. (2019). *A framework for sustainable finance* (Working Paper). Rotterdam: Erasmus University. Retrieved from https://www.rsm.nl/fileadmin/Images_NEW/Erasmus_Platform_for_Sustainable_Value_Creation/A_Framework_for_Sustainable_Finance.pdf

Schoenmaker, D., & Schramade, W. (2019). *Principles of Sustainable Finance*. Oxford University Press.

Solow, R. M. (1991). Sustainability: an economist's perspective. Reprinted. In R. Dorfman & N. S. Dorfman (Eds.), *Economics of the Environment: Selected Readings*. W.W. Norton.

Sommer, S. (2020). Sustainable finance: An overview. *FiBras*. Retrieved from https://www.giz.de/en/downloads/Sustainable%20Finance_English_version.pdf

WB. (1995). *Monitoring Environmental Progress: a Report on Work in Progress*. The World Bank.

ADDITIONAL READING

Apergis, N., Filippidis, I., & Economidou, C. (2007). Financial deepening and economic growth linkages: A panel data analysis. *Review of World Economics, 143*(1), 179–198. doi:10.100710290-007-0102-3

Coulson, A. B. (2003). Sustainable banking and finance: People-the financial sector and the future of the planet. *Futures, 35*(8), 894–895. doi:10.1016/S0016-3287(03)00044-2

Dimitriadis, S., Kouremenos, A., & Kyrezis, N. (2011). Trust-based segmentation: Preliminary evidence from technology-enabled bank channels. *International Journal of Bank Marketing, 29*(1), 5–31. doi:10.1108/02652321111101356

Kaufer, K. (2014). Social responsibility as a core business model in banking: A case study in the financial sector. *Journal of Sustainable Finance & Investment, 4*(1), 76–89. doi:10.1080/20430795.2014.887350

Morrish, S. C., & Lee, C. (2011). Country of origin as a source of sustainable competitive advantage: The case for international higher education institutions in New Zealand. *Journal of Strategic Marketing, 19*(6), 517–529. doi:10.1080/0965254X.2011.599497

Nelson, D., Shrimali, G., Goel, S., Konda, C., & Kumar, R. (2012). *Meeting India's Renewable Energy Targets: The Financing Challenge*. Climate Policy Initiative (CPI). Retrieved from https://climatepolicyinitiative.org/wp-content/uploads/2012/12/Meeting-Indias-Renewable-Targets-The-Financing-Challenge.pdf

Peskin, H. M. (1991). Alternative environmental and resource accounting approaches. In R. Costanza (Ed.), *Ecological Economics: the science and Management of Sustainability*. Columbia University Press.

Rao, R. (2021, September 16). Heed to Heal - Climate Change is the Emerging Financial Risk. *Keynote Address delivered by Deputy Governor, Reserve Bank of India at the CAFRAL Virtual Conference on Green and Sustainable Finance*. Retrieved from https://www.cafral.org.in/sfControl/content/Speech/923202195516AMDG_Speech.PDF

White, M. A. (1996). Environmental finance: Value and risk in an age of ecology. *Business Strategy and the Environment, 5*(3), 198–206. doi:10.1002/(SICI)1099-0836(199609)5:3<198::AID-BSE66>3.0.CO;2-4

Chapter 7
Environmental Financial Reporting Adoption Lag:
The Case of Uganda

Mary Maurice Nalwoga Mukokoma
Kyambogo University, Uganda

Kisenyi Vincent
Uganda Christian University, Uganda

Peter Masaba Nangayi
Uganda Revenue Authority, Uganda

George Kasule
National Water and Sewerage Cooperation, Uganda

ABSTRACT

Financial reporting without integration of environmental issues is not sustainable. The purpose of this chapter is to discuss the need for financial environmental reporting and also to provide empirical evidence for environmental financial reporting disclosure (EFRD) of listed companies in Uganda. Historical, theoretical, and contextual issues of environmental financial reporting are analyzed. Empirical results on the environmental financial reporting disclosure levels in Uganda are presented, and the implications of the current disclosure levels are discussed. The chapter concludes that a low EFRD level demonstrates the lag in the adoption of environmental financial reporting. It is suggested that certain actions are required by the entities to publish environmental financial information and to reduce the lag.

DOI: 10.4018/978-1-6684-5580-7.ch007

INTRODUCTION

Environmental Financial Reporting (EFR) adoption and disclosure by entities are fronted as one of the approaches to address environmental sustainability management challenges (Mähönen, 2020). Unfortunately, limited empirical evidence is available on the adoption and disclosure of environmental related issues in the financial reports by entities (Senn, & Giordano-Spring, 2020). The purpose of this chapter is to contribute to the current debate on the need for financial environmental reporting and also to provide empirical evidence on the level of EFR disclosure of listed companies in Uganda.

Sustainable environmental financial reporting a daunting task and publishing financial reports without such information is failure by such an entity to render accountability for its existence (Tauringana, 2020). The common financial reporting premise is that any financial activity that does not affect an entity's financial position and performance is not measured. This implies that the entity's activities that affect the environment and are not linked to its financial position and performance are not measured. Thus, the financial information reported will be incomplete from a broad societal perspective that cherishes sustainable and responsible environmental reporting.

The world is witnessing increased negative effects due to environmental degradation that include, but are not limited to, deforestation, floods, wildfires, mudslides, diseases, famine, global warming, and the like (World Bank, 2020). Indeed, this year, British Colombia is experiencing unprecedented heat that is claiming people's lives, causing wildfires, and raising air quality concerns (Horgan, 2021). The accounting profession has been continuously challenged and implicated for not doing enough in the impending environmental crisis (Gray *et al.*, 2000; Luft, 2005; Nguyen & Tran, 2019). This is based on the fact that the financial information provided by the accountants in the financial reports is devoid or very shallow on environmental sustainability (Mähönen, 2020). Most importantly, the information provided in the financial statements is the basis for many vital decisions which affect the ecosystem and flow of environmental financing.

Financial reporting is viewed as a process of identifying, recording, summarizing, and communicating the economic information of an entity to various stakeholders. Stakeholders use the information provided in the financial reports to make decisions that affect societal wellbeing and people's livelihoods (World Bank, 2020). This is especially true for countries like Uganda that depend on the natural environment for livelihood. Regardless of the level of national development, the need for entities to report environmental financial information is crucial (Pedron *et al.*, 2021). As noted by Mähönen (2020), the current practice of voluntary environmental disclosure, leaves reporting of such vital information at the discretion of the entity.

Conventional financial reporting has limited itself to events that can be captured in monetary terms with profit being an important concern. Various environmental aspects may not necessarily be easily captured in monetary terms. Some may be treated as contingent liabilities while others would require disclosure (Zabihollah & Ling, 2017). Traditional accounting is premised on the neoclassical economic theory of profit maximization that considers various efficiencies to derive a report (Jensen & Meckling, 1976). The belief is that profit maximization will lead to allocative efficiency, which in turn influences social welfare (Luft, 2005).

This chapter analyzes the historical, theoretical, and contextual issues of environmental financial reporting. It also presents empirical results on the environmental financial reporting disclosure levels in Uganda and discusses the implication of the current disclosure levels. Finally, the need for a move from environmental accounting to sustainable environmental reporting is accentuated.

The information in this chapter communicates to policymakers about their role to legitimize environment-based financial reporting, as well as remind managers, accountants, and auditors to implement such reporting. Additionally, research endeavors will be stimulated, to further the debate on the relevance of environmental financial reporting. Finally, the information in the chapter supplements several interventions by different professions responding to the realization of Sustainable Development Goals (SDGs) on affordable and clean energy, Sustainable Consumption and Production Patterns, and climate action.

Evolution of Environmental Financial Reporting

An entity's financial report without environmental information is deemed out of touch with the call for actions towards sustainable environmental management (Agyemang, *et al.*, 2021). Financial reporting has evolved from an accounting point of view to a broad information sharing scope. This is illustrated, among other things, by the change in the nomenclature of accounting standards from International Accounting Standards (IAS) to International Financial Reporting Standards (IASB, 2020). The change is an attempt to address the needs of financial report users for information that encompasses both financial and non-financial information (Uyar, 2016). Major transformations in the reporting framework have emanated from the corporate scandals which happened between 2002-2008 that corroded public confidence in the accountancy profession and businesses (Pedron *et al.*, 2021). As a way of restoring and insulating the public and investor confidence, the accountancy regulatory bodies across the world called for transparency and an increase in periodic disclosure of both financial and non-financial information (Dancey, 2021). The objective is to enable stakeholders to understand the true value of the business in a broad societal context. Such knowledge would facilitate rational decision making.

The decisions made would in turn influence resource allocation into sectors that contribute to societal wellbeing. Some of the components in the financial reports include social responsibility reports, sustainability reports, intellectual capital reports, and environmental reports.

The past four decades or so from the early 1970s have seen consistent growth in concern for social and environmental reporting, with sustainability reporting emerging in the last fifteen years (Solomon & Warren, 2012). This was also partly accelerated by the Rio De Janeiro summit on the environment, where the term sustainability was coined (Norton, 1992). The environmental reporting concerns have, however, further shifted to integrated reporting which is viewed as the cardinal way to communicate with the shareholders, capturing social, environmental, economic, and financial issues.

Environmental Financial Reporting: Concept and Context

The conceptual definition of environmental reporting has changed over time. Gray *et al.* (1996) defines it as the process of communicating the environmental effects of an organization's economic actions to particular interest groups within society and beyond. Mähönen (2020) adds that it involves extending the accountability of organizations beyond the traditional role of providing a financial account to the owners of capital, in particular, and stakeholders in general. Such an extension is predicated upon the assumption that companies have wider responsibilities than simply creating value for their shareholders. Caputo *et al.* (2021) emphasize that the practice of environmental accounting and reporting has gained popularity globally, given its treatment as an approach that has great potential to unlock value for entities, decision makers and sustainable operations. For this chapter, environmental financial reporting is defined as the process of accounting for and communicating environmental related transactions and occurrences that influence or are likely to influence the financial operations and/or position of an entity.

Environmental financial reporting concerns have continued to be at the center of business continuity (Pedron *et al.*, 2021). These concerns mainly hinge on the consequences of the use of raw materials, energy, water, and waste management by different players in business, culminating in the reduction or depletion of natural resources (Senn & Giordano-Spring, 2020). The reduction in forest cover resulting from cutting down forests, emission of toxic gases into the atmosphere, release of effluents into water bodies, and poor waste management practices, all result in adverse effects on the environment. Over the past decade, the world has witnessed negative effects of environmental degradation, and these include changes in climate, global warming, depletion of the ozone layer, floods, famine, diseases, and many more. These concerns have attracted attention from different countries and professions, including the accounting profession, which has equally been implicated in the impending environmental crisis (Gray *et al.*, 1996).

There are several environmental reporting sustainability standards initiatives across all sectors. Dancey (2021) and Welbeck *et al.*, (2017) report that there are more than 650 different metrics available for companies looking to undertake sustainability reporting, not to mention initiatives from multiple governments and international organizations promoting just climate change reporting. The commonly used matrix is one developed by the Global Reporting Initiative (GRI).

The GRI promotes the use of sustainability reporting as a way for organizations to become more sustainable and contribute to a sustainable global economy (Hummel, 2020). GRI's mission is to make sustainability reporting a standard practice. To enable all companies and organizations report their economic, environmental, social, and governance performance, GRI produces free Sustainability Reporting Guidelines that can be used to generate comprehensive reports. Such comprehensive reports help assess the achievement of the SDGs.

SDGs call for urgent collective action towards global challenges, such as hunger, unemployment, and climate change. The governments of the 191 United Nations (UN) Member States have committed to achieving the SDGs and businesses can help bridge the gap towards achieving the SDGs by enshrining sustainable development in their purpose and core activities (Idowu *et al.*, 2020). Businesses are increasingly realising that there is an inextricable link between a commitment to sustainable development and enduring commercial success through sustainable environmental reporting (Welbeck *et al.*, 2017).

In the same regard, the UN developed the SDGs in 2015 re-emphasizing the importance of social, economic, and environmental sustainability. More than five of the SDGs focus on environmental related issues: SDG 6 on clean water and sanitation, SDG 7 on affordable and clean energy, SDG 13 on climate action, SDG 14 on life below water, SDG 15 on life on land, SDG 11 on sustainable cities and communities. This further highlights the importance of the concern on environment protection, preservation, and conservation.

In Uganda, majority of citizens derive their livelihood from the natural environment (Nsubuga *et al.*, 2021). Thus, environmental protection and sustainability is top on the National Development agenda (MWE, 2020). The Government is committed to National Development Goals (NDGs) of restoring nature for sustainable development (NEMA, 2019). This is manifested in the comprehensive regulatory framework for environmental sustainability and the various support agencies and systems. For example, the legal regulations like the National Environment Act, 2019, the National Environment Regulations, 2020, and the E-Waste Guidelines, 2015, among others, are in place. Despite Government's commitment to environmental sustainability, for the last seven years, the percentage of wetland coverage to total land area has reduced from 10.9% in 2013 to 8.9% in 2020 (MWE, 2020). Besides reduction in wetland coverage, also the forest cover in comparison to the total land area has reduced from 24% in 1990 to 10% in 2017 (MWE, 2020). Additionally, the rate of waste generation is increasing. In Kampala City, for instance, the increase is from 0.26 to 0.47 kg/capita/day (Aryampa *et al.*, 2019).

In terms of climate change, the shift in Uganda's GDP contribution represents challenges and opportunities (Tauringana, 2020). An increasing share of GDP generated from the services and industry sectors, which are less immediately vulnerable to changes in the climate, will increase the economic resilience of Uganda in the face of a changing climate (Nkundabanyanga *et al.*, 2021). These sectors are also typically high value-adding than agriculture, raising the prospect of larger tax revenues to support higher public expenditure that could be directed at climate change-relevant programs.

The state of the environment and level of environmental reporting remain major determinants of the overall national macroeconomic performance and the wellbeing of citizens (NEMA, 2019). Unfortunately, the reports generated by NEMA indicate that the level at which natural resources are being depleted, polluted, and wasted by business entities is alarming (NEMA, 2019). Though NEMA generates national environmental reports, such reports at entity level are not well documented. Decision-makers lack the information that can enable them to appreciate the effect of the business activities on the environment (Tauringana, 2020).

THEORETICAL AND EMPIRICAL ANALYSIS

This section discusses three theories that support environmental financial reporting. Additionally, empirical debates and trends on environmental financial reporting are presented.

Theories Underpinning Environmental Financial Reporting

Several theories have been advanced to explain environmental financial reporting. This sub-section analyses the three outstanding theories, namely: stakeholder, legitimacy, and accountability theories.

The Stakeholder Theory

There are several stakeholders of environmental financial information, hence the relevance of the stakeholder theory, as advocated by Freeman (1984). Freeman defines a stakeholder as any group or individual who can affect or can be affected by the achievement of the firm's objectives. These may include entity owners, suppliers, employees, consumers, government, regulators, the general public, and pressure groups.

The theory recognizes that all activities of an entity are a result of stakeholder interactions and management. Thus, stakeholders need integrated information that demonstrates synergies between the different players and the effect of its actions and decisions on the environment in which the entity operates (Zabihollah & Ling, 2017). Hence, the information disclosed to the stakeholders is value-creating if it includes environmental financial information. Unfortunately, information provided in the financial reports seeks to address the needs of entity owners, downplaying those of other stakeholders (Welbeck *et al.*, 2017). Interestingly, it is these other stakeholders who legitimize the existence of the firm, as explained by the legitimacy theory.

The Legitimacy Theory

Suchman (1995) explains legitimacy theory as society's perception that the actions of an entity are desirable, within the socially constructed norms, beliefs, values, and systems. The legitimacy theory is a system-oriented theory which assumes that the organization is influenced by, and also influences, the society or community where it is domiciled (Tauringana, 2020). Nguyen and Tran (2019) add that the organization has no right to exist or own resources except to the extent that the community decides so, as explained in the stakeholder theory. Hence, the survival of a particular entity is based on a perceived social contract (Oderal *et al.*, 2016).

Legitimacy theory, therefore, implies that any information deemed necessary for society to develop an appropriate perception of the entity's operations should be disclosed. The disclosure of such information is a way of rendering accountability for the firm's existence, as explained by the accountability theory.

The Accountability Theory

According to Gray *et al.* (1996), accountability "*is the responsibility to provide an account or reckoning of those actions for which one is held responsible*" (p.67). The theory illustrates a two-way relationship, where stakeholders expect an explanation from entity managers about the actions of the organization. Managers, in return, have an obligation to account for the operations of the entity they are responsible for. Thus, accountability requires the disclosure of the extent to which the purpose and objective for which resources were entrusted to, have been achieved (Senn & Giordano-Spring, 2020).

The social contract stipulates the responsibility and the right to information, thereby determining accountability. The accountability theory presents a moral case for an organization's disclosure of environmental information to individuals and groups with a right to such information (La Torre *et al.*, 2018).

The Synergy of Theories Underpinning Environmental Financial Reporting

The stakeholder theory is a blend of the legitimacy and accountability theories. In the broad perspective, the stakeholder theory illustrates the contract between economic resource owners and society (Ja'afar, Bala & Lawal, 2021). The general view is that society, under the guidance of a political government, owns the resources an entity uses to operate. The entity, therefore, has a social obligation to disclose information to the public on how resources are managed and, in particular, the environment.

The stakeholder theory is supported by the accountability theory. This is so, since there are many groups affected by the operations of any entity, thus, accountability illustrates the entity's concern for its stakeholders, whether direct or indirect. The direct interest stakeholders are usually the center of concern for voluntary and mandatory disclosures. On the other hand, the indirect interest groups like environmentalists, politicians, journalists and educationalists, among others, represent a society that legitimizes the operations of an entity.

Empirical Debates on Environmental Financial Reporting

The empirical debates are addressing the role of the accounting profession in and level of environmental financial reporting.

The Role of Accounting Professions in Environmental Reporting

Many stakeholders have accused the accounting profession of not doing enough to address environmental reporting concerns (Dancey, 2021; Odera *et al*, 2016; Welbeck *et al*, 2017). A study by Odera *et al.* (2016) found out that the attitude of accountants is one of the factors influencing environmental disclosure. A similar study by Welbeck *et al.* (2017) emphasized the outstanding role of accountants in environmental disclosures of listed firms in Ghana. Accountants have a major influence on environmental financial reports and their disclosure levels. Malik and Kanwal (2018) discovered that information provided by an accountant in financial reports is devoid of such environmental information or has limited disclosure on such issues. This is a serious concern since the information provided in the financial statements is the basis of many decisions which affect the ecosystem. Indeed, accountants have a critical role to play since accounting is viewed as a process of identifying, recording, summarizing, and communicating the economic information of an entity to users for decision making (Zabihollah & Ling, 2017).

The call by Dancey (2021) is for International Accounting Standards Board and International Public Sector Accounting Board, together with National Accounting regulators and accountants, to work as a team (Dancey, 2021). The Accounting standard setters are expected to address issues of measurement and disclosure of environmental matters in the financial reports (Mähönen, 2020). Society on the other hand expects accountants to communicate the effect of the firm's activities in the financial reports as part of responsibility accounting (Senn & Giordano-Spring, 2020). The increasing pressure of the societal expectation on the accounting profession has been on since 1960 (Ja'afar, Bala & Lawal, 2021; Jensen & Meckling, 1976). However, the integration of environmental accounts into annual financial reports is still an ongoing process, though the pace is alarmingly low. A study by Worimegbe and Uyewole (2021) revealed low levels of environmental financial reporting by Nigerian manufacturing firms, especially in the area of material, energy, emissions, effluent and wastage, water, and biodiversity. Nguyen and Tran (2019) also reported low disclosure levels of environmental accounting information in Vietnam.

The accounting profession has been continuously challenged and implicated in the impending environmental crisis (Dancey, 2021). From numerous studies, it is evident that the traditional accounting model is no longer sufficient to meet the information needs of financial report users. Worse still, in most developing countries, disclosure of such information is left at the discretion of the reporting entity, as found out by Agyemang *et al.* (2021).

Level of Environmental Financial Reporting

This section analyses the level and quality of environmental financial reporting disclosures in general and Uganda in particular. As noted in the background of this chapter, there is an increasing demand for organizations to communicate environmental financial information in the annual reports.

Following economic crises and the emerging disruptive pandemics like COVID-19, both the business and financial reporting terrains have radically changed. A study by Tauringana (2020) found out that businesses are increasingly recognizing the impact of their operations on the environment. Entities have become citizens of society and, as a result, the limits of their accountability are changing. This paradigm shift and the need to provide environmental financial information was supported by the study results of Nkundabanyanga *et al.* (2021).

Several factors that drive firms to publish environmental financial reports have been identified (Tauringana, 2020; Agyemang *et al.*, 2021). The factors include ethical motivation, economic motivation, legal compliance, internal organizational factors, pressure from international lending institutions and multinational companies. Ethical motivation to environmental reporting is premised on the financial reporting scandals that rocked the accounting profession, which made stakeholders treat financial reports with suspicion (Luft, 2005). In a bid to restore public confidence, organizations offer comprehensive financial reports that illustrate how the firm is operating in an environmentally responsible way (Dancey, 2021). Economic factors like the stock market trends and the level of competition motivate organizations to provide environmental financial reports.

Empirical studies (Ja'afar, Bala & Lawal, 2021; Pedron *et al.*, 2021) have demonstrated that the level of an entity's environmental disclosure affects the company's returns and market value. Regulatory compliance is another issue that motivates firms to present environmental accountability reports (Worimegbe & Oyewole, 2021). Several regulatory frameworks require entities to provide information on environmental accountability. Internal organizational factors like policy requirements, competitiveness, attitude towards information disclosure, and social responsibility strategies drive organizations to publish environmental accountability reports (Nguyen & Tran, 2019). Finally, international lending institutions and multinational organizations put pressure on organizations to present their environmental accountability reports (Senn & Giordano-Spring, 2020).

Efforts to implement environmental-based reporting have been frustrated by the complexity involved in gathering accurate information on activities outside the entity (Nkundabanyanga *et al.*, 2021). The overarching debate on the scope of activities that an organization should report on is not yet resolved. Guidance on measuring and reporting environment-related assets, liabilities, or expenses is sketchy and segmented (Tauringana, 2020). To address this challenge of harmonization, the Global Reporting Initiative (GRI) came up with standards to help member organizations understand and disclose their environmental footprint (WB, 2020).

A study by Worimegbe and Oyewole, (2021) on environmental disclosures in manufacturing companies found low disclosure levels, especially in areas of materials, energy, emissions, effluent and wastage, water and biodiversity. In contrast, the same study revealed higher disclosure levels for environmental expenditure and investment. Conversely, a related study of manufacturing firms in Egypt (Seyed *et al.*, 2021) revealed low disclosures of environmental investments and expenditure by entities.

There has been an attempt in Uganda to encourage entities in different sectors to report on their environmental footprint in their financial reports (Tauringana, 2020). The Institute of Certified Public Accountants in Uganda (ICPAU) introduced the annual Financial Reporting (FiRe) Awards, intending to promote good reporting. Indeed, one of the components considered in the assessment criteria is environmental reporting. Besides the Institute, the Uganda Securities Exchange requires its members to report on environmental sustainability. Despite the endeavors advanced to environmental financial reporting in Uganda, the level of disclosure has not been investigated.

METHODOLOGY

To examine the level of environmental financial reporting, a disclosure index was computed using the content analysis method. The content analysis method has been used by studies that have computed disclosure indices (Romito & Vurro, 2020; Worimegbe & Oyewole, 2021). The attraction to this method is the use of relatively unobtrusive process and ease of replication. The content of the annual financial reports and websites for sixteen companies registered on the Uganda Stock Exchange was used to calculate the disclosure index. Seventeen companies are registered with the Uganda Securities Exchange (USE). One company that has been trading on the securities exchange for fewer than five years was left out. Thus, the total number of observations used in the analysis was eighty. The sixteen companies used in the analysis cover five sectors, namely, Consumer goods (19%), Consumer Services (19%), Financial services (50%), Manufacturing (6%), and Utilities (6%).

As a benchmark, the study used the Global Reporting Initiative (GRI) index on content disclosed by the entities in the audited financial reports. According to the GRI Sustainable Development Report Guidelines, the total number of environmental related items that are mandatory for disclosure is thirty-four (Bednárová, *et al.*, 2019).

Table 1. Environmental Aspects Examined for Disclosure

Environmental Aspect for Disclosure	No. of Items to Be Disclosed
Natural resources utilization	6
Environmental protection	5
Energy usage	5
Emission & pollution	3
Waste management	4
Safety of people	4
Environmental policies & strategies	4
Environmental expenses and liabilities	3
	34

Source: GRI, 2013; Categories generated by the authors

As indicated in Table I, the thirty-four items were categorized into eight major themes for easy analysis and interpretation.

A scale of two was used on each of the thirty-four scores, where zero was given where there was no information; one, where there was partial information and two, where there was full disclosure. The Environment Financial Reporting Disclosure Index (EFRDI) was therefore calculated using the formula indicated:

$$EFRDI = \frac{\sum_{i=1}^{n} Yi}{N}$$

Where: n = number of items disclosed by the firm; N= total number of items expected to be disclosed, i = items for disclosure, and Yi = the score of information items (i) published by the firm.

Follow-up interviews were conducted to gain an in-depth understanding of the environmental financial reporting disclosure levels. A total of twelve interviews were held, each lasting between 20 to 30 minutes. The respondents included financial reporting regulators, auditors and accountants. Companies with low disclosure levels were particularly targeted and key personnel responsible for preparing financial reports.

The interview responses were validated by triangulating the data sources. Thus, the responses of those responsible for preparing financial reports were validated with views of regulators. Additionally, for respondents who consented to recording the interviews, their views were played back to confirm the facts shared. The interview responses were captured using audio and manual recording. This was done to mitigate the risk of the recordings getting corrupted. The interview responses were written, categorized, and emerging themes identified following guidance from Miles and Huberman (1994).

RESULTS AND DISCUSSIONS

The total number of organizations listed on the Uganda Securities Exchange since 2015 is sixteen. Analysis was done for five years from 2015 to 2019. Table 2 shows the annual EFRDI means for the five sub-sectors over five years and the overall average.

Overall, the EFRDI of 36% for all industries over the five years is low since the ideal score is 100%. The low score implies that of all the thirty-four environmental-related issues companies are expected to disclose according to the GRI Index, on average, only 36% are reported. The low environmental financial reporting disclosure is in harmony with the empirical results of the study by Worimegbe and Uyewole (2021) which showed that the number of environmental items reported in the financial reports is still low. However, an analysis of the annual mean indices shows an increase from 29.6% in 2015 to 43.9% in 2019. This implies that, whereas the information disclosed in the financial reports on environmental related matters is still limited, there is an increase in the number of items being disclosed, as supported by Mähönen (2020). This is in agreement with the results of the study by Nguyen and Tran (2019) which indicated a positive trend of disclosing environmental financial information by entities in emerging economies.

Table 2. Environment Financial Reporting Disclosure Indices of Listed Companies in Uganda.

Industry	No.	Year					
		2015	2016	2017	2018	2019	Overall Average
Consumer services	3	0.418	0.372	0.366	0.449	0.461	0.413
Consumer goods	3	0.285	0.285	0.363	0.384	0.425	0.349
Finance	8	0.289	0.390	0.420	0.448	0.476	0.404
Manufacturing	1	0.195	0.196	0.243	0.3	0.396	0.266
Utilities	1	0.295	0.319	0.369	0.41	0.436	0.366
		0.296	0.312	0.352	0.398	0.439	
Total	**16**						**0.359**

Source: Published annual reports, 2015 – 2019.

Also, the results in Table 2 reveal that disclosure levels are not uniform across the different industries. Companies in the consumer services and finance industry segments with indices of 41% and 40% respectively, score higher than the overall average. What is common with the two segments is the relatively high level of regulation. In the consumer services segment, some companies are cross-listed facing regulation from two stock exchange markets while the finance segments are regulated by the Bank of Uganda and the stock exchange. For the banking sector, most banks recognize the importance of environmental reporting and, as such, have a general statement that reflects environmental awareness. These findings are supported by the conclusion made from the study by Tauringana (2020) that environmental disclosure levels in the annual financial reports of entities vary from industry to industry.

Apart from environmental financial reporting disclosure levels differing among industries, serious differences were noted among companies, with the highest average disclosure index being 57% while the lowest was 19%. One of the companies with higher disclosure levels was Stanbic bank. The bank consistently provides information on energy efficiency, water and material consumption and travel. According to the Stanbic annual report (2019), there has been a deliberate attempt to sustainably improve environmental reporting. For instance, efforts have been taken to use more energy-efficient technologies and reduce paper consumption (Stanbic Bank Uganda, 2019). Indeed, specific percentages are given on energy saved and reduction in paper consumption. Also, the bank was the Financial Reporting award winner for sustainability reporting in 2019. Sustainability reporting is a sub-component of environmental financial reporting. Other companies provided environmental information narratives without concrete data. For example, Uganda Clays reported the plan of energy saving using rice husks.

As regards expenditure on energy, scanty information is available. Except for Stanbic Bank, which reported a percentage reduction in the fuel used (5%-9%), other entities have little information on fuel usage. On the other hand, many companies have taken up tree planting and some, like East African Breweries, seem to be taking it a notch higher by committing a lot of resources in the restoration of an indigenous tree in Gangu and other places.

Of the environmental financial information that should be disclosed, items on emissions and pollution were not reported by all the companies for the five years. This finding raises a serious concern since the operations of most companies produce emissions and pollutant substances that affect the lives of people. As indicated in the stakeholder theory (Zabihollah & Ling, 2017), society has an interest and supports entity operations. The entity therefore has an obligation to report on how its operations support environmental sustainability as suggested by La Torre *et al.* (2018).

The analysis of the information in the entity reports still indicates that no company reported information on environmental-related costs, liabilities and assets. Also, no company provided information on the amount of research and product innovation expense devoted to environmental sustainability. A similar finding was reported in a study by Agyemang *et al.* (2021) that entities in China hardly disclosed environmental related costs and liabilities in their financial reports. The major reasons identified by Ja'afar, Bala and Lawal (2021) and Romito and Vurro (2020) are: the difficulty of identifying and isolating environmental costs from others, lack of a clear definition of environmental expenses, limited reporting guidelines, and lack of enforcement mechanisms.

Another finding was that most companies that attempted to report skewed their information towards the positive side of their contribution to the environment, with limited disclosure of the negative impact. A similar finding was revealed by Caputo *et al.* (2021) that managers of organizations, especially the Board and accountants, tend to report favorable information and sidelining non-favorable information. Managers' report favorable information by utilizing reporting impression management strategies. Such strategies make society doubt the credibility and completeness of the information reported. For instance, one company in the consumer services category did not adequately report on their environmental footprint, even though their inputs are extracted from the environment. Another company that extracts clay for use in the production process revealed limited information on sustainability of the key material needed for the survival of the entity.

Responses got from the twelve follow-up interviews with some accountants who generate the reports and regulators revealed four major themes as reasons for the low environmental financial reporting disclosure, as reported in Table 3.

Table 3. Emerging Themes from Interviews.

Emerging Theme	Number of Times It Is Featuring
Regulatory requirement for environmental reporting	11
Competences to prepare environmental reports	9
Time available to prepare financial reports	8
Attitude towards preparing environmental financial reports	6

Source: Primary data, 2021.

One of the reasons for the low disclosure that came out from the interview responses was lack of a law and concrete standards compelling accountants to publish environmental financial reports. One accountant said, "(…) the preparation and disclosure of environmental financial reporting information is voluntary. Without environmental reporting, the auditor will issue a report indicating that the information presented in the reports is true and fair, complying with International Financial Reporting Standards and the Company's Act 2012". Responding to the same issue, one regulator said, "(…) disclosing environmental financial information is still at the discretion of the entity. That makes it so challenging to enforce especially for companies whose owners are obsessed with profits, with limited regard to environmental sustainability."

Another key theme used to explain low environmental disclosure is lack or limited competences to capture, prepare and report environmental information. A number of accountants confessed to lack of competences to prepare such reports. In addition, lack of time to prepare environmental reports, on top of the heavy workload, featured prominently in the responses. One accountant emphasized thus, "(…)

even if I had passion to include environmental financial information as required by international good practice, I don't have the time and the company is not willing to offer support to do so since employee costs would increase." Related to this reason was the difficulty of identifying and isolating environmental costs from others and the negative attitude of accountants to disclose environmental information.

Synthesis and Implication

The results have revealed that the EFRDI of listed companies in Uganda is low, though attempts are being made by various companies to publish environmental financial reports. Research has emphasized regulation and enforcement (Ja'afar, Bala & Lawal, 2021), attitude of accountants and auditors towards environmental disclosure, and expertise in environmental reporting (Tauringana, 2020) as key factors driving disclosure levels. However, of all the reasons, regulation is outstanding, as pointed out by Senn and Giordano (2020). This implies that the regulatory framework that encourages firms to publish environmental financial reports should be strengthened and supplemented with the need for a positive attitude towards environmental financial reporting.

Organizations do not operate in a vacuum; they owe their sustainability to society and vice versa. Given the legitimacy theory, entities, therefore, must report comprehensive and credible information to society (Worimegbe & Oyewole, 2021). This is based on the backdrop that non-financial information affects the entity's sustainability and financial results (Filipiak & Dylewski, 2020). Caputo *et al.*, (2021) recognize the need that sustainable environmental reporting contributes to the inter-linkages between sustainability, financial results of entities, and society's wellbeing. This implies that sustainable environmental information takes center stage in the financial reports generated by entities.

Society's expectation for companies to account for the effect of their operations on the environment has not yet been satisfied. This is contrary to the provisions of the accountability theory which places an obligation to companies to account for their actions and decisions. By using the impression management strategies in environmental reporting, entities would be sidelining the precepts of the accountability theory.

Debates have emerged from several stakeholders about the need for organizations to make a move from just environmental accounting to sustainable environmental financial reporting (Mähönen, 2020). Advocates are referring to environmental degradation as a result of activities by manufacturing companies (Caputo *et al.*, 2021). Sustainable environmental reporting has had a long season of debates and the need is to move it to implementation. Regulators like the European Banking Authority and the Foundation for International Financial Reporting Standards have proposed and are still fine-tuning guidelines on sustainable environmental reporting (Hummel, 2020). Global challenges, like the current COVID-19 pandemic, are eye-openers to re-directing financial resources to environmentally sustainable projects (Dancey, 2021). This is with the view of meeting the 2030 target on climate and energy sustainability. The call is for entities to become more resilient against climate and environmental risks and shocks (Seyed, *et al.* (2021). The Institute of Certified Professional Accountants of Uganda (ICPAU), supported by other Government bodies such as the Auditor General's Office, Accountant General and necessary financial support from the Government of Uganda are advocating sustainable environmental reporting. However, other than advocacy, more concrete actions are yet to be taken to enhance sustainability financial reporting adoption in Uganda.

As chief stewards of business information, professional accountants are well-positioned to champion sustainable environmental reporting. Indeed, stakeholders desire better information on the entity operations and the effect of such operations on the environment. This desire has not been addressed by voluntary disclosure, as reported by Dancey (2021).

RECOMMENDATIONS AND CONCLUSION

This chapter contributes to the demand for deliberate actions by entities to implement environmental financial reporting. The low EFRD level of listed companies is clear evidence in support of the demand to provide more accountability on the actions of the entity that affect the environments where firms operate. Accountants need to move towards sustainable environmental-based financial reporting if they are to navigate the rugged terrain.

Based on the environmental financial reporting disclosure levels in Uganda, this study recommends that the existing environmental reporting standards be harmonized for easy reporting and compliance monitoring. Additionally, global accountancy regulatory bodies should develop an international standard on environmental reporting to be adopted by member bodies. Finally, clear guidelines on environmental reporting should be developed to address the needs of various sectors customized to the national context.

This chapter has explored the concept of environmental financial reporting, the theories that underpin it, the level of environmental financial disclosure, worldwide and specifically, in Uganda. Additionally, the Environmental Financial Reporting Index for companies listed on the Uganda Security Exchange market has been computed. The computed index of 36% shows that the level of environmental financial reporting in Uganda is still low. Indeed, a discussion has been generated on the need to move from environmental accountability to sustainable environmental reporting. A general recommendation to boost discloser levels is for regulators to put in place enforceable and clear regulatory framework supported by a positive mindset of those in charge of preparing sustainable environmental financial reports.

DISCLAIMER

The contents and views of this chapter are expressed by the authors in their personal capacities. It is not necessary for the Editor and the Publisher to agree with these viewpoints and they are not responsible for any duty of care in this regard.

ACKNOWLEDGMENT

The authors extend sincere gratitude to:

- The Editor and the International Editorial Advisory Board (IEAB) of this book who initially desk reviewed, arranged a rigorous double/triple blind review process and conducted a thorough, minute and critical final review before accepting the chapter for publication.
- All anonymous reviewers who provided very constructive feedbacks for thorough revision, improvement, extension and fine tuning of the chapter.
- All colleagues, assistants and well-wishers who assisted the authors to complete this task.

REFERENCES

Agyemang, A. O., Yusheng, K., Twum, A. K., Ayamba, E. C., Kongkuah, M., & Musah, M. (2021). Trend and relationship between environmental accounting disclosure and environmental performance for mining companies listed in China. *Environment, Development and Sustainability*, *23*(8), 12192–12216. doi:10.100710668-020-01164-4 PMID:33424427

Aryampa, S., Maheshwari, B., Sabiiti, E., Bateganya, N. L., & Bukenya, B. (2019). Status of Waste Management in the East African Cities: Understanding the Drivers of Waste Generation, Collection and Disposal and Their Impacts on Kampala City's Sustainability. *Sustainability*, *11*(19), 5523. doi:10.3390u11195523

Bednárová, M., Klimko, R., & Rievajová, E. (2019). From Environmental Reporting to Environmental Performance. *Sustainability*, *11*(9), 2549. doi:10.3390u11092549

Caputo, F., Pizzi, S., Ligorio, L., & Leopizzi, R. (2021). Enhancing environmental information transparency through corporate social responsibility reporting regulation. *Business Strategy and the Environment, 30*(8), 1–15. doi:10.1002/bse.2814

Dancey, K. (2021). *Professional Accountants Leading Reporting and Assurance on Sustainability*. IFAC.

Filipiak, B. Z., & Dylewski, M. (2020). Sustainable financial reporting in the context of ensuring sustainability of financial systems. In *Finance and sustainable development* (pp. 235–267). Routledge. doi:10.4324/9781003011132-14

Freeman, R. E. (1984). *Strategic Management: A Stakeholder Approach*. Pitman Publishing.

Gray, R. H. (2000). Current developments and trends in social-environmental auditing and attestation. *International Journal of Auditing*, *4*(3), 247–268. doi:10.1111/1099-1123.00316

Gray, R. H., Owen, D. L., & Adams, C. (1996). *Accounting and Accountability: Changes and challenges in corporate social and environmental reporting*. Prentice-Hall.

GRI. (2013). *Sustainability Reporting Guidelines.* Amsterdam: Global Reporting Initiative. Retrieved from https://www.globalreporting.org/standards/2013.asp

Horgan, J. (2021). *B.C Premier Comments about heat wave deaths*. Rogers Media.

Hummel, K. (2020). *The European Union Non-Financial Reporting Directive: Evidence on Regulatory Parameters and Firm-Value Consequences*. Retrieved from https://papers.ssrn.com/sol3/papers.cfm?abstract_id=3744653

IASB. (2020). *International Financial Reporting Standards*. International Accounting Standards Board.

Idowu, S. O., Schmidpeter, R., & Zu, L. (2020). *The Future of the UN Sustainable Development Goals*. Springer. doi:10.1007/978-3-030-21154-7

Ja'afar, Y., Bala, H., & Lawal, A. M. (2021). Determinants of Corporate Environmental Accounting Disclosure of Oil and Gas Firms in Nigeria. *Global Business and Management Research, 13*(1), 16–36.

Jensen, M. C., & Meckling, W. H. (1976). Theory of the firm: Managerial behavior, agency costs and ownership structure. *Journal of Financial Economics*, *3*(4), 305–360. doi:10.1016/0304-405X(76)90026-X

La Torre, M., Sabelfeld, S., Blomkvist, M., Tarquinio, L., & Dumay, J. (2018). Harmonising non-financial reporting regulation in Europe: Practical forces and projections for future research. *Meditari Accountancy Research*, *26*(4), 598–621. doi:10.1108/MEDAR-02-2018-0290

Luft, J. M. (2005). Mandatory environmental disclosures in a legitimacy theory context. *Accounting, Auditing & Accountability Journal*, *18*(4), 492–517. doi:10.1108/09513570510609333

Mähönen, J. (2020). Comprehensive Approach to Relevant and Reliable Reporting in Europe: A Dream Impossible? *Sustainability*, *12*(13), 52–77. doi:10.3390u12135277

Malik, M. S., & Kanwal, L. (2018). Impact of corporate social responsibility disclosure on financial performance: A case study of listed pharmaceutical firms of Pakistan. *Journal of Business Ethics*, *150*(1), 69–78. doi:10.100710551-016-3134-6

Miles, M. B., & Huberman, M. (1994). Data management and analysis methods. In N. K. Denzin & Y. S. Lincoln (Eds.), *Handbook of Qualitative Research*. Sage.

MWE. (2020). *Sector Performance Report 2020*. Ministry of Water & Environment, GOU.

NEMA. (2019). *National State of the Environment Report 2018 -19*. National Environment Management Authority, GOU.

Nguyen, L., & Tran, M. (2019). Disclosure levels of environmental accounting information and financial performance: The case of Vietnam. *Management Science Letters*, *9*(4), 557–570. doi:10.5267/j.msl.2019.1.007

Nkundabanyanga, S. K., Muramuzi, B., & Alinda, K. (2021). Environmental management accounting, board role performance, company characteristics, and environmental performance disclosure. *Journal of Accounting & Organizational Change*, *17*(5), 633–659. doi:10.1108/JAOC-03-2020-0035

Norton, B. (1992). Sustainability. *Human Welfare, and Ecosystem Health*, *1*, 97–111.

Nsubuga, F. N., Mearns, K. F., Davis, N. C., Kalumba, A. M., & Komen, K. (2021). Exploring the influence of climate change and capital assets on livelihood formations in central region of Uganda. *Environment, Development and Sustainability*, *23*(6), 9223–9242. doi:10.100710668-020-01020-5

Odera, O., Scott, A. H., & Gow, J. (2016). Factors influencing corporate social and environmental disclosures: A systematic review. *International Journal of Business Governance and Ethics*, *11*(2), 116–134. doi:10.1504/IJBGE.2016.078199

Pedron, A. P. B., Macagnan, C. B., Simon, D. S., & Vancin, D. F. (2021). Environmental disclosure effects on returns and market value. *Environment, Development and Sustainability, 23*(3), 4614–4633. doi:10.100710668-020-00790-2

Romito, S., & Vurro, C. (2020). Non-financial disclosure and information asymmetry: A stakeholder view on US listed firms. *Corporate Social Responsibility and Environmental Management, 28*(2), 595–605. doi:10.1002/csr.2071

Senn, J., & Giordano-Spring, S. (2020). The limits of environmental accounting disclosure: Enforcement of regulations, standards and interpretative strategies. *Accounting, Auditing & Accountability Journal, 33*(6), 1367–1393. doi:10.1108/AAAJ-04-2018-3461

Seyed, M. A., Hashem, V. & Seyed, Y. Z. (2021). Factors affecting Financial and Non-financial Reporting of the Environment in Gachsaran oil and gas exploitation Company. *PalArch's Journal of Archaeology of Egypt / Egyptology, 18*(8), 146-158.

Solomon, J., & Warren, M. (2012). *Integrated Reporting: The Influence of King III on social, ethical and environmental reporting*. ACCA.

Stanbic Bank Uganda. (2019). *Stanbic Bank Annual Report 2019.* Stanbic Uganda Holdings Limited.

Stanbic Uganda Holdings Limited. (2019). *Annual Report.* SUH.

Suchman, M. (1995). Managing legitimacy: Strategic and institutional approaches. *Academy of Management Review, 20*(3), 571–610. doi:10.2307/258788

Tauringana, V. (2020). Sustainability reporting adoption in developing countries: Managerial perception-based determinants evidence from Uganda. *Journal of Accounting in Emerging Economies, 11*(2), 149–175. doi:10.1108/JAEE-07-2020-0184

Uyar, A. (2016). Evolution of Corporate Reporting and Emerging Trends. *Journal of Corporate Accounting & Finance, 27*(4), 27–30. doi:10.1002/jcaf.22157

Welbeck, E. E., Owusu, G. M. Y., Bekoe, R. A., & Kusi, J. A. (2017). Determinants of environmental disclosures of listed firms in Ghana. *International Journal of Corporate Social Responsibility, 2*(1), 1–12. doi:10.118640991-017-0023-y

Worimegbe, T. M., & Oyewole, T. (2021). Environmental accounting disclosure practices of quoted manufacturing companies in Nigeria. *Global Journal of Business. Economics and Management: Current Issues, 11*(1), 42–47.

World Bank. (2020). *Sustainability Review.* Retrieved from https://www.worldbank.org/en/home

Zabihollah, R., & Ling, T. (2017). Voluntary disclosure of non-financial information and its association with sustainability performance. *Advances in Accounting*, *39*, 47–59. doi:10.1016/j.adiac.2017.08.001

Chapter 8
Social Responsibility for a Sustainable Environment

Živko Bergant
College for Accountancy and Finance, Slovenia

ABSTRACT

Any thinking about preserving the environment is a typical topic of socially responsible action. Today, the notion of social responsibility is abused for various political and business purposes and only left to various civil initiatives. It remains at the level of declarations, voluntary thinking, and philanthropy, albeit it has some impact on corporate practice. The chapter explains that the concept of social responsibility is not something new, as it has accompanied humanity since its inception. Adherence to the principles of social responsibility is a precondition for further successful development, not only of individual companies or countries but of human society in general. It is useful to reflect on the past development regarding the awareness of social responsibility and also the need for future consistent implementation of its principles, especially from the perspective of a sustainable environment. An important direction is to treat the earth as a stakeholder to which companies and individuals are indebted.

INTRODUCTION

Human civilization is facing a major socio-economic transformation. Among other important causes there are climate changes, which reflect the impact of economic development on the environment. The time will come when denying the importance of nature and the environment will no longer be possible. Nature is already billing the human generation (Žakelj, 2020). A sustainable environment has even become

DOI: 10.4018/978-1-6684-5580-7.ch008

a precondition for human survival. Humanity is destroying the physical conditions of its existence, but it is not taking sufficient action. It must be internalized that society and nature form an organic whole.

The current socioeconomic model was not created by workers but by a multitude of dedicated economists, lawyers and engineers who were not made aware of either the environment or the social system by the higher education system. Economics, which now plays a dominant role among the social sciences, will have to submit to ecology. Therefore, its quality will no longer be measured by quantitative criteria, but by qualitative ones.

So, it should not be unexpected that the world has witnessed an increasingly intensive treatment of the concept of social responsibility and its application in practice over the last 60 years. Nevertheless, there is still no single, generally accepted definition of social responsibility today. The development of corporate social responsibility theory is faster than the development of individual social responsibility awareness. The notion of social responsibility is still being abused for various political and business purposes and left to various civil initiatives and movements. In no country it has been consistently introduced into its economic and legal system. Such a situation has negative impact also on sustainable environment. Namely, it remains at the level of declarations, voluntary thinking and philanthropy, but has some impact on corporate practice. In the following, the author wants to contribute to the substantiation of the reasons for a systematic and systemic approach to the understanding and application of the principles of social responsibility in theory and practice.

The chapter shows that the content of social responsibility is not something new, as it has accompanied humanity since its inception. Adherence to the principles of social responsibility is a condition for successful further development, not only of individual companies or countries, but of human society in general. The chapter will reflect on the past development of social responsibility awareness, on current understandings and shortcomings, and on the need for consistent implementation of its principles in the future, especially in terms of a sustainable environment.

BACKGROUND

During the last forty years or so, the concept of social responsibility has transformed from an irrelevant idea into one of widely accepted approaches to understanding business and all global developments as well.

Understanding and addressing the social responsibility (SR) is one of the preconditions for creating and establishing economic democracy towards achieving a sustainable future. The basic justification for the need for economic democracy is already rooted in the fundamental principles of social responsibility. Authors as well as international institutions define social responsibility in many ways. Among them is very important ISO standard (BSI, 2020) with seven principles: responsibility for the impact (accountability), transparency of data, ethical behavior, respect for interests of stakeholders, respect for the rule of law, respect for international norms of behavior, respect for human rights. Here are also a few other short examples: responsibility for future generations, for workers and human creativity, for income inequality, for governance, for the elderly, for entrepreneurship, for health, for politics and for history.

Social responsibility can be considered as the responsibility of various entities and/or activities (states, communities, business, students etc.); however, perhaps the greatest emphasis in the literature is on corporate social responsibility (CSR).[1] Such a view is supported by numerous authors (Wan-Jan, 2006; Khan *et al.*, 2012; Hamidu *et al.*, 2015; Jusoh, 2020) and in the handbooks of the Institute of Corporate Culture Affairs (ICCA, 2006) and A-Z (ICCA, 2010). Nevertheless, in addition to CSR, individuals are a key area for reflection on social responsibility (Benabou & Tirole, 2009; Joseph, 2014; Davis *et al.,* 2017).

The above citations of course, have not exhausted all definitions and aspects of social responsibility in the extensive literature. The existence of a large number of different definitions of social responsibility points to its many aspects as well as its importance. It is therefore understandable that there are also some attempts of systematic approach to various aspects and taxonomies of social responsibility (Bergant, 2020a). Numerous definitions and approaches require some in-depth discussion of the content of social responsibility as a notion.

SOME STARTING POINTS

All human action is based on meeting individual needs. These are therefore the fundamental motivation of everybody's work. Many sciences and authors deal with the treatment, classification and interpretation of human needs and human responses to them. From a psychological point of view, the hierarchy of needs is known, presented by Abraham Maslow (1943), who defined five levels of human needs. The whole economy is based on the rational satisfaction of needs, which is usually defined as the biggest economic problem. Human needs have also been addressed by many other authors also from a sociological point of view, especially in terms of motivation (Alderfer, 1972; McClelland, 1961). Other sciences, such as biology, medicine, anthropology, etc., are also involved in the study of needs. However, differing views on human needs have not contributed enough to a comprehensive approach to addressing them.

Despite several improvements, however, these models do not have a definition of need, they could be called as a "pre-need," which could be (and is) right at the top of the hierarchical scale of needs. Among the authors who identified this need is Pirc (2015) who calls it *the need to survive*. Of course, it is not only about survival, but also about preserving life, which can even lead to paranoid and pathological obsession. The basic need is therefore the existence of man, which is also his fundamental right. Non-recognition of this right means non-recognition of the human right to exist. All other needs arise from it. However, human existence is threatened in different ways and for varied reasons. It is therefore a risk that is constantly perceived by man. Therefore, as a rule, man constantly strives for the greatest possible security, which can only be gained by managing this risk.

Man can manage the risk of his existence only by his work, assuming that he does not exploit other people. This means that the right to work in the broadest sense is only a transformed human right to exist. Any non-recognition of the right to work means non-recognition of the human right to exist. Of course, the right to work also means that a person has a *duty to work* and thus contribute to the management of human risks. In the case of an individual who, for objective reasons, is unable to work to the extent necessary for his existence, but whose work contributes to the greatest extent possible, his right to work is transformed into *a right to solidarity*. Any non-recognition of the right to solidarity means that a person's right to exist is not recognized. True solidarity, then, does not come from the good will or grace of the people. Solidarity is therefore *a right and a duty* based on the interdependence of people. Almsgiving is actually humiliating, so an individual can be justifiably harmed. On the other hand, compassion is based on empathy, and forgiveness, which can also act cohesively in an interdependent group.

Through work (in the broadest sense of the word), man manages risks and creates value added. It is therefore a value that does not reduce the value of wealth or the level of well-being, even though it is fully consumed[2] Based on the above starting points, it is possible to define *the general law of creating and guiding value added* (hereinafter: value-added law). Its dictum includes two aspects:

1. Value addition is the net outcome of the organizational system in risk management, which is inherent in the system and belongs to risk holders in proportion to their contribution to the functioning of the organizational system (aspect of creating value added).
2. Disproportionately high or disproportionately low participation of individual risk carriers in the value added (according to their work contribution) increases the entropy of the organizational system and jeopardizes threatens the realization of its sustainable development (aspect of added-value guidance and its distribution).

The value-added law is general due to its validity in all socio-economic systems (past, present and future), that are focused on sustainable development. The value-added law operates regardless of the wishes or activities of the participants and regardless of the normative organization of the organizational system or its environment. It is therefore completely independent of the human will that created the organizational system. The value-added law has various forms of presence in different economic and political environments and in diverse types of organization (relations between people) of associations.

In addition to raising the level of social well-being, value added also means a reserve for risk management, both for individuals and for their associations and organizations of all kinds.

The contribution to the functioning of the organizational system must be understood in its broadest sense, i.e., in all possible forms (e.g., materialized work, such as real and monetary inputs, knowledge, and of course current physical and intellectual work, including guarantees and opportunity costs or losses of individual participants). Mulej *et al.* (2000) similarly speaks of the "*effort for the lowest entropy*".

Every person is consciously or subconsciously aware of the risks. He or she therefore responds according to the ability to perceive risk and on the ability to respond to that feeling.[3] Human's desire to increase their reserves is therefore natural and they cannot be blamed for unethical behavior. However, this desire becomes unethical when it turns into greed, which is an increase in reserves (or wealth) at the expense of others. This means gaining a larger share of the value added to which an individual is entitled in terms of his or her contribution to risk management. The thinking that greed in capitalism is positive or has developmental effect, it is therefore totally wrong. Namely, greed is not the driver of the development, but the force of decay, according to the second point of the law on value added. This law contains a fundamental ethical principle regarding the distribution of the value added according to the contribution of the individual.

A person is more efficient in creating value addition if it combines in the workplace and exploits the positive synergies of this association. This is achieved through social and technical division of labor. This means that social division of labor must be understood in terms of view of social responsibility. It is different than usual in textbooks. Mainly the specialization of human activities is discussed. However, assuming that the entire human work is an expression of the need for existence, it may be concluded that each subject performs a certain part of the entire work. Therefore, through the usefulness of his work, he contributes to social well-being. From the point of view of social responsibility in the case of individual subjects, social division of labor may be discussed, as practically all subjects in a country or society are included in it.

Both types of division of labor (social and technical) are an expression of an organizational status. With the organization of work, the connection and interdependence between people grow, because organizing in its content means regulating relations between people. Interdependence, however, is one of the fundamental bases of social responsibility, which only increases with the division of labor.

Based on the above findings, there is a short definition:

Social responsibility is the responsibility of individuals and organizational systems of all forms and levels in increasing social well-being.

The basic purpose of all organizations is therefore to create value added, as only on this way it is possible to increase social welfare and thus to increase the reserves for effective risk management.[4] At the same time, the contribution to social well-being is also a fundamental criterion of socially responsible behavior of both companies and individuals.

The above definition of social responsibility is short and relatively concise, but it covers the activities of all people and their organizations. It therefore allows consideration from many aspects that are extremely important for its further development.

Examples of these aspects include internal reporting, solvency, labor and capital, individual behavior, value added, quality of information system, stakeholders, business excellence, social responsibility accounting (Bergant, 2014, 2015, 2018, 2019a, 2019b, 2019c, 2020a, 2020b, 2020c, 2021a, 2021b, 2021c) and of course a sustainable environment.

A LOOK INTO THE PAST

Man, out of concern for his own existence (which was defined as a fundamental need in the previous chapter) soon (already in prehistory) realized that he had to take appropriate action. So, he worked to gain food reserves and thus the ability to manage risk. By today's standards, it could be said that he created surplus value added. The man also realized that he had created more in the group than alone.[5]

The first groups were mainly instinctive, hunting, gathering, genealogy, and later also tribal and regional. Much later (especially in the Middle Ages) higher, i.e., more complex communities and also states developed. To this day, the type of intentional communities has also been preserved[6] with a relatively high interconnectedness. Characteristic of all these communities is the awareness of common interests and beliefs and the consequent interdependence. It is also the basis for some accepted values, such as cooperation, identity, security, freedom, responsibility and solidarity. This also includes a respectful attitude towards the environment.

The feeling of mutual responsibility in people is therefore not new, as it has also been associated with belonging, honor (e.g., chivalry), etc. From today's perspective, social capital within these communities may be discussed, because it captured norms, trust, and networks as its core components. Therefore, the division (distribution) of created value has been a problem and a cause of countless conflicts and wars in the past.[7]

Similarly, the notion of corporate social responsibility is not new in its fundamental content, as "*concern for society has always been present in the business community*" (Gonzalez-Perez, 2013).

In parallel with connecting and uniting people, they were also forced to increase their knowledge by the need for human existence. By increasing knowledge, man has more effectively managed the risks to which he was exposed (and still does so today). Hence his curiosity (joy of knowledge) and desire for knowledge. Both are reflected in three fundamental areas of study. Namely, man practically and theoretically studies and research:

1. Through orientation to the environment, he has developed the natural, technical and information sciences;
2. Through orientation to himself, he has developed the philosophical, psychological, and medical sciences;
3. Through orientation to his role in the social and natural environment, he has developed the social and anthropological and environmental sciences.

The fundamental benefits of these research are the increasing people's knowledge, innovation and ability to manage all types of risks and thus increase the security of society as a whole, including the environment. Exploiting these skills still increases the efficiency of human work today (including removing obstacles to its operation), thereby directly increasing value added. Thus, on the one hand, it is possible to increase the reserves for easier risk management (e.g., retained value added in companies), and on the other hand, the standard of living can also be increased (e.g., in the form of higher participation of employees in the value added). Of course, knowledge can be abused (and today is actually often abused) for narrow interests, indicating a lack of general awareness of the operation of the value-added law. Namely, with the development of knowledge, additional risks appear, which were once considered "side effects", but today have already increased so much that they pose a significant threat to people (Beck, 1992). Perhaps, the most important risk comes from the damaged environment.

An individual who in any way contributes to the value addition and thus to the well-being of society has a sense of usefulness, which is extremely important, as it gives him the joy of working and acquiring knowledge and skills in the broadest sense. Knowledge is therefore the common denominator of all types of work. Even experiences are just accumulated and emotionally valued knowledge that also includes the prevailing values.

In the above starting points, in connection with the value added, the cybernetic model of human activity shown in Figure 1 can be explained.

Figure 1. Creation and guidance of value added
Source: Bergant (2021d)

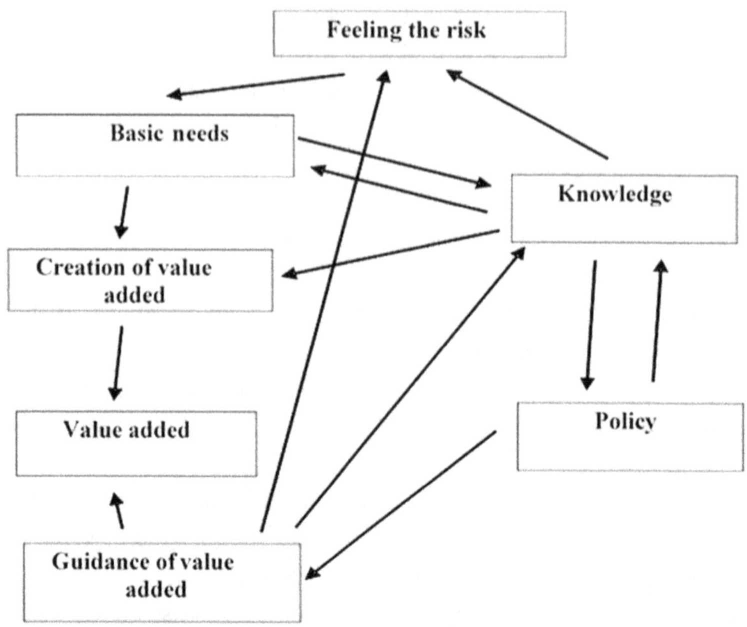

Figure 1 shows in particular:

1. The need for security arises from a sense of risk and from it all other human needs.
2. The need for security forces human being to work, which is his basic activity, and thus to create value added, as well as to increase his knowledge and skills.
3. Applying knowledge through development, innovation and better organization increases the efficiency of value creation.

4. Increasing knowledge has the effect of improving the sense of risk, but at the same time it can increase the risk of misuse of knowledge (e.g., atomic bomb, cyber-attacks).
5. Increasing knowledge also has the effect of increasing needs.
6. The added-value management (i.e., guidance) is strongly influenced by politics in the broadest sense by balancing the needs and interests of stakeholders at all levels and in all organizational processes and all forms of organizations.
7. Policy is directly influenced by the volume of value added created. At the same time the policy influences the creation of knowledge and the guidance of value added.
8. Part of the value added is channeled directly to the development of knowledge and art, which additionally influences the formulation of added-value policy.
9. Proper value-added management increases reserves, enables better risk management and reduces the sense of risk.
10. The above rectangles also include risks arising from the damaged environment, which also affects the policy of creating and allocating (directing) value added.

Figure 1 shows the close links between risk and work, value added and knowledge. Good policy considers all these factors. It includes a sustainable environment policy as well.

The model from Figure 1 can be simplified to a more abstract level shown in Figure 2. Figure 2 summarizes that by using knowledge at work, a person creates value added, which is then in principle directed to:

- Increasing reserves to facilitate risk management (or to increase security);
- Improving the standard of living;
- Development of knowledge to increase value added.

Figure 2. Basic feedback loop
Source: Bergant (2021d)

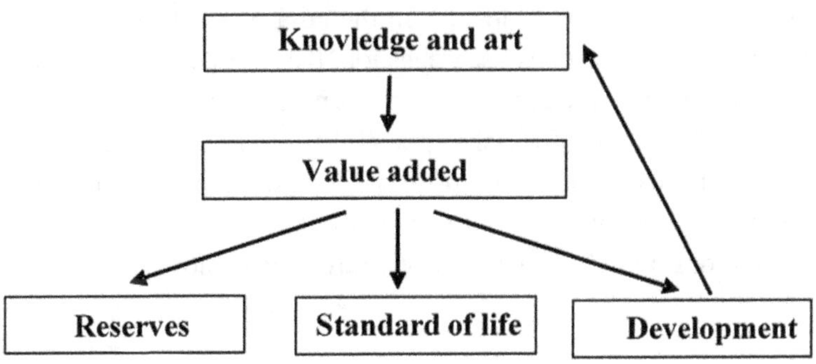

The red thread of human activity is therefore the struggle for survival. The understanding and the content of social responsibility thus developed spontaneously, at the same time as man's efforts for his existence. Humanity destroys the physical conditions of its existence if it neglects the importance of a sustainable environment.

In the professional literature (Gonzalez-Perez, 2013), the first phenomenon and definition of the concept of social responsibility is probably considered to be 1953, when Bowen (1953) defined the social responsibility of businesspeople. They should pursue such a policy that is desirable within the goals and values of society. Other authors have further supplemented this definition.

Social responsibility gained increasing popularity in the following years, especially in the context of the pursuit of independent journalism (Shelton & Safar, 1996). This marked the beginning of the modern era of the development of social responsibility. In this process, the notion of social responsibility often had different meanings for different publics (Gonzalez-Perez, 2013). In further development, the emphasis was mainly on corporate social responsibility, which served primarily as a basis for various theories such as business ethics theory, stakeholder theory, etc. It developed particularly in the 20th century (Gonzalez-Perez, 2013). An important contribution to the development of social responsibilities is to address the aspect of political economy (Mulej *et al.*, 2019).

From a professional point of view, the concept of social responsibility took place in several phases, models and theories, which were also the subject of criticism by various authors. ISO 26000 (ISO, 2010) probably set the pinnacle of this development. The general finding is that social responsibility goes beyond legal regulations but does not replace them (Mulej & Mihec, 2020).

Among the positive doses of this development, the following can be particularly focused on: findings about the positive impact on the sharing of social responsibilities for long-term corporate performance, emphasis on enlightened egoism (enlightened self-interest), integration of companies' competitiveness, adoption of strategic and ethical mechanisms for monitoring business processes, increased attention to human rights in environmental protection, the impact on improving work rights, the development of codes of conduct (e.g. Codes of corporate governance), more attention to monitoring the impact of companies in the environment (development of new standards in successful practices), searches for NGOs, greater emphasis on socially responsible investigation, the growth of various movements and associations for the promotion and enforcement of social responsibility, the rise of recommendations and declarations at various levels, based primarily on voluntary decision-making. The impact of the development of social responsibility is also reflected in the change of some regulations, which, however, worked relatively slowly.

Special emphasis should be placed on extending social responsibility to three domains: economic, social and environmental (Rafay *et al.*, 2020). Many authors speak of a *triple bottom line* (Elkington *et al.,* 1998). Unfortunately, the social and environmental (ecological) areas are somewhat neglected, particularly in terms of setting up an appropriate information system.

Considerable progress in this regard is being made by ISO standards with their principles and recommendations. They make an important contribution to improving business operations of companies as well as to raising people's awareness of the importance of preserving the environment. However, the general awareness of the importance of a sustainable environment is still unsatisfactory and, above all there is not enough will at the level of state policies.

From today's point of view, there are also some other weaknesses that to some extent slow down the development of social responsibility. Undoubtedly, the most important shortcoming is the still unclear definition of the ultimate goal or purpose of companies (Bergant, 2021a), as profit is still considered as a goal of companies, especially in regulations and accounting standards. Therefore, there remains a high risk that recommendations and declarations based primarily on volunteering will end up as a philanthropic activity (Bergant, 2020b).

Another important shortcoming is the greater (perhaps excessive) emphasis on corporate social responsibility compared to the social responsibility of individuals. There is also a lack of emphasis on the social responsibility of society, as it is the duty of governments to influence its dissemination in relevant policy documents (Mulej *et al.,* 2019).

The next shortcoming is still unclear (often also completely wrong) understanding of the concept of stakeholders. Several definitions of stakeholders in a company can be found in the professional literature, especially on corporate social responsibility. They are a basis for discussions on "stakeholder theory" and "stakeholder economy". It means that the word "stakeholder" is quite important particularly in in the economic and sociological sciences. It is therefore important how its meaning is understood (Ramzan *et al.*, 2020). The use of this word is also extremely important for corporate governance and management. However, different authors have different approaches to identify stakeholder groups and often have explanations unrelated to the origin of stakeholder as a category.[8]

From the point of view of social responsibility, the value-added law should be considered. This basis offers a new (better) definition of stakeholders:

Stakeholders are those who contribute to risk management in the company's operations in creating value added.

This contribution means that the stakeholder assumes a certain part of the risk in the company's operations. At the same time, this fact also provides a substantive basis for justifying the company's liability to the stakeholder from in terms of corporate social responsibility (CSR). Such an understanding of stakeholders also includes Earth as a particular stakeholder. Namely it bears the risk caused by activities of both companies and individuals. Earth's participation in the created value added in principle means the operating costs of companies and individuals. These costs are similar to the depreciation of the planet Earth and still they are not fully identified and recognized today.

Social responsibility as an activity is, at least in theory, recognized as a fundamental precondition for achieving a sustainable society and increasing social well-being. Therefore, based on what has been said, an important question arises about the development of social responsibility and sustainable environment in the future, as the well-being and existence of humanity also depend on it.

LOOKING TO THE FUTURE

Increasing inequality among people increases the pressure to close with narrower interest groups, which further increases social risks (Beck, 1992). Therefore, a risk society where risk predominates, differs from an industrial society where scarcity predominates (Mythen, 2004). The contrast between the poor and the rich therefore changing to the contrast the less secure and more secure.[9]

The driving force in society is thus supposed to change from "I am hungry" to "I am afraid" (Mythen, 2004). Today, one can add the fear of climate changes as well. Such a trend is clearly an increasing challenge for the proper response of people and humanity in general. It should be borne in mind that the combination of instincts, emotions and knowledge is different in each person, so everyone feels the risk differently and reacts differently to it. The human response depends primarily on the culture of the nation, the organizational culture, and the culture of the individual (Mythen, 2004).

Therefore, it is important for the future to increase the level of knowledge of all stakeholders in individual organizational systems and thus improve the relevant information systems. It is particularly important to regulate the relationships between mind in the widest sense, emotions, and instincts. The future of the whole society and civilization in general depends on it.

In the future, therefore, in principle, three directions of the company's development are possible:

1. The predominance of mind and positive emotions, which means ensuring an appropriate balance of stakeholder participation in value added and a focus on coexistence, a sustainable environment and the existence of a society that allows not only "to survive" but also "to live";
2. The prevalence of instincts and negative emotions, which means inadequate ratio of stakeholder participation in value added, the predominance of greed and the struggle for supremacy and power, Darwinism, the devaluation and collapse of society as a system, the destruction of the environment, including the climate changes neglecting. Max-Neef (1991) sees two possible scenarios in this direction:
    a. Complete or partial extermination of humanity upon the destruction of nature;
    b. The barbarization of the world, which is also reflected in the retreat of the richest people into their strongholds, which is supposed to separate them from the huge area of poverty outside these barricades;
3. An intermediate state where there is a struggle for the dominance of one or the other direction, which means a crisis situation in society, which requires constant action against the entropy of the social system in the form of finding solutions and negotiations.

The assessment of many authors is that the situation in the world is deteriorating. Berardi (2017) speaks of political impotence, which he defines as the absence of the ability to turn desires into reality, and of globalization, which today means lower wages and a reduced sense of economic and social security. Badiou (2016) points out that everyone knows that terrible inequality cannot be the solution to people's historical destiny.

A similar enumeration of problems, however, is only a treatment of a situation that does not contain effective solutions. Ignoring these problems means the neglecting the manifestations of the operation of value-added law. The result is a lack of professional basis for negotiating and enforcing appropriate changes.

Therefore, it would be difficult to doubt that the world is in crisis. In principle, a crisis occurs in three general cases:

1. When the system reaches a point where a change of direction is required;
2. If the system does not detect the need for changes;
3. If the system misidentifies the causes of the crisis and does not make the right decisions.

The first point, unlike the other two, also means an opportunity not to be missed. Diamond (2005) highlights the second and third points in more detail, lists four categories of factors and continues to break them down:

1. *The system does not recognize signs of upcoming problems:*
    a. *People do not have experience with similar problems or do not expect them at all (they do not know or do not expect the negative consequences of a particular business decision);*
    b. *People have no previous experience (no records or insufficient knowledge);*
    c. *People forget previous experiences (in the case of a boom, for example, they forget that it is necessary to save and create reserves);*
    d. *People incorrectly or inappropriately compare various positions in space and / or time (finding a solution in an unknown position is useful by comparing only in truly comparable positions); in the case of only apparent similarity, especially if the comparisons differ in time and space, they may be misleading and dangerous;*
2. *The system does not detect a problem that has already occurred:*
    a. *The problem is imperceptible in the context of normal business and normal professional and technological methods;*
    b. *Management is remote from what is happening (decision-makers do not have a proper overview and are not aware of what is happening "on the ground");*
    c. *Slow movement reduces the feeling of danger. There is a well-known example of "creeping danger" or "cooked frog syndrome." The management often does the same, ignoring first warnings of negative trends as insignificant and as an exaggeration, "because it's important to follow a basic development trend, not deal with trivial things. The solution of everything is possible with a few bigger deals". Usually, these deals bring additional risks and often the trends only get worse to be solved again with new deals, etc. A similar example is "memory loss" when only minor (insignificant) changes can be observed over a shorter period, and no changes are observed that prove significant when comparing longer periods;*
3. *The system does not attempt to solve an already perceived problem:*
    a. *Decision-makers behave "rationally" but selfishly and immorally (a typical example is "tragedy of common business elements" when "everything is ours"; another example is the "it's not my problem" attitude, which sooner or later turns out to be not true. The following examples are the advantage of short-term interests over long-term ones, lust for power,*

selfishness, concealment of a problem or deception, personal competition and prestige);

   b. *Decision-makers behave "unreasonably" when they stubbornly insist on wrong or ingrained values and solutions (old mistakes are repeated, warning signs are ignored, attachment to old ideas and old solutions is perceived; due to the unwanted risk makes it very difficult to abandon the old way and accept new, it is difficult to reject a solution that seemed to be right, even in this context there is a conflict of short and long term, but as an advantage of personal interest over the common); a special case is "crowd or group psychology", where an individual follows a decision that he or she would not make; this also includes cases of "psychological denial" when a person, in fear of a certain event, simply ignores it or does not believe that it can happen;*

4. *Even when a problem is foreseen, perceived and needs to be solved, this is often not possible, perhaps for the following reasons:*
   a. *The problem is too big to be solved (for example, its weight exceeds the capabilities of those who would like to solve it, while others are not interested in solving it);*
   b. *The solution is too expensive (for example, the resolution costs are higher than other alternative options in the context of a company's bankruptcy);*
   c. *Efforts to resolve it are insufficient (often due to the belief that a particular company cannot be subject to bankruptcy or that, for example, it is the founder's duty to rehabilitate, cover losses, etc.); on the other hand, the founder is often irresponsible when he fails to meet his legal obligations to cover the loss - for example, the state in relation to a public institution; in such a case, the mildest consequence is usually higher costs of later problem solving);*
   d. *Finding a solution is too late (in this context, the "snake look syndrome" is interesting, as it "recognizes the finding that their company is on the verge of bankruptcy, blocks management and paralyzes it like a snake look at victims").* (adapted and supplemented by: Diamond, 2005, pp. 438–457)

Studying the present based on the above findings can be very useful, although it can also lead to pessimistic conclusions. It therefore requires a more complex approach that goes beyond the scope of this chapter, especially with regard to a sustainable environment.

One must be aware that "science does not predict the future and does not create it itself. It identifies possibilities and needs through empirical analysis and theoretical conclusions. However, it can only be realized together with other social factors: politics, the economy, culture and education, and only in this cooperation can be realized the interest of science and the interest of society as a whole" (Grossner, 1970, p. 18).

The above quote indicates a number of areas where changes are needed in relation to social responsibility. In doing so, one must be aware that change in a particular area cannot be successful, as it can only worsen the situation. Therefore, an interdisciplinary approach is needed. Undoubtedly, without systemic change, the dissatisfaction and entropy of associations as organizational systems will increase.

A systematic approach to changes requires considerations in at least the following directions:

- Ensuring an appropriate atmosphere and readiness for change,
- Identification of areas for change,
- Identification of change agents,
- Defining the order of changes,
- Ensuring appropriate dynamics or gradual changes.

The most important initial task is undoubtedly a theoretical discussion without the burdens of past dogmas. It should take place not only in economic area, but also social and philosophical areas. Without such discussions, there will be no change in the mindset that is today trapped in seemingly insurmountable frameworks.

SOLUTIONS AND RECOMMENDATIONS

Undoubtedly, the biggest challenge lies in the academic sphere and education system. This is primarily called for a unified view on accountancy theory,[10] which should also be the basis for changing the general perception of relations in society. Today, this may seem like a big illusion, but an important argument is available. It is a recognition of the operation of the general value-added law, which does not depend on ideological assumptions or individual interests.

Therefore, politicians and politics have a great responsibility to take science and the profession into account in moving towards a sustainable society, including a sustainable environment, and to protect future generations. The changes in policy are always (or should be) the result of changes in people's expectations and demands. These changes can only be realized with a changed education system, for which, again, the academic sphere is responsible. Academics need to end their possible apologetic behavior and expose their independent thinking and suggestions.

Nevertheless, the most crucial factor in the implementation of changes is the state (in its broadest sense), since it defines the fundamental legal order and, in this context, also the basic conditions for the operation of business systems. This has a decisive influence on the manifestations of the general operation of the value-added law in society which are reflected in systemic inequalities.[11]

One of the stakeholders that could require changes to the information system is the trade unions. They should be ultimate bearers of long-term interests and control in organizations. However, they often forget about their power and even more often do not direct it properly. They should be better aware of their social responsibility and become an important driver of changes.

Finally, it must be stressed once again that Earth is a stakeholder par excellence and must be considered.

FUTURE RESEARCH DIRECTIONS

Emerging trends in recent past and present require several and also severe changes, which should be based on scientific findings. Therefore, future research is very important. It must have several directions, for example:

1. Consequences of value-added law in different circumstances:
2. Better definition of organizations' purpose.
3. Better definition of stakeholders.
4. Research on socially responsible behavior of an individual in different circumstances.
5. Research on corporates' impact on a sustainable society.
6. Research on a sustainable environment and an appropriate information system.
7. Research on the need to change the legal system and accounting standards as well.
8. Research on proper communication with people about socially responsible behavior.

CONCLUSION

Social responsibility is not something new in terms of content. Namely, it is an indisputable companion of human activity in its entire past. It is based on human need for existence, which proves to be just as strong in the future. Ignoring this finding and its consequences can also be fatal for many communities. Nowadays, the concept has evolved, but not yet definitively, as it still has many shortcomings.

In the future, it is possible be optimistic about the theory of evolution, but it also requires certain conditions that must be met for positive trends to prevail over negative or good over evil (Wilson (2007). One of the most important conditions is undoubtedly the concern for a sustainable environment.

The influence of current generations on the future is extremely important in this initial creation of appropriate circumstances, especially the integration of knowledge and the creation of an atmosphere of trust. Therefore, the courage to change something is also very important (Lynch & Bobone, 2021).

DISCLAIMER

The contents and views of this chapter are expressed by the author in his personal capacity. It is not necessary for the Editor and the Publisher to agree with these viewpoints, and they are not responsible for any duty of care in this regard.

ACKNOWLEDGMENT

The author extends sincere gratitude to

- The Editor and the International Editorial Advisory Board (IEAB) of this book who initially desk reviewed, arranged a rigorous double/triple blind review process and conducted a thorough, minute and critical final review before accepting the chapter for publication.
- All anonymous reviewers who provided very constructive feedbacks for thorough revision, improvement, extension and fine tuning of the chapter.
- All colleagues, assistants and well-wishers who assisted the authors to complete this task.

REFERENCES

Alderfer, C. (1972). *Existence, Relatedness and Growth.* The Free Press.

Badiou, A. (2015). *Our Wound is Not So Recent.* Lecture delivered at La Commune theatre, Aubervilliers, France. Retrieved from https://miguelabreugallery.com/wp-content/ uploads/2016/09/AlainBadiou_OurWoundisNotSoRecent.pdf

Beck, U. (1992). *Risk Society.* Sage.

Benabou, R., & Tirole, J. (2009). Individual and Corporate Social Responsibility. *Economica, 77*(305), 1–10. doi:10.1111/j.1468-0335.2009.00843.x

Berardi, F. (2017). *Futurability: The Age of Impotence and the Horizon of Possibility*. Verso Books.

Bergant, Ž. (2014, September 2). Corporate responsibility and internal reporting. In *Proceedings of International Conference on Social Responsibility*. IRDO. Retrieved from https://www.irdo.si/skupni-cd/cdji/cd-irdo-2014/referati/d-Bergant-eng.pdf

Bergant, Ž. (2015, September 2). *Social responsibility and corporate's solvency*. Academic Press.

Bergant, Ž. (2018, September 1). Capital, labour and social responsibility. In *Proceedings of International Conference on Social Responsibility*. IRDO., Retrieved from https://www.irdo.si/irdo2018/referati/c-01-Bergant.pdf

Bergant, Ž. (2019). Individual person and social responsibility. In *Proceedings of International Conference on Social Responsibility*. IRDO., Retrieved from https://www.irdo.si/skupni-cd/cdji/cd-irdo-2015/referati/37-zivko-Bergant-paper-final-.pdf

Bergant, Ž. (2019a, September 1). Individual person and social responsibility. In *Proceedings of International Conference on Social Responsibility*. IRDO. Retrieved from https://www.irdo.si/irdo2019/referati/c-1-Bergant.pdf

Bergant, Ž. (2019b). The Relation Between Capital and Labor as a Basis for the Distribution of the Added Value. *International Journal of Science, technology and Society, 7*(3), 50–55.

Bergant, Ž. (2019c). The Quality of Accounting Information and User's Social Responsibility: Social Aspect. *International Journal of Advances in Management and Economics., 8*(5), 8–15. doi:10.31270/IJAME/v08/i05/2019/2

Bergant, Ž. (2020a). Starting Points to Comprehensive Treatment of Social Responsibility. *International Journal of Advances in Management and Economics, 9*(1), 1–7. doi:10.31270/IJAME/v09/i01/2020/1

Bergant, Ž. (2020b). Basic problem of the stakeholder theory from a corporates' social responsibility point of view. *International Journal of Business Marketing and Management, 5*(11), 117–119.

Bergant, Ž. (2020c). Debates on corporate social responsibility are becoming similar to the philanthropy. *International Journal of Advances in Management and Economics, 9*(6), 13–17.

Bergant, Ž. (2021a, September 4). The problem of organization's purpose as a basis for its social responsible behavior. In *Proceedings of International Conference on Social Responsibility*. IRDO. Retrieved from https://www.irdo.si/irdo2021ref/referati/01-b01-zivko.pdf

Bergant, Ž. (2021b). Social responsibility and business excellence. *International Journal of Advanced Engineering Research and Science*, *8*(1), 73–79. doi:10.22161/ijaers.81.11

Bergant, Ž. (2021c). What And Who Is Company's Stakeholder? *International Journal of Science Academic Research*, *2*(1), 770–773.

Bergant, Ž. (2021d). *Accountancy and Social Responsibility. An Innovative New Approach to Accountancy Theory and Practice*. Palgrave Macmillan. doi:10.1007/978-3-030-77928-3

Bowen, R. H. (1953). *Social Responsibilities of the Businessman*. Harper & Row.

BSI. (2020). *ISO* 26000 *Guidance on social responsibility*. British Standard Institution. Retrieved from https://www.bsigroup.com/en-GB/ISO-26000-Social-Responsibility/

Davis, S. L., Rives, L. M., & Maya, S. R. D. (2017). Introducing personal social responsibility as a key element to upgrade CSR. *Spanish Journal of Marketing*, *21*(2), 146–163. doi:10.1016/j.sjme.2017.04.001

Diamond, J. (2005). *Why do Societies Collapsed?* Viking.

Elkington, J., Hailes, J., & Makower, J. (1998). Triple. *The Bottom Line (New York, N.Y.)*, *11*(Appendix). http://archive.babymilkaction.org/pdfs/spinpdfs/appendices/triplebl.pdf

Gonzalez-Perez, M. A. (2013). Corporate Social Responsibility and International Business: A Conceptual Overview. In International Business, Sustainability and Corporate Social Responsibility. Emerald.

Grossner, C. (1970). *Svet v času, ki prihaja* [The world in the time to come]. Ljubljana: Državna založba Slovenije.

Hamidu, A., Haron, M., & Amran, A. (2015). Corporate social responsibility: A review on definitions, core characteristics and theoretical perspectives. *Mediterranean Journal of Social Sciences*, *6*(4), 83–95. doi:10.5901/mjss.2015.v6n4p83

ICCA. (2006). *The ICCA Handbook on Corporate Social Responsibility*. John Wiley & Sons.

ICCA. (2010). *The A to Z of Corporate Social Responsibility*. John Wiley & Sons.

ISO. (2010). *ISO 26000*. International Organization for Standardization. Retrieved from https://www.iso.org/iso/

Joseph, A. (2014). The Need of Personal Responsibility and Integrity in Corporate Social Responsibility Theories. *International Journal of Recent Advances in Organizational Behavior and Decision Sciences, 1*(1), 45–67.

Jusoh, W. N. H. W. (2020). Corporate Social Responsibility: Conventional and Islamic Perspectives. In A. Rafay (Ed.), *Handbook of Research on Theory and Practice of Global Islamic Finance* (pp. 129–149). IGI Global. doi:10.4018/978-1-7998-0218-1.ch007

Khan, T. M., Khan, A. N., Sheraz, A., & Mehfooz, A. (2012). Corporate Social responsibility (CSR) – Definition, Concepts and Scope (A review). *Universal Journal of Management and Social Sciences, 2*(7), 41–51.

Lynch, E., & Bobone, B. (2021, July 21). *The Courage to Change.* Social Europe. Retrieved from https://socialeurope.eu/the-courage-to-change

Maslow, A. (1943, September 8). A Theory of Human Motivation. *Psychological Review, 50*(4), 370–396. doi:10.1037/h0054346

Max-Neef, M. A. (1991). *Human Scale Development: Conception, Application and further Reflections*. The Apex Press.

McClelland, D. (1961). *Achieving society*. The Free Press. doi:10.1037/14359-000

Milanović, B. (2021, October 18). *Can Xi Jinping defeat three stubborn inequalities?* Social Europe. Retrieved from https://socialeurope.eu/can-xi-jinping-defeat-three-stubborn-modern-inequalities

Mulej, M. (2000). *Dialektična in druge mehkosistemske teorije* [Dialectical and other soft system theories]. Maribor: Ekonomsko-poslovna fakulteta.

Mulej, M., Hrast, A., & Mihec, M. (2020). Social Responsibility and Human Selfishness. In *Proceedings of the 6th International Scientific Conference on Contemporary Issues in Economics, Business and Management*. Kragujevac: Faculty of Economics, University of Kragujevac.

Mulej, M., Merhar, V., Žakelj, V., Zore, M., Hrast, A., Toplak, L., ... Ambrožič, B. (2019). *Uvod v politično ekonomijo sodobne družbe* [An Introduction to Political Economy of Modern Society]. Kulturni Center Maribor.

Mythen, G. (2004). *Ulrich Beck. A Critical Introduction to the Risk Society*. Pluto Press.

Pirc, T. (2015). *Postmetafizični ethos ekonomiziranega globalizma* [The postmetaphysical ethos of economized globalism] [Doctoral dissertation]. Ljubljana: Filozofska fakulteta. Retrieved from http://www.pif.si/sites/default/files/inline-files/Pirctadej971.pdf

Rafay, A., Farid, S., Yasser, F., & Safdar, S. (2020). Social Collateral and Repayment Performance: Evidence from Islamic Micro Finance. *Indian Economic Review, 24*(1), 41–74.

Ramzan, M., Ahmad, I., & Rafay, A. (2020). Is Auditor independence influenced by Non-audit services? A stakeholder's viewpoint. *Pakistan Journal of Commerce and Social Sciences*, *14*(1), 388–408.

Shelton, G., & Safar, H. (1996). Social Responsibility Theory Revisited: A Comparative Study of Public Journalism and Developmental Journalism. *Journal of the European Institute for Communication and Culture*, *3*(3), 97–107.

Wan-Jan, S. (2006). Defining corporate social responsibility. *Journal of Public Affairs*, *6*(3–4), 176–184. doi:10.1002/pa.227

Wilson, S. D. (2007). *Evolution for Everyone*. Random House.

Žakelj, V. (2020). Economics in the Anthropocene. Žiri: Self-Published.

ENDNOTES

1 More definitions of corporate social responsibility see also in: Noufe (2016).

2 More about the definition of value added, its structure and distribution, see also in: Bergant (2019a).

3 More about these abilities and responds in: Bergant (2019).

4 More about organization's purpose in: Bergant (2021).

5 Of course, he also realized that it is easier to obtain a risk reserve at the expense of others. This is still evident in society today (dissatisfaction, rebellions, wars, etc.).

6 More about intentional communities in: FIC (2021).

7 This confirms the operation of the value-added law in this period as well.

8 More about these authors and their definitions on stakeholder see in: Bergant (2021b).

9 Such a development is logical from the value-added law point of view, as the rich have greater reserves for risk management than the poor.

10 More about it in Bergant (2921c).

11 More about these inequalities in Milanović (2021).

Chapter 9
Sustainability Risks for ESG:
An Investor's Perspective

Gil Cohen
https://orcid.org/0000-0002-5176-4583
Western Galilee College, Israel

ABSTRACT

Sustainability becomes more important for investors in recent years. This study examined three sustainability risks—environmental, social, and governance (ESG)—which the investors take into consideration before any decision making. It is found that while environmental risks negatively affect excess returns in some years. However, since 2018 investors valued environmental risks, social risks were found to be the most influential factor negatively related to excess returns. Corporate governance risks have been found to be embedded in the traditional systematic risk factor "beta," but no evidence has been found for negative correlations between corporate governance risks and excess returns of stocks. It is also observed that solar energy companies have achieved the highest returns, followed by low-carbon and wind energy producers. Those results insinuate that investors value the solar energy production method as the most cost-effective green energy production technique.

INTRODUCTION

Climate finance seeks to support of actions that will address climate change issues. The Kyoto Protocol 1997 and the Paris Agreement 2015 call for financial assistance from parties with more financial resources to those that are less endowed and more vulnerable. This recognizes that the contribution of countries to climate change and their capacity to prevent it and to cope with its consequences vary enormously.

DOI: 10.4018/978-1-6684-5580-7.ch009

Climate finance is needed for mitigation because large-scale investments are required to significantly reduce emissions. The Paris agreement sets the goal of zero net greenhouse gas emissions from human activity. Each party is obligated to set targets for emissions reduction or limitation, implement domestic measures to achieve those targets, and submit data on its progress for international review and evaluation (Rafay, 2022). The second milestone of 2015 was the adoption of the Sustainable Development Goals (SDGs) by the 194 countries of the UN General Assembly addressing global social issues and environmental challenges that threaten the sustainability of human society. Global goals were set, including poverty eradication, good health and well-being, quality education, clean energy, sustainable cities, responsible consumption and production, and action on climate change. Amid these changes corporate managers began to embrace environmental management, equal opportunity, work-life balance, labor rights, and other socially responsible policies as integral to the management of business risks and opportunities. At the same time, investors began to recognize the importance of ESG (Environmental, Social and Corporate Governance) risks in investment decisions. ESG holds social and environmental responsibilities to corporates that used to sanctify revenues and profits above all other corporate goals and missions ensuring the long life of a company through a combination of financial profitability, environmental protection, and social responsibilities. ESG investment is a set of global guidelines drawn up under UN leadership is stating that investment managers should incorporate ESG factors when making investment decisions and are required to provide information representing their approach to responsible investment. According to Kawaguchi (2017), incorporating ESG factors mean including issues relating to the environment such as: carbon emissions, energy efficiency, resources efficiency, recycling, water resources, renewable energy, preservation of forests and marine resources. Social issues including workplace diversity, working conditions across the supply chain, force labor and modern slavery. Those policies which were regarded as additional costs factors are now being treated differently, since mounting threats to humanity such as climate changes and wealth gaps are now being recognized by consumers, stakeholders, corporates workers and governments.

There are two important aspects of the impact of sustainability on the financial markets as a whole and on the investments and portfolio construction. First, investors are more concerned about ESG issues and prefer to invest in firms that are ware of these issues and are willing to invest resources to reduce their sustainability risks. Second, more and more investment houses are stating that they will not continue to invest in companies that harm the environment. For example, in July 2021, "Altshuler Shaham" which is the largest investment house in Israel, has announced that it intends to end its investment in companies with more than a quarter of their revenues in the future in carbon. Moreover, the investment house argued that the move is not due to climatic activism, but to an economic perspective, in their view, "*climatic risks are investment risks*". Such important move from the leader of the institutional investors that dominates the financial market would essentially drive companies to take care of their environmental issues. However, this revolution had not come without protest and debates initiated by private investors that uses the services of those institutional investors. In their view, not investing in high ESG risk stocks may harm returns on their portfolios and eventually massive abandonment of that investment house by unsatisfied customers. "Altshuler Shaham" is the first swallow in Israel that may be followed by other investment houses. A massive joining this movement by private and institutional investors can really change the world by forcing companies that seek public funds to better care about sustainability issues.

This chapter is designed to examine to what extent ESG risks affect companies returns in recent years (2016-2020). Data of 83 firms from NASDAQ 100 is used for which the ESG risk score is calculated. It is examined that to what extent this risk factors are embedded in the traditional systematic risk "beta" and their impact on stock's excess returns. Such attempt has never been tried before by prior research. Moreover, this research is also unique in its methodology and updated data. Only a few past research have attempted to directly derive from the financial markets the impact of ESG risks on risk and return involved in the investing process. Moreover, past researchers have addressed each ESG risk separately and therefore a more comprehensive approach is adopted in the following research.

LITERATURE REVIEW

The understanding that profitability alone does not ensure long run existence of an organization, is well established by researcher (For example: Elkington, 1997; Lo, 2010; Schaltegger *et al.*, 2013). Shareholders now understand that investing funds and resources in easing environmental and social risk can be beneficial to the stock value as well as their image for the public. Sustainability usually refers to Environmental, Social and corporate Governance (ESG) issues that have public implications. Corporate sustainability has become vital for organizations' long-term success (Eccles *et al.*, 2012; Ortiz-de-Mandojana and Bansal, 2016), and it has been increasingly studied in the academic literature in recent decades. The literature on the subject mainly deals with Corporate Social Responsibility (CSR) that improve employee motivation and the firm's surrounding business atmosphere (Montiel, 2008). Corporate sustainability generally refers to the integration of financial profitability, environmental protection, and social responsibility into organizations' mission declarations and every applied to everyday activities (Elkington, 1997; Lo, 2010; Schaltegger *et al.*, 2013). The world commission on environment and development, 1987[1], defined corporate sustainability as *meeting the needs of a firm's direct and indirect stakeholders such as shareholders, employees, clients, pressure groups, communities, etc., without compromising its ability to meet the needs of future stakeholders as well.* Following these objectives, researchers have dealt with issues such as assessing corporate sustainability (Topple *et al.*, 2017), improving sustainability engagement (Schönherr *et al.*, 2017), providing investment opportunities (Schramade, 2017), and designing sustainable business models (Morioka *et al.*, 2017, 2018). Although many researchers have focus on corporate sustainability models and efforts, not many have tried to document the effect of sustainability risks on the financial markets. Since the financial market are a good futures proxies, a lot about the present and future of different sustainability aspects may be learned. Nizam *et al.* (2019) have studied the impact of sustainability on banks' performance. The concluded that financial performance and social and environmental performance are related, evidence for the banking sector remains limited and inconclusive. Garcia *et al.* (2018) have found that larger companies have higher levels of performance. They also found that companies in sensitive industries present superior environmental performance even when controlling for size and country. Lee *et al.* (2013) examined whether portfolios comprising high-ranked Corporate Social Performance (CSP) firms out/underperform portfolios comprised of low-ranked CSP firms for US sample of firms covering the period from 1998 till 2007. Their results are consistent with the "no-linkage" hypothesis, which argues that no significant difference in the risk-adjusted performance is expected between high- and low-ranked CSP-formed portfolios. Unlike Lee *et al.* (2013) in our research conducted on much more recent data, it is found that corporate environmental and social risks are negatively correlated to excess returns of stocks. While the most consistent influential factor is the social risks. These finding shed light on the enormous importance of investor's value and human business conduction methods.

Environmental Responsibilities

In recent years stakeholders increasingly require organizations to become more environmentally aware adjust their business model towards integration of values such as animal protection and public health preservation. Traditional environmental protection was considered only as a public interest that by imposing sanctions and regulations on the private sector tries protect the environment. In recent years, the private sector has adopted the approach of co-responsibility towards environmental issues. Corporate environmental responsibility is now defined as the way in which organizations incorporate environmental issues into their operations to eliminate waste and emission and reduce to minimum bad effects on the country's natural resources. Li, Liao & Albitar (2020) constructed a Corporate Environmental

Responsibility (CER) engagement measurement to examine the relationship between CER engagement and firm value as based on a sample of 496 China's A-share listed companies from 2008 to 2016. The results show that when firms start to adopt environmental regulations, CER would have a negative effect on firm value. However, at a specific level, CER would start to enhance firm value positively. Unlike Li *et al.* (2020) the research is extended to all ESG ingredients and examine excess return over the NASDAQ 100 benchmark. Moreover, returns of six green energy ETFs (three general and three sectorial) will be examined to better understand how investors view alternative energy investment opportunities. The sectorial ETFs are FAN which invest in wind energy stocks, TAN which invest in solar energy stocks and SMOG which invest in low carbon energy stocks.

Social Responsibilities

Corporate social responsibility is a broad concept whereby companies integrate social concerns in their business operations. As the use of corporate responsibility expands, it is becoming increasingly important to have a socially conscious image. Consumers, employees, and stakeholders prioritize socially responsible companies when choosing a brand or investment opportunity. Businesses can practice social responsibility by donating money, products or services to nonprofit organizations or volunteer its personnel and physical resources for social causes. An important part of social responsibility is ethical labor practices. By treating all employees fairly and ethically without gender or any other discriminations firms gain positive attitude from their business environment including customers, suppliers, competitors, and shareholders. Baohua *et al.* (2020) investigated corporate innovation from the perspective of a firm's employee-related Corporate Social Responsibility (CSR) in China. They found that more employee-related CSR generates more innovation success. Their results also suggest that a firm's incentive to offer better employee-related CSR is an important determinant of its innovation.

Corporate Governance Responsibilities

Corporate governance responsibilities include all measures a company make to ensure that it is managed in such manner that minimize different risks the company face. An adequate corporate governance will minimize chances that one stakeholder group may benefit unfairly at the expense of other stakeholder groups due to a weak control and mal regulated systems. Managers could make poor investment decisions which benefit them but are detrimental to the company's shareholders. A company's exposure to legal, regulatory, and reputational risks could become heightened. The company could also receive lawsuits from one of its customers or stakeholders due to some form of impropriety. These could potentially damage the reputation of the company and lead to significant legal costs. Moreover, a company's ability to honor its debt obligations may become hindered. This exposes it to bankruptcy risk if its creditors decide to take legal action. An example of study in corporate governance conflicts is Georg (2017) who showed that a structural conflict of interest in non-executive boards exists due to missing corporate governance structures and a lack of awareness for legal issues with regard to information security risks. Non-executive boards receive information on strategic security threats as a part of their oversight function to fulfill investor interest in transparency. At the same time, they act as representatives of company stakeholders and have an interest to counteract to information security risks based on the stakeholder's risk disposition.

Green Energy ETFs

One important way to examine the public opinion on the future of green energy is to examine the performances of major ETFs (Exchange Trade Funds) that holds various kind of green energy producing companies. Moreover, the financial market can also help us understand better which green energy production methods are superior to other methods in the eyes of investors. The use of ETFs that holds many stocks in a specific sector enable researchers to avoid individual stock bias and can clarify the financial market attitude towards clean energy production in general and towards specific production techniques within the green energy sector. The analysis is started by examining the returns of the following general clean energy ETFs. ICLN which is a global clean energy ETF, QCLN which is NASDAQ clean energy index fund and PBD which is also a global clean energy ETF. It important to note that these ETFs are composed of global equities in the clean energy sector without distinction of the production methods or technologies. Figure 1 presents their annual returns from 2016 until 2020 along with the annual returns of the NASDAQ index.

Figure 1 shows that an important investor's trend has occurred in 2019. Since then, the green energy ETFs have gained a substantial higher return the NASDAQ index. Moreover, in 2020, The QCLN which contains NASDAQ companies has produced to investor excess returns of 162 percent over the NASDAQ index. The global green energy ETFs examined here, have produced in 2020 an excess return of 104.5 percent for ICLN and 148.2 percent for the PBD over the NASDAQ index. Measuring the risk involved in investing in these ETFs by the standard deviation of their monthly returns over the examined period, it is observed that clean energy ETFs holds more risk than the NASDAQ investment. The standard deviations of the clean energy ETFs were 7.53, 8.41, and 7.30 for ICLN, QCLN and PBD respectively, while the NASDAQ monthly standard deviation was only 4.92. This result was expected since clean energy companies rely on a relatively new disruptive technology that contains higher risks.

Figure 1. General Green Energy ETFs and NASDAQ Annual Returns
Note: ICLN is a global clean energy ETF, QCLN is NASDAQ clean energy index fund and PBD is also a global clean energy ETF.

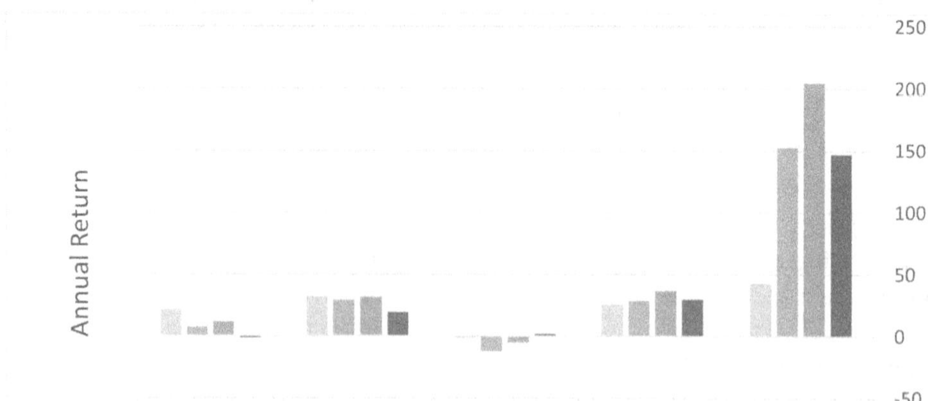

	2016	2017	2018	2019	2020
ICLN	-1.7	19.2	1.7	29.7	147.3
QCLN	11.8	31.6	-5.4	37.1	204.8
PBD	7.4	29.3	-12.1	28.6	152.5
NASDAQ	21.7	31.9	-1.7	25.6	42.8

Green energy sectors are examined to better understand which sector is prefereed by investors. Such information may insinuate on the future of the different green energy production techniques. The ETFs that were examined are: FAN which is a global wind energy ETF, wind is used to produce electricity using the kinetic energy created by air in motion. This is transformed into electrical energy using wind turbines or wind energy conversion systems. Wind first hits a turbine's blades, causing them to rotate and turn the turbine connected to them. TAN which is solar energy ETF, solar power plants use mirrors to concentrate the sun's energy to drive traditional steam turbines or engines that create electricity, and SMOG which is low-carbon energy ETF. Low carbon simply means less carbon dioxide (CO^2). Carbon dioxide is a key greenhouse gas that drives global climate change. The results of the annual returns of those sectors ETFs are summarized in Figure 2.

Figure 2 shows dominance of the solar energy ETF in most of the years, followed by the low-carbon ETF and the lowest return was produced by the examined wind energy ETF. The gap between those ETFs for the entire period was substantial. While TAN has achieved to investors an average yearly return of 58 percent, SMOG has achieved 36.6 percent and FAN only 22 percent. Considering investment risks, FAN monthly returns standard deviation for the entire period is the lowest (5.76) while the TAN is the larger (10.31) and SMOG is in between (7.13).

Figure 2. Green Energy Sectors ETFs Annual Returns
Note: FAN is a global wind energy ETF, TAN is solar energy ETF, and SMOG is low-carbon energy ETF.

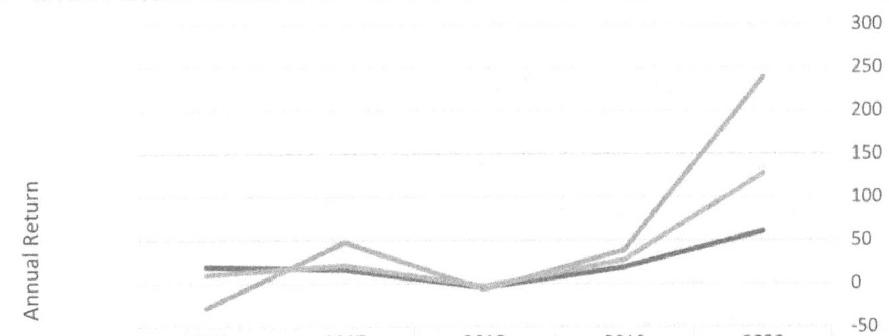

	2016	2017	2018	2019	2020
FAN	19.46	16.11	-4.57	18.68	60.3
TAN	-28.2	47.55	-6.41	38.44	238.4
SMOG	10.1	21.2	-2.91	27.12	127.7

FAN TAN SMOG

ESG Risks and Stocks Returns

The results of a research examined whether sustainability risks affect stocks returns. Our data is consisted of returns of 83 firms that belong to the NASDAQ 100 index from the beginning of 2016 till the end of April 2021, for which Sustainalytics [2] have calculated their ESG risk rating. The rating is consisted of three factors: E represents Environmental risks, S social risks and G Governance risks. According to Sustainalytics, *investors need tools that help them to identify material ESG risks within portfolio companies, understand the potential magnitude of the risk and enable them to compare companies across sectors*. Moreover, Sustainalytics' ESG risk ratings are designed to help investors identify and understand financially material ESG risks at the security and portfolio level and how they might affect the long-term performance for equity and fixed income investments. The ESG risk ratings measure the degree to which a company's economic value is at risk driven by ESG factors or, the magnitude of a company's unmanaged ESG risks.

In the following research it is examined that to what extent Environmental, Social and Governance risks influence excess return over the NASDAQ100 index. The purpose is to understand more about how sustainability risks are reflected in the capital market. It is found that from the three examined risks, the social risk is the most negatively influential factor on the stocks excess return. Moreover, it is found that in recent years the importance of the environmental risk increases. It is also observed that solar energy companies are preferred by investors followed by low-carbon energy production companies.

DATA, MODEL AND RESULTS

Our data contain returns from the beginning of January 2016 till the end of April 2021 for 83 companies that belong to the NASDAQ100 list for which Sustainalytics* has calaulate ESG rating that captures Enviromental, Social and Governance risks. The data ais collected for stock's systematic risk "Beta" factor and returns of three major ETFs that invest in alternative energy[3]. A company's ESG risk rating is comprised of a quantitative score and a risk category. The quantitative score represents units of unmanaged ESG risk with lower scores representing less unmanaged risk. Unmanaged Risk is measured on an open-ended scale starting at zero (no risk) and, for 95% of cases, a maximum score below 50. Based on their quantitative scores, companies are grouped into one of five risk categories (negligible, low, medium, high, severe). These risk categories are absolute, meaning that a 'high risk' assessment reflects a comparable degree of unmanaged ESG risk across all subindustries covered. This means that a bank, for example, can be directly compared with an oil company or any other type of company. Moreover, the ESG risk ratings, combined with qualitative analyses, provide a differentiated risk signal and deeper insights into the materiality of certain ESG issues for a company and what the company is or is not doing to manage them effectively. ESG Risk Ratings is that the world is transitioning to a more sustainable economy and that the effective management of ESG risks should, therefore, be associated with superior long-term enterprise value. For this reason, a negative correlation is expected between ESG risk rating particles and access retern of each company over the NASDAQ100 index. Moreover, our analysis will enable us to examin year by year shifts in investors state of mind towerds different sustainability risks by analysing their action in the financial market. Table 1 show descriptive statistics for our ESG risk rating applied to 83 of NASDAQ 100 stocks.

Table 1. Descriptive Statistics of ESG Risks Ratings of NASDAQ100 stocks

	E	S	G	Total
Averege	4.01	10.12	6.91	21
St.Dev	4.41	3.70	1.95	5.98
Max	19.3	20.3	12.4	35
Min	0	3.5	3.6	11

Notes: E is Environmental risks, S is Social risks and G is corporate Governance risks.

Table 1 shows that the total average score is 21 which represent a "Medium" sustainability risks for the NASDAQ100 examined stocks. Table 1 also show that the variability of the Environmental risk rating (E) is the highest among the three sustainability risks ratings. The analysis is started by examing whether the traditional systematic risk factor "Beta"[4] that captures the risk of an individual assets relativelly to market portfolio risks contains sustainability risks defines by the ESG risk rating. The model and its results are presented in Equations 1 and 2.

$$\beta Si = \beta_1 + \beta_2(Ei) + \beta_3(Si) + \beta_4(Gi) \tag{1}$$

Where: βSi=the "Beta" of stock *i*, *Ei*=Enviromental risk rating of stock *i*, *Si*=Social risk rating of stock *i*, *Gi*=Goverence risk rating of stock i.

$$\underset{Tstat}{\beta Si} = \underset{(6.27)}{0.93} + \underset{(0.70)}{0.01}\left(Ei\right) - \underset{(-2.32)}{0.02}\left(Si\right) + \underset{(2.08)}{0.04}\left(Gi\right) \tag{2}$$

$F=2.63$, $R^2=0.09$, $N=83$

Equation 2 show that the traditional "Beta" risk factor does not contain environmental risks, and it negatively related to social risks. The only risk that is positivelly related to the "Beta" is corportae goverence risks. Those results prove that this traditional systematic risk factor fails to capture environmental risk and social risks. The only risk that is enbeded in the "Beta" is corporate goverence risks. These results empesises the important of the ESG rating espechially the first two risk factors (E+S).

Multiple OLS[5] regression line (Model 3) is contructed which tests the impact of Environmental (E), Social (S) and Governence (G) on excess return over the NASDAQ 100 index. The NASDAQ 100 is used as a benchmark in order to neutralize the Covid 19 pandemic market crash and the volatility in the financial market that followed the pandemic. The model will also enable us to conclude which of the independent variables (ESG) affects significally the dependent variable (excess return) in each of the examined years. A negative correlation is expected between those risk factors and the calculated excess return. The result of Model 3 for the entire sample is described in Equation 4 and year by year in Table 2.

$$RSi - RN = \beta_1 + \beta_2(Ei) + \beta_3(Si) + \beta_4(Gi) \tag{3}$$

Where: *RSi – RN*= Excess return of stock *i* over the NASDAQ 100 index, *Ei*=Enviromental risk rating of stock *i*, *Si*=Social risk rating of stock *i*, *Gi*=Goverence risk rating of stock *i*.

$$\underset{Tstat}{RSi - RN} = \underset{(0.27)}{2.18} - \underset{(-0.57)}{0.25\left(Ei\right)} - \underset{(-2.89)}{1.64\left(Si\right)} + \underset{(2.29)}{2.44\left(Gi\right)} \quad (4)$$

F=3.33, R^2=0.14

Equation 4 demonstrates a negative significant impact of social risks and a positive impact of corporate governance risks on the firm's excess returns. No significant dependency has been spotted between environmental risks and excess returns. These results shed light on the priorities of investors. They value the most social issues and expect companies to treat fairly their workers, customers and other stakeholders. Environmental issues do not seems to influence investors when they decide upon their portfolio ingredients. Corporate governance risks which have been found to be embedded in the systematic risk factor influence positively on excess return, meaning that investors see those risk as legitimate corporate risk for which they can ask higher returns. It is interesting and important to examine Model 3 year by year to seek trends in investors attitudes towards ESG risks.

Table 2. Excess Returns and ESG Risk Rating

Year	β_1	$\beta_2(Ei)$	$\beta_3(Si)$	$\beta_4(Gi)$	F	R^2
2021^	9.16* (1.66)	0.28 (0.93)	-0.86** (-2.19)	-0.06 (-0.08)	2.60	0.09
2020	-68.24** (-2.52)	-0.25 (-0.16)	-0.90 (-0.46)	10.33** (2.83)	2.89	0.10
2019	(12.23) (0.91)	-0.01 (-0.01)	-1.80* (-1.88)	0.40 (0.22)	1.32	0.05
2018	13.50 (1.07)	-0.56 (-0.80)	0.42 (0.46)	-1.30 (-0.77)	0.44	0.02
2017	22.39* (1.78)	-1.17* (-1.70)	-3.30** (-3.36)	2.18 (1.29)	4.95	0.16
2016	22.85 (1.31)	0.41 (0.42)	-3.37** (-2.70)	3.09 (1.32)	2.66	0.09

Notes: *RSi – RN*= Excess return of stock i over the NASDAQ 100 index, *Ei*=Environmental risk rating of stock i, *Si*=Social risk rating of stock i, *Gi*=Governance risk rating of stock i. the numbers in the brackets are T statistics. * significant at 90% significance level, ** significant at 95% significance level.^ the data for 2021 is until the end of April 2021.

Table 2 shows that Environmental risk rating (E) was found to be significantly negatively correlated to excess return only at 2017 while social risk rating (S) was significantly negatively related to excess returns for 2016, 2017, 2019 and 2021[6]. Moreover the corporate governance risk rating (G) was found to be positively correlated to excess return at 2020 meaning that governance risk improved returns but not vice versa. These results point out that investors take into considerations mostly social risks and less environmental or governance risks. These results stress the need for other economic incentives that should be used by governments to encourage corporation to be more environmental friendly rather than to expect the financial market to punish undesired corporate environmental behavior. These measures can be tangible for example tax on pollution of water or air sources or intangible such as a campaign against polluting companies

Data is bifurcated into two bundles according to each ESG rating. The first bundle holds ten the stocks with the highest E risk rating and the second bundle contains ten stocks with the lowest E rating. For each bundle, average excess return is calculated over the NASDAQ100 index. This process is also repreated for S risk rating and G risk rating. The results are presented in Figures 3 to 5.

Figure 3. Environmental Risks and Excess Returns
Note: Excess return is the annual average stocks return minus NASDAQ100 annual return

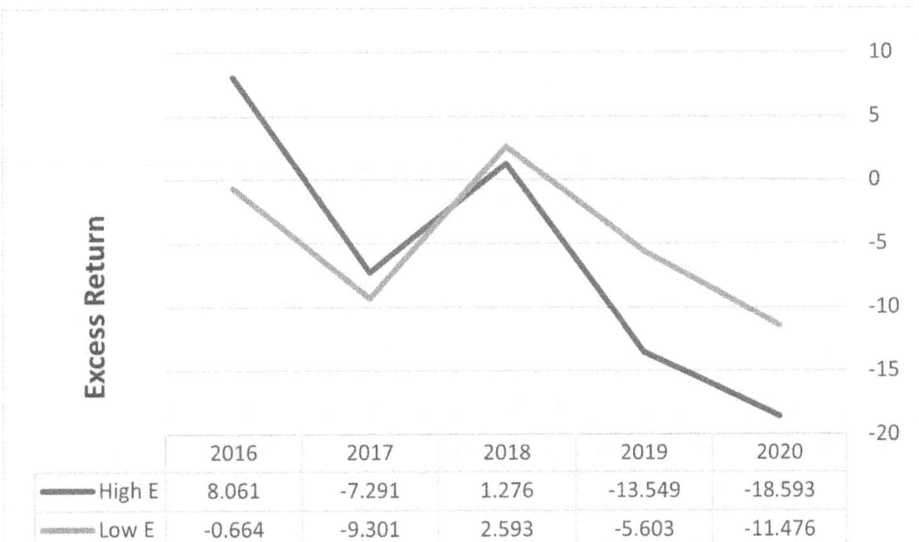

Figure 3 shows that until 2017 the high E risk bundle has produced higher excess returns than the low E risk bundle. However since 2018 and on the opposite has occurred when investors have started to punish companies that caused environmental hazareds.

Figure 4 demonstrates inconsistency in the impact of social risks on both bundles (high S and Low S). At three of the five examined years, the low S risks bundle has produced higher excess returns while at the other two years, the lower S risk bundle has achieved higher excess returns. It is worth reminding here that S risks was demonstrated in Table 2 as the risk factor that effected negatively stock's excess returns.

Figure 4. Social Risks and Excess Returns

Note: Excess return is the annual average stocks return minus NASDAQ100 annual return

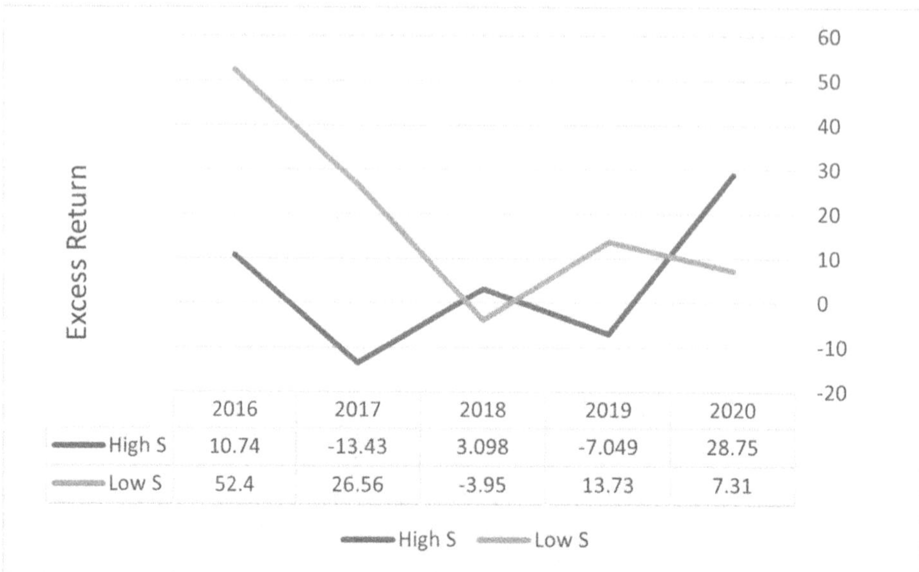

Figure 5 shows that the high G risks bundle has achieved higher excess returns at four out of the five examined years. Those finding show and those summarized in Table 2 prove that G risks does not negatively affects excess returns.

Figure 5. Governance Risks and Excess Returns
Note: Excess return is the annual average stocks return minus NASDAQ100 annual return

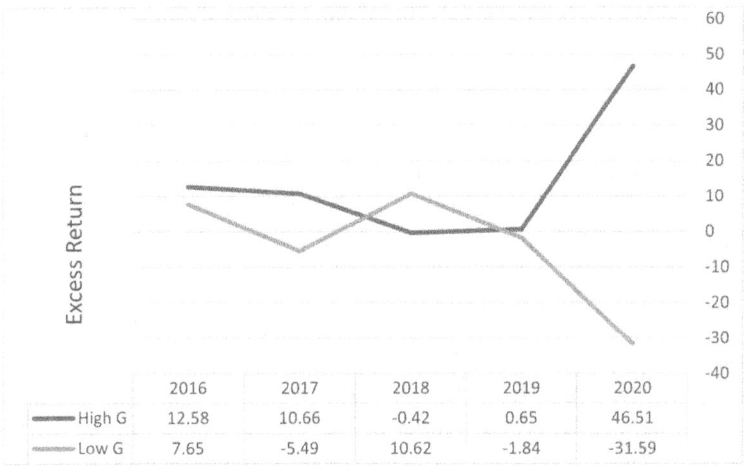

DISCUSSIONS AND IMPLICATIONS

In this study, it is examined that to what extent investors take into their consideration the sustainability risks of three different nature: environmental, social, and corporate governance. Moreover, it is examined that what kind of green energy companies seems most attractive to investors in recent years. It is found that while environmental risks negatively affect excess returns in some years. However, since 2018 investors value environmental risks and punish companies that their activities harm the environment with relatively low returns. Social risks were found to be the most influential factor negatively related to excess returns. This result light the importance of social risks to the valuation of a stock in the capital market. Shareholder that seeks to maximize their share value, should address organizational social issues, and invest funds and other resources to ensure that social risks are mitigated. Corporate governance risks have been found to be embedded in the traditional systematic risk factor “Beta”, but no evidence have been found for negative correlations between corporate governance risks and stock’s excess returns. Examining six green energy ETFs returns in recent years and comparing them to the NASDAQ returns it is found that green energy ETFs have achieved to investors substantial higher return compared to the NASDAQ returns. However, those returns are associated with higher risk that is, in our view, sourced by the disruptive innovative nature of that industry. It is also observed that solar energy companies have achieved the highest returns, followed by low-carbon and wind energy producers. Those result can insinuate that investors value the most solar energy production method as the most cost effective green anergy production technique. The implications of this study are enormous they first wave a stop sign to companies that conduct their businesses without any ESG considerations, stating clearly that such manner will eventually harm shareholders with diminishing share values. Second, this research can serve as guideline to firms to the enormous importance that investors attribute to the way they treat their work force in order to produce products in an exploiting and sometime inhuman manner. Third, these results also stress the need for other economic incetives that should be used by governments to encourage corporation to be more environmental friendly rather than to expect the financial market to punish undesired corporate environmental behavior. These measures can be tangible for example tax on pollution of water or air sources or intangible such as a campaign against polluting companies. The world is advancing to a better ESG managerial approach and companies that will adopt this approach will benefit from higher respect of their surrounding stakeholders including customers, workers, shareholders, and the entire public. Future studies should continue to monitor the influence of ESG risks on the financial market and can also integrate countries comparison.

DISCLAIMER

The contents and views of this chapter are expressed by the author in his personal capacity. It is not necessary for the Editor and the Publisher to agree with these viewpoints and they are not responsible for any duty of care in this regard.

ACKNOWLEDGMENT

The author extends sincere gratitude to

- The Editor and the International Editorial Advisory Board (IEAB) of this book who initially desk reviewed, arranged a rigorous double/triple blind review process and conducted a thorough, minute and critical final review before accepting the chapter for publication.
- All anonymous reviewers who provided very constructive feedbacks for thorough revision, improvement, extension and fine tuning of the chapter.
- All colleagues, assistants and well-wishers who assisted the authors to complete this task.

REFERENCES

Baohua, L., Sun, P. Y., & Zeng, Y. (2020). Employee-related corporate social responsibilities and corporate innovation: Evidence from China. *International Review of Economics & Finance*, *70*, 357–372. doi:10.1016/j.iref.2020.07.008

Eccles, R., Ioannou, I., & Serafeim, G. (2012, January 6). Is sustainability now the key to corporate success? *The Guardian*. Retrieved from https://www.theguardian.com/sustainable-business/sustainability-key-corporate-success

Elkington, J. (1997). *Cannibals with Forks: The Triple Bottom Line of 21st Century Business*. Capstone Publishing Ltd.

Garcia, A. S., Mendes-Da-Silva, W., & Orsato, R. J. (2019). Corporate sustainability, capital markets, and ESG performance. In W. Mendes-Da-Silva (Ed.), *Individual Behaviors and Technologies for Financial Innovations*. Springer. doi:10.1007/978-3-319-91911-9_13

Georg, L. (2017). Information security governance: Pending legal responsibilities of non-executive boards. *The Journal of Management and Governance*, *21*(4), 793–814. doi:10.100710997-016-9358-0

Kawaguchi, M. (2017, June 6). *The Evolution of ESG Investing: from Ethical Concern to Corporate value*. The Tokyo Foundation for Policy Research. Retrieved from https://www.tkfd.or.jp/en/research/detail.php?id=407

Lee, D. D., Faff, R. W., & Rekker, S. A. C. (2013). Do high and low-ranked sustainability stocks perform differently? *International Journal of Accounting & Information Management*, *21*(2), 116–132. doi:10.1108/18347641311312267

Li, Z., Liao, G., & Albitar, K. (2020). Does corporate environmental responsibility engagement affect firm value? The mediating role of corporate innovation. *Business Strategy and the Environment*, *29*(3), 1045–1055. doi:10.1002/bse.2416

Lo, S. F. (2010). Performance Evaluation for Sustainable Business: A Profitability and Marketability Framework. *Corporate Social Responsibility and Environmental Management*, *17*(6), 311–319. doi:10.1002/csr.214

Montiel, I. (2008). Corporate social responsibility and corporate sustainability: Separate pasts, common futures. *Organization & Environment*, *21*(3), 245–269. doi:10.1177/1086026608321329

Morioka, S. N., Bolis, I., & Carvalho, M. M. (2018). From an ideal dream towards reality analysis: Proposing Sustainable Value Exchange Matrix (SVEM) from systematic literature review on sustainable business models and face validation. *Journal of Cleaner Production*, *178*, 76–88. doi:10.1016/j.jclepro.2017.12.078

Morioka, S. N., Bolis, I., Evans, S., & Carvalho, M. M. (2017). Transforming sustainability challenges into competitive advantage: Multiple case studies kaleidoscope converging into sustainable business models. *Journal of Cleaner Production*, *167*, 723–738. doi:10.1016/j.jclepro.2017.08.118

Nizam, E., Ng, A., Dewandaru, G., Nagayev, R., & Nkoba, M. A. (2019). The impact of social and environmental sustainability on financial performance: A global analysis of the banking sector. *Journal of Multinational Financial Management*, *49*, 35–53. doi:10.1016/j.mulfin.2019.01.002

Ortiz-de-Mandojana, N., & Bansal, P. (2016). The long-term benefits of organizational resilience through sustainable business practices. *Strategic Management Journal*, *37*(8), 1615–1631. doi:10.1002mj.2410

Rafay, A. (2022). *Handbook of Research on Energy and Environmental Finance 4.0*. IGI Global. doi:10.4018/978-1-7998-8210-7

Schaltegger, S., Beckmann, M., & Hansen, E. G. (2013). Transdisciplinary in corporate sustainability: Mapping the field. *Business Strategy and the Environment*, *22*(4), 219–229. doi:10.1002/bse.1772

Schönherr, N., Findler, F., & Martinuzzi, A. (2017). Exploring the interface of CSR and the sustainable development goals. *Transnational Corporations*, *24*(3), 33–47. doi:10.18356/cfb5b8b6-en

Schramade, W. (2017). Investing in the UN Sustainable Development Goals: Opportunities for Companies and Investors. *Journal of Applied Corporate Finance*, *29*(2), 87–99. doi:10.1111/jacf.12236

Topple, C., Donovan, J. D., Masli, E. K., & Borgert, T. (2017). Corporate sustainability assessments: MNE engagement with sustainable development and the SDGs. *Transnational Corporations*, *24*(3), 61–71. doi:10.18356/2ae5911c-en

ENDNOTES

1 https://sustainabledevelopment.un.org/content/documents/5987our-common-future.pdf

2 https://www.sustainalytics.com/

3 Provided by finance.yahoo.com.

4 The "Beta" was provided by Finance.yahoo.com and it was calculated using five years monthly data.

5 OLS =Ordinary least square.

6 The data for 2021 is untill the end of April 2021

Chapter 10
Crowdfunding for Sustainable Utilities Tunnel Projects:
The Case of China

Feng Sun
South China Normal University, China

Tayo Oke
Afe Babalola University, Nigeria

Marie G. Nakitende
Uganda Martyrs University, Uganda

ABSTRACT

G-S interactive finance framework is the ideal one to enhance the success rate and efficiency of utilities tunnel projects. Government/non-profit organizations/individuals (G part) and profitable social organizations/individuals (S part) are the counterparties to the G-S interactive finance framework. Utilities tunnel projects flexibly select one funding model or several funding modes to maximize the management revenue. Choice of suitable funding mode (like debt funding, equity funding, internet finance) is important to acquire enough construction capital for these types of projects. According to the number of investors, size of the financing, financing tenure, and finance procedure convenience, every funding mode has its own special character, usage, scope, and procedure. This chapter explores crowdfunding pledging analysis for these types of projects. Small projects of utilities tunnels can use crowdfunding mode, and big projects of utilities tunnels can use crowdfunding mode gradually.

DOI: 10.4018/978-1-6684-5580-7.ch010

INTRODUCTION

Utilities tunnel projects have been rapidly constructed and developed in China. These projects have made great contribution to the working and living of the people in cities. Rational finance design and funding mode will improve the construction and operation for utilities tunnel projects. This chapter uses G-S interactive finance framework to analyze the fulfillment of utilities tunnel projects and their funding modes in China and gives an exploratory crowdfunding analysis for the fulfillment of utilities tunnel project.

This chapter first analyzes non-profitable government and other organizations or individuals (G part) and profitable social organizations or individuals (S part) to construct and operate utilities tunnel project together. A framework of G-S interactive finance is used to give exact analysis for the construction and operation of utilities tunnel project in China. The cooperation between G part and S part increases the successful rate and efficiency. G part and S part can flexibly adopt many different styles such as franchise BOT (build-operate-transfer). Government organizations will give this project to social companies to design, construct and operate in certain franchise period. When franchise period is over, social companies will transfer utilities tunnel project to government with no returns. All life cycle management can be used to increase the efficiency of utilities tunnel project. In all life cycle management mode, the design, construction, operation and supervision are managed together to fully make use of every stage's character and to balance every stage's development to realize high efficiency running and economic revenue.

Second, this chapter introduces several funding modes for utilities tunnel project, including bank loan, bond, equity, securities fund and Internet finance funding modes in China, which are helpful to acquire enough construction capital timely and efficiently. Every funding mode has its special character and usage scope and procedure, and the advantage of every funding mode should be fulfilled for utilities tunnel project. According to project scale, geography location, construction cost and operation management, these funding modes have different management requirements and procedures. Utilities tunnel project should flexibly select one funding mode or several funding modes to maximize the management revenue. All funding modes should be satisfied with the lowest weighted capital cost. Finance risks probably produced by all kinds of funding modes should be fully considered, and the risk that is unable to get the capital timely and the risk that is unable to repay finance capital should be avoided.

Third, this chapter gives an exploratory crowdfunding pledging analysis for fulfillment of utilities tunnel. Crowdfunding projects are fulfilled on Internet platform, and founders pose project introduction on this platform and backers supply pledged capital also on this platform. The management of crowdfunding platform usually includes "All-or-Nothing" and "Keep-it-All" two types. One utilities tunnel project should choose suitable type of crowdfunding platform to fulfill. Utilities tunnel project can use crowdfunding to increase funding modes besides traditional debt and equity funding modes and can use flexible crowdfunding strategy and procedure to fulfill. Crowdfunding mode can be flexibly used to pledge construction capital in middle and small utilities tunnel projects now.

This chapter contributes to the literature mainly in the following points. First, it gives an exploratory pledging analysis for crowdfunding mode in utilities tunnel project. To the best of the author's knowledge, this chapter is the first to give analysis on crowdfunding mode used in utilities tunnel project. Second, it uses non-profitable organizations or individuals, profitable social companies and profitable other social organizations or individuals to analyze the finance bodies for the construction and operation of utilities tunnel project. Third, it uses G-S interactive finance framework to analyze the process and character of bank loan, bond, equity and other funding modes for utilities tunnel project.

BACKGROUND

The construction for utilities tunnel belongs to an important part in urban underground space construction. By constructing corridor in some depth underground, water supply and drainage, electric power, telecommunication, gas, rubbish and other pipelines are laid inside the tunnel. These pipelines can be constructed and maintained together to make full use of resource and to decrease cost expenditure. Utilities tunnel is a complicated engineering project with large scale, including underground space technology, engineering design, construction, pipeline technology, operation management etc. So, its design and construction involve with many engineering fields, whose cooperation and management are necessary for the successful fulfillment of utilities tunnel project.

Different with traditional pipeline "open-cut" operation style, utilities tunnel has many advantages. First, it can avoid resource wasting and inconvenience to society, because traditional open-cut style need dig the ground many times. Bad pipelines need to be taken out from underground and new pipelines need to be laid inside, which can create traffic problem for maintenance. Second, it can decrease safety questions and can repair timely for pipeline obstacle. For traditional style, some pipelines such as electric lines in the air can create safety problem and are not good for municipal appearance, and a lot of maintenance time will be wasted to solve pipeline obstacle (Canto-Perello *et al.*, 2013; Phillips, 2016; Zhang *et al.*, 2019). Third, utilities tunnel usually has long term operation and usage period, and this will improve the sustainable development level of cities and update of total municipal functions.

After long term research and improvement, the technology for utilities tunnel is very mature and many countries have constructed tunnel projects, which are widely used for pipeline construction and energy transportation (Canto-Perello *et al.*, 2016; Goel, 2001; Hulme & Burchell, 1999; Legrand *et al.*, 2004; Yan *et al.*, 2021). The utilities tunnel kilometers per thousand people in some cities are: Stockholm 2.1, Tokyo 2, Osaka 2, Madrid 1.6, Taiwan 1.3, Moscow 1.2, China 0.24 (Yang & Peng, 2016). Utilities tunnel will have a wide development prospect in the future accompanying with the rapid construction of cities in the world.

Engineering projects for utilities tunnels are generally fulfilled as public projects in China. Because their constructions need large scale cost expenditure, and these projects belong to urban management infrastructure, the local governments often take part in the construction and management. The characters of utilities tunnel projects are non-competitiveness and exclusiveness. Non-competitiveness means that one pipeline using unit won't affect the usage of another pipeline using unit and many pipeline using units can share one or more tunnel pipelines. Exclusiveness means that managing unit for utilities tunnel public project can charge to pipeline using units and can exclude those pipeline using units if they don't pay the fee.

Because of quasi-public goods attributes for utilities tunnel public project in China, it can't allocate resources individually by market mechanism, which belongs to a field of market failure. There is seldom one company can afford the high-cost expenditure of utilities tunnel, and the local government often gives much bonus for the construction of utilities tunnel infrastructure. The supply of quasi-public goods for utilities tunnel should be mainly guided by government sector. Government sector should macroscopically adjust and control resources allocation to fulfill the function and efficiency for utilities tunnel public project.

This chapter uses G-S interactive finance framework to analyze utilities tunnel projects and their funding modes in China and gives an exploratory crowdfunding pledging analysis for fulfillment of utilities tunnel project.[1] China's fulfillment and practice for utilities tunnel project can give useful experiences for other countries to construct and operate utilities tunnel.

Crowdfunding is a new type of Internet funding tool, whose character is that the capital can be pledged from many backers with the advantage of Internet platform, and it can supply pledged capital to project founder in short time (Baber, 2020). Project founder poses project introduction on Internet platform, and backers select suitable and different crowdfunding projects to supply pledged capital on the basis of project introduction posed by founder (Husin & Haron, 2020).

Crowdfunding mode is seldom used in engineering projects now. The first crowdfunding photovoltaic project is Mosaic Solar House Roof for crowdfunding mode in US in 2011, which has pledged 600 thousand dollars and has engineering design for 18MW. The first crowdfunding photovoltaic project in China is built in 2014, which has pledged 10 million RMB and has engineering design for 1MW.

MAIN FOCUS OF THE CHAPTER

G-S Interactive Finance Framework for Utilities Tunnel Public Project in China

Analysis of G-S Interactive Finance Framework for Utilities Tunnel

Generally, there are three finance types for utilities tunnel project. First, all the construction and operation finance are supported only by non-profitable organizations or individuals. Second, all the construction and operation finance are supported only by profitable organizations or individuals. Third, all the construction and operation finance are supported by non-profitable organizations or individuals and profitable organizations or individuals together (Sun *et al.*, 2017).

Because of the attribute of public infrastructure, these quasi-public goods can be supplied individually by government sector, and their costs can be spent from government finance incomes. They can also be supplied by cooperation of government sector and social capital. In this mode, government sector should mainly guide and social capital should cooperate. Because utilities tunnel has big scale construction, high investment amount and long recycle period, it will create much finance expenditure pressure to government sector if government sector affords total investment individually. In addition, because of information asymmetry, the government hasn't the complete information and knowledge for the construction and management of utilities tunnel. This is not good to timely supply the public project, so government sector and social capital should supply utilities tunnel public project together in China.

In reality, non-profitable government organizations, other organizations or individuals (G part) and profitable social organizations or individuals (S part) usually construct and operate utilities tunnel together. In China, the project is mainly fulfilled by non-profitable government sector and profitable social companies.

Government sector and social companies can design rational G-S interactive finance framework to acquire high efficiency and good economic revenue. G-S interactive finance framework is a new type of analysis angle for utilities tunnel project (Sun *et al.*, 2017). It analyzes the finance design from the cooperation between non-profitable organizations or individuals and profitable organizations or individuals. This chapter uses G-S interactive finance framework to analyze finance design, construction and operation, and investment revenue of government organizations and social companies for utilities tunnel public project in China. This chapter uses non-profitable organizations or individuals, profitable social companies and profitable other social organizations or individuals to analyze the finance bodies from another angle. Profitable social companies manage the construction and operation for the public project to make a living, and they have abundant technology and management experiences for project (Rafay, 2019). Profitable other social organizations or individuals take part in the project only as an investment way.

Assume during construction period for the public project of utilities tunnel in China, the financial capital is from $i(i=1,2,\ldots,n_G)$ non-profitable government organizations(other non-profitable organizations or individuals can also be included in G part), and *No.i* government organization invests $I_{Gi}(I_{Gi}>0)$. The financial capital is also from $j_1(j_1=1,2,\ldots,n_{s1})$ profitable social companies and from $j_2(j_2=1,2,\ldots,n_{s2})$ other profitable social organizations or individuals. *No.*j_1 social company invests I_{Sj_1}, and *No.*j_2 other social organization or individual invests $I_{Sj_2}\left(I_{Sj_1}>0, I_{Sj_2}\geq 0\right)$. $I_{Sj_2}=0$ means *No.*j_2 other social organization or individual doesn't invest, and the public project is supplied by government organizations and social companies.

During construction period, the finance weights of G part and S part(ω_{S1} is social companies, and ω_{S2} is other social organizations or individuals) are:

$$\omega_G=\frac{\sum_{i=1}^{n_G} I_{Gi}}{\sum_{i=1}^{n_G} I_{Gi}+\sum_{j_1=1}^{n_{s1}} I_{Sj_1}+\sum_{j_2=1}^{n_{s2}} I_{Sj_2}} \quad (0<\omega_G<1) \tag{1}$$

$$\omega_{S1}=\frac{\sum_{j_1=1}^{n_{s1}} I_{Sj_1}}{\sum_{i=1}^{n_G} I_{Gi}+\sum_{j_1=1}^{n_{s1}} I_{Sj1}+\sum_{j_2=1}^{n_{s2}} I_{Sj2}} \quad (0<\omega_{S1}<1) \tag{2}$$

$$\omega_{S2}=\frac{\sum_{j_2=1}^{n_{s2}} I_{Sj2}}{\sum_{i=1}^{n_G} I_{Gi}+\sum_{j_1=1}^{n_{s1}} I_{Sj1}+\sum_{j_2=1}^{n_{s2}} I_{Sj2}} \quad (0\leq\omega_{S2}<1,\ \omega_G+\omega_{S1}+\omega_{S2}=1). \tag{3}$$

Operation period is usually long for several decades and assume there are T_γ periods (γ=1,2,…,m). During T_γ period, *No.i* government organization invests F_{GiT_γ} $(F_{GiT_\gamma} \geq 0)$. *No.j*$_1$ social company and *No.j*$_2$ social organization or individual invest $F_{Sj_1T_\gamma}$ and $F_{Sj_2T_\gamma}$ respectively $(F_{Sj_1T_\gamma} \geq 0, F_{Sj_2T_\gamma} \geq 0)$. The capital discount rate is R_{T_γ}. Assume that P and Q_{T_γ} are service price and service number of utilities tunnel. C_{XT_γ} and C_{YT_γ} are fixed cost and varying cost.

Then the net revenue of utilities tunnel is revenue minus cost $B_{T_\gamma} - C_{T_\gamma}$:

$$B_{T_\gamma} - C_{T_\gamma} = (P - C_{YT_\gamma})Q_{T_\gamma} + \sum_{i=1}^{n_G} F_{GiT_\gamma} + \sum_{j_1=1}^{n_{s1}} F_{Sj_1T_\gamma} + \sum_{j_2=1}^{n_{s2}} F_{Sj_2T_\gamma} - C_{XT_\gamma}. \tag{4}$$

Assume that net revenue is continuous distribution function among interval $[a_{T_\gamma}, b_{T_\gamma}]$, and $f(\bullet)$ is probability density function. Then cumulative probability distribution function is:

$$F(X_{T_\gamma}) = P(X \leq X_{T_\gamma}) = \int_{a_{T_\gamma}}^{X_{T_\gamma}} f(X)dX. \tag{5}$$

$$F(X_{T_\gamma}) \in [0,1] \tag{6}$$

Net revenue expectation is:

$$\begin{aligned} E(B_{T_\gamma} - C_{T_\gamma}) = \int_{a_{T_\gamma}}^{b_{T_\gamma}} [(P - C_{YT_\gamma})Q_{T_\gamma} + \sum_{i=1}^{n_G} F_{GiT_\gamma} + \sum_{j_1=1}^{n_{s1}} F_{Sj_1T_\gamma} + \sum_{j_2=1}^{n_{s2}} F_{Sj_2T_\gamma} - C_{XT_\gamma}]f((P - C_{YT_\gamma})Q_{T_\gamma} \\ + \sum_{i=1}^{n_G} F_{GiT_\gamma} + \sum_{j_1=1}^{n_{s1}} F_{Sj_1T_\gamma} + \sum_{j_2=1}^{n_{s2}} F_{Sj_2T_\gamma} - C_{XT_\gamma})d((P - C_{YT_\gamma})Q_{T_\gamma} + \sum_{i=1}^{n_G} F_{GiT_\gamma} + \sum_{j_1=1}^{n_{s1}} F_{Sj_1T_\gamma} \\ + \sum_{j_2=1}^{n_{s2}} F_{Sj_2T_\gamma} - C_{XT_\gamma}) = \int_{a_{T_\gamma}}^{b_{T_\gamma}} (B_{T_\gamma} - C_{T_\gamma})f(B_{T_\gamma} - C_{T_\gamma})d(B_{T_\gamma} - C_{T_\gamma}). \end{aligned} \tag{7}$$

Net revenue variance is:

$$V(B_{T_\gamma} - C_{T_\gamma}) = E(B_{T_\gamma} - C_{T_\gamma} - \int_{a_{T_\gamma}}^{b_{T_\gamma}} (B_{T_\gamma} - C_{T_\gamma})f(B_{T_\gamma} - C_{T_\gamma})d(B_{T_\gamma} - C_{T_\gamma}))^2. \tag{8}$$

If:

$$f(B_{T_\gamma} - C_{T_\gamma}) = e^{-(B_{T_\gamma} - C_{T_\gamma})^2/2} / \sqrt{2\pi} \tag{9}$$

The net revenue is satisfied with standard normal distribution.

For one utilities tunnel public project, government organizations and social companies should cooperate and adopt rational management measures to increase net revenue expectation $E(B_{T_\gamma} - C_{T_\gamma})$.[2] To acquire stable net revenue, government organizations and social companies should adopt rational measures to decrease the variance $V(B_{T_\gamma} - C_{T_\gamma})$.

On the one hand, pipeline using units are charged for the usage of utilities tunnel, and there are different types of charge, which constitute main parts of revenue B_{T_γ} of utilities tunnel. The charge number can be decided according to the area of pipeline cross section, and pipeline using units should pay more for the more section area. The charge number can also be decided according to the occupied space in utilities tunnel by pipeline using units, and pipeline using units should pay more for the more occupied space. Rational charge procedure should be designed to increase the revenue B_{T_γ} of utilities tunnel. On the other hand, there are maintenance and management cost for utilities tunnel during operation period, and rational measures should be adopted to decrease cost expenditure C_{T_γ}.

To measure volatility risk and find out abnormal risk periods for utilities tunnel public project, the varying coefficient should be used. The absolute value of varying coefficient can be computed as follows:

$$VC_{T_\gamma} = \left| \frac{V(B_{T_\gamma} - C_{T_\gamma})}{E(B_{T_\gamma} - C_{T_\gamma})} \right|. \tag{10}$$

If VC_{T_γ} value is high in one period, it shows the volatility risk is big in this period. Government organizations and social companies should analyze and find out the influence factors to create so high VC_{T_γ} value. To acquire stable revenue flowing, government organizations and social companies need use some measures to decrease the high VC_{T_γ}. The risks of utilities tunnel projects include construction, operation and funding risks, etc. Wu *et al.* (2021) propose an integrated model based on dynamic hazard scenario identification (DHSI), Bayesian network (BN) modeling and risk analysis for risk assessment of urban utilities tunnel.

The total revenue W for utilities tunnel during construction period and operation period is:

$$W = \sum_{\gamma=1}^{m} \frac{\int_{a_{T_\gamma}}^{b_{T_\gamma}} (B_{T_\gamma} - C_{T_\gamma}) f(B_{T_\gamma} - C_{T_\gamma}) d(B_{T_\gamma} - C_{T_\gamma})}{(1 + R_{T_\gamma})^{\gamma}} - \sum_{i=1}^{n_G} I_{Gi} - \sum_{j_1=1}^{n_{s1}} I_{Sj_1} - \sum_{j_2=1}^{n_{s2}} I_{Sj_2} \cdot \tag{11}$$

Assume that $Q=F(P)$. Then extreme optimal solution P^* for utilities tunnel is satisfied with:

$$\frac{\partial W}{\partial P} = [\sum_{\gamma=1}^{m} \frac{\int_{a_{T_\gamma}}^{b_{T_\gamma}} (B_{T_\gamma} - C_{T_\gamma}) f(B_{T_\gamma} - C_{T_\gamma}) d(B_{T_\gamma} - C_{T_\gamma})}{(1 + R_{T_\gamma})^{\gamma}} - \sum_{i=1}^{n_G} I_{Gi} - \sum_{j_1=1}^{n_{s1}} I_{Sj_1} - \sum_{j_2=1}^{n_{s2}} I_{Sj_2}] \Bigg|_P^{/} = 0 \cdot \tag{12}$$

Extreme optimal solution Q^* is satisfied with:

$$\frac{\partial W}{\partial Q} = [\sum_{\gamma=1}^{m} \frac{\int_{a_{T_\gamma}}^{b_{T_\gamma}} (B_{T_\gamma} - C_{T_\gamma}) f(B_{T_\gamma} - C_{T_\gamma}) d(B_{T_\gamma} - C_{T_\gamma})}{(1 + R_{T_\gamma})^{\gamma}} - \sum_{i=1}^{n_G} I_{Gi} - \sum_{j_1=1}^{n_{s1}} I_{Sj_1} - \sum_{j_2=1}^{n_{s2}} I_{Sj_2}] \Bigg|_Q^{/}$$

$$= [\sum_{\gamma=1}^{m} \frac{\int_{a_{T_\gamma}}^{b_{T_\gamma}} (B_{T_\gamma} - C_{T_\gamma}) f(B_{T_\gamma} - C_{T_\gamma}) d(B_{T_\gamma} - C_{T_\gamma})}{(1 + R_{T_\gamma})^{\gamma}} - \sum_{i=1}^{n_G} I_{Gi} - \sum_{j_1=1}^{n_{s1}} I_{Sj_1} - \sum_{j_2=1}^{n_{s2}} I_{Sj_2}] \Bigg|_P^{/} [F^{-1}(Q)]^{/} = 0. \tag{13}$$

During T_γ period, *No.i* government organization gets revenue D_{GiT_γ}, and *No.*j_1 social company and *No.*j_2 other social organization or individual get revenue $D_{Sj_1T_\gamma}$ and $D_{Sj_2T_\gamma}$. Then the revenue proportions of government organizations and social companies are:

$$\omega_{G_{T_\gamma}} = \frac{\sum_{\gamma=1}^{m}\sum_{i=1}^{n_G} D_{GiT_\gamma} / (1+R_{T_\gamma})^\gamma}{\sum_{\gamma=1}^{m}\sum_{i=1}^{n_G} D_{GiT_\gamma} / (1+R_{T_\gamma})^\gamma + \sum_{\gamma=1}^{m}\sum_{j_1=1}^{n_{s1}} D_{Sj_1T_\gamma} / (1+R_{T_\gamma})^\gamma + \sum_{\gamma=1}^{m}\sum_{j_2=1}^{n_{s2}} D_{Sj_2T_\gamma} / (1+R_{T_\gamma})^\gamma} \tag{14}$$

$$\omega_{S_{1T_\gamma}} = \frac{\sum_{\gamma=1}^{m}\sum_{j_1=1}^{n_{s1}} D_{Sj_1T_\gamma} / (1+R_{T_\gamma})^\gamma}{\sum_{\gamma=1}^{m}\sum_{i=1}^{n_G} D_{GiT_\gamma} / (1+R_{T_\gamma})^\gamma + \sum_{\gamma=1}^{m}\sum_{j_1=1}^{n_{s1}} D_{Sj_1T_\gamma} / (1+R_{T_\gamma})^\gamma + \sum_{\gamma=1}^{m}\sum_{j_2=1}^{n_{s2}} D_{Sj_2T_\gamma} / (1+R_{T_\gamma})^\gamma}. \tag{15}$$

The investment revenue H_G of government organizations and the investment revenue H_{S1} and H_{S2} of social companies and other social organizations or individuals are:

$$H_G = \sum_{\gamma=1}^{m}\sum_{i=1}^{n_G} \frac{D_{GiT_\gamma}}{(1+R_{T_\gamma})^\gamma} / \left(\sum_{i=1}^{n_G} I_{Gi} + \sum_{\gamma=1}^{m}\sum_{i=1}^{n_G} \frac{F_{GiT_\gamma}}{(1+R_{T_\gamma})^\gamma}\right) \tag{16}$$

$$H_{S1} = \sum_{\gamma=1}^{m}\sum_{j_1=1}^{n_{s1}} \frac{D_{Sj_1T_\gamma}}{(1+R_{T_\gamma})^\gamma} / \left(\sum_{j_1=1}^{n_{s1}} I_{Sj_1} + \sum_{\gamma=1}^{m}\sum_{j_1=1}^{n_{s1}} \frac{F_{Sj_1T_\gamma}}{(1+R_{T_\gamma})^\gamma}\right) \tag{17}$$

$$H_{S2} = \sum_{\gamma=1}^{m}\sum_{j_2=1}^{n_{s2}} \frac{D_{Sj_2T_\gamma}}{(1+R_{T_\gamma})^\gamma} / \left(\sum_{j_2=1}^{n_{s2}} I_{Sj_2} + \sum_{\gamma=1}^{m}\sum_{j_2=1}^{n_{s2}} \frac{F_{Sj_2T_\gamma}}{(1+R_{T_\gamma})^\gamma}\right) \tag{18}$$

$$H_{S1} > H_{S2}. \tag{19}$$

The investment revenue H_{Gi} of *No.i* government organization and the investment revenue H_{Sj_1} of $No.j_1$ social company are:

$$H_{Gi} = \sum_{\gamma=1}^{m} \frac{D_{GiT_\gamma}}{(1+R_{T_\gamma})^\gamma} / \left(I_{Gi} + \sum_{\gamma=1}^{m} \frac{F_{GiT_\gamma}}{(1+R_{T_\gamma})^\gamma}\right) \tag{20}$$

$$H_{Sj_1} = \sum_{\gamma=1}^{m} \frac{D_{Sj_1T_\gamma}}{(1+R_{T_\gamma})^\gamma} / (I_{Sj_1} + \sum_{\gamma=1}^{m} \frac{F_{Sj_1T_\gamma}}{(1+R_{T_\gamma})^\gamma}). \tag{21}$$

The main character of G-S interactive finance framework for utilities tunnel public project in China is listed in Table 1.

Operation and Management for Utilities Tunnel Public Project in China

The first Chinese utilities tunnel public project was built in Beijing in 1958. The public projects were built with big scale in the early stage of 21 century. According to data statistics, 69 cities in China began to construct utilities tunnel public projects about 1,000 kilometers in 2015. Its total investment was about 88 billion RMB. The utilities tunnel public projects length was rapidly developed to about 6,600 kilometers until December 2017. In the future, the planning construction length will surpass 30,000 kilometers in China, and its total investment will arrive at 1,800 billion RMB. Utilities tunnel public projects will be built in many cities in China, e.g., utilities tunnel length in Beijing is between 150 and 200 kilometers until 2020.

Among plans of city construction, the new main roads and new industrial parks should construct utilities tunnel projects in the future (Wang, 2016). China government pays more attention to construct infrastructure in cities, and construction and operation for utilities tunnel public projects will be developed in more cities. Utilities tunnel public projects will have wide development prospect in China.

Utilities tunnel public project has the character of big scale construction and high investment, that is, the total investment $\sum_{i=1}^{n_G} I_{Gi} + \sum_{j_1=1}^{n_{s1}} I_{Sj_1} + \sum_{j_2=1}^{n_{s2}} I_{Sj_2}$ is high. Generally, the total investment will be mainly supported by government organizations and social companies. Government organizations investment ω_G and social companies' investment ω_{S1} are main proportion for total investment. $\sum_{i=1}^{n_G} I_{Gi} + \sum_{j_1=1}^{n_{s1}} I_{Sj_1} + \sum_{j_2=1}^{n_{s2}} I_{Sj_2}$ mainly includes the building and installation expense for the tunnel and additional engineering projects, and operation cost $C_{YT_\gamma} Q_{T_\gamma} + C_{XT_\gamma}$ mainly includes running, maintenance, renewal expense (Liu, 2016). According to the character of utilities tunnel public project, it is very important to design rational construction and operation mechanism. For both government organizations and social companies, rational investment proportion, construction and operation duty and right should be regulated.

Government organizations and social companies should use their separate advantages to cooperate to acquire good performance of utilities tunnel.

For a long time, the construction and operation for utilities tunnel public project had been done by government organizations individually. Because of incomplete information about construction and operation of utilities tunnel for government organizations, the efficiency and function for utilities tunnel public project couldn't be completely fulfilled. In 2014 the government proposed to adopt franchise, investment bonus and government purchasing service styles to encourage social capital to invest utilities tunnel public projects in cities.[3] In 2015 the government proposed to amplify the cooperation between government organizations and social companies to encourage social capital to build project corporation to take part in construction and operation. In 2019 the government proposed to improve certifying service program for the construction, and engineering construction for all kinds of pipelines should be fulfilled with united management.

According to data statistics, there were 515 utilities tunnel projects to be built in 2017, among which about half projects had adopted the cooperation between government organizations and social companies. Now the cooperation between government organizations and social companies has been widely used in the operation for utilities tunnel public projects in China.

According to detailed status for utilities tunnel public project, the cooperation between government organizations and social companies can flexibly adopt many different styles. Franchise BOT(build-operate-transfer) is a typical operation style, and many styles can be created based on BOT. If utilities tunnel public project adopts BOT style, government organizations will give this public project to social companies to design and construct. Social companies have license of certain franchise period after this public project has been built. During franchise period, *No.*j_1 social company operates utilities tunnel public project and can get revenue H_{Sj_1} from $B_{T_\gamma} - C_{T_\gamma}$, and H_{Sj_1} should surpass its aim revenue rate. When franchise period is over, social companies will transfer utilities tunnel public project to government with no returns.

As quasi-public goods, utilities tunnel public project has the character of big scale construction, high investment and long recycle period. To build utilities tunnel public project, it is necessary to dig in some depth underground to build one way, two ways or multi ways corridors. The light, ventilation, supervision, telecommunication and other systems need to be built inside the corridors. The construction cost for utilities tunnel public project is high because many systems need be constructed together. To acquire timely high $\sum_{i=1}^{n_G} I_{Gi} + \sum_{j_1=1}^{n_{s1}} I_{Sj_1} + \sum_{j_2=1}^{n_{s2}} I_{Sj_2}$

for utilities tunnel public project, government organizations and social companies' cooperation can be used.

Table 1. G-S interactive finance framework for utilities tunnel public project in China

Finance Bodies	Finance Weights	Investment Revenue	Project Revenue
non-profitable government organizations	$0<\omega_G<1$ ($\omega_G+\omega_{S1}+\omega_{S2}=1$)	$H_G>0$. H_G should surpass aim revenue rate.	Max. $E(B_{T_\gamma} - C_{T_\gamma})$
profitable social companies	$0<\omega_{S1}<1$	$H_{S1}>0$. H_{S1} should surpass aim revenue rate. H_{S1}-floating value according to performance.	Min. $V(B_{T_\gamma} - C_{T_\gamma})$ Min. VC_{T_γ}
other profitable social organizations or individuals	$0\leq\omega_{s2}<1$	$H_{S2}>0$. $H_{S1}>H_{S2}$. H_{S2} should surpass aim revenue rate. H_{S2}-constant value.	$W>0$ $\frac{\partial^2 W}{\partial Q^{*2}} < 0$

The investment revenue H_{Gi} of *No.i* government organization and the investment revenue H_{Sj_1} of *No.*j_1 social company should both surpass their aim revenue rates. Because other social organizations or individuals take part in project only as an investment way, the investment revenue H_{S2} can be designed as a constant value, which is more than corresponding bank deposit rate. Because social companies manage construction and operation for project, the investment revenue H_{S1} can be designed as floating value according to performance.

Utilities tunnel public project should adopt all life cycle management mode to improve efficiency for the construction and operation. In all life cycle management mode, the design, construction, operation and supervision for utilities tunnel public project are managed together to fully make use of every stage's character and to balance every stage's development to realize high efficiency running and economic revenue. The total revenue should satisfy:

$$W = \sum_{\gamma=1}^{m} \frac{\int_{a_{T_\gamma}}^{b_{T_\gamma}} (B_{T_\gamma} - C_{T_\gamma}) f(B_{T_\gamma} - C_{T_\gamma}) d(B_{T_\gamma} - C_{T_\gamma})}{(1 + R_{T_\gamma})^{\gamma}} - \sum_{i=1}^{n_G} I_{Gi} - \sum_{j_1=1}^{n_{s1}} I_{Sj_1} - \sum_{j_2=1}^{n_{s2}} I_{Sj_2} > 0. \tag{22}$$

Government organizations and social companies should adopt rational measures to increase *W* value. Rational extreme optimal solution P^* and Q^* should be adopted. Assume that there is unique extreme optimal solution, then *W* should satisfy:

$$\frac{\partial^2 W}{\partial Q^{*2}} = [\sum_{\gamma=1}^{m} \frac{\int_{a_{T_\gamma}}^{b_{T_\gamma}} (B_{T_\gamma} - C_{T_\gamma}) f(B_{T_\gamma} - C_{T_\gamma}) d(B_{T_\gamma} - C_{T_\gamma})}{(1+R_{T_\gamma})^\gamma} - \sum_{i=1}^{n_G} I_{Gi} - \sum_{j_1=1}^{n_{s1}} I_{Sj_1} - \sum_{j_2=1}^{n_{s2}} I_{Sj_2}] \Bigg|_{Q}^{//} < 0. \tag{23}$$

If $W>0$, the total revenue $W(Q^*)$ will arrive at maximum profit value. If $W<0$, the total revenue $W(Q^*)$ will arrive at minimum loss value.

During design stage for utilities tunnel public project, the district status, engineering condition, finance and expense should be fully considered.[4] The design, engineering, operation and supervision sides must coordinate each other to improve running efficiency in all life cycle for public project.

For the construction and operation for utilities tunnel public project, the realization of investment revenue for government organizations and social companies should be fully considered. Government organizations and social companies should select suitable portfolio such as stocks and bonds to increase investment revenue. As quasi-public goods, utilities tunnel public project not only can acquire economic revenue, but also can acquire social benefits. Non-profitable government organizations should fully consider the realization of investment revenue for profitable social organizations or individuals. During operation periods for utilities tunnel public project, the net revenue $B_{T_\gamma} - C_{T_\gamma}$ should first compensate the constant value revenue H_{S2} of profitable other social organizations or individuals. Then the net revenue $B_{T_\gamma} - C_{T_\gamma}$ should compensate the floating value revenue H_{S1} of social companies. If it is not enough for H_{Sj_1} of $No.j_1$ social company to surpass aim revenue rate, government organizations can give extra bonus to social companies.

Rational investment recycles and profit style for social companies should be designed. For example, the profit style for France government organizations and social companies' cooperation mainly includes three types. First, directly charge to terminal consumers. Second, pay the total fee by public finance or country tax, that is, government sector pays the total fee. Third, mix the two modes and repay the fee in many periods (Xu, 2016). To get the investment of social companies timely for the construction of utilities tunnel public project, many channels of profit mode should be designed for social companies. During operation period, utilities tunnel public project can charge the fee entering into tunnel and daily maintenance fee to pipeline using units.[5]

Funding Modes Analysis for Utilities Tunnel Project in China

Utilities tunnel projects have been greatly developed in these years in China, and the prospect for utilities tunnel construction and operation is in good condition. Just as above mentioned, utilities tunnel belongs to large scale engineering projects involving with many engineering fields, and it has the character of high construction cost. To construct utilities tunnel project, enough investment is necessary. There are many types of funding modes for utilities tunnel in China, and rational funding mode selection can guarantee the successful fulfillment of the construction. The funding modes mainly include bank loan, bond, stock, cash and other modes in China now, and utilities tunnel project can select one or more funding modes together to construct. This part analyzes the different funding types for utilities tunnel in China.

Analysis of Bank Loan Funding Mode for Utilities Tunnel Project in China

The most common funding mode for utilities tunnel project in China is that government organizations and social companies and other social organizations or individuals invest and cooperate together. When government organizations and social companies and other social organizations or individuals afford high construction cost together for utilities tunnel project, debt finance can be chosen to get required capital. To operate utilities tunnel project, government organizations and social companies and other social organizations or individuals can use own capital, or act as debtor to get debt capital from creditor and repay the capital and pay the interest according to regulated debt term.

There are many commercial banks in China now, and they can supply loans for the funding needs from companies and social institutions. These commercial banks include nationally owned banks, and other local commercial banks. There are four big national commercial banks in China, including Bank of China, Industrial and Commercial Bank of China, China Construction Bank, Agricultural Bank of China. Utilities tunnel project can apply loan from these commercial banks and uses net revenue $B_{T_\gamma} - C_{T_\gamma}$ to refund the loan. These commercial banks belong to profitable social companies, and they give investment I_{Sj_1} to utilities tunnel project. To avoid investment risk, these commercial banks usually make strict apply requirement for loan, and mortgage and warrant often are necessary to acquire the loan. For utilities tunnel project, it usually has stable net revenue flowing during operation period, which can be used to pay the capital and interest to bank.

Assume utilities tunnel project acquires loans from some commercial banks, then the total investment of these banks is:

$$I_{S_j} = \sum_{j_1=1}^{n_{s1}} I_{s_{j_1}} \tag{24}$$

The total revenue acquired by these banks at T_j period under continuous interest rate R_{S_j} is:

$$K_{s_j} = \sum_{j_1=1}^{n_{s1}} I_{sj_1} e^{R_{sj_1} T_{j_1}} \tag{25}$$

The total investment revenue rate for these banks is:

$$H_{s_j} = \sum_{j_1=1}^{n_{s1}} I_{s_{j_1}} e^{R_{s_{j_1}} T_{j_1}} / \sum_{j_1=1}^{n_{s1}} I_{s_{j_1}} \tag{26}$$

Analysis of Bond Funding Mode for Utilities Tunnel Project in China

When utilities tunnel project uses bond funding mode to acquire construction capital, social companies and other social organizations or individuals can supply the investment for utilities tunnel. The total investment for social companies and other social organizations or individuals is $\sum_{j_1=1}^{n_{s1}} I_{s_{j_1}} + \sum_{j_2=1}^{n_{s2}} I_{s_{j_2}}$.

Assume the total investment for social companies and other social organizations or individuals is paid according to bond par value. Annual bond interest rate is C_r, and interest is paid V times in one year with time period T_m. Interest is paid for α years, and θ is interest payment times. Maturity revenue rate R_{T_γ} keeps constant for utilities tunnel project.

The duration investment value during the period is:

$$\Phi_1 = \sum_{\theta=1}^{\alpha V-1} \left[\theta T_m \left(\sum_{j_1=1}^{n_{s1}} I_{s_{j_1}} + \sum_{j_2=1}^{n_{s2}} I_{s_{j_2}} \right) C_r / V^2 \right] / \left(1 + R_{T_\gamma}\right)^{\theta} \tag{27}$$

The duration investment value at the end of the period is:

$$\Phi_2 = \alpha T_m \left(\sum_{j_1=1}^{n_{s1}} I_{s_{j_1}} + \sum_{j_2=1}^{n_{s2}} I_{s_{j_2}} \right) \left(C_r / V + 1 \right) / \left(1 + R_{T_\gamma} \right)^{\alpha V} \tag{28}$$

The investment during the period is:

$$\Phi_3 = \sum_{\theta=1}^{\alpha V - 1} \left[\left(\sum_{j_1=1}^{n_{s1}} I_{s_{j_1}} + \sum_{j_2=1}^{n_{s2}} I_{s_{j_2}} \right) C_r / V \right] / \left(1 + R_{T_\gamma} \right)^{\theta} \tag{29}$$

The investment at the end of the period is:

$$\Phi_4 = \left(\sum_{j_1=1}^{n_{s1}} I_{s_{j_1}} + \sum_{j_2=1}^{n_{s2}} I_{s_{j_2}} \right) \left(C_r / V + 1 \right) / \left(1 + R_{T_\gamma} \right)^{\alpha V} \tag{30}$$

Macaulay duration M_d for utilities tunnel project is:

$$M_d = (\Phi_1 + \Phi_2) / (\Phi_3 + \Phi_4) \tag{31}$$

Because operation cycle is usually long for utilities tunnel project, the bond term is usually long and bond duration M_d is also long, which means that it needs long time to recycle the investment. If maturity revenue rate R_{T_γ} is increased for utilities tunnel bond, then bond duration M_d will be decreased.

$$\Phi_5 = \sum_{\theta=1}^{\alpha V} \left[\theta \left(\theta + 1 \right) \left(\sum_{j_1=1}^{n_{s1}} I_{s_{j_1}} + \sum_{j_2=1}^{n_{s2}} I_{s_{j_2}} \right) C_r / V \right] / \left(1 + R_{T_\gamma} \right)^{\theta + 2} \tag{32}$$

$$\Phi_6 = \alpha V \left(\alpha V + 1 \right) \left(\sum_{j_1=1}^{n_{s1}} I_{s_{j_1}} + \sum_{j_2=1}^{n_{s2}} I_{s_{j_2}} \right) / \left(1 + R_{T_\gamma} \right)^{\alpha V + 2} \tag{33}$$

The bond number acquired by social companies and other social organizations or individuals is N_b. Then bond convexity C_d for utilities tunnel project is:

$$C_d = (\Phi_5 + \Phi_6) / N_b \tag{34}$$

Order that bond price S_b is a continuous function of maturity revenue rate.

$$S_b = F\left(R_{T_\gamma}\right) \tag{35}$$

Assume that bond price S_b is an order continuous derivative function, and $R_{T_{\gamma 0}}$ is base point, then $\nexists\varphi>0$:

$$F\left(R_{T_\gamma}\right) = F\left(R_{T_{\gamma 0}}\right) + F^{/}\left(R_{T_{\gamma 0}}\right)\left(R_{T_\gamma} - R_{T_{\gamma 0}}\right) + F^{//}\left(R_{T_{\gamma 0}}\right)\left(R_{T_\gamma} - R_{T_{\gamma 0}}\right)^2 / 2! + \cdots$$
$$+F^{(n)}\left(R_{T_{\gamma 0}}\right)\left(R_{T_\gamma} - R_{T_{\gamma 0}}\right)^n / n! + F^{(n+1)}\left(\varphi\right)\left(R_{T_\gamma} - \varphi\right)^{(n+1)} / \left(n+1\right)! \tag{36}$$

There is:

$$\Phi_7 = \sum_{\theta=1}^{\alpha V}\left[\theta\left(\sum_{j_1=1}^{n_{s1}} I_{s_{j_1}} + \sum_{j_2=1}^{n_{s2}} I_{S_{j_2}}\right)C_r / V\right] / \left(1 + R_{T_{\gamma 0}}\right)^{\theta+1} \tag{37}$$

$$\Phi_8 = \alpha V\left(\sum_{j_1=1}^{n_{s1}} I_{S_{j_1}} + \sum_{j_2=1}^{n_{s2}} I_{S_{j_2}}\right) / \left(1 + R_{T_{\gamma 0}}\right)^{\alpha V+1} \tag{38}$$

$$\Phi_9 = \sum_{\theta=1}^{\alpha V}\left[\theta\left(\theta+1\right)\left(\sum_{j_1=1}^{n_{s1}} I_{S_{j_1}} + \sum_{j_2=1}^{n_{s2}} I_{S_{j_2}}\right)C_r / V\right] / \left(1 + R_{T_{\gamma 0}}\right)^{\theta+2} \tag{39}$$

$$\Phi_{10} = \alpha V\left(\alpha V+1\right)\left(\sum_{j_1=1}^{n_{s1}} I_{S_{j_1}} + \sum_{j_2=1}^{n_{s2}} I_{S_{j_2}}\right) / \left(1 + R_{T_{\gamma 0}}\right)^{\alpha V+2} \tag{40}$$

Bond price S_b second-order Taylor approximation is listed as follows, which can be used to estimate S_b value:

$$F\left(R_{T_\gamma}\right) \approx F\left(R_{T_{\gamma 0}}\right) - \left(\Phi_7 + \Phi_8\right)\left(R_{T_\gamma} - R_{T_{\gamma 0}}\right) / N_b + \left(\Phi_9 + \Phi_{10}\right)\left(R_{T_\gamma} - R_{T_{\gamma 0}}\right)^2 / 2!\,N_b \tag{41}$$

When government organizations and social companies and other social organizations or individuals issue bond for utilities tunnel project, they need estimate maturity revenue rate R_{T_γ} to guarantee that the pricing of bond S_b is rational. If the pricing of S_b is high then they perhaps can't get enough funding capital, and if the pricing of S_b is low then the issuers perhaps have certain amount loss.

To get required capital for utilities tunnel project, government organizations can issue government bond in China. Government organizations can issue national bond or local government bond to get capital from social companies and other social organizations or individuals, and regulate par value, coupon C_r/V and term to maturity α and pay bond interest and repay principal according to certain payment term. Government bond is guaranteed by government credit, and its credit level is very high and can be deemed as non-risk bond. National bond is issued by central government and has the highest credit level such as AAA level and is suitable for large scale utilities tunnel project or is suitable to fulfill several utilities tunnel projects together.

To operate utilities tunnel project, government organizations can issue government bond in short term, middle term or long term. Short term bond is mainly used to get emergency capital (for example, temporary bond issuing no more than one year to satisfy emergency fund needs for utilities tunnel construction), and middle term and long-term bonds are mainly used to get large capital. Because operation period is long, middle term bond and long-term bond are main funding types.

To get required capital for utilities tunnel project, social companies and other social organizations can issue enterprise bond. They can regulate bond kinds, par value, coupon C_r/V, term to maturity α, etc. Nonmortgage credit bond guaranteed by enterprise credit can be issued for finance, and mortgage bond guaranteed by utilities tunnel infrastructure and product as mortgage goods can be issued for finance. Enterprise can issue secured bond by secured support. Social companies and other social organizations can issue enterprise bond in short term, middle term or long term. Short term bond is mainly used to get emergency capital while middle term and long-term bonds are mainly used to get large amount capital.

Finance institution can directly take part in project operation for utilities tunnel as finance body and can also supply capital as creditor to government organizations and social companies and other social organizations or individuals. Whether as finance body or as creditor, finance institution should strictly check and supervise project operation for utilities tunnel. Finance institution can check and supervise capital usage, organization construction, personnel management, resource and material usage during the process of feasibility study, design, engineering, running for utilities tunnel project.[6]

Analysis of Equity Funding Mode for Utilities Tunnel Project in China

To acquire the construction capital for utilities tunnel project in China, equity funding is another important funding mode. Stocks for utilities tunnel project can be issued to government organizations and social companies and other social organizations or individuals. Different with bond funding mode, these investors can't acquire fixed interest income with bond interest rate C_r, but they may get dividend from the revenue of utilities tunnel project. They can also get capital revenue by selling the stocks to other investors in Shanghai Stock Exchange and Shenzhen Stock Exchange, etc.

The total investment for utilities tunnel project is:

$$I_T = \sum_{i=1}^{n_G} I_{G_i} + \sum_{j_1=1}^{n_{s1}} I_{s_{j_1}} + \sum_{j_2=1}^{n_{s2}} I_{s_{j_2}} \tag{42}$$

Assume that the starting dividend for utilities tunnel stock is D_0, and the par value for utilities tunnel stock is U. The utilities tunnel stock is sold at price S_t at capital market.

When utilities tunnel stock is issued, its issuing price probably deviates from par value. If issuing price S_p is lower than par value($S_p<U$), it means that issuing price is in certain discount range. If issuing price is higher than par value($S_p>U$), it means that issuing price is in certain premium range. Assume utilities tunnel stock is issued at par value for simplicity of analysis($S_p=U$).

The investors may acquire dividend from the stock of utilities tunnel project, and the total dividend of these investors is:

$$D_T = \sum_{i=1}^{n_G} \left(I_{G_i} / U\right)\left(D_0 / R_{T_\gamma}\right) + \sum_{j_1=1}^{n_{s1}} \left(I_{S_{j_1}} / U\right)\left(D_0 / R_{T_\gamma}\right) + \sum_{j_2=1}^{n_{s2}} \left(I_{S_{j_2}} / U\right)\left(D_0 / R_{T_\gamma}\right) \tag{43}$$

The investment revenue rate for keeping utilities tunnel stock is:

$$H_T = D_T / I_T \tag{44}$$

The investment revenue rate for government organizations for keeping utilities tunnel stock is:

$$H_{T_G} = \sum_{i=1}^{n_G} \left(I_{G_i} / U\right)\left(D_0 / R_{T_\gamma}\right) / \sum_{i=1}^{n_G} I_{G_i} \tag{45}$$

The investment revenue rate for social companies for keeping utilities tunnel stock is:

$$H_{T_{S1}} = \sum_{j_1=1}^{n_{s1}} \left(I_{S_{j_1}} / U\right)\left(D_0 / R_{T_\gamma}\right) / \sum_{j_1=1}^{n_{s1}} I_{S_{j_1}} \tag{46}$$

The investment revenue rate for other social organizations or individuals for keeping utilities tunnel stock is:

$$H_{T_{S2}} = \sum_{j_2=1}^{n_{s2}} \left(I_{S_{j_2}} / U\right)\left(D_0 / R_{T_\gamma}\right) / \sum_{j_2=1}^{n_{s2}} I_{S_{j_2}} \tag{47}$$

If the investors sell utilities tunnel stock at π period, the total capital revenue for utilities tunnel stock is:

$$C_T = \sum_{i=1}^{n_G} \left(S_{t_{G_i}} - U\right)\left(I_{G_i} / U\right) / \left(1 + R_{T_\gamma}\right)^{\pi_{G_i}}$$
$$+ \sum_{j_1=1}^{n_{s1}} \left(S_{t_{j_1}} - U\right)\left(I_{S_{j_1}} / U\right) / \left(1 + R_{T_\gamma}\right)^{\pi_{j_1}} + \sum_{j_2=1}^{n_{s2}} \left(S_{t_{j_2}} - U\right)\left(I_{S_{j_2}} / U\right) / \left(1 + R_{T_\gamma}\right)^{\pi_{j_2}} \tag{48}$$

The total dividend for government organizations and social companies and other social organizations or individuals becomes:

$$D_T = \sum_{i=1}^{n_G} \left(I_{G_i} / U\right)\left(D_0 / R_{T_\gamma}\right)\left(1 - 1 / \left(1 + R_{T_\gamma}\right)^{\pi_{G_i}}\right)$$
$$+ \sum_{j_1=1}^{n_{s1}} \left(I_{S_{j_1}} / U\right)\left(D_0 / R_{T_\gamma}\right)\left(1 - 1 / \left(1 + R_{T_\gamma}\right)^{\pi_{j_1}}\right) + \sum_{j_2=1}^{n_{s2}} \left(I_{S_{j_2}} / U\right)\left(D_0 / R_{T_\gamma}\right)\left(1 - 1 / \left(1 + R_{T_\gamma}\right)^{\pi_{j_2}}\right) \tag{49}$$

The total investment revenue rate for utilities tunnel project becomes:

$$H_T = (D_T + C_T) / I_T \tag{50}$$

The investment revenue rate for government organizations becomes:

$$H_{T_G} = \left(\sum_{i=1}^{n_G} \left(S_{t_{G_i}} - U\right)\left(I_{G_i} / U\right) / \left(1 + R_{T_\gamma}\right)^{\pi_{G_i}} + \sum_{i=1}^{n_G} \left(I_{G_i} / U\right)\left(D_0 / R_{T_\gamma}\right)\left(1 - 1 / \left(1 + R_{T_\gamma}\right)^{\pi_{G_i}}\right)\right) / \sum_{i=1}^{n_G} I_{G_i} \tag{51}$$

The investment revenue rate for social companies becomes:

$$H_{T_{s1}} = \left(\sum_{j_1=1}^{n_{s1}} \left(S_{t_{j_1}} - U\right)\left(I_{S_{j_1}} / U\right) / \left(1 + R_{T_\gamma}\right)^{\pi_{j_1}} + \sum_{j_1=1}^{n_{s1}} \left(I_{S_{j_1}} / U\right)\left(D_0 / R_{T_\gamma}\right)\left(1 - 1 / \left(1 + R_{T_\gamma}\right)^{\pi_{j_1}}\right) \right) / \sum_{j_1=1}^{n_{s1}} I_{S_{j_1}} \quad (52)$$

The investment revenue rate for other social organizations or individuals becomes:

$$H_{T_{s2}} = \left(\sum_{j_2=1}^{n_{s2}} \left(S_{t_{j_2}} - U\right)\left(I_{S_{j_2}} / U\right) / \left(1 + R_{T_\gamma}\right)^{\pi_{j_2}} + \sum_{j_2=1}^{n_{s2}} \left(I_{S_{j_2}} / U\right)\left(D_0 / R_{T_\gamma}\right)\left(1 - 1 / \left(1 + R_{T_\gamma}\right)^{\pi_{j_2}}\right) \right) / \sum_{j_2=1}^{n_{s2}} I_{S_{j_2}} \quad (53)$$

When government organizations and social companies and other social organizations or individuals invest utilities tunnel stock, they have revenue allocation right and management supervision right to the enterprise issuing stocks, but revenue allocation must be done after the enterprise has fulfilled the repayment duties for loan from finance institution, bond and other debts (Capponi & Frei, 2017; Fracassi, 2017; He *et al.*, 2018; Maskowitz *et al.*, 2012; Zhao, 2017).

Equity finance for utilities tunnel project can take many ways to fulfill according to stock kinds, rights and duties etc. Preference share gives stockholders rights acquiring fixed dividend from unallocated profit of enterprise in advance. The capital risk for preference share is lower than that of ordinary share, but preference share stockholders haven't extra revenue claim right and management voting right which are owned by ordinary share stockholders. Ordinary share is commonest equity finance way for utilities tunnel project. Different with debt finance which need pay interest and repay principal according to fixed term, equity finance needn't pay fixed amount compensation and repay principal according to fixed term.

The construction cost is high for utilities tunnel project, and the finance capital can be drawing back from operation revenue $B_{T_\gamma} - C_{T_\gamma}$. Operation revenue mainly includes the fee entering into tunnel and daily maintenance fee which are charged from pipeline using institutions.[7] Operation revenue is usually stable, which is suitable for long term revenue such as equity finance.

Other Funding Modes and Modes Selection in China

To add funding modes for utilities tunnel project, investment fund can be absorbed in project operation, whose strong portfolio management ability and capital operating ability can be used. Securities funds such as pension fund and insurance fund can be absorbed in utilities tunnel project operation to fully make use of their operation management ability. When investors select funds, they often consider the issuing fee amount. A few factors will influence the choice for funds with different fees. Grinblatt *et al.* (2016) find that investors with high-IQ, having a university or business degree, working in the finance profession tend to own low-fee funds.

Because now big data, cloud computing and other techniques become more mature, Internet finance develops rapidly (Rafay, 2019). Utilities tunnel project should fully make use of Internet finance's convenience and quickness to enhance capital acquiring ability and to increase funding modes and sources. Crowdfunding is an effective funding mode of Internet finance, which can get pledged capital from many social individuals by construction of Internet finance platform. It can fully gather and use diversified social funds. The investors can be compensated from the operation revenue $B_{T_\gamma} - C_{T_\gamma}$ of utilities tunnel project.

For many above funding modes, utilities tunnel project can select one or more suitable funding modes to get the investment capital. Every funding mode has different funding characters and operation procedures, and utilities tunnel project should fully make use of the advantages of these modes to acquire best funding practice.

To the number of investors, bank loan usually only involves several finance institutions, while bond finance and equity finance will involve many social companies and other social organizations or individuals. Internet finance will also involve many small amounts fund investors. This means that investor management for these funding modes should be different. To finance scale, finance institution usually has strong investment ability and loan amount is high. For utilities tunnel project with stable revenue $B_{T_\gamma} - C_{T_\gamma}$ and good prospect, bond finance and equity finance usually can easily get large amount fund from social companies and other social organizations or individuals. On the contrary, Internet finance is emerging funding mode, which now is probably uneasy to get large amount fund.

To finance using period, finance institution can supply short term loan, middle term loan and long-term loan according to project condition (Rafay & Farid, 2019). Bond finance can issue short term bond, middle term bond and long-term bond. Equity finance hasn't term limitation unless funding enterprise meets bankruptcy or liquidation etc. Internet finance now is usually impossible to give long term funding capital. To finance procedure convenience, utilities tunnel project can get bank loan after passing through credit census and loan condition check for finance institution. Because bond finance and equity finance will be issued to social companies and other social organizations or individuals, finance body usually gives the funding issuing or underwriting to finance institution or securities institution for substitution. Internet finance needs good web technology and web safety to guarantee the finance to be fulfilled safely and effectively.

When funding modes are chosen, the weighted capital cost for all kinds of funding modes should be lowest in principle. Finance risks probably produced by all kinds of funding modes should be fully considered, and the risk that is unable to get the capital timely and the risk that is unable to repay finance capital should be avoided. Suitable funding mode choice will decrease finance risk, while unsuitable funding mode choice will increase finance risk for utilities tunnel project in China.[8] During the operation process, construction cost and running cost should be controlled rationally, and engineering construction risk, tunnel using risk, operation risk and other risks should be controlled at the lowest level (Henk, 1998; Russell *et al.*, 1999; Rostami *et al.*, 2013; Špačková *et al.*, 2013; Aldoseri & Worthington, 2020).

Crowdfunding Mode for Utilities Tunnel Project

The funding mode, procedure and management of crowdfunding are greatly different with traditional funding modes (Butticè *et al.*, 2017; Schulz *et al.*, 2015; Zhou *et al.*, 2018). Mollick (2014) points out that crowdfunding refers to the efforts by entrepreneurial individuals and groups-cultural, social, and for-profit-to fund their ventures by drawing on relatively small contribution from a relatively large number of individuals using the Internet, without standard financial intermediaries. Schwienbacher (2010) defines crowdfunding—an open call, essentially through the Internet, for the provision of financial resources either in form of donation or in exchange for some form of reward and/or voting rights in order to support initiatives for specific purposes.[9]

Crowdfunding projects are fulfilled on Internet platform, and founders pose project introduction on this platform and backers supply pledged capital also on this platform (Anglin *et al.*, 2018; Read, 2013; Steigenberger & Wilhelm, 2018; Rafay, 2020). The early crowdfunding platforms appear nearly 2008-2009 in the world, and there are more and more crowdfunding platforms founded all over the world. Figure 1 shows the rapid growth tendency for crowdfunding in recent years compiled with 2015 data (Hobey, 2015). The biggest crowdfunding platform is Kickstarter, and most of big crowdfunding platforms mainly focus on US and European now.

When crowdfunding project is fulfilled, the personal character of founder may affect the fulfillment of crowdfunding project. Rakesh *et al.* (2015) expand project-based features into four different categories: temporal traits, personal traits, geo-location traits, and network traits. They provide several unique insights about these features and their effects on the success of Kickstarter projects. They analyze various interesting knowledge about the behaviors of Kickstarter users with respect to their backing frequency, social network, geo-location and other personality-based traits. Greenberg and Mollick (2017) use lab experiments and field data to show that activist choice homophily provides an explanation for why women are more likely to succeed at crowdfunding than men and why women are most successful in industries in which they are least represented.[10]

Figure 1. Crowdfunding Market Development Tendency All Over the World

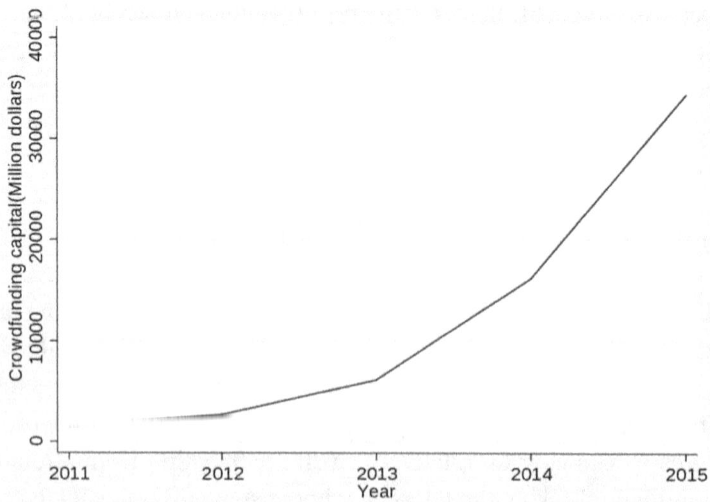

When founder poses crowdfunding project on Internet platform, the pledged goal, pledged date, delivery date, reward and other introduction of project will be posted on crowdfunding platform. This kind of introduction often includes videos, photos and words, which is a funding signal of good prospect and will attract backers to supply pledged capital at short period (Cecere *et al.*, 2017; Colombo, 2021; Ge & Luo, 2016; Kim *et al.*, 2015; Salahaldin *et al.*, 2019; Zheng *et al.*, 2017). The management of crowdfunding platform to project usually includes two types. One type is "All-or-Nothing". The founder can get pledged capital from backers if pledged capital surpasses pledged goal, and backers needn't supply pledged capital if pledged capital doesn't arrive at pledged goal. The typical crowdfunding platform of "All-or-Nothing" is Kickstarter. Another type is "Keep-it-All". The founder can get pledged capital supplied by backers whether or not pledged capital arrives at pledged goal. The typical crowdfunding platform of "Keep-it-All" is famous Indiegogo platform.

Veuger (2015) analyzes the role of crowdfunding platforms, which include platform size, the degree of regulation, funding models of platform such as "All-or-Nothing" and "Keep-it-All", and their effect on the overall platform success rate. Li and Jarvenpaa (2015) investigate how the use of stretch goals influences project performance using online crowdfunding on Kickstarter as an example. Empirical results show that the use of stretch goal is associated with better project funding performance, and this positive effect is even stronger for projects with higher levels of community engagement. Ariel *et al.* (2016) presents the findings of three online surveys conducted in the second half of 2015 at the European level regarding perceptions about crowdfunding in the renewable energy sector.

Crowdfunding is a new and flexible type of funding mode, and crowdfunding projects with different scales can be got according to different kinds and characters of projects posed by founder. On Kickstarter platform, the main kinds for crowdfunding projects include Theater, Technology, Publishing, Photography, Music, Journalism, Games, Food, Film & Video, Fashion, Design, Dance, Crafts, Comics, Art. Figure 2 lists launched projects of different categories on Kickstarter platform until May 2021. The number of launched projects for Film & Video is biggest, which arrives at 77,043 projects. Dance has smallest number of launched projects at 4,334 projects.

Figure 2. Launched Projects of Different Categories on Kickstarter Platform until May 2021

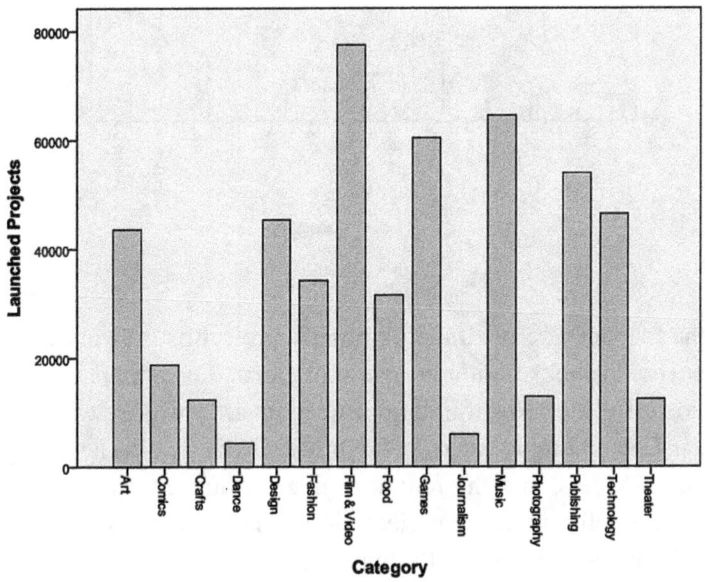

From small innovative design project with several hundred dollars to big project with several million dollars till several hundreds of millions of dollars, all can be fulfilled with crowdfunding mode, which has strong and flexible funding advantages. Figure 3 lists total pledged capital for different categories on Kickstarter platform until May 2021. The number of pledged capitals for Games is biggest, which arrives at 1.6 billion dollars. Dance has smallest number of pledged capitals at 15.19 million dollars.

Figure 3. Total Pledged Capital for Different Categories on Kickstarter Platform until May 2021

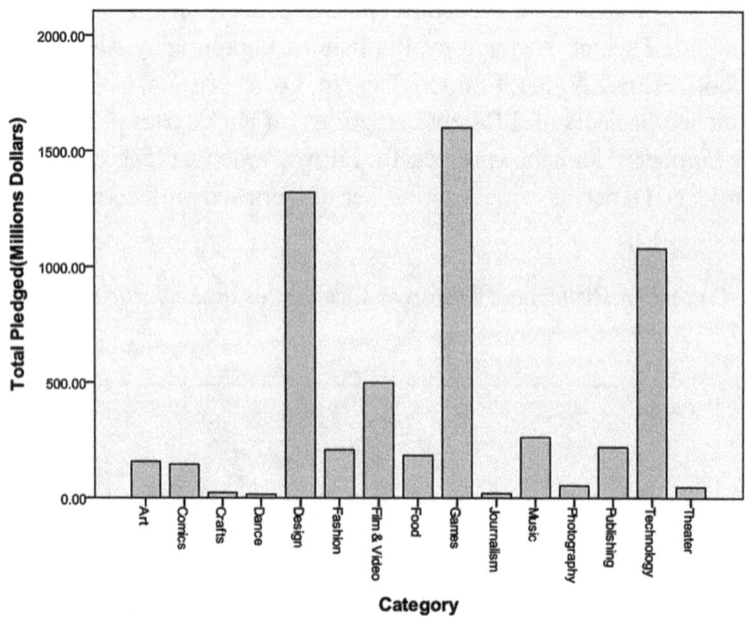

When the founder of crowdfunding poses a project on crowdfunding platform, this founder should choose suitable type of platform. For example, some platforms in the world fulfill the crowdfunding projects mainly with reward type, such as Kickstarter in US and Jingdong Crowdfunding in China. The backers supply pledged capital to the founders, and the founders give certain reward such as product to the backers after delivery of the project. Some platforms in the world operate the crowdfunding projects mainly with donation type, such as gofundme.com in US and gongyi.qq.com in China.

There isn't crowdfunding mode used in utilities tunnel project until now. But because of the advantages of crowdfunding mode, it can be used in the design and fulfillment of utilities tunnel projects in the future. Utilities tunnel project can use crowdfunding to increase funding modes besides traditional debt and equity funding modes and can use flexible crowdfunding strategy and procedure to fulfill. According to advantages of crowdfunding mode, small projects of utilities tunnel can be tried to use crowdfunding mode, and big projects of utilities tunnel can use crowdfunding mode gradually. Another method is part of utilities tunnel project can use crowdfunding mode to fulfill, while other part of the project can use traditional funding mode.

For utilities tunnel project, the corridor is built at some space underground, in which water supply and drainage, electric power, telecommunication, gas, rubbish and other pipelines are laid. According to construction scale, project condition, operation and other factors, suitable crowdfunding mode can be chosen to pledge capital for utilities tunnel project. Crowdfunding mode can be flexibly used to pledge construction capital in middle and small utilities tunnel projects now.

When crowdfunding founder for utilities tunnel project fulfills crowdfunding, it is necessary to take some measures to increase the investment confidence of backers (Buengeler *et al.*, 2021; Hirshleifer *et al.*, 2019; Mclean & Zhao, 2014; Morellec *et al.*, 2015; Nanda & Rhodes-Kropf, 2017; Walker, 2017). Because backers search the Internet platform to find suitable investment projects from many platform projects, the introduction posed by founder of crowdfunding for utilities tunnel project is important. Excellent videos, photos and words will attract more backers in short time and increase the confidence of founders to acquire pledged capital for utilities tunnel project.

FUTURE RESEARCH DIRECTIONS

This chapter uses G-S interactive finance framework to analyze utilities tunnel projects and their funding modes in China and gives an exploratory crowdfunding pledging analysis for fulfillment of utilities tunnel project. Because there aren't empirical crowdfunding data for utilities tunnel, quantitative analysis on crowdfunding for utilities tunnel is impossible now. The future research can consider quantitative analysis after acquiring crowdfunding data for utilities tunnel, such as the analysis on the influence factors for the success rate of utilities tunnel crowdfunding.

CONCLUSION

In reality, non-profitable government and other organizations or individuals (G part) and profitable social organizations or individuals (S part) usually construct and operate engineering project for utilities tunnel together. This chapter uses G-S interactive finance framework to analyze finance design for utilities tunnel public project in China.

The Chinese engineering projects for utilities tunnel are usually fulfilled as public projects and belong to urban management infrastructure, and government organizations and social companies supply utilities tunnel public projects together in most cases, which can fully make use of their respective advantages for the projects.

When utilities tunnel project is acquiring the construction capital, it can adopt bank loan funding mode, bond funding mode, stock funding mode, securities fund mode and Internet finance funding mode. According to the character of every funding mode, utilities tunnel project should flexibly choose one or more funding modes to increase the efficiency to acquire construction capital.

This chapter gives an exploratory crowdfunding pledging analysis for fulfillment of utilities tunnel project. According to advantages of crowdfunding mode, small projects of utilities tunnel can be tried to use crowdfunding mode, and big projects of utilities tunnel can use crowdfunding mode gradually.

DISCLAIMER

The contents and views of this chapter are expressed by the authors in their personal capacities. It is not necessary for the Editor and the Publisher to agree with these viewpoints and they are not responsible for any duty of care in this regard.

ACKNOWLEDGMENT

The authors extend sincere gratitude to:

- The Editor and the International Editorial Advisory Board (IEAB) of this book who initially desk reviewed, arranged a rigorous double/triple blind review process and conducted a thorough, minute and critical final review before accepting the chapter for publication.
- All anonymous reviewers who provided very constructive feedbacks for thorough revision, improvement, extension and fine tuning of the chapter.
- All colleagues, assistants and well-wishers who assisted the authors to complete this task.

REFERENCES

Ahlers, G. K. C., Cumming, D., Günther, C., & Schweizer, D. (2015). Signaling in equity crowdfunding. *Entrepreneurship Theory and Practice*, *39*(4), 955–980. doi:10.1111/etap.12157

Aldoseri, M., & Worthington, A. C. (2020). Operational Risk Management of Islamic Banks. In A. Rafay (Ed.), *Handbook of Research on Theory and Practice of Global Islamic Finance* (pp. 455–470). IGI Global. doi:10.4018/978-1-7998-0218-1.ch025

Anglin, A. H., Short, J. C., Drover, W., Stevenson, R. M., Mckenny, A. F., & Allison, T. H. (2018). The power of positivity? The influence of positive psychological capital language on crowdfunding performance. *Journal of Business Venturing*, *33*(4), 470–492. doi:10.1016/j.jbusvent.2018.03.003

Ariel, B., Stephanie, B., Bruce, B., Kathrin, K., Thomas, M., & Matthias, K. (2016). *Survey results on public perceptions and the views of crowdfunding platforms and project developers.* Retrieved from https://discovery.dundee.ac.uk/en/publications/survey-results-on-public-perceptions-and-the-views-of-crowdfundin

Baber, H. (2020). Crowdfunding Framework in Islamic Finance. In A. Rafay (Ed.), *Handbook of Research on Theory and Practice of Global Islamic Finance* (pp. 307–320). IGI Global. doi:10.4018/978-1-7998-0218-1.ch017

Buengeler, C., Diccolo, R. F., & Locklear, L. R. (2021). LMX differentiation and group outcomes: A framework and review drawing on group diversity insights. *Journal of Management*, *47*(1), 260–287. doi:10.1177/0149206320930813

Butticè, V., Colombo, M. G., & Wright, M. (2017). Serial crowdfunding, social capital, and project success. *Entrepreneurship Theory and Practice*, *41*(2), 183–207. doi:10.1111/etap.12271

Canto-Perello, J., Curiel-Esparza, J., & Calvo, V. (2013). Criticality and threat analysis on utility tunnels for planning security policies of utilities in urban underground space. *Expert Systems with Applications*, *40*(11), 4707–4714. doi:10.1016/j.eswa.2013.02.031

Canto-Perello, J., Curiel-Esparza, J., & Calvo, V. (2016). Strategic decision support system for utility tunnel's planning applying A'WOT method. *Tunnelling and Underground Space Technology*, *55*, 146–152. doi:10.1016/j.tust.2015.12.009

Capponi, A., & Frei, C. (2017). Systemic influences on optimal equity-credit investment. *Management Science*, *63*(8), 2756–2771. doi:10.1287/mnsc.2016.2460

Cecere, G., Le Guel, F., & Rochelandet, F. (2017). Crowdfunding and social influence: An empirical investigation. *Applied Economics*, *49*(57), 5802–5813. doi:10.1080/00036846.2017.1343450

Colombo, O. (2021). The use of signals in new-venture financing: A review and research agenda. *Journal of Management*, *47*(1), 237–259. doi:10.1177/0149206320911090

Fracassi, C. (2017). Corporate finance policies and social networks. *Management Science*, *63*(8), 2420–2438. doi:10.1287/mnsc.2016.2433

Ge, L., & Luo, X. C. (2016). Team rivalry and lending on crowdfunding platforms: An empirical analysis. *Financial Innovation*, *2*(1), 17. doi:10.118640854-016-0035-8

Goel, R. K. (2001). Status of tunnelling and underground construction activities and technologies in India. *Tunnelling and Underground Space Technology*, *16*(2), 63–75. doi:10.1016/S0886-7798(01)00035-9

Greenberg, J., & Mollick, E. (2017). Activist choice homophily and the crowdfunding of female founders. *Administrative Science Quarterly*, *62*(2), 341–374. doi:10.1177/0001839216678847

Grinblatt, M., Ikäheimo, S., Keloharju, M., & Knüpfer, S. (2016). IQ and mutual fund choice. *Management Science*, *62*(4), 924–944. doi:10.1287/mnsc.2015.2166

He, H. Y., Luo, Q., & Chen, T. (2018). Research on PPP financing model of utilities tunnel based on investors' perspective. *The Engineering Economist*, *28*(5), 60–65.

Henk, G. G. (1998). Privatization and the public/private partnership. *Journal of Management Engineering*, *14*(4), 28–29. doi:10.1061/(ASCE)0742-597X(1998)14:4(28)

Hirshleifer, D., Levi, Y., Lourie, B., & Teoh, S. H. (2019). Decision fatigue and heuristic analyst forecasts. *Journal of Financial Economics*, *133*(1), 83–98. doi:10.1016/j.jfineco.2019.01.005

Hobey, E. (2015, March 31). *Global crowdfunding market to reach 34.4B in 2015.* Massolution Posts Research Findings. Retrieved from https://www.crowdfundinsider.com/2015/03/65302-massolution-posts-research-findings-crowdfunding-market-grows-167-in-2014-crowdfunding-platforms-raise-16-2-billion/

Hulme, T. W., & Burchell, A. J. (1999). Tunnelling projects in Singapore: An overview. *Tunnelling and Underground Space Technology*, *14*(4), 409–418. doi:10.1016/S0886-7798(00)00004-3

Husin, M. M., & Haron, R. (2020). Financial Sustainability of SMEs through Islamic Crowdfunding. In A. Rafay (Ed.), *Handbook of Research on Theory and Practice of Global Islamic Finance* (pp. 321–337). IGI Global. doi:10.4018/978-1-7998-0218-1.ch018

Kim, J. H., Newberry, P., & Qiu, C. (2015). *An empirical analysis of a crowdfunding platform*. (Working Paper No., 15-12). NET Institute.

Legrand, L., Blanpain, O., & Buyle-Bodin, F. (2004). Promoting the urban utilities tunnel technique using a decision-making approach. *Tunnelling and Underground Space Technology*, *19*(1), 79–83. doi:10.1016/S0886-7798(03)00041-5

Li, Z. X., & Jarvenpaa, S. L. (2015). *Motivating IT-Mediated crowds: the effect of goal setting on project performance in online crowdfunding*. (Working Paper No., 15-07). NET Institute.

Lin, M. F., & Viswanathan, S. (2016). Home bias in online investments: An empirical study of an online crowd funding market. *Management Science*, *62*(5), 1393–1414. doi:10.1287/mnsc.2015.2206

Liu, F. R. (2016). Utilities tunnel investment and financial mechanism needs deep research in Beijing. *China Investment*, *15*, 74–75.

Maskowitz, T. J., Ooi, Y. H., & Pedersen, L. H. (2012). Time series momentum. *Journal of Financial Economics*, *104*(2), 228–250. doi:10.1016/j.jfineco.2011.11.003

Mclean, R. D., & Zhao, M. X. (2014). The business cycle, investor sentiment, and costly external finance. *The Journal of Finance*, *69*(3), 1377–1409. doi:10.1111/jofi.12047

Mollick, E. (2014). The dynamics of crowdfunding: An exploratory study. *Journal of Business Venturing*, *29*(1), 1–16. doi:10.1016/j.jbusvent.2013.06.005

Morellec, E., Valta, P., & Zhdanov, A. (2015). Financing investment: The choice between bonds and bank loans. *Management Science*, *61*(11), 2580–2602. doi:10.1287/mnsc.2014.2005

Nanda, R., & Rhodes-Kropf, M. (2017). Financing risk and innovation. *Management Science*, *63*(4), 901–918. doi:10.1287/mnsc.2015.2350

Phillips, J. (2016). A quantitative evaluation of the sustainability or unsustainability of three tunnelling projects. *Tunnelling and Underground Space Technology*, *51*, 387–404. doi:10.1016/j.tust.2015.09.009

Rafay, A. (Ed.). (2019). *FinTech as a Disruptive Technology for Financial Institutions*. IGI Global. doi:10.4018/978-1-5225-7805-5

Rafay, A. (Ed.). (2020). *HandBook of Research on Theory and Practice of Global Islamic Finance*. IGI Global. doi:10.4018/978-1-7998-0218-1

Rafay, A., & Farid, S. (2019). Islamic Banking System: A Credit Channel of Monetary Policy – Evidence from an Emerging Economy. *Economic Research Journal*, *32*(1), 742–754. doi:10.1080/1331677X.2019.1579662

Rakesh, V., Choo, J., & Reddy, C. K. (2015). Project recommendation using heterogeneous traits in crowdfunding. *Ninth International AAAI Conference on Web and Social Media.*

Read, A. (2013). Crowdfunding: an empirical and theoretical model of non-profit support. *Economics Theses, 91*. Retrieved from https://soundideas.pugetsound.edu/economics_theses/91

Rostami, J., Sepehrmanesh, M., Gharahbagh, E. A., & Mojtabai, N. (2013). Planning level tunnel cost estimation based on statistical analysis of historical data. *Tunnelling and Underground Space Technology, 33*, 22–33. doi:10.1016/j.tust.2012.08.002

Russell, A. D., Udaipurwola, A., Alldritt, M., & El-Guindy, K. (1999). Computer system for the selection of trenchless and conventional methods for underground utilities. *Tunnelling and Underground Space Technology, 14*, 1–12. doi:10.1016/S0886-7798(00)00019-5

Salahaldin, L., Angerer, M., Kraus, S., & Trabelsi, D. (2019). A duration-based model of crowdfunding project choice. *Finance Research Letters, 29*, 404–410. doi:10.1016/j.frl.2018.11.005

Schulz, M., Haas, P., Blohm, I., & Leimeister, J. M. (2015). How idea creativity and hedonic value influence project success in crowdfunding. *12th International Conference on Wirtschaftsinformatik.*

Schwienbacher, A., & Larralde, B. (2010). Crowdfunding of small entrepreneurial ventures. In D. Cumming (Ed.), *The Oxford handbook of Entrepreneurial Finance*. Oxford University Press.

Špačková, O., Novotná, E., Šejnoha, M., & Šejnoha, J. (2013). Probabilistic models for tunnel construction risk assessment. *Advances in Engineering Software, 62*, 72–84. doi:10.1016/j.advengsoft.2013.04.002

Steigenberger, N., & Wilhelm, H. (2018). Extending signaling theory to rhetorical signals: Evidence from crowdfunding. *Organization Science, 29*(3), 529–546. doi:10.1287/orsc.2017.1195

Sun, F., Liu, C., & Zhou, X. G. (2017). Utilities tunnel's finance design for the process of construction and operation. *Tunnelling and Underground Space Technology, 69*, 182–186. doi:10.1016/j.tust.2017.06.005

Veuger, J. W. (2015). Crowdfunding: the role of platforms in project success. *5th IBA Bachelor Thesis Conference.*

Walker, D. M. (2017). Crowdfunding: An innovative way to fund your project. *Nurse Researcher*, *25*(1), 24–29. doi:10.7748/nr.2017.e1425 PMID:28639522

Wang, P. (2016). Construction experience of urban underground pipe gallery in Suzhou. *Construction Economics*, *2*, 113–115.

Wu, J. S., Bai, Y. P., Fang, W. P., Zhou, R., Reniers, G., & Khakzad, N. (2021). An integrated quantitative risk assessment method for urban underground utility tunnels. *Reliability Engineering & System Safety*, *213*, 107792. doi:10.1016/j.ress.2021.107792

Xu, L. (2016). Legal issues of French public-private partnership(government organizations and social companies). *Administrative Law Review*, *3*, 116–127.

Yan, Y. F., Huang, Q. B., Xie, Y. L., Lin, T., Xu, Q., Fan, F. F., & Wang, Y. L. (2021). Failure analysis of urban open-cut utility tunnel under ground fissures environment in Xi'an, China. *Engineering Failure Analysis*, *127*, 105529. doi:10.1016/j.engfailanal.2021.105529

Yang, C., & Peng, F. L. (2016). Discussion on the development of underground utility tunnels in China. *Procedia Engineering*, *165*, 540–548. doi:10.1016/j.proeng.2016.11.698

Zhang, Z., Ren, J. R., Xiao, K. C., Lin, Z. Z., Xu, J. Y., Wang, W., & Pei, C. X. (2019). Cost allocation mechanism design for urban utility tunnel construction based on cooperative game and resource dependence theory. *Energies*, *12*(17), 3309. doi:10.3390/en12173309

Zhao, G. (2017). Confidence, bond risks, and equity returns. *Journal of Financial Economics*, *126*(3), 668–688. doi:10.1016/j.jfineco.2017.09.007

Zheng, H. C., Xu, B., Wang, T., & Chen, D. Y. (2017). Project implementation success in reward-based crowdfunding: An empirical study. *International Journal of Electronic Commerce*, *21*(3), 424–448. doi:10.1080/10864415.2016.1319233

Zhou, M. J., Lu, B. Z., Fan, W. G., & Wang, G. A. (2018). Project description and crowdfunding success: An exploratory study. *Information Systems Frontiers*, *20*(2), 259–274. doi:10.100710796-016-9723-1 PMID:29755287

ADDITIONAL READING

Shiller, R. J. (1981). Do stock prices move too much to be justified by subsequent changes in dividends? *The American Economic Review*, *71*(3), 421–436.

Špačková, O., Šejnoha, J., & Straub, D. (2013). Probabilistic assessment of tunnel construction performance based on data. *Tunnelling and Underground Space Technology*, *37*, 62–78. doi:10.1016/j.tust.2013.02.006

KEY TERMS AND DEFINITIONS

"All-or-Nothing" Mode: The founder can get pledged capital from backers if pledged capital surpasses pledged goal, and backers needn't supply pledged capital if pledged capital doesn't arrive at pledged goal.

BOT Style: A typical operation style for utilities tunnel project. It mainly includes the process of build-operate-transfer.

Crowdfunding: A new type Internet funding tool, whose character is the capital can be pledged from many backers to supply the project of founder with the advantage of Internet platform.

G-S Interactive Finance Framework: A framework used to analyze the finance design for construction and operation of utilities tunnel project.

"Keep-it-All" Mode: The founder can get pledged capital supplied by backers whether or not pledged capital arrives at pledged goal.

Platform: An Internet platform tool used for crowdfunding. The pledged goal, pledged date, delivery date, reward and other introduction of project using videos, photos and words will be posted on the platform.

Utilities Tunnel: By constructing corridor in some depth underground, water supply and drainage, electric power, telecommunication, gas, rubbish and other pipelines are laid inside utilities tunnel, which can be used to construct and maintain together.

ENDNOTES

1. Suitable funding mode choice is important to acquire enough construction capital for utilities tunnel project, which can directly lead to the success of utilities tunnel project whether or not.
2. Because net revenues are different in different periods, the volatility levels are also different.
3. The government also proposed to try government organizations and social companies' cooperation for utilities tunnel public project.
4. The needs for pipeline using units and maintenance should also be fully considered.

5 Some measures can be flexibly adopted to increase the activeness of social companies.

6 Finance institution regulates loan rate and sets mortgage requirement. The capital and interest can be compensated from operation revenue of utilities tunnel project.

7 Because utilities tunnel project usually has not only economic benefits but also social benefits, government perhaps gives extra bonus to make up capital shortage.

8 For example, Internet funding mode isn't a suitable funding mode now for a large-scale utilities tunnel project, and in this case debt or equity funding mode should be chosen.

9 Lin and Viswanathan (2016) think crowdfunding is that contributors or investors provide funds to an individual or business either as donations or in return for a debt repayable over time, an equity share, or a reward.

10 Ahlers et al. (2015) examine the impact of firms' financial roadmaps (e.g., preplanned exit strategies such as IPOs or acquisitions), external certification (awards, government grants and patents), internal governance (such as board structure), and risk factors (such as amount of equity offered and the presence of disclaimers) on funding success. The data highlight the importance of financial roadmaps and risk factors as well as internal governance for successful equity crowdfunding, but external certification has little impact.

Chapter 11
Renewable Energy Framework for Sustainability:
The Case of Spain

Maria Jesus Garcia
University of Valencia, Spain

ABSTRACT

Urban environments (areas in which multiple activities developed by human beings are brought together) have a strong environmental impact. Therefore, in those areas, rational use of natural resources and efficient consumption of energy must be promoted. Energy efficiency must also be accompanied by a policy of diversifying the sources used in energy production, which opens the door to the use and promotion of renewable energies. Energy efficiency consists not only measures to save and contain demand, but also requires the regulation and management of the supply of renewable energy sources. As a result, clean energy is represented by the low level of emissions into the atmosphere.

INTRODUCTION

The idea of sustainable development has to relate to other concepts and ideas within the framework of which it finds its justification and its content. Sustainable development cannot be discussed without first placing it in a broader context from which it owes. In this sense, a reference to the principle of sustainable development, energy efficiency and the idea of urban renovation is necessary. These are generic concepts within the framework of which energy renovation is framed and which also lend its justification and reason for being.

DOI: 10.4018/978-1-6684-5580-7.ch011

The first term to which it is necessary to allude to explain the idea of energy renovation has to do with the concept of sustainable development, which for some time now has been used in our domestic legislation and whose legal implementation has been carried out mainly through Law 2/2011, of 4th March, on Sustainable Economy.

Sustainable development is a concept that combines three interrelated elements and has traditionally been treated differently in Spanish legislation. Perhaps that is why it can be said that in our legal system the concept is relatively new in that it interrelates different objectives that converge in the different sectoral areas, emphasizing the interdependence between them rather than in their singular treatment (Steven & Majumdar, 2012). These three elements or pillars that converge in the concept of sustainable development are: social, economic and environmental. "*Sustainable development is a type of development that advocates first of all the harmonization between economic development and environmental protection, adding social progress; it would therefore be development in which high and stable growth in the production of goods and services is compatible with widespread social progress, environmental protection and prudent and efficient use of natural resources."; it is therefore a delicate building supported by three main pillars: social, economic and environmental in which none of them prevails over the others*".

Accordingly, sustainability has an integrated character, preceded as it is by the objectives of economic recovery, environmental sustainability and social cohesion. It is a general principle with transversal or horizontal projection, capable of crossing different and varied sectoral areas, as many as are relevant to achieve its integrating objectives (Curry & Pragasen, 2012).

Among the different sectorial areas transferred by the idea of sustainable development is undoubtedly the field of urban planning and housing. The activity generated in cities has an important environmental impact, so it is necessary to orient urban structures, homes and buildings under premises that are as respectful as possible with the environment, also taking advantage of its economic potential and its effect on the social fabric that inhabits it. It is about promoting integrated actions in the urban environment that are in tune with the objectives also integrating sustainable development.

Since sustainable development is an integrative concept, its influence on the urban and housing sector could not fail to have these same connotations, insofar as sustainable urbanism is nothing but a projection of sustained development in a specific area. Urban planning must respond to the requirements of sustainable development, minimizing its commitment to growth and betting on the regeneration of the existing city in order to achieve a sustainable and inclusive urban model, environmentally, socially and economically that improves the quality of life of citizens in urban spaces. In short, integrated objectives of sustainability applied to urban planning are explained, in which the duty of conservation plays a fundamental role.

BACKGROUND

Spanish Constitution is devoid of explicit references to sustainable development since it is a relatively new concept in our domestic law. However, the relationship between this principle and certain constitutional rights is evident, since the idea of sustainable urbanism advocates the preservation of urban spaces and buildings in which the constitutional right to decent housing and an adequate environment can be realized. From the perspective of the principle of sustainability, urban planning must be oriented towards renovation in order to comply with article 45 of the Constitution, since renovation does not consume land and makes it possible to exploit and use, rather to reuse, the existing heritage. In this sense, the implications between sustainable development and protection and the right to an adequate environment that guarantees the quality of life are fully established. Sustainable urban development would comply with article 45 of the Constitution in its two aspects: as a requirement imposed on the public authorities to ensure their protection and as the right of citizens to enjoy an adequate environment in order to ensure a certain quality of life. The observation that the urban environment is also the environment, or in other words, that the environment is also integrated by the urban environment, is clearly deduced from this and other recently adopted laws in our legal system. Thus, article 1 of Royal Legislative Decree 7/2015, of 30th October, approving the revised text of the Land Law, when defining its object, shows that the actions that are carried out try to ensure citizens an adequate quality of life, and the effectiveness of their right to enjoy a decent and adequate housing. Article 5 of the Act also establishes the rights of the citizen to whose satisfaction the act is subject, including the right to enjoy a decent, adequate and accessible home that is free of noise or other polluting emissions, as well as the right to enjoy an environment and a suitable landscape (Droege, 2008).

On the other hand, Law 7/85 of 2nd April, regulating the bases of local regime, in its most recent amendment, also highlighted this point when it speaks in its article 25 of the competence of the municipalities in matters relating to the urban environment.

The connections with the constitutional right to housing are also clear in the extent maintaining the housing in proper condition for use, ensuring the maintenance of the existing population in a way that promotes the social and economic texture of this urban area.

In short, this is indicative that the actions of renovation, renewal and regeneration referred to from the point of view of sustainable development has its legal basis in articles 45 and 46 of the Constitution, without denying the implications that such a treatment of environmental protection will have on the economic and social aspects, such as the revival of economic activity, among others.

And precisely with this integrative purpose, the Law on renovation, renovation and urban regeneration is enacted, which combines the treatment of urban development actions in the urban environment and actions on housing and the architectural park from the point of view of the umbrella of sustainability. The point of view from which this Law rushing to the processing of such sectoral domains was certainly novel, as if, until then, it is accustomed to witness the treatment sector of the subjects on the basis of its consideration of the substantive, that is, as a sectoral domains where the material determined the content of the Law, in the case of the mentioned norm, the unifying element of the different precepts contained in it is not the substantive scope or material one, but the principle under which this treatment acted as an element of cohesion of the different precepts. The principle of sustainability is referred, which justified those regulations are found under the umbrella of the same law sectoral areas as varied as urban legislation, precepts on urban renovation, urban leasing legislation or horizontal property. Nothing new if Law 2/2011 of 4th March, Sustainable Economy is considered. Royal Legislative Decree 7/2015, of 30th October, approving the revised text of the Land Law and Urban Renovation serves now to a more specific, as it regulates subjects with a greater connection to each other that are all grouped under the generic concept of "urban", or more accurately, "urban environment". The content of this Law seems to consider the regulation of urban planning, as it affects consolidated urban land, susceptible to renovation, regeneration or renovation actions or new urbanization actions. But the truth is that the Law seems to be aimed at regulating urban development actions based on the principle of sustainable development.

Obviously, within this perspective of environmental sustainability present in the idea of sustainable urbanism one of the most relevant aspects from the point of view of its impact on the environment is that it has to do with the use and exploitation of energy and the use of certain forms of energy that maximize their consumption causing the minimum environmental impact. And focused as sustainable urbanism is on the idea of maintenance and conservation of the already made city and the existing buildings, this objective is to accommodate the buildings and the existing real estate park to these new energy demands. That is why energy renovation is discussed, meaning a set of actions in the urban environment and in existing buildings and homes that try to adapt the pre-existing elements (housing, but not only this, but also endowments, services and equipment) to the principles of efficiency and energy saving in accordance with the legal framework provided by Law 38/1999, of 5th November, on Building Planning and Royal Decree 314/2006, of 17th March, Technical Building Code.

Directive 2012/27/EU states that buildings represent 40% of energy consumption in the European Union, so it becomes clear the need to influence the building sector and improve its energy performance (Lund, 2012).

These objectives, it is found in article 3 of Royal Legislative Decree 7/2015, of 30th October, consolidated text of the Law of Soil and Urban Renovation, which speaks of minimizing polluting emissions and greenhouse gases, water and energy consumption and waste production. Also, in paragraph i) of the same article these objectives are highlighted, when the Law refers to the need to prioritize renewable energies over the use of fossil energy sources and combat energy poverty with measures in favor of efficiency and energy saving. And finally, subparagraph (h) refers to the need to promote the protection of the atmosphere and the use of clean materials, products and technologies that reduce pollutant emissions and greenhouse gases from the construction sector, as well as reused and recycled materials that contribute to improving resource efficiency.

Energy efficiency is therefore one of the goals to be achieved in the urban environment aimed at achieving the objectives of environmental sustainability that underlie the generic concept of sustainable urban development. Thus, when article 3 of Royal Legislative Decree 7/2015, of 30th October, refers to the purposes to which public policies will tend in the urban environment, it bets on a concept of sustainability from the economic, social, environmental point of view that promotes the rational use of natural resources and energy efficiency. The Law seems to understand that energy efficiency is capable of promoting sustainable environmental conditions by itself and contributing to economic sustainability by generating jobs and employment, which is why its treatment is singled out as an emerging sector with great potential, not only environmental, but also economic.

To this end, energy efficiency must also be accompanied by a policy of diversifying the sources used in energy production, which opens the door to the use, promotion and use of renewable energies. The much-discussed energy efficiency cannot consist only of measures aimed at saving and containing demand, but also requires the regulation and management of supply that promotes the introduction of renewable energy sources, which is in turn clean energy given its low level of emissions into the atmosphere (Purohit & Pallav, 2013).

In accordance with the above, energy renovation, based on the principle of energy efficiency, would be aimed at:

- Prioritize renewable energies.
- Promote energy savings.
- Reduce pollutant emissions and waste production.

ENERGY EFFICIENCY IN THE CONTEXT OF EUROPEAN UNION REGULATIONS

It should not be forgotten that European legislation sets specific targets for energy efficiency and emission reductions. In this sense it is necessary to make reference to the Directive 2010/31/EU of the European Parliament and of the Council of 19th May 2010 on the energy performance of buildings (object transposition part in the Royal Decree 235/2013 of April 5) and Directive 2012/27/EU of the European Parliament and of the Council of 25th October 2012 on energy efficiency, which aims to update the community legal order in the context of the general objective of the Europe 2020 Strategy, this implies the objectives of a 20% reduction in greenhouse gas emissions, an increase in the contribution of renewable energies by 20% and a 20% improvement in energy efficiency. The Directive also sets more ambitious targets for 2050 aimed at reducing the level of CO2 emissions by 80-90% compared with 1990 levels. The measures identified by the said Directive concern key areas and sectors for achieving energy efficiency targets, such as building renovation. In this context, the Directive requires not only a significant percentage of central Government buildings to be renovated annually in order to improve their energy efficiency, but also that Member States also establish a strategy to mobilize investment in the renovation of residential buildings in order to improve the energy efficiency of the entire housing stock. The formulas to achieve these objectives are through the control of demand, promoting actions aimed at ensuring savings measures, but also through actions of management and regulation of supply, which includes its diversification, prioritizing the use of renewable energies for energy production over the use of fossil energies.

In this context, the Renewable Energy Plan (PER) 2011-2020 has been approved by resolution of the Council of Ministers of November 11, 2011, setting objectives that are in line with Directive 2009/28/EC of the European Parliament and of the Council of 23rd April 2009 on the promotion of the use of energy from renewable sources, and in response to the mandates of the Royal Decree 661/2007, which regulates the activity of electricity production under the special regime and the Law 2/2011 of 4th March, Sustainable Economy. The PER has the objective of achieving, as indicated by the Community Directive, that in the year 2020 at least 20% of the gross final consumption of energy in Spain comes from the use of renewable sources.

Law 8/2013 of 26th June on urban renovation, regeneration and renewal served these purposes by partially transposing Directive 2012/27/EU, on energy efficiency, so that the principle of energy rationality is one of the pillars of the standard. The aforementioned standard established among its objectives those of minimizing the consumption of energy in homes constituting habitual residence and prioritizing renewable energies with measures in favor of efficiency and energy saving. This applies not only to new buildings and installations, but also to existing ones that are the subject of intervention. The content of this rule has become part of the Royal Legislative Decree 7/2015, of 30th October, consolidated text of the Land and Urban Renovation Law. In this context, the urban duty of conservation is considered as an instrument at the service of energy renovation, to the extent that its content is divided into a series of strata that support actions aimed at adapting the existing real estate to the demands of energy efficiency that the rules that regulate the building are demanding.

SOME CLARIFICATIONS ON THE CONCEPT OF RENOVATION IN THE CURRENT REGULATIONS

Law 8/2013, of 26th June, established a new nomenclature when formulating actions in the urban environment that differs from the nomenclature used in previous legislation, where the concept of urban renovation was comprehensive of a set of isolated or integrated actions that could even involve the demolition of buildings and urban elements incompatible with actions of sanitation or urban regeneration. Thus, two types of renovation were distinguished: isolated renovation and integrated renovation. The first considered the real estate in its own individuality, without implications or connections with the surrounding elements. On the contrary, integrated renovation considered the affected heritage as part of a larger space in which it was integrated. Integrated renovation consisted of the renovation of urban spaces, which without dispensing with the renovation of individual elements, transcended their effects to project on other elements of the environment, considering it as a whole.

According to the new nomenclature introduced by Law 8/2013, of 26th June, renovation is the term that refers to singular actions in buildings, while those that affect the urban fabric is called regeneration or urban renewal, according to entail the demolition of any of the elements of urban pre-existing. Based on this distinction, article 2 of Royal Legislative Decree 7/2015 of 30th October, establishes possible actions to be carried out in the urban environment, differentiating between renovation of buildings and regeneration and urban renewal. According to the cited article, performances on the urban environment are those that are intended to perform renovation work, when there are situations of failure or degradation of the basic requirements of functionality, safety and habitability of buildings, and the regeneration and urban renewal will be those that affect, both buildings as urban structure, including works of new building in the replacement of buildings previously demolished.

With reference to the basic requirements of functionality, safety, and livability, the idea of renovation of building is spacious and accommodates works and activities related to energy efficiency of the buildings, which introduces the concept of energy renovation, which involves performing actions on the real estate existing in a situation of failure or degradation in relation to the basic requirements of the building to adapt it to the demands of efficiency and energy savings.

EFFICIENCY AND ENERGY RENOVATION WITHIN THE FRAMEWORK OF THE URBAN DUTY OF CONSERVATION AND THE USE OF RENEWABLE ENERGIES

Both the renovation of buildings and the integrated actions of urban renewal and regeneration are actions of urban significance, so on these actions must be projected the urban instruments and techniques that affect the situation of buildings and homes. So, what sets the Real Decreto legislativo 7/2015, of 30th October, which in its article 2.1 states that all of these actions will apply to the statutory scheme basic duties and charges to which they are entitled in accordance with the performance of urban transformation or building that behave, in accordance with the provisions of article 7.

One of these duties is the duty of urban conservation, whose content is integrated by reference to Law 38/1999, of 5th November, on Building Planning, which in turn refers to Royal Decree 314/2006, of 17th March, which approves the Technical Building Code. The requirements of energy efficiency are incorporated into the duty of conservation through the regulation made in the Technical Building Code in its reference to living conditions, since they are applicable not only to new buildings, but also to existing ones when they are the subject of some intervention. Among these requirements are those related to the use of renewable energies.

But in addition, the Building Planning Law configures the duty of conservation in open terms by reference to the regulations that may be applicable in each case. The Act points to the Technical Building Code may be supplemented with the requirements of other regulations issued by the competent Authorities and is regularly updated according to the evolution of technology and the demand of the society, which emphasizes the open-ended character of the setting of the duty of conservation.

THE CONTENT OF THE DUTY OF CONSERVATION: THE THREE LEVELS

The duty of urban conservation is regulated in article 15 of the consolidated text of the Law on Land and Urban Renovation, article that reformulates the wording of the duty of conservation established by Royal Legislative Decree 2/2008, of 20th June in the terms in which it was drafted after Law 8/2013, of 26th June of urban renovation, regeneration and renewal.

The aforementioned precept establishes different duties and burdens that configure the urban content of the property right, among which is the duty of conservation. According to the statement of reasons of the Law on urban renovation, regeneration and renovation, of which the aforementioned article 15 brings cause, the duty of conservation is articulated in three levels depending on the content that results from it for the owner.

At its basic level, the duty of conservation entails the duty to allocate the buildings to uses compatible with territorial and urban planning and the need to guarantee the safety, health, accessibility and decoration of the real estate. In this way, the duty of conservation includes the three basic requirements of the building, referring to functionality, safety and habitability. So far, the duty of conservation coincides with its traditional formulation. However, the Law of renovation, regeneration and renewing urban added to article 9 of the Consolidated Text of the Land Act, Royal legislative Decree 2/2008 of 20th June, a new section under which the duty of conservation also includes the realization of the work and the necessary works in order to satisfy, in general, the basic requirements of the building set forth in article 3.1 of the Law 38/1999, of 5th November on building renovation. This explicit reference to the previous Law is no longer included in article 15 of Royal Legislative Decree 7/2015 of 30th October, but is implicit in said article insofar as the aforementioned precept establishes the duty to preserve buildings in the legal conditions of safety, health, universal accessibility, ornament and the others required by the laws to serve as support for the uses for which they are intended and are compatible with territorial and urban planning, from which an implicit reference to the Building Planning Law and the Technical Building Code is inferred.

A second level, in which the duty of conservation includes the works and works necessary to adapt and progressively update the buildings, in particular the facilities, to the legal norms that are explicitly required at all times. Law 8/2013, of June 26, started from the consideration of an open conservation duty, whose content was not delimited by article 9 of Royal Legislative Decree 2/2008, of June 20, consolidated text of the Land Law, but subject to variations or extensions from other subsequent laws. Thus, Article 9, paragraph 2, established the competent administration could impose at any time the realization of works to comply with the legal duty of conservation in accordance with the provisions of the applicable state and autonomous community legislation. This provision, due to its obviousness, is also absent in article 15 of Royal Legislative Decree 7/2015 of 30th October, which does not prevent considering the duty of conservation as a duty of an evolutionary nature and subject to the variation of the technical requirements that are foreseen in the different applicable regulations. In this way, the duty of conservation will also include the necessary works to adapt the buildings and update their facilities to the legal norms that are required at any time, as the regulations of the sector introduce modifications in order to maintain the conditions of use of the buildings. The duty of conservation is thus in open terms, by reference to the regulations that may be applicable in each case.

Finally, a third level includes additional works, carried out for reasons of general interest, in respect of which the Law distinguishes two cases:

- those carried out for tourist or cultural reasons that constitute an assumption already included in the previous legislation, although under the consideration of improvement and forced renovation works.
- those carried out for the improvement of the quality and sustainability of the urban environment, assumption that now introduces Law of renovation, regeneration and urban renewal in the modification that makes of the Consolidated Text of the Law of the Land.

THE INITIAL CONTENT OF THE DUTY OF CONSERVATION: ENERGY SAVING AND THE USE OF RENEWABLE ENERGY

The preservation of buildings in conditions of safety, health and public decoration constitutes a legal duty imposed on the owner on the basis of the social function of the property in accordance with article 33 of the Constitution. To the duty of the owner to maintain the buildings in the aforementioned conditions, it is now also added that of universal accessibility, and in addition, it is implicitly integrated into the duty of conservation the realization of the works and the works necessary to satisfy in general, the basic requirements of the building established in article 3.1 of Law 38/1999, of 5th November, of Building Planning.

Article 3.1 of the Building Planning Act establishes three basic requirements for buildings aimed at ensuring the safety of people, the welfare of society and the protection of the environment. These are requirements relating to functionality, safety and habitability. And precisely in this last section the measures relating to energy saving and thermal insulation are established so that a rational use of the energy necessary for the proper use of the building is achieved. The efficiency and energy savings are part of the duty of conservation to the extent that this duty entails keeping the buildings in terms of serving to its use, which leads to the need to satisfy the basic requirements of the building, within which are located relative to energy savings, thermal insulation and rational use of energy, and that is conducive to the simultaneous execution of conservation work directed to maintain the buildings in terms of safety, sanitation and beautification works and aimed to enhancc the energy efficiency of the same. Therefore, it is better to take advantage of the realization of conservation works in the most traditional sense of the term to promote the realization of actions related to energy renovation, which are now integrated into the duty of conservation.

The requirements of energy efficiency have been incorporated into the duty of conservation through the regulation carried out by the Technical Building Code, Royal Decree 314/2006, of 17th March. and are applicable not only to newly constructed buildings, but also to those undergoing repair or renovation. The aforementioned Royal Decree is issued in implementation of Law 38/1999 of 5th November, on Building Planning, whose second provision empowers the Government to approve a regulatory norm that establishes the basic requirements that buildings must meet in relation to the requirements relating to safety and habitability listed in paragraphs b) and c) of article 3.1 of the Building Planning Law.

Among the requirements relating to habitability, Article 15 of the said Code regulates the basic requirements of energy saving. These basic requirements apply and must be met both by new buildings and by existing buildings that are subject to modification, reform, extension or renovation and are basic, so that their requirements are mandatory throughout the national territory. The eleventh Final Provision of the Law 8/2013, of June 26, has widened the scope of application of Technical Building Code to modify its article 1 that the basic requirements must be met, as established by the regulations set in the project, the construction, the maintenance, preservation and use of buildings and facilities, as well as in interventions in existing buildings. Likewise, the aforementioned rule has modified Article 2 of the Technical Code, so that its basic requirements will be required not only to new buildings but also to all those existing buildings that are the subject of intervention.

The basic requirements for energy savings set out in the Technical Code are five, namely: limitation of energy demand, performance of thermal installations, energy efficiency of lighting installations, minimum solar contribution of domestic hot water and minimum photovoltaic contribution of electrical energy. The purpose for which it is intended with this energy saving enters into what was formerly defined as energy efficiency, as it is to get a rational and sustainable use of the energy used in the building or home, and also enhance the consumption comes from renewable energy sources.

For this reason, among these basic requirements it is necessary to highlight those that refer to solar contributions, and above all, those that refer to the production of domestic hot water, which " have the character of minimums, and can be extended as a result of additional provisions issued by the competent administrations"

And this raises the question of which Administration is competent to regulate this question. Some autonomous communities have adopted their own regulations on renewable energy. This is the case of the Autonomous Community of Andalusia and its Law 2/2007, on the promotion of renewable energies and energy savings and efficiency in Andalusia. The aforementioned Law is developed by Decree 169/2011, of 31st May, whose Chapter II "*Basic requirements for the use of renewable energies, savings and energy efficiency*", complies with the provisions of the Technical Building Code by adapting these requirements to the energy needs and climatic characteristics of Andalusia. However, the Andalusian regulations do not establish additional requirements of contribution to the minimum contributions of thermal energy required in the state regulations through the Technical Building Code.

By applying the principle of linking negative in the interpretation of the principle of legality, the judgments of the Supreme Court of 22nd May 2015 (RJ 2015/2620 and 2015/2016) consider such other competent authorities are, in addition to the autonomous communities, local authorities and that the criteria listed in the Technical Building Code constitute minimum values that the local authorities have to respect, but that can increase.

According to the jurisprudential criterion established after the judgments of the Supreme Court of May 22, 2015 (RJ 2015/2620 and 2015/2016), this reference to the competent administrations, also includes local entities that can thus adapt the state provisions to their own peculiarities and the needs that conform their specific local interests.

Thus, some municipalities, in the context of sustainable urbanism, have adopted ordinances aimed at promoting energy savings and promoting the use of renewable energies such as solar energy based on the competences that local legislation recognizes them in matters such as urbanism and the environment. Such is the case of the municipal Ordinance on the collection and use of solar thermal energy in buildings, of the City of Burgos . Also, the Ordinance of the same name of the City of Pamplona as well as the municipal Ordinance of eco-energy efficiency and use of renewable energy in buildings and their facilities, of the City of Zaragoza among others.

The approval of the Technical Building Code, Royal Decree 314/2006, of 17th March, has come to provide the legal authorization whose absence motivated the challenge of the local ordinances on energy use to understand that the Law of Bases of Local Regime did not provide sufficient legal authorization for municipalities to approve ordinances in this sense. The judgments of the Supreme Court of May 22, 2015 (RJ 2015/2620 and 2015/2016) indicate that from the approval of the Technical Building Code the normative coverage of the ordinances relating to the use of solar energy is accommodated in the aforementioned legal text, which has the character of basic legislation

ENERGY EFFICIENCY AS AN ADDITIONAL CONTENT TO THE DUTY OF CONSERVATION: THE IMPROVEMENT OF ENERGY EFFICIENCY AND THE USE OF RENEWABLE ENERGY SOURCES

The duty of conservation will also include the adaptation of the building to the use of renewable energies indirectly when renovation actions are carried out that update the duty of conservation.

The duty to initial conservation is added to the duty to perform additional work for tourism or cultural, or to improve the quality and sustainability of the urban environment, since the distinction between the duty of conservation based on the fulfillment of the social function of property and the duty of conservation based on reasons of general interest has been a constant in the planning legislation that the different laws have been addressed in a different way, but always on the basis of their recognition . The content of these additional works is defined by reference to the Technical Building Code and may consist of partial or complete adaptation to all or some of the basic requirements established therein. In accordance with this article, the Administration may order the owners to carry out works aimed at improving the quality or sustainability of the urban environment, including works to improve energy efficiency and including those aimed at encouraging the installation of renewable energy sources in buildings.

The attention to renewable energies is framed by both in the works additional ordering the administration to improve the quality and sustainability of the urban environment imposed by reasons of general interest, and is justified in the community legislation and in particular Directive 2012/27/EU, noting that buildings represent 40% of energy consumption in the European Union compels the member states to develop strategies that include the realization of investment in the renovation of residential and commercial buildings . The Directive requires not only the annual renovation of a percentage of public buildings of the central State Administration (thus underlining the exemplary nature of public actions), but also the mobilization of investments aimed at the renovation of buildings for commercial or residential uses with the aim of improving their energy efficiency.

The characteristic of these actions is that the law empowers the public administrations to impose them for reasons of general interest beyond the limits that govern the duty of conservation, in which case, the Law indicates, the ordering Administration will be responsible for the works that exceed this limit to obtain improvements of general interest. Additional conservation is discussed which involves carrying out additional works and financing measures to improve the energy efficiency of buildings. This implies the renovation of buildings through internal strategies of mobilization of real estate investments where the legal limit for the owner is that of the duty of conservation and the administration has to contribute to the financing of the rest, since they are improvements of general interest. In this case, the duty of conservation goes beyond the particular objective of adaptation of the building in question to identify with a broader objective of general interest focused on the consolidated urban environment where it is located and on the fulfillment of energy efficiency objectives that are deduced from European policies, for which the mobilization of investments aimed at the renovation of residential and commercial buildings is foreseen. The additional content of the duty of conservation must be framed within integral actions and policies of economic, social, environmental regeneration and cohesion of the city as a whole, perspective from which the duty of conservation transcends the individual level to achieve improvements of general interest. And from this perspective, not only building renovation actions are imposed, but also actions that include actions to implement renewable energy not only at the building level, but also through urban development actions in urban fabrics that involve urban regeneration or renewal (Dilip & Tatsutani, 2019).

However, article 15 of Royal Legislative Decree 7/2015, of 30th October, does not seem to require any additional requirements for the imposition of such additional conservation works. Since it is an additional duty that transcends the individual plan of the property to which it refers to have an impact on the urban environment, it could be considered consubstantial to the general interest alleged that the property was included in some type of legal instrument of renovation. Well established, for example in the article 111 of the Law of Sustainable Economy, repealed by the Law 8/2013, of June 26, in which it is stated that the competent authority could command, in the form, terms and deadlines set by the applicable law, the execution of works of improvement up to the maximum amount of statutory duty, in addition to for reasons cultural and tourist collected by the applicable legislation, in the course of the construction or the building that were to become affected by a program, plan or any other legal instrument for the renovation of housing approved and in force, and refers to works designed to guarantee the rights recognized by law to individuals, or to be imposed by legal norms supervened for reasons of safety, adequacy of facilities and minimum services, reduction of polluting emissions and emissions of any kind and those necessary to reduce water and energy consumption.

ENERGY RENOVATION AND THE LIMIT OF THE DUTY OF CONSERVATION

Law 8/2013, of 26th June, introduced some modifications regarding the limits of the duty of conservation and that were fixed by reference to quantitative criteria. These amendments are now incorporated in article 15 of the consolidated text of the Law on Land and Urban Renovation. In this sense, the limit of the duty of conservation is established at half of the current construction value of a new plant property, equivalent to the original in relation to the constructive characteristics and the useful surface, carried out in the necessary conditions so that its occupation is authorized, or where appropriate, is in a position to be legally destined for its own use. By establishing this limit, the state legislation configures the content of the duty of conservation by reference to an objective criterion, thus preventing the autonomous legislation from establishing its own limits with respect to that duty. Law 8/2013, of June 26, introduced an important novelty in the duty of urban conservation and in the regulation that until now had been carried out of it by the Consolidated Text of the Land Law of 2008, by quantifying the limit of the duty of conservation, which were doing the autonomous regulations in some cases. This modification should be subject to positive evaluation, as in this way, the limit is set up with basic character and binding on the legislator autonomous, so that in accordance with the provisions of article 149.1.1 of the Constitution, defines the legal positions of the owners in relation to their duty of conservation, and imposes rules equal and uniform to all property owners of buildings.

The duty of conservation is established by reference to an objective limit and individualized by reference to each particular property, which is fixed by reference to a percentage applied on the current value of a new construction of similar functional and structural characteristics and equal useful surface. In short, the Law addresses the value or cost of replacement by considering not the value of the damaged building (current value of the building), but a new building whose valuation will serve to contrast the cost of repair works and set the limit of the duty of conservation. The valuation system deals exclusively with the replacement value, that is, the hypothetical value of a construction of the same structure and building typology that allows a use of similar characteristics to that of the construction with respect to which the declaration of ruin is intended. The evaluation of these repairs will have to be carried out based on current techniques and materials that allow to maintain or return to the construction the original functionality. The legislation considers the economic profitability of the extension of the useful life of the constructions through the conservation or renovation of the same ones. In this sense, the limit of the profitability of the conservation of the buildings is fixed in the disbursement by the owner of expenses that remain below half of the cost of a new construction with characteristics similar to the existing one.

But the limit of the duty of conservation is solved based on economic criteria where the cost of replacement works is only one of the terms of the equation. The second is related to the content and extent of the works to be made to understand fulfilled the aforementioned duty. In this sense, it should be noted that the conservation works are not merely the works necessary to maintain the property in conditions of safety, health and ornament (Sawyer, 2009). It is already indicated in the previous section that the duty of conservation also involves the realization of works necessary to ensure universal accessibility, as well as those others that are necessary to meet the basic requirements of the building established in article 3.1 of Law 38/1999 of 5th November on Building Planning, where interventions related to energy efficiency are registered, including both those that are deduced from the current regulations and those others that are explicitly required to adapt and update their facilities to the standards. In short, this means going to the Technical Building Code, in which the basic requirements of the building are specified, which in terms of energy saving also implies the need to include among these works, those relating to the installation of collection systems, transformation, storage and use of solar energy. In addition, the values derived from this basic requirement will be considered minimum, without prejudice to stricter values that may be established by the competent administrations and that contribute to sustainability according to the characteristics of their location and territorial scope.

It could be thought that since one of the terms of the equation expands with respect to what was the traditional duty of conservation, the logical consequence will be that the limit of the duty of conservation will be easily exceeded by including more demanding actions in the maintenance of buildings that also meet criteria of saving and energy efficiency. However, this possible consequence is remedied if the second comparative term focuses on the replacement cost of the property. This clarification is important since urban planning legislation has not always made use of this criterion to delimit the cessation of the duty of conservation. Thus, for example, article 247 of the Consolidated Text of the Land Act of 1992, when referring to the declaration of ruin (which implied the cessation of the duty of conservation), referred to the present value of the building or plants concerned, excluding the value of the land. This meant taking as a reference the value of the building at the time when it was planned to carry out the repair works on it, which implied valuing the building applying criteria indicative of the depreciation suffered by the property depending on age and state of conservation among others. Obviously, this means that the building is quantified at a lower magnitude easily exceeded by the cost of maintenance and renovation works carried out in it. The option to include the replacement cost of a similar building of new plant allows to increase quantitatively the second term of the equation.

CONCLUSION

The Law 8/2013 introduced within the duty of urban conservation the realization of additional works that had as a common denominator the fact that its imposition is based on reasons of general interest, and that the Consolidated Text of the Land Law of 2008 considered as works of improvement. Royal Legislative Decree 7/2015, of 30th October, refers to them in article 15.1 c). These additional works include those carried out for tourism and cultural reasons, to which are added those focused on improving the quality and sustainability of the urban environment, introduced by Law 2/2011 of 4th March on Sustainable Economy and where those actions related to energy efficiency are framed. The content of these additional works for the improvement of quality and sustainability is determined by reference to the Technical Building Code.

Well, these works additional to the duty of conservation which now also include those related to the improvement of the quality and sustainability of the urban environment, has a particular legal regime, since the law establishes the possibility for the administration to force the landlord to the realization of the same, even once exceeded the limit of the duty of conservation. In this case, the administration that orders or imposes the realization of such works must pay the economic excess that entails the realization of the same. And this economic excess is fixed by reference to the limit of the duty of conservation referred to above. In this way, the limit of the duty of conservation (half of the current value of construction of a building of a new plant, equivalent to the original in connection with the construction features and the useful surface, taken with the conditions necessary for their occupation is approvable or, in your case is in a position to be legally intended for use by own) it is also the limit of the works to be executed at the expense of the owners when the Administration of the order to the improvement of the quality or sustainability of the urban environment. The Law assumes the criterion of the joint participation of the owner and the Administration in the maintenance of the property, as deduced from article 9.1 of the Land Law after the wording given to it by the Law on urban renovation, regeneration and renovation.

Royal Legislative Decree 7/2015, October 30, considers the importance of these renovation actions in the urban environment and the need to adapt them to the limits of the legal duty of conservation through the economic viability report, regulated in article 22. This memory, it is expected not only in cases in which they carry out activities of regeneration and renewal, but also in the case of actions of renovation of building, isolated or included in a scope of work (by areas or spaces), establishing as one of its aims to ensure the least possible impact on the personal wealth of the individuals, adjusted in any case the limits of the duty to bequeath conservation.

DISCLAIMER

The contents and views of this chapter are expressed by the author in her personal capacity. It is not necessary for the Editor and the Publisher to agree with these viewpoints and they are not responsible for any duty of care in this regard.

ACKNOWLEDGMENT

The author extends sincere gratitude to

- The Editor and the International Editorial Advisory Board (IEAB) of this book who initially desk reviewed, arranged a rigorous double/triple blind review process and conducted a thorough, minute and critical final review before accepting the chapter for publication.
- All anonymous reviewers who provided very constructive feedbacks for thorough revision, improvement, extension and fine tuning of the chapter.
- All colleagues, assistants and well-wishers who assisted the authors to complete this task.

REFERENCES

Curry, N., & Pragasen, P. (2012). Biogas prediction and design of a food waste to energy system for the urban environment. *Renewable Energy*, *41*(5), 200–209. doi:10.1016/j.renene.2011.10.019

Dilip, A., & Tatsutani, M. (2019). *Sustainable energy for developing countries*. Oxford University.

Droege, P. (2008). *Urban Energy Transition: From Fossil Fuels to Renewable Power*. Elsevier. doi:10.1016/B978-0-08-045341-5.00029-3

Lund, P. (2012). Large-scale urban renewable electricity schemes. Integration and interfacing aspects. *Energy Conversion and Management*, *63*(11), 162–172. doi:10.1016/j.enconman.2012.01.037

Purohit, I., & Pallav, P. (2013). Evaluating the potential of concentrating solar power generation in North-western India. *Energy Policy*, *62*, 157–175. doi:10.1016/j.enpol.2013.06.069

Sawyer, S. (2009). *Un-habitat, Local Governments for Sustainability, and the United Nations Environment Programme. In Sustainable Urban Energy Planning: A handbook for cities and towns in developing countries*. UNEP.

Steven, C., & Majumdar, A. (2012). Opportunities and challenges for a sustainable energy future. *Nature*, *488*(8), 294–303. PMID:22895334

Compilation of References

Abbasi, F., & Riaz, K. (2016). CO_2 emissions and financial development in an emerging economy: An augmented VAR approach. *Energy Policy*, *90*, 102–114. doi:10.1016/j.enpol.2015.12.017

Agyemang, A. O., Yusheng, K., Twum, A. K., Ayamba, E. C., Kongkuah, M., & Musah, M. (2021). Trend and relationship between environmental accounting disclosure and environmental performance for mining companies listed in China. *Environment, Development and Sustainability*, *23*(8), 12192–12216. doi:10.100710668-020-01164-4 PMID:33424427

Ahamed, M. M., & Mallick, S. K. (2019). Is financial inclusion good for bank stability? International evidence. *Journal of Economic Behavior & Organization*, *157*, 403–427. doi:10.1016/j.jebo.2017.07.027

Ahlers, G. K. C., Cumming, D., Günther, C., & Schweizer, D. (2015). Signaling in equity crowdfunding. *Entrepreneurship Theory and Practice*, *39*(4), 955–980. doi:10.1111/etap.12157

Ahmad, F. (2013). The effect of oil prices on unemployment: Evidence from Pakistan. *Business and Economics Research Journal*, *4*(1), 43–57.

Ahmadov, I. (2016). Azerbaijan's New Macroeconomic Reality: How to Adapt to Low Oil Prices. *Caucasus Analytical Digest*, *83*, 2–6.

Aimer, N. M. M., & Moftah, M. (2016). The effects of fluctuations of oil price on economic growth of Libya. *Energy Economics Letters*, *3*(2), 17–29. doi:10.18488/journal.82/2016.3.2/82.2.17.29

Akinlo, T., & Apanisile, O. T. (2015). The impact of volatility of oil price on the economic growth in sub-Saharan Africa. *Journal of Economics. Management and Trade*, *5*(3), 338–349.

Akyol, H., & Baltaci, N. (2018). Ülke Kredi Risk Düzeyi, Petrol Fiyatlari Ve Temel Makroekonomik Göstergelerin Hisse Senedi Getirilerine Etkisi: BIST 100 Örneği. *Kafkas Universitesi. Sosyal Bilimler Enstitu*, *22*, 459–476.

Alagoz, M., Alacahan, N. D., & Akarsu, Y. (2017). Petrol fiyatlarının makro ekonomi üzerindeki etkisi-ülke karşılaştırmaları ile panel veri analizi. *Karamanoğlu Mehmetbey Üniversitesi Sosyal Ve Ekonomik Araştırmalar Dergisi*, *19*(33), 144–150.

Alderfer, C. (1972). *Existence, Relatedness and Growth*. The Free Press.

Aldoseri, M., & Worthington, A. C. (2020). Operational Risk Management of Islamic Banks. In A. Rafay (Ed.), *Handbook of Research on Theory and Practice of Global Islamic Finance* (pp. 455–470). IGI Global. doi:10.4018/978-1-7998-0218-1.ch025

Ali, H. S., Yusop, Z. B., & Hook, L. S. (2015). Financial development and energy consumption nexus in Nigeria: An application of autoregressive distributed lag bound testing approach. *International Journal of Energy Economics and Policy*, *5*(3), 816–821.

Alkahteeb, T. T. Y., & Sultan, Z. A. (2019). Oil price and economic growth: The case of Indian economy. *International Journal of Energy Economics and Policy*, *9*(3), 274–279. doi:10.32479/ijeep.7602

Amri, F. (2016). The relationship amongst energy consumption, foreign direct investment and output in developed and developing countries. *Renewable & Sustainable Energy Reviews*, *64*, 694–702. doi:10.1016/j.rser.2016.06.065

Anenberg, S. C., Miller, J., Minjares, R., Du, L., Henze, D. K., Lacey, F., & Heyes, C. (2017). Impacts and mitigation of excess diesel-related NO x emissions in 11 major vehicle markets. *Nature*, *545*(7655), 467–471. doi:10.1038/nature22086 PMID:28505629

Anglin, A. H., Short, J. C., Drover, W., Stevenson, R. M., Mckenny, A. F., & Allison, T. H. (2018). The power of positivity? The influence of positive psychological capital language on crowdfunding performance. *Journal of Business Venturing*, *33*(4), 470–492. doi:10.1016/j.jbusvent.2018.03.003

Anifowose, M. A., Rashid, H. M., Annuar, H. A., & Ibrahim, H. (2018). Intellectual capital efficiency and corporate book value: Evidence from Nigerian economy. *Journal of Intellectual Capital*, *19*(3), 644–668. doi:10.1108/JIC-09-2016-0091

Arcand, J. L., Berkes, E., & Panizza, U. (2015). Too much finance? *Journal of Economic Growth*, *20*(2), 105–148. doi:10.100710887-015-9115-2

Arellano, M., & Bond, S. (1991). Some tests of specification for panel data: Monte Carlo evidence and an application to employment equations. *The Review of Economic Studies*, *58*(2), 277–297. doi:10.2307/2297968

Arellano, M., & Bover, O. (1995). Another look at the instrumental variable estimation of error-components models. *Journal of Econometrics*, *68*(1), 29–51. doi:10.1016/0304-4076(94)01642-D

Ariel, B., Stephanie, B., Bruce, B., Kathrin, K., Thomas, M., & Matthias, K. (2016). *Survey results on public perceptions and the views of crowdfunding platforms and project developers*. Retrieved from https://discovery.dundee.ac.uk/en/publications/survey-results-on-public-perceptions-and-the-views-of-crowdfundin

Arora, V., & Tanner, M. (2013). Do oil prices respond to real interest rates? *Energy Economics*, *36*, 546–555. doi:10.1016/j.eneco.2012.11.001

Aryampa, S., Maheshwari, B., Sabiiti, E., Bateganya, N. L., & Bukenya, B. (2019). Status of Waste Management in the East African Cities: Understanding the Drivers of Waste Generation, Collection and Disposal and Their Impacts on Kampala City's Sustainability. *Sustainability*, *11*(19), 5523. doi:10.3390u11195523

Asaleye, A. J., Aremu, C. O., Lawal, A. I., Inegbedion, H., Popoola, O., Adewara, S. O., & Obasaju, B. O. (2019). Oil price shock and macroeconomic performance in Nigeria: Implication on employment. *International Journal of Energy Economics and Policy*, *9*(5), 451–457. doi:10.32479/ijeep.7768

Asian Development Bank. (2017). *Responding to External Shocks Hitting the Economy of Kazakhstan*. Retrieved from https://www.adb.org/sites/default/files/project-documents/49045/49045-001-dpta-en_8.pdf

Aslanli, K. (2016). *Lower Oil Revenues, Higher Public Debt: The Fiscal Policy Implications of Low Oil Prices in Azerbaijan*. National Reports. Retrieved from https://www.socialwatch.org/node/17465

Asongu, S. A., & Nnanna, J. (2019). Foreign Aid, Instability, and Governance in Africa. *Politics & Policy*, *47*(4), 807–848. doi:10.1111/polp.12320

Asongu, S. A., & Odhiambo, N. M. (2020a). Governance, CO_2 emissions and inclusive human development in sub-Saharan Africa. *Energy Exploration & Exploitation*, *38*(1), 18–36. doi:10.1177/0144598719835594

Asongu, S. A., & Odhiambo, N. M. (2020b). Inequality thresholds, governance and gender economic inclusion in sub-Sahran Africa. *International Review of Applied Economics*, *34*(1), 91–114. doi:10.1080/02692171.2019.1645817

Atil, A., Nawaz, K., Lahiani, A., & Roubaud, D. (2020). Are natural resources a blessing or a curse for financial development in Pakistan? The importance of oil prices, economic growth and economic globalization. *Resources Policy*, *67*, 101683. doi:10.1016/j.resourpol.2020.101683

Awolaja, G. O., & Musa, D. C. (2017). Asymmetric Oil Price Shocks and Stock Prices in Nigeria. *MPRA Paper*, 1–27.

Ayisi, R. K. (2020). The asymmetry effect of oil price changes on inflation, and the welfare implication for Ghana. *African Journal of Economic and Management Studies*, *12*(1), 55–70. doi:10.1108/AJEMS-01-2020-0009

Ba, L., Gasmi, F., & Noumba, P. (2010). *Is the level of financial sector development a key determinant of private investment in the power sector?* (Working Paper No. 5373). World Bank.

Baber, H. (2020). Crowdfunding Framework in Islamic Finance. In A. Rafay (Ed.), *Handbook of Research on Theory and Practice of Global Islamic Finance* (pp. 307–320). IGI Global. doi:10.4018/978-1-7998-0218-1.ch017

Badiou, A. (2015). *Our Wound is Not So Recent*. Lecture delivered at La Commune theatre, Aubervilliers, France. Retrieved from https://miguelabreugallery.com/wp-content/uploads/2016/09/AlainBadiou_OurWoundisNotSoRecent.pdf

Bagehot, W. (1873). *Lombard Street: A description of the money market*. Wiley & Sons.

Bai, R., Lam, J. C., & Li, V. O. (2018). A review on health cost accounting of air pollution in China. *Environment International*, *120*, 279–294. doi:10.1016/j.envint.2018.08.001 PMID:30103126

Baloch, R. M., Maesano, C. N., Christoffersen, J., Banerjee, S., Gabriel, M., Csobod, E., & Dewolf, M. C. (2020). Indoor air pollution, physical and comfort parameters related to schoolchildren's health: Data from the European SINPHONIE study. *The Science of the Total Environment*, *739*, 139870. doi:10.1016/j.scitotenv.2020.139870 PMID:32544681

Baohua, L., Sun, P. Y., & Zeng, Y. (2020). Employee-related corporate social responsibilities and corporate innovation: Evidence from China. *International Review of Economics & Finance*, *70*, 357–372. doi:10.1016/j.iref.2020.07.008

Barclays. (2020, August 13). *ESG funds: Looking beyond the label*. Retrieved from https://www.investmentbank.barclays.com/our-insights/3-point-perspective/esg-funds-looking-beyond-the-label.html

Baskurt, B. B., Celik, S., Oke, T., & Rafay, A. (2022). FDI and Environmental Degradation: Evidence from a developed country. In A. Rafay (Ed.), *Handbook of Research on Energy and Environmental Finance 4.0* (pp. 446–471). IGI Global. doi:10.4018/978-1-7998-8210-7.ch018

Bayramov, V., & Abbas, G. (2017). Oil shock in the Caspian Basin: Diversification policy and subsidized economies. *Resources Policy*, *54*, 149–156. doi:10.1016/j.resourpol.2017.10.006

Bayramov, V., Breban, D., & Mukhtarov, E. (2019). Economic effects estimation for the Eurasian Economic Union: Application of regional linear regression. *Communist and Post-Communist Studies*, *52*(3), 209–225. doi:10.1016/j.postcomstud.2019.07.001

Bayramov, V., & Orujova, L. (2017). Volatility, Diversification and Oil Shock in Resource-Rich Turkic Countries: Avenues for Recovery. *Bilig*, *83*, 303–329.

Beck, T., Demirguc-Kunt, A., Laeven, L., & Levine, R. (2004). *Finance, firm size, and growth* (Working Paper No. 10983). NBER.

Beck, T., Demirguc-Kunt, A. S. L. I., Laeven, L., & Levine, R. (2008). Finance, firm size, and growth. *Journal of Money, Credit and Banking*, *40*(7), 1379–1405. doi:10.1111/j.1538-4616.2008.00164.x

Beck, U. (1992). *Risk Society*. Sage.

Bednárová, M., Klimko, R., & Rievajová, E. (2019). From Environmental Reporting to Environmental Performance. *Sustainability*, *11*(9), 2549. doi:10.3390u11092549

Beirne, P. (1999). For a nonspeciesist criminology: Animal abuse as an object of study. *Criminology*, *37*(1), 117–148. doi:10.1111/j.1745-9125.1999.tb00481.x

Bekhet, H. A., Matar, A., & Yasmin, T. (2017). CO_2 emissions, energy consumption, economic growth, and financial development in GCC countries: Dynamic simultaneous equation models. *Renewable & Sustainable Energy Reviews*, *70*, 117–132. doi:10.1016/j.rser.2016.11.089

Benabou, R., & Tirole, J. (2009). Individual and Corporate Social Responsibility. *Economica*, *77*(305), 1–10. doi:10.1111/j.1468-0335.2009.00843.x

Benramdane, A. (2017). Oil price volatility and economic growth in Algeria. *Energy Sources. Part B, Economics, Planning, and Policy*, *12*(4), 338–343. doi:10.1080/15567249.2015.1128015

Berardi, F. (2017). *Futurability: The Age of Impotence and the Horizon of Possibility*. Verso Books.

Berbena, R., & Jansen, W. (2009). Bond market and stock market integration in Europe: A smooth transition approach. *Applied Economics*, *41*(24), 3067–3080. doi:10.1080/00036840701367572

Berensmann, K., Volz, U., Alloisio, I., Bak, C., Bhattacharya, A., Leipold, G., Schindler, H., & MacDonald, L., Huifang, T., & Yang, Q. (2017). *Fostering Sustainable Global Growth through Green Finance—What Role for the G20*. The World Bank. Retrieved from https://collaboration.worldbank.org/content/usergenerated/asi/cloud/ attachments/sites/collaboration-for-development/en/groups/green-finance-community-of-practice/documents/jcr:content/content/primary/blog/green_finance_educat-LVNC/Climate_Green-Finance_V2.pdf

Bergant, Ž. (2015, September 2). *Social responsibility and corporate's solvency*. Academic Press.

Bergant, Ž. (2019b). The Relation Between Capital and Labor as a Basis for the Distribution of the Added Value. *International Journal of Science, technology and Society, 7*(3), 50–55.

Bergant, Ž. (2014, September 2). Corporate responsibility and internal reporting. In *Proceedings of International Conference on Social Responsibility*. IRDO. Retrieved from https://www.irdo.si/skupni-cd/cdji/cd-irdo-2014/referati/d-Bergant-eng.pdf

Bergant, Ž. (2018, September 1). Capital, labour and social responsibility. In *Proceedings of International Conference on Social Responsibility*. IRDO., Retrieved from https://www.irdo.si/irdo2018/referati/c-01-Bergant.pdf

Bergant, Ž. (2019). Individual person and social responsibility. In *Proceedings of International Conference on Social Responsibility*. IRDO., Retrieved from https://www.irdo.si/skupni-cd/cdji/cd-irdo-2015/referati/37-zivko-Bergant-paper-final-.pdf

Bergant, Ž. (2019c). The Quality of Accounting Information and User's Social Responsibility: Social Aspect. *International Journal of Advances in Management and Economics.*, *8*(5), 8–15. doi:10.31270/IJAME/v08/i05/2019/2

Bergant, Ž. (2020a). Starting Points to Comprehensive Treatment of Social Responsibility. *International Journal of Advances in Management and Economics*, *9*(1), 1–7. doi:10.31270/IJAME/v09/i01/2020/1

Bergant, Ž. (2020b). Basic problem of the stakeholder theory from a corporates' social responsibility point of view. *International Journal of Business Marketing and Management*, *5*(11), 117–119.

Bergant, Ž. (2020c). Debates on corporate social responsibility are becoming similar to the philanthropy. *International Journal of Advances in Management and Economics*, *9*(6), 13–17.

Bergant, Ž. (2021a, September 4). The problem of organization's purpose as a basis for its social responsible behavior. In *Proceedings of International Conference on Social Responsibility*. IRDO. Retrieved from https://www.irdo.si/irdo2021ref/referati/01-b01-zivko.pdf

Bergant, Ž. (2021b). Social responsibility and business excellence. *International Journal of Advanced Engineering Research and Science*, *8*(1), 73–79. doi:10.22161/ijaers.81.11

Bergant, Ž. (2021c). What And Who Is Company's Stakeholder? *International Journal of Science Academic Research*, *2*(1), 770–773.

Bergant, Ž. (2021d). *Accountancy and Social Responsibility. An Innovative New Approach to Accountancy Theory and Practice*. Palgrave Macmillan. doi:10.1007/978-3-030-77928-3

Bergset, L. (2015). The rationality and irrationality of financing green start-ups. *Administrative Sciences*, *5*(4), 260–285. doi:10.3390/admsci5040260

Berument, M. H., Ceylan, N. B., & Dogan, N. (2010). The impact of oil price shocks on the economic growth of selected MENA1 countries. *Energy Journal*, *31*(1), 149–176. doi:10.5547/ISSN0195-6574-EJ-Vol31-No1-7

Bhusal, T. P. (2010). Econometric analysis of oil consumption and economic growth in Nepal. *Economic Journal of Development Issues*, *11/12*, 135–143.

Boogaard, H., Walker, K., & Cohen, A. J. (2019). Air pollution: The emergence of a major global health risk factor. *International Health*, *11*(6), 417–421. doi:10.1093/inthealth/ihz078 PMID:31613318

Borio, C. (2011). Rediscovering the macroeconomic roots of financial stability policy: Journey, challenges, and a way forward. *Annual Review of Financial Economics*, *3*(1), 87–117. doi:10.1146/annurev-financial-102710-144819

Boutabba, M. A. (2014). The impact of financial development, income, energy and trade on carbon emissions: Evidence from the Indian economy. *Economic Modelling*, *40*, 33–41. doi:10.1016/j.econmod.2014.03.005

Bouzid, A. (2012). The relationship of oil prices and economic growth in Tunisia: A vector error correction model analysis. *The Romanian Economic Journal*, *XV*(43), 3–22.

Bowen, R. H. (1953). *Social Responsibilities of the Businessman*. Harper & Row.

Brown, S. P. A., Yucel, M. K., & Thompson, J. (2003). *Business cycles: the role of energy prices* (Working Paper 0304). Federal Reserve Bank of Dallas.

Brown, S. P., & Yücel, M. K. (2002). Energy prices and aggregate economic activity: An interpretative survey. *The Quarterly Review of Economics and Finance*, *42*(2), 193–208. doi:10.1016/S1062-9769(02)00138-2

Brunnschweiler, C. N. (2010). Finance for renewable energy: An empirical analysis of developing and transition economies. *Environment and Development Economics*, *15*(3), 241–274. doi:10.1017/S1355770X1000001X

BSI. (2020). *ISO* 26000 *Guidance on social responsibility*. British Standard Institution. Retrieved from https://www.bsigroup.com/en-GB/ISO-26000-Social-Responsibility/

Buckland, R., & Fraser, P. (2000). *Abnormal returns in the UK water industry since privatisation* (Working Paper No. 00-10). Aberdeen Papers in Accountancy, Finance and Management. University of Aberdeen.

Buckland, R., & Williams, J. (2013). *Volatility and regulation in water supply and distribution: A post-privatization comparison of UK and US water utilities*. University of Aberdeen. Retrieved from https://aura.abdn.ac.uk/bitstream/2164/2968/1/WaterUtilityPaperforAURA.pdf

Buckland, R., Beecher, J., & Williams, J. (2015). Risk and regulation in water utilities: A cross-country comparison of evidence from the CAPM. *Journal of Regulatory Economics*, *47*(2), 117–145. doi:10.100711149-014-9261-z

Buengeler, C., Diccolo, R. F., & Locklear, L. R. (2021). LMX differentiation and group outcomes: A framework and review drawing on group diversity insights. *Journal of Management*, *47*(1), 260–287. doi:10.1177/0149206320930813

Butticè, V., Colombo, M. G., & Wright, M. (2017). Serial crowdfunding, social capital, and project success. *Entrepreneurship Theory and Practice*, *41*(2), 183–207. doi:10.1111/etap.12271

Canto-Perello, J., Curiel-Esparza, J., & Calvo, V. (2013). Criticality and threat analysis on utility tunnels for planning security policies of utilities in urban underground space. *Expert Systems with Applications*, *40*(11), 4707–4714. doi:10.1016/j.eswa.2013.02.031

Canto-Perello, J., Curiel-Esparza, J., & Calvo, V. (2016). Strategic decision support system for utility tunnel's planning applying A'WOT method. *Tunnelling and Underground Space Technology*, *55*, 146–152. doi:10.1016/j.tust.2015.12.009

Capponi, A., & Frei, C. (2017). Systemic influences on optimal equity-credit investment. *Management Science*, *63*(8), 2756–2771. doi:10.1287/mnsc.2016.2460

Caputo, F., Pizzi, S., Ligorio, L., & Leopizzi, R. (2021). Enhancing environmental information transparency through corporate social responsibility reporting regulation. *Business Strategy and the Environment*, *30*(8), 1–15. doi:10.1002/bse.2814

Carpejani, G., Assad, A. S., Godoi, L. R., Waters, J., & de Andrade, J. B. (2020). The Anthropocene: Conceptual Analysis with Global Climate Change, Planetary Boundaries and Gaia 2.0. In Water, Energy and Food Nexus in the Context of Strategies for Climate Change Mitigation (pp. 301-314). Springer Nature.

CBI. (2021). Sustainable Debt Market: Summary H1 2021. *Climate Bonds Initiative*. Retrieved from https://www.climatebonds.net/files/reports/cbi_susdebtsum_h12021_02b.pdf

CecchettiS. G.KharroubiE. (2015). *Why does financial sector growth crowd out real economic growth?* (Discussion Paper No. DP10642). CEPR. Retrieved from https://ssrn.com/abstract=2615882

Cecere, G., Le Guel, F., & Rochelandet, F. (2017). Crowdfunding and social influence: An empirical investigation. *Applied Economics*, *49*(57), 5802–5813. doi:10.1080/00036846.2017.1343450

Central Bank of the Republic of Azerbaijan. (2017). *Annual Report*. Retrieved from https://www.cbar.az/home?language=en

CESD. (2019). *Social consequences of the oil price shock in the resource rich post-soviet countries*. Center for Economic and Social Development. Retrieved from https://www.cesd.az/

CFA. (2018). *Coal vs Renewables: Financial Analysis*. New Delhi: Centre for Financial Accountability. Retrieved from https://carboncopy.info/wp-content/uploads/COAL-VS-RENEWABLES-REPORT_NOV-19-2.pdf

Chandran, V. G. R., & Tang, C. F. (2013). The impacts of transport energy consumption, foreign direct investment and income on CO_2 emissions in ASEAN-5 economies. *Renewable & Sustainable Energy Reviews*, *24*, 445–453. doi:10.1016/j.rser.2013.03.054

Charfeddine, L., & Khediri, K. B. (2016). Financial development and environmental quality in UAE: Cointegration with structural breaks. *Renewable & Sustainable Energy Reviews*, *55*, 1322–1335. doi:10.1016/j.rser.2015.07.059

Chen, S., Chen, D., & Härdle, W. K. (2014). *The influence of oil price shocks on china's macroeconomy: a perspective of international trade*. Retrieved from https://papers.ssrn.com/sol3/papers.cfm?abstract_id=2634637

Chen, F., & Chen, Z. (2021). Cost of economic growth: Air pollution and health expenditure. *The Science of the Total Environment*, *755*, 142543. doi:10.1016/j.scitotenv.2020.142543 PMID:33035980

Chitioui, S. (2012). Does economic growth and financial development spur energy consumption in Tunisia? *Journal of Economics and International Finance*, *4*(7), 150–158. doi:10.5897/JEIF12.014

Choi, S., Furceri, D., Loungani, P., Mishra, S., & Poplawski-Ribeiro, M. (2018). Oil prices and inflation dynamics: Evidence from advanced and developing economies. *Journal of International Money and Finance*, *82*, 71–96. doi:10.1016/j.jimonfin.2017.12.004

Churchill, A. A., & Saunders, R. J. (1989). *Financing the energy sector in developing countries* (Working Paper Energy Series No. 14). World Bank.

Cihak, M., Demirgüç-Kunt, A., Feyen, E., & Levine, R. (2012). *Benchmarking financial systems around the world* (Policy Research Working Paper No. WPS6175). World Bank.

Çoban, S., & Topcu, M. (2013). The nexus between financial development and energy consumption in the EU: A dynamic panel data analysis. *Energy Economics*, *39*, 81–88. doi:10.1016/j.eneco.2013.04.001

Colbeck, I. (2007). Air pollution: history of actions and effectiveness of change. In *The Handbook of Environment and Society* (pp. 374–384). Sage. doi:10.4135/9781848607873.n26

Colombo, O. (2021). The use of signals in new-venture financing: A review and research agenda. *Journal of Management*, *47*(1), 237–259. doi:10.1177/0149206320911090

Costanza, R., & Daly, H. E. (1992). Natural capital and sustainable development. *Conservation Biology*, *6*(1), 37–46. doi:10.1046/j.1523-1739.1992.610037.x

Cuestas, J. C., & Gil-Alana, L. A. (2018). Oil price shocks and unemployment in Central and Eastern Europe. *Economic Systems*, *42*(1), 164–173. doi:10.1016/j.ecosys.2017.05.005

Currie, J., Neidell, M., & Schmieder, J. F. (2009). Air pollution and infant health: Lessons from New Jersey. *Journal of Health Economics*, *28*(3), 688–703. doi:10.1016/j.jhealeco.2009.02.001 PMID:19328569

Curry, N., & Pragasen, P. (2012). Biogas prediction and design of a food waste to energy system for the urban environment. *Renewable Energy*, *41*(5), 200–209. doi:10.1016/j.renene.2011.10.019

Da Silva, P. P., Cerqueira, P. A., & Ogbe, W. (2018). Determinants of renewable energy growth in Sub-Saharan Africa: Evidence from panel ARDL. *Energy*, *156*, 45–54. doi:10.1016/j.energy.2018.05.068

Dabla-Norris, M. E., & Srivisal, M. N. (2013). *Revisiting the link between finance and macroeconomic volatility* (Working Paper No. 13/29). International Monetary Fund.

Dancey, K. (2021). *Professional Accountants Leading Reporting and Assurance on Sustainability*. IFAC.

Davis, S. L., Rives, L. M., & Maya, S. R. D. (2017). Introducing personal social responsibility as a key element to upgrade CSR. *Spanish Journal of Marketing*, *21*(2), 146–163. doi:10.1016/j.sjme.2017.04.001

De Gregorio, J., & Guidotti, P. E. (1995). Financial development and economic growth. *World Development*, *23*(3), 433–448. doi:10.1016/0305-750X(94)00132-I

Derrick, A. (1998). Financing mechanisms for renewable energy. *Renewable Energy*, *15*(1-4), 211–214. doi:10.1016/S0960-1481(98)00159-1

Diamond, J. (2005). *Why do Societies Collapsed?* Viking.

Dickey, D. A., & Fuller, W. A. (1981). Likelihood ratio statistics for autoregressive time series with a unit root. *Econometrica*, *49*(4), 1057–1072. doi:10.2307/1912517

Dikkaya, M., & Doyar, B. V. (2017). Causality among Oil Prices, GDP and Exchange Rate: Evidence from Azerbaijan and Kazakhstan. *Bilig*, *83*, 79–98.

Dilip, A., & Tatsutani, M. (2019). *Sustainable energy for developing countries*. Oxford University.

Dogan, E., & Seker, F. (2016). The influence of real output, renewable and non-renewable energy, trade and financial development on carbon emissions in the top renewable energy countries. *Renewable & Sustainable Energy Reviews*, *60*, 1074–1085. doi:10.1016/j.rser.2016.02.006

Dogrul, H. G., & Soytas, U. (2010). Relationship between oil prices, interest rate, and unemployment: Evidence from an emerging market. *Energy Economics*, *32*(6), 1523–1528. doi:10.1016/j.eneco.2010.09.005

Droege, P. (2008). *Urban Energy Transition: From Fossil Fuels to Renewable Power*. Elsevier. doi:10.1016/B978-0-08-045341-5.00029-3

Dutta, K. D., & Saha, M. (2020). Nexus of governance, macroprudential policy and financial risk: Cross-country evidence. *Economic Change and Restructuring*, *54*(4), 1253–1298. doi:10.100710644-020-09301-9

Eccles, R., Ioannou, I., & Serafeim, G. (2012, January 6). Is sustainability now the key to corporate success? *The Guardian*. Retrieved from https://www.theguardian.com/sustainable-business/sustainability-key-corporate-success

Edelstein, P., & Kilian, L. (2007). *Retail energy prices and consumer expenditures*. Retrieved from https://papers.ssrn.com/sol3/papers.cfm?abstract_id=1135493

Elkington, J. (1997). *Cannibals with Forks: The Triple Bottom Line of 21st Century Business*. Capstone Publishing Ltd.

Elkington, J., Hailes, J., & Makower, J. (1998). Triple. *The Bottom Line (New York, N.Y.)*, *11*(Appendix). http://archive.babymilkaction.org/pdfs/spinpdfs/appendices/triplebl.pdf

Environmental Protection Agency. (2015). *Air Quality Index Report*. United States Environmental Protection Agency.

Enzensberger, N., Fichtner, W., & Rentz, O. (2003). Financing renewable energy projects via closed-end funds—A German case study. *Renewable Energy*, *28*(13), 2023–2036. doi:10.1016/S0960-1481(03)00080-6

Esen, O., & Bayrak, M. (2015). Enerji Açığının Belirleyicilerinin Teorik Perspektiften İncelenmesi. *Anemon Muş Alparslan Üniversitesi Sosyal Bilimler Dergisi*, *3*(1), 45–61. doi:10.18506/anemon.26550

Eze, I. C., Schaffner, E., Fischer, E., Schikowski, T., Adam, M., Imboden, M., Tsai, M., Carballo, D., Von Eckardstein, A., Künzli, N., Schindler, C., & Probst-Hensch, N. (2014). Long-term air pollution exposure and diabetes in a population-based Swiss cohort. *Environment International*, *70*, 95–105. doi:10.1016/j.envint.2014.05.014 PMID:24912113

Fangmin, L., & Jun, W. (2011). Financial system and renewable energy development: Analysis based on different types of renewable energy situation. *Energy Procedia*, *5*, 829–833. doi:10.1016/j.egypro.2011.03.146

Filipiak, B. Z., & Dylewski, M. (2020). Sustainable financial reporting in the context of ensuring sustainability of financial systems. In *Finance and sustainable development* (pp. 235–267). Routledge. doi:10.4324/9781003011132-14

Fiorelli, C., & Mele, M. (2017). Water gain: As a common good becomes a financial opportunity. *International Journal of Economics and Financial Issues*, *7*(2), 626–630.

Fisman, R., & Love, I. (2004). Financial development and intersectoral allocation: A new approach. *The Journal of Finance*, *59*(6), 2785–2807. doi:10.1111/j.1540-6261.2004.00716.x

Force, G. F. T. (2015). *Establishing China's green financial system. Report of the Green Finance Task Force*. People's Bank of China & United Nations Environment Programme. Retrieved from https://2degrees-investing.org/wp-content/uploads/2015/04/Establishing-Chinas-green-financial-system-April-2015.pdf

Fracassi, C. (2017). Corporate finance policies and social networks. *Management Science*, *63*(8), 2420–2438. doi:10.1287/mnsc.2016.2433

Freeman, R. E. (1984). *Strategic Management: A Stakeholder Approach*. Pitman Publishing.

Friedman, M. (1970, September 13). The Social Responsibility of Business is to Increase its Profits. *The New York Times*. Retrieved from https://link.springer.com/chapter/10.1007/978-3-540-70818-6_14

Garcia, A. S., Mendes-Da-Silva, W., & Orsato, R. J. (2019). Corporate sustainability, capital markets, and ESG performance. In W. Mendes-Da-Silva (Ed.), *Individual Behaviors and Technologies for Financial Innovations*. Springer. doi:10.1007/978-3-319-91911-9_13

Ge, L., & Luo, X. C. (2016). Team rivalry and lending on crowdfunding platforms: An empirical analysis. *Financial Innovation*, *2*(1), 17. doi:10.118640854-016-0035-8

Gelb, A. (2010). Economic Diversification in Resource Rich Countries. Center for Global Development.

Geman, H., & Kanyinda, A. (2007). Water as the next commodity. *Journal of Alternative Investments*, *10*(2), 23–30. doi:10.3905/jai.2007.695264

Gennaioli, N., Shleifer, A., & Vishny, R. (2012). Neglected risks, financial innovation, and financial fragility. *Journal of Financial Economics*, *104*(3), 452–468. doi:10.1016/j.jfineco.2011.05.005

Georg, L. (2017). Information security governance: Pending legal responsibilities of non-executive boards. *The Journal of Management and Governance*, *21*(4), 793–814. doi:10.100710997-016-9358-0

Ghalayini, L. (2011). The interaction between oil price and economic growth. *Middle Eastern Finance and Economics*, *13*(21), 127–141.

Gielen, D., Boshell, F., Saygin, D., Bazilian, M. D., Wagner, N., & Gorini, R. (2019). The role of renewable energy in the global energy transformation. *Energy Strategy Reviews*, *24*, 38–50. doi:10.1016/j.esr.2019.01.006

Gilroy, B. M., Schreckenberg, H., & Seiler, V. (2013). *Water as an alternative asset* (Working Paper No. 2012-09). Center for International Economic. Retrieved from http://groups.unipaderborn.de/fiwi/RePEc/Working%20Paper%20neutral/WP55%20-%20 2012-09.pdf

Goel, R. K. (2001). Status of tunnelling and underground construction activities and technologies in India. *Tunnelling and Underground Space Technology*, *16*(2), 63–75. doi:10.1016/S0886-7798(01)00035-9

Gonzalez-Perez, M. A. (2013). Corporate Social Responsibility and International Business: A Conceptual Overview. In International Business, Sustainability and Corporate Social Responsibility. Emerald.

Gorus, M. S., Ozgur, O., & Develi, A. (2019). The relationship between oil prices, oil imports and income level in Turkey: Evidence from Fourier approximation. *OPEC Energy Review*, *43*(3), 327–341. doi:10.1111/opec.12159

Gray, R. H. (2000). Current developments and trends in social-environmental auditing and attestation. *International Journal of Auditing*, *4*(3), 247–268. doi:10.1111/1099-1123.00316

Gray, R. H., Owen, D. L., & Adams, C. (1996). *Accounting and Accountability: Changes and challenges in corporate social and environmental reporting*. Prentice-Hall.

Greenberg, J., & Mollick, E. (2017). Activist choice homophily and the crowdfunding of female founders. *Administrative Science Quarterly*, *62*(2), 341–374. doi:10.1177/0001839216678847

GRI. (2013). *Sustainability Reporting Guidelines*. Amsterdam: Global Reporting Initiative. Retrieved from https://www.globalreporting.org/standards/2013.asp

Grinblatt, M., Ikäheimo, S., Keloharju, M., & Knüpfer, S. (2016). IQ and mutual fund choice. *Management Science*, *62*(4), 924–944. doi:10.1287/mnsc.2015.2166

Griskevicius, V., Tybur, J. M., Delton, A. W., & Robertson, T. E. (2011). The influence of mortality and socioeconomic status on risk and delayed rewards: A life history theory approach. *Journal of Personality and Social Psychology*, *100*(6), 1015–1026. doi:10.1037/a0022403 PMID:21299312

Gronwald, M., Mayr, J., & Orazbayev, S. (2009). *Estimating the effects of oil price shocks on the Kazakh economy* (Working Paper No. 81). ifo Institut – Leibniz-Institut für Wirtschaftsforschung an der Universität München.

Grossner, C. (1970). *Svet v času, ki prihaja* [The world in the time to come]. Ljubljana: Državna založba Slovenije.

Guliyev, F. (2016). Azerbaijan: Low Oil Prices and their Social Impact. *Caucasus Analytical Digest*, *83*, 16–25.

Gundogan, H., & Tok, D. (2019). Petrole bağımlı ülkelerde petrol fiyatlarının sanayi üretimine etkisi: Panel nedensellik çalışması. *Ege Academic Review*, *19*(1), 131–140.

Guo, Y., Zeng, H., Zheng, R., Li, S., Pereira, G., Liu, Q., Chen, W., & Huxley, R. (2017). The burden of lung cancer mortality attributable to fine particles in China. *The Science of the Total Environment*, *579*, 1460–1466. doi:10.1016/j.scitotenv.2016.11.147 PMID:27913022

Hamidu, A., Haron, M., & Amran, A. (2015). Corporate social responsibility: A review on definitions, core characteristics and theoretical perspectives. *Mediterranean Journal of Social Sciences*, *6*(4), 83–95. doi:10.5901/mjss.2015.v6n4p83

Hanabusa, K. (2009). Causality relationship between the price of oil and economic growth in Japan. *Energy Policy*, *37*(5), 1953–1957. doi:10.1016/j.enpol.2009.02.007

Haris, M., Yao, H., Tariq, G., Malik, A., & Javaid, H. M. (2019). Intellectual capital performance and profitability of banks: Evidence from Pakistan. *Journal of Risk and Financial Management*, *12*(2), 56. doi:10.3390/jrfm12020056

Hashim, D., & Boffetta, P. (2014). Occupational and environmental exposures and cancers in developing countries. *Annals of Global Health*, *80*(5), 393–411. doi:10.1016/j.aogh.2014.10.002 PMID:25512155

He, H. Y., Luo, Q., & Chen, T. (2018). Research on PPP financing model of utilities tunnel based on investors' perspective. *The Engineering Economist*, *28*(5), 60–65.

He, L., Liu, R., Zhong, Z., Wang, D., & Xia, Y. (2019). Can green financial development promote renewable energy investment efficiency? A consideration of bank credit. *Renewable Energy*, *143*, 974–984. doi:10.1016/j.renene.2019.05.059

Henk, G. G. (1998). Privatization and the public/private partnership. *Journal of Management Engineering*, *14*(4), 28–29. doi:10.1061/(ASCE)0742-597X(1998)14:4(28)

Hira, T. K. (2012). Promoting sustainable financial behaviour: Implications for education and research. *International Journal of Consumer Studies*, *36*(5), 502–507. doi:10.1111/j.1470-6431.2012.01115.x

Hirshleifer, D., Levi, Y., Lourie, B., & Teoh, S. H. (2019). Decision fatigue and heuristic analyst forecasts. *Journal of Financial Economics*, *133*(1), 83–98. doi:10.1016/j.jfineco.2019.01.005

Hobey, E. (2015, March 31). *Global crowdfunding market to reach 34.4B in 2015.* Massolution Posts Research Findings. Retrieved from https://www.crowdfundinsider.com/2015/03/65302-massolution-posts-research-findings-crowdfunding-market-grows-167-in-2014-crowdfunding-platforms-raise-16-2-billion/

Horgan, J. (2021). *B.C Premier Comments about heat wave deaths.* Rogers Media.

Hulme, T. W., & Burchell, A. J. (1999). Tunnelling projects in Singapore: An overview. *Tunnelling and Underground Space Technology*, *14*(4), 409–418. doi:10.1016/S0886-7798(00)00004-3

Humbatova, S., Tanriverdiyev, S., Garayev, A., & Hajiyev, N. (2019). Analysis of the oil, price and currency factor of economic growth in Azerbaijan. *Entrepreneurship and Sustainability Issues*, *6*(3), 1335–1353. doi:10.9770/jesi.2019.6.3(20)

Hummel, K. (2020). *The European Union Non-Financial Reporting Directive: Evidence on Regulatory Parameters and Firm-Value Consequences*. Retrieved from https://papers.ssrn.com/sol3/papers.cfm?abstract_id=3744653

Husin, M. M., & Haron, R. (2020). Financial Sustainability of SMEs through Islamic Crowdfunding. In A. Rafay (Ed.), *Handbook of Research on Theory and Practice of Global Islamic Finance* (pp. 321–337). IGI Global. doi:10.4018/978-1-7998-0218-1.ch018

IASB. (2020). *International Financial Reporting Standards*. International Accounting Standards Board.

ICCA. (2006). *The ICCA Handbook on Corporate Social Responsibility*. John Wiley & Sons.

ICCA. (2010). *The A to Z of Corporate Social Responsibility*. John Wiley & Sons.

Idowu, S. O., Schmidpeter, R., & Zu, L. (2020). *The Future of the UN Sustainable Development Goals*. Springer. doi:10.1007/978-3-030-21154-7

Idrisov, G., Kazakova, M., & Polbin, A. (2015). A theoretical interpretation of the oil prices impact on economic growth in contemporary Russia. *Russian Journal of Economics*, *1*(3), 257–272. doi:10.1016/j.ruje.2015.12.004

IEA. (2014). *Africa Energy Outlook. A Focus on Energy Prospects in Sub-Saharan Africa*. World Energy Outlook Special Report. Retrieved from https://www.usaid. gov/sites/default/files/documents/1860/IE47A-Africa-Energy-Outlook-2014.pdf

IEA. (2015). *World Energy Outlook Special Report: India Energy Outlook*. International Energy Agency. Retrieved from https://www.iea.org/reports/india-energy-outlook-2015

IFC. (2017). *Blended Concessional Finance for Private Sector Projects – Summary Report*. International Finance Corporation. Retrieved from https://www.ifc.org/wps/wcm/connect/a8398ed6-55d0-4cc4-95aa-bcbabe39f79f/DFI+Blended+Concessional+Finance+for+Private+Sector+Operations_Summary+R....pdf?MOD=AJPERES&CVID=lYCLe0B

IFC. (2021). *Emerging Market Green Bonds Report 2020*. The World Bank Group. Retrieved from https://www.ifc.org/wps/wcm/connect/publications_ext_ content/ifc_external_publication_site/publications_listing_page/emerging-market-green-bonds-report-2020

IREDA. (2021). *IREDA Annual Report*. New Delhi: Indian Renewable Energy Development Agency Limited. Retrieved from https://www.ireda.in/home

ISO. (2010). *ISO 26000*. International Organization for Standardization. Retrieved from https://www.iso.org/iso/

Iwayemi, A., & Fowowe, B. (2011). Impact of oil price shocks on selected macroeconomic variables in Nigeria. *Energy Policy, 39*(2), 603–612. doi:10.1016/j.enpol.2010.10.033

Ja'afar, Y., Bala, H., & Lawal, A. M. (2021). Determinants of Corporate Environmental Accounting Disclosure of Oil and Gas Firms in Nigeria. *Global Business and Management Research, 13*(1), 16–36.

Jalil, A., & Feridun, M. (2011). The impact of growth, energy and financial development on the environment in China: A cointegration analysis. *Energy Economics, 33*(2), 284–291. doi:10.1016/j.eneco.2010.10.003

Jans, J., Johansson, P., & Nilsson, J. P. (2018). Economic status, air quality, and child health: Evidence from inversion episodes. *Journal of Health Economics, 61*, 220–232. doi:10.1016/j.jhealeco.2018.08.002 PMID:30193188

Javid, M., & Sharif, F. (2016). Environmental Kuznets curve and financial development in Pakistan. *Renewable & Sustainable Energy Reviews, 54*, 406–414. doi:10.1016/j.rser.2015.10.019

Jensen, M. C., & Meckling, W. H. (1976). Theory of the firm: Managerial behavior, agency costs and ownership structure. *Journal of Financial Economics, 3*(4), 305–360. doi:10.1016/0304-405X(76)90026-X

Jeucken, M. (2010). *Sustainable finance and banking: The financial sector and the future of the planet*. Routledge. doi:10.4324/9781849776264

Jiang, L., Zhou, H.-F., Bai, L., & Zhou, P. (2017). Does foreign direct investment drive environmental degradation in China? An empirical study based on air quality index from a spatial perspective. *Journal of Cleaner Production, 176*, 864–872. doi:10.1016/j.jclepro.2017.12.048

Jiménez-Rodríguez, R., & Sánchez, M. (2005). Oil price shocks and real GDP growth: Empirical evidence for some OECD countries. *Applied Economics, 37*(2), 201–228.

Jin, Y., Li, B., Roca, E., & Wong, V. (2016). Water as an investment: Liquid yet illiquid. *Applied Economics, 48*(9), 731–745. doi:10.1080/00036846.2015.1085646

Jin, Y., Reza, R., Li, B., Roca, E., & Wong, V. (2019). Water as an investment and the impact of regulatory risk. *Financial Planning Research. Journal, 5*(1), 55–81.

Jin, Y., Roca, E., Li, B., Wong, V., & Cheung, A. (2015). Sprinkle your investment portfolio with water! *International Journal of Water, 9*(1), 43–59. doi:10.1504/IJW.2015.067445

Johansen, S. (1988). Statistical analysis of cointegration vectors. *Journal of Economic Dynamics & Control, 12*(2-3), 231–254.

Joseph, A. (2014). The Need of Personal Responsibility and Integrity in Corporate Social Responsibility Theories. *International Journal of Recent Advances in Organizational Behavior and Decision Sciences, 1*(1), 45–67.

Jusoh, W. N. H. W. (2020). Corporate Social Responsibility: Conventional and Islamic Perspectives. In A. Rafay (Ed.), *Handbook of Research on Theory and Practice of Global Islamic Finance* (pp. 129–149). IGI Global. doi:10.4018/978-1-7998-0218-1.ch007

Justice, S. (2009). *Private financing of renewable energy – A guide for policymakers*. Retrieved from https://www.chathamhouse.org/sites/default/files/public/Research/Energy,%20Environment%20and%20Development/1209_financeguide.pdf

Kahn, M. E., & Mansur, E. T. (2010). How do energy prices, and labor and environmental regulations affect local manufacturing employment dynamics? A regression discontinuity approach (No. w16538). National Bureau of Economic Research.

Kang, X., Khan, F. U., Ullah, R., Arif, M., Rehman, S. U., & Ullah, F. (2021). Does Foreign Direct Investment Influence Renewable Energy Consumption? Empirical Evidence from South Asian Countries. *Energies*, *14*(12), 3470. doi:10.3390/en14123470

Kankaria, A., Nongkynrih, B., & Gupta, S. K. (2014). Indoor air pollution in India: Implications on health and its control. *Indian Journal of Community Medicine*, *39*(4), 203. doi:10.4103/0970-0218.143019 PMID:25364142

Karanasos, M. (2001). Prediction in ARMA models with GARCH in mean effects. *Journal of Time Series Analysis*, *22*(5), 555–576. doi:10.1111/1467-9892.00241

Karekezi, S. (2002). Renewables in Africa—Meeting the energy needs of the poor. *Energy Policy*, *30*(11-12), 1059–1069. doi:10.1016/S0301-4215(02)00058-7

Karl, T. R., Melillo, J. M., Peterson, T. C., & Hassol, S. J. (2009). *Global climate change impacts in the United States*. Cambridge University Press.

Kassomenos, P., Kelessis, A., Petrakakis, M., Zoumakis, N., Christidis, T., & Paschalidou, A. (2012). Air quality assessment in a heavily polluted urban Mediterranean environment through air quality indices. *Ecological Indicators*, *18*, 259–268. doi:10.1016/j.ecolind.2011.11.021

Katırcıoğlu, S. T., Sertoglu, K., Candemir, M., & Mercan, M. (2015). Oil price movements and macroeconomic performance: Evidence from twenty-six OECD countries. *Renewable & Sustainable Energy Reviews*, *44*, 257–270.

Kawaguchi, M. (2017, June 6). *The Evolution of ESG Investing: from Ethical Concern to Corporate value*. The Tokyo Foundation for Policy Research. Retrieved from https://www.tkfd.or.jp/en/research/detail.php?id=407

Kelishadi, R., & Poursafa, P. (2010). Air pollution and non-respiratory health hazards for children. *Archives of Medical Science*, *6*(4), 483–495. doi:10.5114/aoms.2010.14458 PMID:22371790

Kennedy, B. (2020, May 6). The returns and fundamentals of ESG integrated investing. *DGFM*. Retrieved from https://www.davygfm.com/insights/esg-investing-series/the-returns-and-fundamentals-of-esg-integrated-investing.html

Kennedy, P. (2003). *A guide to econometrics* (5th ed.). MIT Press.

Keser, Ö. (2003). Energy, environment, and education relationship, in developing countries' policies: A case study for Turkey. *Energy Sources, 25*(2), 123–133.

Khan, T. M., Khan, A. N., Sheraz, A., & Mehfooz, A. (2012). Corporate Social responsibility (CSR) – Definition, Concepts and Scope (A review). *Universal Journal of Management and Social Sciences, 2*(7), 41–51.

Khoshnevis Yazdi, S., & Khanalizadeh, B. (2017). Air pollution, economic growth and health care expenditure. *Economic research-. Ekonomska Istrazivanja, 30*(1), 1181–1190. doi:10.1080/1331677X.2017.1314823

Kiani, A. (2011). Impact of high oil prices on Pakistan's economic growth. *International Journal of Business and Social Science, 2*(17), 209–217.

Kilci, E. N. (2019). Analysis of the causality relationship between Brent crude oil prices and energy import in Turkey under structural breaks. *Business and Economics Research Journal, 10*(4), 777–788.

Kilian, L., & Vega, C. (2011). Do energy prices respond to US macroeconomic news? A test of the hypothesis of predetermined energy prices. *The Review of Economics and Statistics, 93*(2), 660–671.

Kilinc-Ata, N. (2022). Oil Prices, Macroeconomic Performance and Sustainability: The Case of Turkey. In A. Rafay (Ed.), *Finance for Sustainability in a Turbulent Economy*. IGI Global. doi:10.4018/978-1-6684-5580-7.ch004

Kim, J. H., Newberry, P., & Qiu, C. (2015). *An empirical analysis of a crowdfunding platform*. (Working Paper No., 15-12). NET Institute.

Kim, J., & Park, K. (2015). *Financial development and deployment of renewable energy technologies* (Working Paper No. 2015-023). KAIST College of Business.

Kocaarslan, B., Soytas, M. A., & Soytas, U. (2020). The asymmetric impact of oil prices, interest rates and oil price uncertainty on unemployment in the US. *Energy Economics, 86*, 104625.

Kocabiyik, T., & Fattah, A. S. (2020). Makroekonomik Değişkenlerin Borsa Endeksleri Üzerine Etkisi: Türkiye Ve Abd Karşılaştırması. *Finansal Araştırmalar Ve Çalışmalar Dergisi, 12*(22), 116–151.

Koenker, R., & Bassett, G. (1978). Regression quantiles. *Econometrica, 46*(1), 33–50. doi:10.2307/1913643

Konstantinos, D., Patlitzianas, A., & Christos, K. (2011). Sustainable energy investments in Hellenic urban areas: Examining modern financial mechanisms. *Renewable & Sustainable Energy Reviews, 15*(9), 5186–5188. doi:10.1016/j.rser.2011.03.006

Kurihara, Y. (2015). Oil prices and economic growth in developed countries. *International Journal of Business and Social Science, 6*(11), 40–46.

La Torre, M., Sabelfeld, S., Blomkvist, M., Tarquinio, L., & Dumay, J. (2018). Harmonising non-financial reporting regulation in Europe: Practical forces and projections for future research. *Meditari Accountancy Research*, *26*(4), 598–621. doi:10.1108/MEDAR-02-2018-0290

Labatt, S., & White, R. R. (2003). *Environmental Finance: A Guide to Environmental Risk Assessment and Financial Products*. Wiley.

Lardic, S., & Mignon, V. (2008). Oil prices and economic activity: An asymmetric cointegration approach. *Energy Economics*, *30*(3), 847–855.

LeBlanc, M., & Chinn, M. D. (2004). *Do high oil prices presage inflation? The evidence from G-5 countries* (Working Paper No. 561). Santa Cruz: University of California.

Lee, D. D., Faff, R. W., & Rekker, S. A. C. (2013). Do high and low-ranked sustainability stocks perform differently*? International Journal of Accounting & Information Management*, *21*(2), 116–132. doi:10.1108/18347641311312267

Legrand, L., Blanpain, O., & Buyle-Bodin, F. (2004). Promoting the urban utilities tunnel technique using a decision-making approach. *Tunnelling and Underground Space Technology*, *19*(1), 79–83. doi:10.1016/S0886-7798(03)00041-5

Lenton, T. M., & Latour, B. (2018). Gaia 2.0. *Science*, *361*(6407), 1066–1068. doi:10.1126cience.aau0427 PMID:30213897

Levine, R. (1997). Financial development and economic growth: Views and agenda. *Journal of Economic Literature*, *35*(2), 688–726.

Li, Z. X., & Jarvenpaa, S. L. (2015). *Motivating IT-Mediated crowds: the effect of goal setting on project performance in online crowdfunding*. (Working Paper No., 15-07). NET Institute.

Liming, H. (2009). Financing rural renewable energy: A comparison between China and India. *Renewable & Sustainable Energy Reviews*, *13*(5), 1096–1103. doi:10.1016/j.rser.2008.03.002

Lindlein, P., & Mostert, W. (2005). *Financing Renewable Energy. Instruments, Strategies, Practice Approaches* (Discussion Paper No. 38). Frankfurt: KfW.

Lin, M. F., & Viswanathan, S. (2016). Home bias in online investments: An empirical study of an online crowd funding market. *Management Science*, *62*(5), 1393–1414. doi:10.1287/mnsc.2015.2206

Linnenluecke, M. K., Smith, T., & McKnight, B. (2016). Environmental finance: A research agenda for interdisciplinary finance research. *Economic Modelling*, *59*, 124–130. doi:10.1016/j.econmod.2016.07.010

Liu, F. R. (2016). Utilities tunnel investment and financial mechanism needs deep research in Beijing. *China Investment*, *15*, 74–75.

Liu, H., Erdem, E., & Shi, J. (2011). Comprehensive evaluation of ARMA–GARCH(-M) approaches for modeling the mean and volatility of wind speed. *Applied Energy*, *88*(3), 724–732. doi:10.1016/j.apenergy.2010.09.028

Li, Z., Liao, G., & Albitar, K. (2020). Does corporate environmental responsibility engagement affect firm value? The mediating role of corporate innovation. *Business Strategy and the Environment*, *29*(3), 1045–1055. doi:10.1002/bse.2416

Ljung, G. M., & Box, G. E. P. (1978). On a measure of a lack of fit in time series models. *Biometrika*, *65*(2), 297–303. doi:10.1093/biomet/65.2.297

Lokonon, B. O. K., & Salami, A. O. (2017). *Climate Change and Renewable Energy Generation in Africa* (Working Paper No. 269). Abidjan: African Development Bank.

Lo, S. F. (2010). Performance Evaluation for Sustainable Business: A Profitability and Marketability Framework. *Corporate Social Responsibility and Environmental Management*, *17*(6), 311–319. doi:10.1002/csr.214

Lovelock, J. (2006). *The Revenge of Gaia: Earth's Climate Crisis & the Fate of Humanity*. Basic Books.

Lovelock, J., & Margulis, L. (1974). Atmospheric homeostasis by and for the biosphere: The Gaia hypothesis. *Tellus*, *26*(2), 2–10.

Lucas, R. E. Jr. (1988). On the mechanics of economic development. *Journal of Monetary Economics*, *22*(1), 3–42. doi:10.1016/0304-3932(88)90168-7

Luft, J. M. (2005). Mandatory environmental disclosures in a legitimacy theory context. *Accounting, Auditing & Accountability Journal*, *18*(4), 492–517. doi:10.1108/09513570510609333

Lund, P. (2012). Large-scale urban renewable electricity schemes. Integration and interfacing aspects. *Energy Conversion and Management*, *63*(11), 162–172. doi:10.1016/j.enconman.2012.01.037

Luttenberger, N., & Zedlitz, J. (2018). Standard International Trade Classification. *Business & Information Systems Engineering*, *60*(4), 305–316. doi:10.100712599-017-0495-z

Lynch, E., & Bobone, B. (2021, July 21). *The Courage to Change*. Social Europe. Retrieved from https://socialeurope.eu/the-courage-to-change

Lynch, M. J., Long, M. A., & Stretesky, P. B. (2019). Gaia and a Green Theory of Justice. In *Green Criminology and Green Theories of Justice* (pp. 127–149). Palgrave Macmillan. doi:10.1007/978-3-030-28573-9_6

Ma, H., Oxley, L., Gibson, J., & Li, W. (2010). A survey of China's renewable energy economy. *Renewable & Sustainable Energy Reviews*, *14*(1), 438–445. doi:10.1016/j.rser.2009.07.029

Mahmood, H., & Murshed, M. (2021). Oil price and economic growth nexus in Saudi Arabia: Asymmetry analysis. *International Journal of Energy Economics and Policy*, *11*(1), 29.

Mähönen, J. (2020). Comprehensive Approach to Relevant and Reliable Reporting in Europe: A Dream Impossible? *Sustainability, 12*(13), 52–77. doi:10.3390u12135277

Malik, A. H., Md Isa, A. H., Jais, M., Ur Rehman, A., & Ali Khan, M. (2021). Financial stability of Asian Nations: Governance quality and financial inclusion. *Borsa Istanbul Review, 22*(2), 377–387. doi:10.1016/j.bir.2021.05.005

Malik, M. S., & Kanwal, L. (2018). Impact of corporate social responsibility disclosure on financial performance: A case study of listed pharmaceutical firms of Pakistan. *Journal of Business Ethics, 150*(1), 69–78. doi:10.100710551-016-3134-6

Mammadov, J. (2016). Oil Price Shocks and Monetary Policy in Azerbaijan: Challenges and Opportunities. *Caucasus Analytical Digest, 83*, 6–11.

Marathe, S. R., & Guntur, A. R. (2020). Does Crude Oil Prices have Effect on Exports, Imports and GDP on BRICS Countries?-An Empirical Evidence. *International Journal of Energy Economics and Policy, 10*(6), 524.

Martinot, E. (2004). Global Renewable Energy Markets & Policies. *New Academy Review, 3*, 56–67.

Maskowitz, T. J., Ooi, Y. H., & Pedersen, L. H. (2012). Time series momentum. *Journal of Financial Economics, 104*(2), 228–250. doi:10.1016/j.jfineco.2011.11.003

Maslow, A. (1943, September 8). A Theory of Human Motivation. *Psychological Review, 50*(4), 370–396. doi:10.1037/h0054346

Max-Neef, M. A. (1991). *Human Scale Development: Conception, Application and further Reflections*. The Apex Press.

McClelland, D. (1961). *Achieving society*. The Free Press. doi:10.1037/14359-000

McKinnon, R. I. (1973). *Money and capital in economic development*. The Brookings Institution Press.

Mclean, R. D., & Zhao, M. X. (2014). The business cycle, investor sentiment, and costly external finance. *The Journal of Finance, 69*(3), 1377–1409. doi:10.1111/jofi.12047

Mensi, W., Rehman, M. U., & Al-Yahyaee, K. H. (2020). Time-frequency co-movements between oil prices and interest rates: Evidence from a wavelet-based approach. *The North American Journal of Economics and Finance, 51*, 100836.

Milanović, B. (2021, October 18). *Can Xi Jinping defeat three stubborn inequalities?* Social Europe. Retrieved from https://socialeurope.eu/can-xi-jinping-defeat-three-stubborn-modern-inequalities

Miles, M. B., & Huberman, M. (1994). Data management and analysis methods. In N. K. Denzin & Y. S. Lincoln (Eds.), *Handbook of Qualitative Research*. Sage.

Minsky, H. P. (1974). The modeling of financial instability: An introduction. *Modelling and Simulation (Anaheim), 5*(1), 267–272.

Mohammadi, M. (2017). Prediction of α -stable G.A.R.C.H. and ARMA-G.A.R.C.H.-M models. *Journal of Forecasting*, *36*(7), 859–866. doi:10.1002/for.2477

Mollick, E. (2014). The dynamics of crowdfunding: An exploratory study. *Journal of Business Venturing*, *29*(1), 1–16. doi:10.1016/j.jbusvent.2013.06.005

Montiel, I. (2008). Corporate social responsibility and corporate sustainability: Separate pasts, common futures. *Organization & Environment*, *21*(3), 245–269. doi:10.1177/1086026608321329

Morellec, E., Valta, P., & Zhdanov, A. (2015). Financing investment: The choice between bonds and bank loans. *Management Science*, *61*(11), 2580–2602. doi:10.1287/mnsc.2014.2005

Morioka, S. N., Bolis, I., & Carvalho, M. M. (2018). From an ideal dream towards reality analysis: Proposing Sustainable Value Exchange Matrix (SVEM) from systematic literature review on sustainable business models and face validation. *Journal of Cleaner Production*, *178*, 76–88. doi:10.1016/j.jclepro.2017.12.078

Morioka, S. N., Bolis, I., Evans, S., & Carvalho, M. M. (2017). Transforming sustainability challenges into competitive advantage: Multiple case studies kaleidoscope converging into sustainable business models. *Journal of Cleaner Production*, *167*, 723–738. doi:10.1016/j.jclepro.2017.08.118

Mosley, S. (2014). Environmental history of air pollution and protection. In *The Basic Environmental History* (pp. 143–169). Springer. doi:10.1007/978-3-319-09180-8_5

Mukhtarov, S., Aliyev, S., & Zeynalov, J. (2020). The Effect of Oil Prices on Macroeconomic Variables: Evidence from Azerbaijan. *International Journal of Energy Economics and Policy*, *10*(1), 72–80.

Mukhtarov, S., Humbatova, S., Mammadli, M., & Hajiyev, N. (2021). The Impact of Oil Price Shocks on National Income: Evidence from Azerbaijan. *Feature Papers in Energy, Environment and Well-Being*, *14*(6), 1695.

Mularova, D. (2017). *Towards a green finance framework: Opportunities and challenges for banks in the existing regulatory context*. Brussels: European Banking Federation. Retrieved from https://www.ebf.eu/ebf-media-centre/towards-a-green-finance-framework/

Mulej, M. (2000). *Dialektična in druge mehkosistemske teorije* [Dialectical and other soft system theories]. Maribor: Ekonomsko-poslovna fakulteta.

Mulej, M., Hrast, A., & Mihec, M. (2020). Social Responsibility and Human Selfishness. In *Proceedings of the 6th International Scientific Conference on Contemporary Issues in Economics, Business and Management*. Kragujevac: Faculty of Economics, University of Kragujevac.

Mulej, M., Merhar, V., Žakelj, V., Zore, M., Hrast, A., Toplak, L., ... Ambrožič, B. (2019). *Uvod v politično ekonomijo sodobne družbe* [An Introduction to Political Economy of Modern Society]. Kulturni Center Maribor.

MWE. (2020). *Sector Performance Report 2020*. Ministry of Water & Environment, GOU.

Mythen, G. (2004). *Ulrich Beck. A Critical Introduction to the Risk Society*. Pluto Press.

Nanda, R., & Rhodes-Kropf, M. (2017). Financing risk and innovation. *Management Science*, *63*(4), 901–918. doi:10.1287/mnsc.2015.2350

Narayan, P. K., Sharma, S., Poon, W. C., & Westerlund, J. (2014). Do oil prices predict economic growth? New global evidence. *Energy Economics*, *41*, 137–146.

Nasir, M., Ahmad, F. K., Ahmed, M., & Wu, J. (2015). Financial and economic stability as 'two sides of a coin': Non-crisis regime evidence from the UK based on VECM. *Journal of Financial Economic Policy*, *7*(4), 327–353. doi:10.1108/JFEP-01-2015-0006

Nasreen, S., & Rafay, A. (2022). Technological Innovation and Financialization for Environment: The Case of Pakistan. In A. Rafay (Ed.), *Handbook of Research on Energy and Environmental Finance 4.0* (pp. 333–353). IGI Global. doi:10.4018/978-1-7998-8210-7.ch013

National Bank of Kazakhstan. (2019). *Kazakhstan: Balance of Payments and External Debt*. Retrieved from https://nationalbank.kz/kz?switch=english

Nazir, S., & Qayyum, A. (2014). Impact of oil price and shocks on economic growth of Pakistan: Multivariate analysis. *MPRA Paper,* 1–24.

NEMA. (2019). *National State of the Environment Report 2018 -19*. National Environment Management Authority, GOU.

Nguyen, L., & Tran, M. (2019). Disclosure levels of environmental accounting information and financial performance: The case of Vietnam. *Management Science Letters*, *9*(4), 557–570. doi:10.5267/j.msl.2019.1.007

Nieto, M. (2017). *Banks and Environmental Sustainability: Some reflections from the perspective of financial stability*. CEPS.

Nizam, E., Ng, A., Dewandaru, G., Nagayev, R., & Nkoba, M. A. (2019). The impact of social and environmental sustainability on financial performance: A global analysis of the banking sector. *Journal of Multinational Financial Management*, *49*, 35–53. doi:10.1016/j.mulfin.2019.01.002

Nkundabanyanga, S. K., Muramuzi, B., & Alinda, K. (2021). Environmental management accounting, board role performance, company characteristics, and environmental performance disclosure. *Journal of Accounting & Organizational Change*, *17*(5), 633–659. doi:10.1108/JAOC-03-2020-0035

Noh, H. J. (2018). *Financial strategy to accelerate green growth* (Working Paper No. 866). Manila: Asian Development Bank.

Norton, B. (1992). Sustainability. *Human Welfare, and Ecosystem Health*, *1*, 97–111.

Noureen, S., & Mahmood, Z. (2016). Explaining Trends and Factors Affecting Export Diversification in ASEAN and SAARC Regions: An Empirical Analysis. *Nust Journal of Social Sciences and Humanities*, *2*(1), 1–28.

Nsubuga, F. N., Mearns, K. F., Davis, N. C., Kalumba, A. M., & Komen, K. (2021). Exploring the influence of climate change and capital assets on livelihood formations in central region of Uganda. *Environment, Development and Sustainability*, *23*(6), 9223–9242. doi:10.100710668-020-01020-5

Nusair, S. A. (2020). The asymmetric effects of oil price changes on unemployment: Evidence from Canada and the US. *Journal of Economic Asymmetries*, *21*, e00153.

Odera, O., Scott, A. H., & Gow, J. (2016). Factors influencing corporate social and environmental disclosures: A systematic review. *International Journal of Business Governance and Ethics*, *11*(2), 116–134. doi:10.1504/IJBGE.2016.078199

OECD. (2008). *OECD environmental outlook to 2030*. Organisation for Economic Co-operation and Development. Retrieved from https://www.OECD-ilibrary.org/environment/OECD-environmental-outlook-to-2030_9789264040519-en

OECD. (2016). *Economic Consequences of Outdoor Air Pollution*. Organisation for Economic Co-operation and Development.

OECD. (2020). *Coronavirus (COVID-19): SME Policy Responses*. Retrieved from https://www.oecd.org/coronavirus/policy-responses/coronavirus-covid-19-sme-policy-responses-04440101/

Oji, K. C. (2015). *Models of Financing Renewable Energy for Sustainable Development: An African Perspective* [Ph.D. thesis]. Faculty of Commerce, Law and Management, University of the Witwatersrand, Johannesburg, South Africa.

Okoro, E. G. (2014). Oil price volatility and economic growth in Nigeria: A Vector Auto-Regression (VAR) approach. *Acta Universitatis Danubius. Œconomica*, *10*(1), 70–82.

Omojolaibi, J. A., & Egwaikhide, F. (2013). A panel analysis of oil price dynamics, fiscal stance and macroeconomic effects: The case of some selected African countries. *Economic and Financial Review*, *51*(1), 4.

Omri, A., Daly, S., Rault, C., & Chaibi, A. (2015). Financial development, environmental quality, trade and economic growth: What causes what in MENA countries? *Energy Economic*, *48*, 242–252. doi:10.1016/j.eneco.2015.01.008

Ortiz-de-Mandojana, N., & Bansal, P. (2016). The long-term benefits of organizational resilience through sustainable business practices. *Strategic Management Journal*, *37*(8), 1615–1631. doi:10.1002mj.2410

Ozturk, I., & Acaravci, A. (2013). The long-run and causal analysis of energy, growth, openness and financial development on carbon emissions in Turkey. *Energy Economics*, *36*, 262–267. doi:10.1016/j.eneco.2012.08.025

Painuly, J. P. (2001). Barriers to renewable energy penetration; a framework for analysis. *Renewable Energy*, *24*(1), 73–89. doi:10.1016/S0960-1481(00)00186-5

Panwar, N. L., Kaushik, S. C., & Kothari, S. (2011). Role of renewable energy sources in environmental protection: A review. *Renewable & Sustainable Energy Reviews*, *15*(3), 1513–1524. doi:10.1016/j.rser.2010.11.037

Parajuli, I., Lee, H., & Shrestha, K. R. (2016). Indoor air quality and ventilation assessment of rural mountainous households of Nepal. *International Journal of Sustainable Built Environment*, *5*(2), 301–311. doi:10.1016/j.ijsbe.2016.08.003

Patrick, H. T. (1966). Financial development and economic growth in underdeveloped countries. *Economic Development and Cultural Change*, *14*(2), 174–189. doi:10.1086/450153

Pedron, A. P. B., Macagnan, C. B., Simon, D. S., & Vancin, D. F. (2021). Environmental disclosure effects on returns and market value. *Environment, Development and Sustainability*, *23*(3), 4614–4633. doi:10.100710668-020-00790-2

Pena, M. S. B., & Rollins, A. (2017). Environmental exposures and cardiovascular disease: A challenge for health and development in low-and middle-income countries. *Cardiology Clinics*, *35*(1), 71–86. doi:10.1016/j.ccl.2016.09.001 PMID:27886791

Peri, M., Vandone, D., & Baldi, L. (2017). Volatility Spillover between Water, Energy and Food. *Sustainability*, *9*(6), 1071. doi:10.3390u9061071

Pescetto, G. M. (2008). Regulation and Systematic Risk: The Case of the Water Industry in England and Wales. *Applied Financial Economics*, *18*(1), 61–73. doi:10.1080/09603100601057847

Petrică, A. C., Stancu, S., & Tindeche, A. (2016). Limitation of ARIMA models in financial and monetary economics. *Theoretical and Applied Economics*, *23*(4), 19–42.

Pfeiffer, B., & Mulder, P. (2013). Explaining the diffusion of renewable energy technology in developing countries. *Energy Economics*, *40*, 285–296. doi:10.1016/j.eneco.2013.07.005

Phillips, J. (2016). A quantitative evaluation of the sustainability or unsustainability of three tunnelling projects. *Tunnelling and Underground Space Technology*, *51*, 387–404. doi:10.1016/j.tust.2015.09.009

Piñeiro-Chousaa, J., López-Cabarcosb, M. A., & Ribeiro-Soriano, D. (2020). Does investor attention influence water companies' stock returns? *Technological Forecasting and Social Change*, *158*, 120115. doi:10.1016/j.techfore.2020.120115

Pirc, T. (2015). *Postmetafizični ethos ekonomiziranega globalizma* [The postmetaphysical ethos of economized globalism] [Doctoral dissertation]. Ljubljana: Filozofska fakulteta. Retrieved from http://www.pif.si/sites/default/files/inline-files/Pirctadej971.pdf

Purohit, I., & Pallav, P. (2013). Evaluating the potential of concentrating solar power generation in North-western India. *Energy Policy*, *62*, 157–175. doi:10.1016/j.enpol.2013.06.069

PwC. (2013). *Exploring green finance incentives in China*. Shenzhen: PricewaterhouseCoopers Consultants. Retrieved from https://www.pwchk.com/en/migration/pdf/green-finance-incentives-oct2013-eng.pdf

Qianqian, Z. (2011). The impact of international oil price fluctuation on China's economy. *Energy Procedia*, *5*, 1360–1364.

Rafay, A. (Ed.). (2019). *FinTech as a Disruptive Technology for Financial Institutions*. IGI Global., doi:10.4018/978-1-5225-7805-5

Rafay, A. (Ed.). (2020). *HandBook of Research on Theory and Practice of Global Islamic Finance*. IGI Global. doi:10.4018/978-1-7998-0218-1

Rafay, A. (Ed.). (2022). *Handbook of Research on Energy and Environmental Finance 4.0*. IGI Global. doi:10.4018/978-1-7998-8210-7

Rafay, A., & Farid, S. (2015). An Analysis of Oil Price Volatility using VAR: Evidence from Pakistan. *Lahore Journal of Business*, *4*(1), 23–36. doi:10.35536/ljb.2015.v4.i1.a2

Rafay, A., & Farid, S. (2019). Islamic Banking System: A Credit Channel of Monetary Policy – Evidence from an Emerging Economy. *Economic Research Journal*, *32*(1), 742–754. doi:10.1080/1331677X.2019.1579662

Rafay, A., Farid, S., Yasser, F., & Safdar, S. (2020). Social Collateral and Repayment Performance: Evidence from Islamic Micro Finance. *Indian Economic Review*, *24*(1), 41–74.

Rafay, A., Sadiq, R., & Ajmal, M. M. (2017). Uniform Framework for Sukuk-Al-Ijara – A proposed model for all Madhahib. *Journal of Islamic Accounting and Business Research*, *8*(4), 420–454. doi:10.1108/JIABR-09-2015-0042

Rahimli, N., & Nazirov, M. (2020). Impact of Oil Price On Azerbaijan Economy: Relationship Between Oil Prices, Real Effective Exchange Rates and Real GDP. *Journal of Social and Economic Studies*, *3*(1), 37–45.

Rajan, R. G., & Zingales, L. (1998). Financial dependence and growth. *The American Economic Review*, *88*(3), 559–586.

Rakesh, V., Choo, J., & Reddy, C. K. (2015). Project recommendation using heterogeneous traits in crowdfunding. *Ninth International AAAI Conference on Web and Social Media*.

Ramzan, M., Ahmad, I., & Rafay, A. (2020). Is Auditor independence influenced by Non-audit services? A stakeholder's viewpoint. *Pakistan Journal of Commerce and Social Sciences*, *14*(1), 388–408.

Rashed, A., Chen, Y. C., & Soon, S. (2022). FDI and the Gap of Clean Power Finance: The Case of Africa. In A. Rafay (Ed.), *Handbook of Resaerch on Energy & Environmental Finance 4.0*. IGI Global. doi:10.4018/978-1-7998-8210-7.ch009

RBI. (2021). Green Finance in India: Progress and Challenges. *RBI Bulletin*. Retrieved from https://rbidocs.rbi.org.in/rdocs/Bulletin/PDFs/ 04AR_2101202185D9B6905ADD465CB7DD280B88266F77.PDF

Read, A. (2013). Crowdfunding: an empirical and theoretical model of non-profit support. *Economics Theses, 91*. Retrieved from https://soundideas.pugetsound.edu/economics_theses/91

Reinhart, C. M., & Reinhart, V. R. (2015). Financial crises, development, and growth: A long-term perspective. *The World Bank Economic Review, 29*(suppl_1), S53–S76. doi:10.1093/wber/lhv011

REN21. (2014). *Renewables 2014: Global Status Report 2014*. Paris: Renewable Energy Policy Network for the 21st Century (REN21).

Reza, R., & Tularam, G. A. (2021). The Determinants of capital structure: evidence from the global water industry. In K. Marleau (Ed.), Advances in Capital Structure Research (pp. 119–149). Nova Science.

Reza, R. (2017). *An investigation of water investment performance: Analysis of the global water industry [PhD Thesis]*. Griffith University. Retrieved from https://research-repository.griffith.edu.au/handle/10072/371256

Reza, R., Tularam, G. A., & Li, B. (2017). An investigation into the interdependence of global water indices: A VAR analysis. *Applied Economics, 49*(8), 769–796. doi:10.1080/00036846.2016.1205725

Reza, R., Tularam, G. A., & Li, B. (2018). Returns and volatility of water investments. *Cogent Economics & Finance, 6*(3), 1438724. doi:10.1080/23322039.2018.1438724

Reza, R., Tularam, G. A., & Li, B. (2021). A review of global research on private investment in the water sector. *Utilities Policy, 72*, 101283. doi:10.1016/j.jup.2021.101283

Rifkin, J. (2011). *The third industrial revolution: how lateral power is transforming energy, the economy, and the world*. Macmillan.

Robeco, S. A. M. (2015). *Water: The market of the future*. Zurich: Carbon Neutral Publication. Retrieved from http://www.RobecoSAM.com/images/Water_ Study_en.pdf

Robinson, J. (1952). *The Generalisation of the General Theory in the Rate of Interest and Other Essays*. Macmillan.

Roca, E. D., & Tularam, G. A. (2012). Which way does water flow? An econometric analysis of the global price integration of water stocks. *Applied Economics, 44*(23), 2935–2944. doi:10.1080/00036846.2011.568403

Roca, E., Tularam, G. A., & Reza, R. (2015). Fundamental signals of investment profitability in the global water industry. *International Journal of Water, 9*(4), 395–424. doi:10.1504/IJW.2015.072155

Romano, G., & Guerrini, A. (2019). Paying Returns to Shareholders of Water Utilities: Evidence from Italy. *Sustainability, 11*(7), 2033. doi:10.3390u11072033

Romito, S., & Vurro, C. (2020). Non-financial disclosure and information asymmetry: A stakeholder view on US listed firms. *Corporate Social Responsibility and Environmental Management, 28*(2), 595–605. doi:10.1002/csr.2071

Rompotis, G. G. (2016). Evaluating a new hot trend: The case of water exchange-traded funds. *The Journal of Index Investing*, *6*(4), 103–128. doi:10.3905/jii.2016.6.4.103

Roodman, D.OECD. (2009). How to do xtabond2: An introduction to difference and system GMM in Stata. *The Stata Journal*, *9*(1), 86–136. doi:10.1177/1536867X0900900106

Rostami, J., Sepehrmanesh, M., Gharahbagh, E. A., & Mojtabai, N. (2013). Planning level tunnel cost estimation based on statistical analysis of historical data. *Tunnelling and Underground Space Technology*, *33*, 22–33. doi:10.1016/j.tust.2012.08.002

Rostin, R., Adam, P., Nur, M., Saenong, Z., & Baso, J. N. (2019). The effect of crude oil prices on inflation, interest rates and economic growth in Indonesia. *International Journal of Energy Economics and Policy*, *9*(5), 14.

Roubaud, D., & Shahbaz, M. (2017). Financial development, economic growth, and electricity demand: A sector analysis of an emerging economy. *Journal of the Energy Division*, *43*(1/2), 47–98.

Russell, A. D., Udaipurwola, A., Alldritt, M., & El-Guindy, K. (1999). Computer system for the selection of trenchless and conventional methods for underground utilities. *Tunnelling and Underground Space Technology*, *14*, 1–12. doi:10.1016/S0886-7798(00)00019-5

Sadorsky, P. (1999). Oil price shocks and stock market activity. *Energy Economics*, *21*(5), 449–469.

Sadorsky, P. (2010). The impact of financial development on energy consumption in emerging economies. *Energy Policy*, *38*(5), 2528–2535. doi:10.1016/j.enpol.2009.12.048

Sağlam, Y., & Güreşçi, G. (2018). Petrol Şoklarının Makroekonomik Göstergeler Üzerine Etkileri: OPEC İçin Yapısal VAR Analizi. *Finans Politik ve Ekonomik Yorumlar*, *55*(640), 27–47.

Salahaldin, L., Angerer, M., Kraus, S., & Trabelsi, D. (2019). A duration-based model of crowdfunding project choice. *Finance Research Letters*, *29*, 404–410. doi:10.1016/j.frl.2018.11.005

Salahuddin, M., Alam, K., Ozturk, I., & Sohag, K. (2018). The effects of electricity consumption, economic growth, financial development and foreign direct investment on CO_2 emissions in Kuwait. *Renewable & Sustainable Energy Reviews*, *81*, 2002–2010. doi:10.1016/j.rser.2017.06.009

Sandor, R. L. (2016). *How I Saw It: Analysis and Commentary on Environmental Finance (1999–2005)*. World Scientific Publishing Company.

Sarangi, G. K. (2018). *Green Energy Finance in India: Challenges and Solutions* (Working Paper No. 863). Manila: Asian Development Bank.

Sardo, F., & Serrasqueiro, Z. (2017). A European empirical study of the relationship between firms' intellectual capital, financial performance and market value. *Journal of Intellectual Capital*, *18*(4), 771–778. doi:10.1108/JIC-10-2016-0105

Sarkar, A., & Singh, J. (2010). Financing energy efficiency in developing countries—Lessons learned and remaining challenges. *Energy Policy*, *38*(10), 5560–5571. doi:10.1016/j.enpol.2010.05.001

Saunders, R. W., Gross, R. J. K., & Wade, J. (2012). Can premium tariffs for micro-generation and small scale renewable heat help the fuel poor, and if so, how? Case studies of innovative finance for community energy schemes in the UK. *Energy Policy, 42*, 78–88. doi:10.1016/j.enpol.2011.11.045

Sawyer, S. (2009). *Un-habitat, Local Governments for Sustainability, and the United Nations Environment Programme. In Sustainable Urban Energy Planning: A handbook for cities and towns in developing countries*. UNEP.

Schaltegger, S., Beckmann, M., & Hansen, E. G. (2013). Transdisciplinary in corporate sustainability: Mapping the field. *Business Strategy and the Environment, 22*(4), 219–229. doi:10.1002/bse.1772

Schoenmaker, D. (2019). *A framework for sustainable finance* (Working Paper). Rotterdam: Erasmus University. Retrieved from https://www.rsm.nl/fileadmin/Images_NEW/Erasmus_Platform_for_Sustainable_Value_Creation/A_Framework_for_Sustainable_Finance.pdf

Schoenmaker, D., & Schramade, W. (2019). *Principles of Sustainable Finance*. Oxford University Press.

Scholtens, B., & Veldhuis, R. (2015). *How Does the Development of the Financial Industry Advance Renewable Energy? A Panel Regression Study of 198 Countries Over Three Decades*. Retrieved from http://www.hdl.handle.net/10419/113114

Schönherr, N., Findler, F., & Martinuzzi, A. (2017). Exploring the interface of CSR and the sustainable development goals. *Transnational Corporations, 24*(3), 33–47. doi:10.18356/cfb5b8b6-en

Schramade, W. (2017). Investing in the UN Sustainable Development Goals: Opportunities for Companies and Investors. *Journal of Applied Corporate Finance, 29*(2), 87–99. doi:10.1111/jacf.12236

Schulz, M., Haas, P., Blohm, I., & Leimeister, J. M. (2015). How idea creativity and hedonic value influence project success in crowdfunding. *12th International Conference on Wirtschaftsinformatik.*

Schumpeter, J. A. (1911). *The Theory of Economic Development*. Harvard University Press.

Schwienbacher, A., & Larralde, B. (2010). Crowdfunding of small entrepreneurial ventures. In D. Cumming (Ed.), *The Oxford handbook of Entrepreneurial Finance*. Oxford University Press.

Selin, N. E., Wu, S., Nam, K. M., Reilly, J. M., Paltsev, S., Prinn, R. G., & Webster, M. D. (2009). Global health and economic impacts of future ozone pollution. *Environmental Research Letters, 4*(4), 044014. doi:10.1088/1748-9326/4/4/044014

Senn, J., & Giordano-Spring, S. (2020). The limits of environmental accounting disclosure: Enforcement of regulations, standards and interpretative strategies. *Accounting, Auditing & Accountability Journal, 33*(6), 1367–1393. doi:10.1108/AAAJ-04-2018-3461

Senzangakhona, P., & Choga, I. (2015). Crude oil prices and unemployment in South Africa: 1990–2010. *Mediterranean Journal of Social Sciences*, *6*(2), 407.

Seyed, M. A., Hashem, V. & Seyed, Y. Z. (2021). Factors affecting Financial and Non-financial Reporting of the Environment in Gachsaran oil and gas exploitation Company. *PalArch's Journal of Archaeology of Egypt / Egyptology, 18*(8), 146-158.

Shahbaz, M., Jam, F. A., Bibi, S., & Loganathan, N. (2016a). Multivariate Granger causality between CO_2 emissions, energy intensity and economic growth in Portugal: Evidence from cointegration and causality analysis. *Technological and Economic Development of Economy*, *22*(1), 47–74. doi:10.3846/20294913.2014.989932

Shahbaz, M., Nasir, M. A., & Roubaud, D. (2018). Environmental degradation in France: The effects of FDI, financial development, and energy innovations. *Energy Economics*, *74*, 843–857. doi:10.1016/j.eneco.2018.07.020

Shahbaz, M., Shahzad, S. J. H., Ahmad, N., & Alam, S. (2016b). Financial development and environmental quality: The way forward. *Energy Policy*, *98*, 353–364. doi:10.1016/j.enpol.2016.09.002

Shahbaz, M., Solarin, S. A., Mahmood, H., & Arouri, M. (2013). Does financial development reduce CO_2 emissions in Malaysian economy? A time series analysis. *Economic Modelling*, *35*, 145–152. doi:10.1016/j.econmod.2013.06.037

Shaw, E. (1973). *Financial Deepening in Economic Development*. Oxford University Press.

Shelton, G., & Safar, H. (1996). Social Responsibility Theory Revisited: A Comparative Study of Public Journalism and Developmental Journalism. *Journal of the European Institute for Communication and Culture*, *3*(3), 97–107.

Sheng, X., & Gupta, R. (2022). Oil Price Shocks and Income Inequality: Evidence From the US. In A. Rafay (Ed.), *Handbook of Research on Energy and Environmental Finance 4.0* (pp. 144–158). IGI Global. doi:10.4018/978-1-7998-8210-7.ch005

Shrestha, R. M. (2007). *Financing mechanisms for renewable energy, extract of course on bio-energy for achieving MGDs*. Asian Institute of Technology.

Sieferle, R. (2001). *The subterranean forest: energy systems and the industrial revolution*. White Horse Press.

Sodeyfi, S., & Katircioglu, S. (2016). Interactions between business conditions, economic growth and crude oil prices. *Economic Research-Ekonomska Istraživanja*, *29*(1), 980–990.

Solomon, J., & Warren, M. (2012). *Integrated Reporting: The Influence of King III on social, ethical and environmental reporting*. ACCA.

Solow, R. M. (1991). Sustainability: an economist's perspective. Reprinted. In R. Dorfman & N. S. Dorfman (Eds.), *Economics of the Environment: Selected Readings*. W.W. Norton.

Sommer, S. (2020). Sustainable finance: An overview. *FiBras*. Retrieved from https://www.giz.de/en/downloads/Sustainable%20Finance_English_version.pdf

Špačková, O., Novotná, E., Šejnoha, M., & Šejnoha, J. (2013). Probabilistic models for tunnel construction risk assessment. *Advances in Engineering Software*, *62*, 72–84. doi:10.1016/j.advengsoft.2013.04.002

Stanbic Bank Uganda. (2019). *Stanbic Bank Annual Report 2019*. Stanbic Uganda Holdings Limited.

Stanbic Uganda Holdings Limited. (2019). *Annual Report*. SUH.

Statistical Committee of the Republic of Azerbaijan. (2017). *Reports*. Retrieved from https://www.stat.gov.az/?lang=en

Steigenberger, N., & Wilhelm, H. (2018). Extending signaling theory to rhetorical signals: Evidence from crowdfunding. *Organization Science*, *29*(3), 529–546. doi:10.1287/orsc.2017.1195

Steven, C., & Majumdar, A. (2012). Opportunities and challenges for a sustainable energy future. *Nature*, *488*(8), 294–303. PMID:22895334

Stutz, J. (2010). The three-front war: pursuing sustainability in a world shaped by explosive growth. *Sustainability: Science. Practice and Policy*, *6*(2), 49–59.

Suchman, M. (1995). Managing legitimacy: Strategic and institutional approaches. *Academy of Management Review*, *20*(3), 571–610. doi:10.2307/258788

Sun, F., Liu, C., & Zhou, X. G. (2017). Utilities tunnel's finance design for the process of construction and operation. *Tunnelling and Underground Space Technology*, *69*, 182–186. doi:10.1016/j.tust.2017.06.005

Tamazian, A., Chousa, J. P., & Vadlamannati, K. C. (2009). Does higher economic and financial development lead to environmental degradation: Evidence from BRIC countries. *Energy Policy*, *37*(1), 246–253. doi:10.1016/j.enpol.2008.08.025

Tamazian, A., & Rao, B. B. (2010). Do economic, financial and institutional developments matter for environmental degradation? Evidence from transitional economies. *Energy Economics*, *32*(1), 137–145. doi:10.1016/j.eneco.2009.04.004

Tang, W., Wu, L., & Zhang, Z. (2010). Oil price shocks and their short-and long-term effects on the Chinese economy. *Energy Economics*, *32*, S3–S14.

Tauringana, V. (2020). Sustainability reporting adoption in developing countries: Managerial perception-based determinants evidence from Uganda. *Journal of Accounting in Emerging Economies*, *11*(2), 149–175. doi:10.1108/JAEE-07-2020-0184

Tobin, J. (1984). On the Efficiency of the Financial System. *Lloyds Bank Review*, 1-15.

Toke, D., & Lauber, V. (2007). Anglo-Saxon and German approaches to neoliberalism and environmental policy: The case of financing renewable energy. *Geoforum*, *38*(4), 677–687. doi:10.1016/j.geoforum.2006.11.016

Topple, C., Donovan, J. D., Masli, E. K., & Borgert, T. (2017). Corporate sustainability assessments: MNE engagement with sustainable development and the SDGs. *Transnational Corporations*, *24*(3), 61–71. doi:10.18356/2ae5911c-en

Trang, N. T. N. (2017). The impact of oil price on the growth, inflation, unemployment and budget deficit of Vietnam. *International Journal of Energy Economics and Policy*, *7*(3), 42–49.

Tran, N. P., Van, L. T.-H., & Vo, D. H. (2020). The nexus between corporate governance and intellectual capital in Vietnam. *Journal of Asia Business Studies*, *14*(5), 637–650. doi:10.1108/JABS-01-2020-0007

Tran, N. P., & Vo, D. H. (2020). Human capital efficiency and firm performance across sectors in an emerging market. *Cogent Business & Management*, *7*(1), 1738832. doi:10.1080/23311975.2020.1738832

Tularam, G. A., & Reza, R. (2019). Subsurface Acid Sulphate Pollution and Salinity Intrusion in Coastal Groundwater Environments. In N. Narayanan, B. Mohanadhas & V. Mangottiri (Eds.), Flow and Transport in Subsurface Environment (pp. 189–214). Springer.

Tularam, G. A. (2014). Investing in water for a green economy. *Australian Plants*, *51*(4), 372–373. doi:10.1080/07293682.2014.948987

Tularam, G. A., & Krishna, M. (2009). Long term consequences of groundwater pumping in Australia: A review of impacts around the globe. *Journal of Applied Sciences in Environmental Sanitation*, *4*(2), 151–166.

Tularam, G. A., & Marchisella, P. (2014). Water scarcity in Asia and its long-term water and border security implications for Australia. In R. M. Clark & S. Hakim (Eds.), *Securing Water and Wastewater Systems* (pp. 189–211). Springer. doi:10.1007/978-3-319-01092-2_9

Tularam, G. A., & Murali, K. K. (2015). Water security problems in Asia and longer-term implications for Australia. In W. L. Filho & V. Sümer (Eds.), *Sustainable Water Use and Management Green Energy and Technology* (pp. 119–149). Springer. doi:10.1007/978-3-319-12394-3_7

Tularam, G. A., & Properjohn, M. (2011). An investigation into water distribution network security: Risk and implications. *Security Journal*, *24*(4), 283–301. doi:10.1057j.2010.4

Tularam, G. A., & Reza, R. (2016). Water exchange traded funds: A study on idiosyncratic risk using Markov switching analysis. *Cogent Economics & Finance*, *4*(1), 1139437. doi:10.1080/23322039.2016.1139437

Tularam, G. A., & Reza, R. (2017). The Critical Importance of Groundwater in Coastal Areas: Impact of Climate Change on Bangladesh Freshwater Resources. *Journal of Climate Change*, *3*(1), 59–70. doi:10.3233/JCC-170006

Tularam, G. A., & Saeed, T. (2016). Oil-price forecasting based on various univariate time-series models. *American Journal of Operations Research*, *6*(3), 226–235. doi:10.4236/ajor.2016.63023

UN. (2015). *World population projected to reach 9.7 billion by 2050.* Department of Economic and Social Affairs, United Nations.

UNEPFI. (2012). *Financing renewable energy in developing countries – Drivers and barriers for private finance in sub-Saharan Africa*. United Nations Environmental Program Finance Initiative.

Uyanto, S. S. (2019). Monte Carlo power comparison of seven most commonly used heteroscedasticity tests. *Communications in Statistics. Simulation and Computation*, 1–18.

Uyar, A. (2016). Evolution of Corporate Reporting and Emerging Trends. *Journal of Corporate Accounting & Finance*, *27*(4), 27–30. doi:10.1002/jcaf.22157

Van Eyden, R., Difeto, M., Gupta, R., & Wohar, M. E. (2019). Oil price volatility and economic growth: Evidence from advanced economies using more than a century's data. *Applied Energy*, *233*, 612–621.

Vandone, D., Peri, M., Vandone, D., Baldi, L., & Tanda, A. (2018). The impact of energy and agriculture prices on the stock performance of the water industry. *Water Resources and Economics*, *23*, 14–27. doi:10.1016/j.wre.2018.02.002

Veuger, J. W. (2015). Crowdfunding: the role of platforms in project success. *5th IBA Bachelor Thesis Conference*.

Vo, D. H. (2018). Should bankers be concerned with Intellectual capital? A study of the Thai banking sector. *Journal of Intellectual Capital*, *19*(5), 897–914. doi:10.1108/JIC-12-2017-0185

Vo, D. H., Nguyen, N. T., & Van, L. T. H. (2021). Financial inclusion and stability in the Asian region using bank-level data. *Borsa Istanbul Review*, *21*(1), 36–43. doi:10.1016/j.bir.2020.06.003

Walker, D. M. (2017). Crowdfunding: An innovative way to fund your project. *Nurse Researcher*, *25*(1), 24–29. doi:10.7748/nr.2017.e1425 PMID:28639522

Wang, P. (2016). Construction experience of urban underground pipe gallery in Suzhou. *Construction Economics*, *2*, 113–115.

Wang, Y. S., & Chueh, Y. L. (2013). Dynamic transmission effects between the interest rate, the US dollar, and gold and crude oil prices. *Economic Modelling*, *30*, 792–798.

Wan-Jan, S. (2006). Defining corporate social responsibility. *Journal of Public Affairs*, *6*(3–4), 176–184. doi:10.1002/pa.227

WB. (1995). *Monitoring Environmental Progress: a Report on Work in Progress*. The World Bank.

Wei, Y., & Guo, X. (2016). An empirical analysis of the relationship between oil prices and the Chinese macro-economy. *Energy Economics*, *56*, 88–100.

Welbeck, E. E., Owusu, G. M. Y., Bekoe, R. A., & Kusi, J. A. (2017). Determinants of environmental disclosures of listed firms in Ghana. *International Journal of Corporate Social Responsibility*, *2*(1), 1–12. doi:10.118640991-017-0023-y

WHO. (2021a). *Household air pollution and health*. Retrieved from https://www.who .int/news-room/fact-sheets/detail/household-air-pollution-and-health

WHO. (2021b). *Household air pollution: Disease impacts*. World Health Organisation.

Wild, D., Francke, C. J., Menzli, P., & Schon, U. (2007). *Water: A Market of the Future*. Switzerland, Zurich: SAM Sustainable Asset Management. Retrieved from https:// venturecenter.co.in/water/pdf/Sam%20Group-Water%20Market%20Report%202007.pdf

Wilson, S. D. (2007). *Evolution for Everyone*. Random House.

Winpenny, J. (2015). *Water: Fit to Finance? Catalyzing National Growth through Investment in Water Security*. Report of the High-Level Panel on Financing Infrastructure for a Water-Secure World. Water Council, OECD. Retrieved from https://www.worldwatercouncil.org/en/publications/water-fit-finance

Wiser, R. H. (1997). Renewable energy finance and project ownership: The impact of alternative development structures on the cost of wind power. *Energy Policy*, *25*(1), 15–27. doi:10.1016/S0301-4215(96)00115-2

Worimegbe, T. M., & Oyewole, T. (2021). Environmental accounting disclosure practices of quoted manufacturing companies in Nigeria. *Global Journal of Business. Economics and Management: Current Issues*, *11*(1), 42–47.

World Bank. (2020). *A Slow Recovery through the COVID-19 Crisis*. Retrieved from https://www.worldbank.org/en/country/kazakhstan

World Bank. (2020). *Navigating the crisis* (Working Paper 2020). Retrieved from https://www.worldbank.org/en/country/kazakhstan

World Bank. (2020). *Sustainability Review*. Retrieved from https://www.worldbank.org/en/home

World Bank. (2020). *The Global Economic Outlook during the COVID-19 pandemic: A Changed World*. Retrieved from https://www.worldbank.org/en/country/kazakhstan

Wu, J. S., Bai, Y. P., Fang, W. P., Zhou, R., Reniers, G., & Khakzad, N. (2021). An integrated quantitative risk assessment method for urban underground utility tunnels. *Reliability Engineering & System Safety*, *213*, 107792. doi:10.1016/j.ress.2021.107792

Xie, Y., Dai, H., Dong, H., Hanaoka, T., & Masui, T. (2016). Economic impacts from PM2. 5 pollution-related health effects in China: A provincial-level analysis. *Environmental Science & Technology*, *50*(9), 4836–4843. doi:10.1021/acs.est.5b05576 PMID:27063584

Xie, Y., Dai, H., Zhang, Y., Wu, Y., Hanaoka, T., & Masui, T. (2019). Comparison of health and economic impacts of PM2. 5 and ozone pollution in China. *Environment International*, *130*, 104881. doi:10.1016/j.envint.2019.05.075 PMID:31200152

Xu, L. (2016). Legal issues of French public-private partnership(government organizations and social companies). *Administrative Law Review*, *3*, 116–127.

Yang, C., & Peng, F. L. (2016). Discussion on the development of underground utility tunnels in China. *Procedia Engineering*, *165*, 540–548. doi:10.1016/j.proeng.2016.11.698

Yang, J., & Zhang, B. (2018). Air pollution and healthcare expenditure: Implication for the benefit of air pollution control in China. *Environment International*, *120*, 443–455. doi:10.1016/j.envint.2018.08.011 PMID:30142582

Yan, Y. F., Huang, Q. B., Xie, Y. L., Lin, T., Xu, Q., Fan, F. F., & Wang, Y. L. (2021). Failure analysis of urban open-cut utility tunnel under ground fissures environment in Xi'an, China. *Engineering Failure Analysis*, *127*, 105529. doi:10.1016/j.engfailanal.2021.105529

Zabihollah, R., & Ling, T. (2017). Voluntary disclosure of non-financial information and its association with sustainability performance. *Advances in Accounting*, *39*, 47–59. doi:10.1016/j.adiac.2017.08.001

Žakelj, V. (2020). Economics in the Anthropocene. Žiri: Self-Published.

Zeneli, F. (2016). Analysis of risks and investments' opportunities in water sector. *Academicus International Scientific Journal*, *7*(13), 128–137. doi:10.7336/academicus.2016.13.10

Zhang, J., & Mu, Q. (2018). Air pollution and defensive expenditures: Evidence from particulate-filtering facemasks. *Journal of Environmental Economics and Management*, *92*, 517–536. doi:10.1016/j.jeem.2017.07.006

Zhang, X., Chen, X., & Zhang, X. (2018). The impact of exposure to air pollution on cognitive performance. *Proceedings of the National Academy of Sciences of the United States of America*, *115*(37), 9193–9197. doi:10.1073/pnas.1809474115 PMID:30150383

Zhang, Y. J. (2011). The impact of financial development on carbon emissions: An empirical analysis in China. *Energy Policy*, *39*(4), 2197–2203. doi:10.1016/j.enpol.2011.02.026

Zhang, Z., Ren, J. R., Xiao, K. C., Lin, Z. Z., Xu, J. Y., Wang, W., & Pei, C. X. (2019). Cost allocation mechanism design for urban utility tunnel construction based on cooperative game and resource dependence theory. *Energies*, *12*(17), 3309. doi:10.3390/en12173309

Zhao, G. (2017). Confidence, bond risks, and equity returns. *Journal of Financial Economics*, *126*(3), 668–688. doi:10.1016/j.jfineco.2017.09.007

Zhao, L., Zhang, X., Wang, S., & Xu, S. (2016). The effects of oil price shocks on output and inflation in China. *Energy Economics*, *53*, 101–110.

Zheng, H. C., Xu, B., Wang, T., & Chen, D. Y. (2017). Project implementation success in reward-based crowdfunding: An empirical study. *International Journal of Electronic Commerce*, *21*(3), 424–448. doi:10.1080/10864415.2016.1319233

Zhou, M. J., Lu, B. Z., Fan, W. G., & Wang, G. A. (2018). Project description and crowdfunding success: An exploratory study. *Information Systems Frontiers*, *20*(2), 259–274. doi:10.100710796-016-9723-1 PMID:29755287

Zhu, H., Duan, L., Guo, Y., & Yu, K. (2016). The effects of FDI, economic growth and energy consumption on carbon emissions in ASEAN-5: Evidence from panel quantile regression. *Economic Modelling*, *58*, 237–248. doi:10.1016/j.econmod.2016.05.003

About the Contributors

Abdul Rafay is a practitioner cum academician. For more than 25 years, Mr. Rafay has been working as a freelance advisor, consultant & trainer to a wide variety of public & private sector national and multinational companies in the areas of Corporate Finance, Financial Policy & Implementation, Auditing & Assurance, Accountancy, Corporate Tax Management, Financial Technology, and System Consultancy. He has been providing consultancy to various industries including Textile, Auto Assembling, Footwear, Industrial/Agro Chemicals, Ice Cream/Dairies, Glass/Ceramics, Healthcare, Mining/Natural Resources, Packaging/Paper Sacking, Steel/Pipe Casting, Rice Processing, Brokerage/Co-operative Financing, Software Development, Real Estate, Printing/Publishing, and Construction/Civil Engineering, etc. Mr. Rafay is a Fellow member of the Institute of Chartered Accountants of Pakistan. He is also a member of various national and international professional bodies including the Institute of Internal Auditors (IIA), USA; Association of Certified Fraud Examiners (ACFE), USA. Since 2001, he has been a lifetime member of the Lahore Tax Bar Association. He has served as Co-regional Director (Founding) of Lahore-Islamabad Chapter of Professional Risk Managers International Association (PRMIA), Washington, USA (2011-2013). In 2012, he was nominated as Member: Education & Training Committee (ETCOM) of The Institute of Chartered Accountants of Pakistan (ICAP). He is also a member of ICAP's "Islamic Finance working group" which is closely in liaison with the State Bank of Pakistan and other stakeholders for Islamic Finance Accounting and Auditing Standards. He is an Alumnus of Rausing Executive Development Center (REDC), Lahore University of Management Sciences (LUMS), Pakistan. In 2014, International Finance Corporation (World Bank Group) selected him for Training of Trainers (ToT) for Corporate Governance Action Planning for SMEs. He is also an approved trainer for the Institute of Financial Markets of Pakistan (IFMP) established by the Securities and Exchange Commission of Pakistan (SECP), the corporate regulator. In 2013, his name got included in the list of "Certified Directors" as per Clause (xi) of The Code of Corporate Governance 2012 issued by SECP. Currently, he is on the board of a Listed Company as an Independent Director. For the last 27 years, Mr. Rafay has also been associated with teaching in some of the top business schools of Pakistan. His specialized subjects of interest include Strategic Corporate Finance, Financial Crimes, Financial Derivatives, Investments/Portfolio Analysis, International Financial Reporting Standards, Corporate Restructuring (Mergers & Acquisitions), Financial Statement Analysis & Corporate Taxation. He also served as an instructor in Civil Services Academy, Pakistan to train the CSS Officers selected by the Federal Public Service Commission of Pakistan (FPSC). Currently, he is a Professor of Finance & Accounting at the University of Management & Technology, Pakistan. He has published more than two dozen research papers in SSCI, ESCI and Scopus indexed journals published by reputed global publishers including Emerald, Sage, Taylor & Francis, and IGI Global. He contributed multiple chapters in Books edited by International Editors. For many years, he authored/edited multiple international books on FinTech, Islamic Finance, Financial Crimes, Money Laundering, Terrorism Financing, Energy Finance, and Environmental Finance published by IGI Global, USA.

* * *

Vugar Bayramov holds a PhD in economics from the Azerbaijan State University of Economics. He is a Professor for 12 years at the Azerbaijan State University of Economics. His research interests include socio-economic issues. He possesses 16 years of experience as a chairman of the Center for Economic and Social Development. He published more than 65 articles.

Živko Bergant holds a PhD in business organization sciences from the University of Ljubljana, Slovenia. Currently, he is Assistant Professor at the College for Accountancy and Finance in Ljubljana Slovenia. His research interests include accountancy, finance, organization, and social responsibility. He possesses 25 years of experience and published more than 400 papers and 17 books. He is also a Palgrave Hamilton author.

Alhassan Bunyaminu holds a PhD in Finance from the University of Central Nicaragua, Nicaragua. Currently, he is a Lecturer at the University of Professional Studies, Ghana. His research interests include Energy Finance, Financial Modelling, Financial Market and institutions, corporate finance & Corporate Governance. Dr. Bunyaminu is a Chartered Global Investment Analyst (CGIA) and a member of the Chartered Global Financial and Investment Institute in the USA and Ghana. He possesses over 15 years of experience as a local governance expert and offers consultancy and research services to Metropolitan, Municipal, and District Assemblies (MMDAs) across Ghana. Dr. Bunyaminu is also a capacity building and training provider for public and private organizations in management and finance. He has published more than 20 papers/book chapters/books. Dr. Bunyaminu serves as a reviewer to a number of journals published by Emerald, Taylor & Francis, SAGE and Springer.

Gil Cohen holds a PhD in Finance from the University of Haifa, Israel. Currently, he is a Professor and Head of the Management department at Western Galilee College, Israel. His research interests include Finance, Sustainability, Risks, Trading. He possesses 25 years of experience as a financial market expert and published many articles research papers on financial behavior and anomalies.

María Jesús García holds a PhD in Law from the University of Valencia, Spain. Currently, she is a Professor at the University of Valencia. Her research interests include European Law, Environmental Law, Public Law. She has published more than 40 papers and book chapters and authored 7 books.

M. Maschendar Goud holds a PhD in Finance from Osmania University, India. He was a recipient of the Indian Council of Social Science Research (ICSSR) Doctoral Research Fellowship for the doctoral program. He possesses more than three years of experience in teaching and research. He has worked in various projects sponsored by the Indian Council of Social Science Research (ICSSR), University Grants Commission (UGC), MoHRD, Government of India, Karnataka Evaluation Authority (KEA), National Agricultural Bank for Rural Development (NABARD), Swachha Andhra Corporation (SAC), Andhra Pradesh, Swachh Bharat Mission (SBM), and other Private Organisations like Thermal Powertech Corporation India Ltd. (TPCIL) and currently working on Performance of State Level Public Enterprises, Government of India. His areas of interest include Economics, Accounting, Financial Management, and Rural Development.

Nigar Islamli holds a B.Sc. Degree in economics from the Azerbaijan State University of Economics. Currently, she is a researcher on macroeconomics at the Center for Economic and Social Development. Her research interests include socio-economic issues. She possesses 2 years of experience as a researcher to the first think tank in Azerbaijan.

Kiranmai J. holds an MPhil in Management from the University of Madhuai-Karmaraj University, India. Currently, she is an Assistant Professor at the Institute of Public Enterprise. Her research interests include Accounting, Finance, Green finance, corporate governance, and CSR. She possesses 14 years of consultancy experience and published more than 30 papers/book chapters/books. She is an Editor with the Indian Journal of Corporate Governance published by SAGE and IPE Journal of Management.

Aasia Kanwal holds MBBS and MPhil from Rawalpindi Medical University, Pakistan and the University of Health Sciences, Pakistan respectively. Her areas of interest are Nutritional Physiology and Health Economics. Currently, she is affiliated with Shalamar Medical & Dental College, Lahore, Pakistan.

George Kasule holds a Masters in Business Administration from Makerere University, Uganda. Currently he is a Manager at National Water and Sewerage Co-operation. His research interests include Water Management and Business. He possesses eighteen years of experience as an advisor to Government companies.

Nurcan Kilinc-Ata holds a PhD degree in Economics from the University of Stirling, UK. Currently, she is a research fellow at National Research University Higher School of Economics, Institute of Economics and Utility Regulation, Moscow, Russian Federation. Her main research interests are energy and natural resource Economics, energy policies, renewable energy system, energy efficiency and environmental economics.

Naveed Lashari possesses MBBS, FCPS (Rheumatology), FCPS (Medicine), MRCP SCE Rheumatology (UK), FACR Rheumatology (USA), FRCP (Glasgow), FACP (USA), EULAR (Europe) CC Rheumatology PG Dip: Diabetes Meltus (UK) 'Rheumatologist. He is currently working as a Classified Medical Specialist & Diabetologist at Fazaia Medical College & PAF Hospital-9, Islamabad.

Arsalan Haneef Malik is a PhD scholar at the Faculty of Economics and Business, University of Malaysia Sarawak. His research interest includes corporate social responsibility and sustainability practices, financial inclusion, financial stability, and environmental and social sustainability. He possesses eight years of experience in accountancy and finance by working in an audit firm, manufacturing, and construction sector. He has published several research papers.

Ram Kumar Mishra holds a PhD from the University of Rajasthan, India. He is ONGC Subir Raha Chair Professor on Corporate Governance, Senior Professor and Former Director, Institute of Public Enterprise (IPE), Hyderabad, did his PhD from University of Rajasthan, India. He is a visiting fellow at London Business School (UK) and also attended the International Teachers Programme at SDA Bocconi, Milan. Dr. Mishra has taught at the University of Bradford and was a Visiting Professor at Maison Des Sciences De L' Hommes, Paris, and Faculty of Economics, University of Ljubljana, Slovenia. He is a member of the UN Task Force on International Standards of Excellence in Public Administration and Education. He is a special invite to the OECD Working Group on Privatization and Corporate Governance of SOEs and the Asian Network of Corporate Governance. He is a Non-Executive Director on some of the public and private enterprise boards in India. He has considerable experience in teaching and guiding research for the doctoral degree in management, economics, public administration, and commerce.

Mary Maurice Mukokoma holds a PhD in Business from School of Management, University of Maastricht, Netherlands.. Currently she is a Senior Lecturer at Kyambogo University. Her research interests include Environmental Financial Reporting, Sustainable Financial Reporting and Business Management. She possesses Twenty years of experience as a consultant to National Financial Reporting Agency and Business enterprises. She published more than fifteen papers/book chapters/books.

Marie G. Nakitende holds a PhD in Management from Cardinal Stritch University, USA. Currently, she is Dean, Faculty of Business Administration and Management at Uganda Martyrs University, Uganda. She published many research papers in international journals.

Peter Masaba Nangayi holds a Masters in Business Administration from Uganda Martyrs University. Currently he is a Domestic Taxes Officer at Uganda Revenue Authority. His research interests include Banking, Finance and Reporting. He possesses eight years of experience as an advisor to Government. He published more than 3 papers/book chapters/books.

Tayo Oke holds a PhD and is a principal partner at the financial and economic law firm; ASIKO Chambers. Currently, he is also a senior academician at Afe Babalola University, Ado-Ekiti, Nigeria.

Rajibur Reza holds a PhD in Finance from the Department of Accounting, Finance and Economics (AFE), Griffith University, Australia. His research interests lie at the banking and insurance, corporate finance, environmental and sustainability finance, and social housing finance. His research expertise in the areas of water finance and investment. He has published seven articles in peer-reviewed journals and two book chapters.

Feng Sun holds a PhD in Management from the University of Science and Technology Beijing, China. Currently, he is Senior Economist at the South China Normal University. His research interests include financial econometrics and statistics, applied analysis for economics and management, etc. He possesses twenty years of experience as a consultant to Government, multinational companies, local companies, and research fields. He published many papers/book chapters as the first author.

Gurudeo Anand Tularam holds a PhD in Mathematics from the Queensland University of Technology, Australia. Currently he is a Senior Researcher (Science), at Griffith University, Australia. His research expertise in time series and stochastic calculus methods in business and finance applications such as investment, portfolio analysis and risk assessment. He has published more than hundred papers in reputed international journals.

Awais ur Rehman holds a PhD in finance from Universiti Malaysia Sarawak. He also holds degrees in management sciences, Islamic finance, and laws. Currently, he is working at the University of Central Punjab. He possesses more than five years of professional experience. He has published more than thirty research papers.

Kisenyi Vincent holds a Masters in Accounting and Finance from the University of Dundee, UK. Currently he is a Lecturer and Dean at Uganda Christian University. His research interests include Environmental Management and Financial Management. He possesses over twenty years of experience as a consultant to organizations on Environmental management and Reporting. He published more than eight papers/book chapters/books.

Ibrahim Nandom Yakubu obtained his PhD degree in Banking and Finance from Ankara Yildirim Beyazit University, Turkey. He is a recipient of the prestigious Commonwealth Shared Scholarship under which he completed his MSc. study at the University of Liverpool, UK. He also received his BSc. in Banking and Finance from the University of Professional Studies, Accra where he graduated with First Class. Dr. Ibrahim holds an Investment Foundations Certificate from the CFA Institute (USA). He had also worked as a Teaching Assistant and Part-time Tutor at the Faculty of Business, Tamale Technical University, Ghana. His research focuses on corporate finance, financial markets and institutions, and energy finance. Dr. Ibrahim has over 30 publications including articles and book chapters. His research works have appeared in various internationally ranked journals and he has presented his research findings in international and national conferences. He also serves as an ad hoc reviewer for a number of journals published by Emerald, Taylor & Francis, SAGE, and Springer.

Index

V

W

www.ingramcontent.com/pod-product-compliance
Lightning Source LLC
LaVergne TN
LVHW061544290926
849162LV00004B/896
* 9 7 8 1 6 6 8 4 5 5 8 0 7 *